WOMEN IN THE NEW MILLENNIUM

The Global Revolution

Anne R. Breneman
Rebecca N. Mbuh

Hamilton Books
A member of
The Rowman & Littlefield Publishing Group
Lanham · Boulder · New York · Toronto · Oxford

Library of Congress Control Number: 2005932948
ISBN-13: 978-0-7618-3342-0 (paperback : alk. ppr.)
ISBN-10: 0-7618-3342-0 (paperback : alk. ppr.)

Dedicated
In Memoriam to
our friends and colleagues
Professor Grace Chen
and
Professor Mary Francis Greene

ଔଞ୍ଚ

CONTENTS

Figures and Tables

Preface

There are times in the course of one's life, which can be described as liminal. That is, a confluence of events engages the mind, spirit and emotion in a holistic manner, so that one aspect of being cannot be separated from the other. There seems to be a certain fluidity as an aspect of consciousness flows into another quite seamlessly. Such experiences act as doors to new understandings and insights about the individual's relationship to all else, including society, individuals, place, knowledge and consciousness. The spirit and intellect seem more clear, expansive and inclusive. Emotions seem freer to integrate with those of others, whether in the same social environment and occasion or elsewhere in time and place. An individual emerges from such an epiphany with fresh perspectives, perceptions, and visions. Such were the experiences of the authors, who were present at the opening event of the United Nations (UN) Fourth World Women's Conference in Beijing in August 1995 and the Beijing +5 Follow-up in Manhattan in June 2000. Anne Breneman describes her experience at the Beijing Conference:

> After a number of delays in the American delegation's efforts to obtain travel documents, originating with clashes between the Chinese and US governments over human rights issues concerning dissident Harry Wu, and strident expressions of outrage by some international women's groups upon hearing that the conference had been moved during the planning stages from Beijing to Hairou, a city about an hour away,—the Nongo
> vernmental Organizations (NGOs Forum formally convened with a grand opening in a large stadium about half way between the two locations. Over 38,000 women and a small portion of supportive men from most nations of the world, including hundreds of ethnicities, were welcomed by the Chinese nation and people with an extravagant ceremony involving over a thousand Chinese women, men and children.
>
> In Hairou, we found a global city of women, with nearly 5000 NGOs setting up booths, tents, events, posters, and decorations. The peoples of that city had been evacuated temporarily to make way for jurisdiction, which was under the UN rule of law, rather than the Chinese government, during the course of the two-week-long conference.
>
> From America many NGO delegations had come, representing the great diversity of culture and perspective, but we were not alone. As we were swept into the stadium by our eager Chinese hostesses, with passes pressed into our hands, we found ourselves in the company of dancing and chanting Indian and African women from many cultures and backgrounds. The rising spirits of victorious women were impossible to resist! Many of the African delegations wore garments made from cloth especially designed for the Conference.
>
> A script had been written and posted on an electronic board, using phrases such as: "women and men: two wings of the bird of peace" and "equality, education, and development." An all women's orchestra, dressed in flowing white garments and seated on an s-shaped stage, uplifted us with an original opera

praising women and assuring us of the heights possible as equal partners with men. Human simulations of a sailboat of equality formed before our eyes, then embarked upon a sea as its sail unfurled. On cue, as the words "We are two wings of a bird" appeared on the electronic board and the music reached a crescendo, 5000 white doves were released, winged their path around the stadium then disappeared. During the grand finale hundreds of children, youth and men walked around the stadium, paying tribute to women as mothers, wives, and daughters capable of achieving any goals they set before themselves.

Looking around the stadium at the women of the world representing all the conditions, concerns and hopes of those unable to be present, I felt inexplicably drawn into a community of women from past, present and future: those who suffered indignities and limitations, sometimes violence; many now struggling for protection, equality, and dignity; girls and women of the future who will stand on the shoulders of these and achieve a measure of equality, fulfillment, achievement, and respect unimaginable to all who have preceded them. As the torch was passed from Nigerian women leaders to Chinese women leaders-symbolizing the continuity of the struggle, the convening of the Fourth UN World Women's Conference, and its global context- the seed was planted for Women in the New Millennium: the Global Revolution.

The seed planted within our consciousness during these seminal events was nourished by our friendship. We shared very different life experiences growing up in Cameroon and the United States, yet we felt welded together by common interests and experiences in the academy. Both of us had experienced the ardors of graduate school, though at different universities and in different disciplines. We had also been colleagues at Allen University in Columbia, South Carolina, for more than a decade. One afternoon at a coffee shop in Columbia, we conceived of inviting women scholars from a variety of cultures to reflect upon their experiences as women within gendered cultures and upon their visions of prospects for gender equality and empowerment. Some women responded to an invitation to share their experiences and visions of a more egalitarian world with its concomitant lifestyles, relationships, and opportunities. This process of gathering data from women of varying cultures and nations continued during the Beijing +5 conference in New York City 2000.

Unlike Beijing 1995, when the entire world community was buzzing about the various human rights issues and the implications for women's delegations and NGOs attending the conference in China, a communist nation considered by the West to be lacking in recognition of human rights, the Beijing +5 conference seemed lost in the hustle and bustle of New York City. The New York Times gave minimal coverage to the conference, one of hundreds of conferences held in the great metropolis annually. Even the sponsoring body, the UN, seemed unprepared to receive the numerous international women's delegations. Consequently, more than half of those who were present to attend the opening ceremonies in Dag Hammerskjold Square were sent from one official line to another for registration, after having been sent to the opposite end of Manhattan the day before for the same purpose. And so we were among the many who spent that entire June morning in a line that wound around several city blocks, missing the opening ceremony, just blocks away. Security guards near the United Nations informed us that what was going on around the block was the beginning of some kind of a protest march for the handicapped! We wondered: did such a varied group of international women seem "handicapped" through a traditional male lens?

Nonetheless, resigned to a long period of waiting to be registered, the women began to introduce themselves to one another, take photos, and exchange business cards and invitations to one another's workshops. A Japanese group of women passed out small crafts made by participants in a project for rehabilitating girls who had been abused or shunned by families and community. The gifts were accompanied by invitations to a workshop and dinner featuring the project and other activities by these enthusiastic women. A congresswoman from Bermuda, a Bangladeshi feminist, a Malawian dignitary dressed in tribal regalia, a delegate from Peru, an Italian activist, and several Ghanaian women lawyers posed for snapshots together, then exchanged business cards and began conversing in a variety of languages, including sign language. The informal conference began in the long colorful line of waiting women, accompanied by several men, just as much as the formal conference convened a few blocks away in the square, with fanfare and speeches.

The symbolic nature of these seemingly small incidents and interactions was not lost on the women standing in line, as they did what many women learn to do early in life- make the most of a constricted circumstance. The subject of women as "handicapped" came up in several conversations and caused both amusement and dismay. As it turned out, there were handicapped women whose courage and achievement were featured during the opening events of the conference—which we missed while standing in line for duplicate credentials. The security guard had jumped to the easy conclusion that the rationale for the large numbers of unusual looking women, among whom were several handicapped, was that the Beijing +5 conference was a convention for the handicapped.

On our part, we began utilizing our interview schedule to collect data about this cross section of women of the world, recognizing that they were both representative of women in their native lands and unique women at the same time. As representatives of various delegations, they each shared the hopes, concerns and dreams of other women like themselves. Yet, women who travel internationally, overcome hardships and obstacles, negotiate and articulate the concerns of other women in large and small groups at the regional, national and international levels are not average women. They are rather symbols to other women of what is possible for the masses of women still toiling under difficult circumstances, restrictions, and vestiges of male dominated societies, in which women are expected to carry a heavier load of daily work in their families, maintain silence when decisions are made, confine their education and life work to the domestic sphere, submit themselves to the "ways of men", and in many cases live in fear of violence and abuse from male partners and, in times of war, from enemies.

The Manhattan conference, shared by both authors, is described by Rebecca Mbuh in relation to our conceptualization of this book:

On the opening day of the Beijing +5 Conference held in New York from

June 5-8, 2000, women from all over the world came to be seen, scrutinized, heard, questioned and understood. Each present had a personal agenda as well as the agenda of the army of women represented. Together these women amassed a force that was determined to shake and shape government foundations and move them to visible action. The cool, breezy and drizzling day set the backdrop for an agenda that was as diversified as the women present; yet the unifying theme echoing from the conference rooms to the streets and beyond was the same. "Women 2000: Gender Equality, Development and Peace in the 21st Century" was printed on all handouts, agendas, news headlines, posters, and conference materials. These women were further energized by the instant feedback and support from their respective countries as a flurry of exchanged email messages urged them to speak out forcefully.

During a special session of the UN General Assembly, UN Secretary General Kofi Annan referred to the Beijing +5 Conference purpose, "Undoubtedly there has been progress, but at the same time much remains to be done to bring equality to both men and women." Then US First Lady Hillary Clinton, speaking at a UNIFEM Symposium, added, "Our work is far from done." She was not only echoing the voices of women delegates present, but also sending a message to all women.

More than 15,000 women from 150 countries attended the Beijing +5 Conference. These countries are classified by western standards as "developed, developing, in transition, or undeveloped"- replacing the older, more ethnocentric language of "First, Second, Third and Fourth World" countries. Observing the gathering of these determined women (from what might have seemed to many as another planet), I was impressed with the kaleidoscopic vision of African, European, Asian, Middle Eastern, Pacific-Island and South and North American women. Most were dressed in their traditional or national attires, showing both their pride of origin and the importance they attached to participating in such an historic event, an event that was sure to change the way society views and treats women. The conference promised to contribute to the charting of a new course in the history of mankind.

My colleague and friend, a Caucasian American, and I, an African- Cameroonian American, felt exhilarated to be among this group of remarkable women struggling to make a difference, not only in the lives of women, but of humankind. We were also motivated to launch our initial research and to present a paper that grew out of the Beijing Fourth World Women's Conference in 1995. Thus engrossed in the spirit of womanhood and inspired by the thousands of strong women at the Beijing +5 Conference of 2000, in Manhattan, we enthusiastically aspired towards the current manuscript.

Inspired by these events and experiences that brought us into contact with an international community of women yearning for a new way of life, we have conceived of a volume which explores how a women's movement has grown from specific situations and belief systems of the world, gained national momentum in the 19th and 20th centuries, and emerged at the end of the 20th century and the opening of the 21st as a global revolution. In the cooperative mode preferred by many women, we invited colleagues from China, Sweden, Korea, Cameroon, Indonesia, Nigeria, Cameroon and the USA to assist us with our project and include their valuable perspectives and reflections, which are in the form of both scholarly work and interview material. The result may best be described by Danticat in her book, *Krik? Krak!*, "When you write, it's like braiding your hair. Taking a handful of coarse, unruly strands and attempting to bring them to unity. Some of the braids are long, others are short, some are thick. Others are thin. Some are heavy. Others are light."1

Aware that many such volumes will be written in the future which will gather more comprehensive histories and facts, our intent is to make a contribution, rather than to assume our work as definitive. Faculty and students concerned with social movements, revolutions, women's studies, gender equality, multicultural studies, the sociology of gender relations, or women and the emergence of a global community- may find this book useful to their purposes. Thoughtful people will be interested in the provocative concepts and diverse, global perspectives presented in this volume. The authors consider this work an urgently needed one, as it brings together elements of the gender revolution on a new level of thought, one which has the potential of reconciling the gender divide while moving both females and males toward a way of life which transcends any current form of social organization on the planet, whether east or west, north or south, urban or rural, conservative or liberal, traditional or modern. It is our belief that the complete attainment of gender equality will ultimately unglue civilization as we know it and reconstruct it in a manner that is conducive to human prosperity everywhere on our planet.

We approach our task by dividing the body of our work into five parts and 15 chapters. Reference materials, such as the Fourth World Conference on Women Platform for Action, our interview schedule, a religious statement on gender equality by the National Spiritual Assembly of the Bahá'í's of the US, UN data on women in government, and several related documents have been included in the appendixes for the reader's reference. The first part, "Beginnings," explores the origins of women's movements in many regions of the world, their commonalities and their uniqueness.

Part Two, "Women Awakening", analyzes some of the unique ways women in the Middle East, Mexico and Southwestern USA, Sweden and Cameroon have responded to the long histories of inequalities and resulting injuries and oppressions, which more often than not have characterized the lives of women throughout the world.

In Part Three, "Women Arising", we explore the role the UN has played since its inception in 1945 in the conceptualization, organization and systemization of a global movement to empower women through education, regional, and international conferences, collaboration, and goal setting. This part also highlights the continent of Africa and the effects of the UN's policy and sponsorship of programs and conferences which empower women, particularly after the UN sponsored International Women's Conference in Nairobi in 1985.

Part Four, Hazards of Growing up Female, addresses what for many women are the horrendous obstacles, which prevent the achievement of equality. Without legal and moral enforcement of laws that protect both girls and women from various forms of customary male privilege and some of the dire results, gender equality would only be a vague ideal. The UN Beijing Platform has designated both the spread of AIDS and violence toward women as among the most critical areas of concern. Mark DeLancey, an American political scientist currently on the faculty of Sookmyung Women's College in Korea, teams up with Mokgadi Moletsane, a South African scholar, to describe and analyze the effects of the AIDS scourge on African women.

The final part is entitled Reflections and Prospects and features the insights of Wu Xiaoqun, a historian, Bret Breneman, a writer and English professor, and the authors, Mbuh and Breneman, on the Chinese women's movement, adjusted images of manhood, redefinitions of male and female roles in African societies, the changing nature of motherhood, and challenges to be overcome as various national movements struggle between both traditional conceptions and egalitarian visions of social structures.

Patriarchy is conceptualized as an antique model of gender relations which will need to be replaced gradually by a more progressive model of egalitarianism and mutual cooperation. *Women in the New Millennium* aims to contribute to a public awareness of the gender revolution that is sweeping the globe while focusing on several regions of the world to examine the origins and direction of the movement. The authors do not attempt to encompass all of the cultures, nationalities and issues inherent within such a broad-based movement, even within the United States. Many significant groups, such as African American, Native American and Jewish women, are not represented directly by their own voices as authors, though their experience, struggle and presence in history are recognized as critical to the founding of the multiple movements that are converging in a global revolution. We hope that this book will invite women of all backgrounds to the ongoing dialogue and the creation of action plans which will ultimately shape the direction of the new world which is emerging. We believe that it is propitious that the book will be launched at a women's conference, which bears the same title and organization as our book, at Hampton University, Hampton, Virginia during March 2005. On the other side of the planet, a panel of Women in the New Millennium authors will be presenting their perspectives during the Women's Worlds Conference at Ewha University in Seoul, Korea a few months later, in June 2005.

Women in the New Millennium is not intended as a manual which instructs others on how to approach gender problems, nor does it address specific policies and political strategies for activism, as valuable as such works may be. Rather it explores the evolution of such a remarkable and far-reaching revolution in the minds and experiences of women, and to some extent, men, from diverse cultures. *Women in the New Millennium*, as its title suggests, aims to use our understanding of the past as a basis for envisioning a new world of possibilities for both women and men. That is, if war does indeed begin in the minds of men who grow up in patriarchal social structures, then it must be within the minds of both men and women that we create the foundations for a more egalitarian, prosperous and peaceful world.

Our intent in writing this book is to speak generally to thinking readers who are concerned with moving individuals, families and communities toward a structural change in gender relations, which in turn will impact social, economic and, ultimately, political realities in each culture and nation. We also speak to our colleagues and students, who as members of the academy are often in the forefront of social change as they seek knowledge, insight and skills, which will ultimately challenge the ways in which the social world has been conceived.

We would like to recognize the contributions made by our colleagues, friends and supporting institutions during the extended course of our research, writing and preparation of this manuscript. Our contributing authors have become our friends and collaborators over the years of working together on our writing project. Supporters include Fakhereh Mottahed, a Nigerian Baha' delegate to the Beijing Women's Conference who collected our first 34 interviews from Nigerian women, Cheryl Walker, who painstakingly edited parts of our manuscript, Monica Suroosh, who saved us with her manuscript production skills and willingness to take on the long hours of intensely tedious and exacting work, Dr John Waddell, who provided encouragement during the early stages of our work and on our respective sabbaticals from Allen University, the United Negro College Fund for financial support, Lynne Yancey, who reviewed the manuscript on behalf of the National Spiritual Assembly of the Bahá'ís of the U.S., and Hampton University and Sookmyung Women's University, our current employers. Further, our deepest appreciation goes to Mark DeLancey and Bret Breneman, for their participation as authors, their encouragement as our husbands, and their continuous assistance in the editing of the manuscript in its various stages of production. Anne's daughters, Michelle, Yvonne, and Suzanne, and son, Julian Mihdi, have contributed to the manuscript in ways that only families can know. Rebecca's sister, Florence Mbuh, and brother, Justice Mbuh, assisted with data collection and editing; while other brothers and sisters provided emotional support and encouragement. Rebecca also acknowledges her father as the first educated man in his village to open doors for the equal education of male and female children.

Both Rebecca and Anne acknowledge their respective mothers, Mechi Margaret and Lucy E. Rowley, as their primary role models and inspiration for embracing a vision of women who rise to new possibilities with courage, dignity and grace.

Anne R. Breneman	Rebecca A. Mbuh
Hampton University	Sookmyung Women's University
Hampton, VA USA	Séoul, Korea
April 2005	

Preface Notes

1. Edwidge Danticat, *Krik? Krak!* (New York: Soho Press, 1994).

LIST OF ACRONYMS

ACAFEJ: Association of Women Lawyers in Cameroon
ACDI: Canadian International Development Agency
ACW: African Center for Women
ATRCW: African Training and Research Center for Women
BUN: Buea University Newsletter
CEDAW: Convention on the Elimination of All Forms of Discrimination
    Against Women
CNU: Cameroon National Union
FAO: UN Food and Agricultural Organization
FGM: Female Genital Mutilation
GEM: Gender Equality Measurement
GNI: Gender-Related Development Index
HELP: Home Education Livelihood Program
HRAF: Human Relations Area Files
ILO: International Labor Organization
MIDENO: Northwest Province Development Authority (Cameroon)
MINEDUC: Ministry of Education
MTCT: Mother To Child Transmission
NGO: Non-Governmental Organizations (Associated with the UN)
NIC: National Information Center
OECD: Organization for Economic Co-Operation and Development
RHR: Reproductive Health and Research
UN: United Nations
UNDP: United Nations Development Program
UNESCO: United Nations Educational, Scientific and Cultural Organization
UNFPA: United Nations Population Fund
UNGA: United Nations General Assembly
UNHCR: United Nations High Commissioner for Refugees
UNICEF: United Nations Children's Fund
UNIFEM: United Nations Development Fund for Women
UNITA: National Union for the Total Independence of Angola
WEDO: Women's Environment and Development Organization
WGG: Working Group on Girls
WHO: World Health Organization

PART I

BEGINNINGS

Introduction to Part I:

Beginnings

How do revolutions begin? Are they ideas whose time have come; are they diffused through traders, boatmen, and caravans; are they passed along through women's conversations; or are they seeds of discontent planted within the human psyche until ripe enough to burst forth into action? Could they be visions given to clairvoyants in every society or teachings and prophecies of the Prophets signaling the return of the Spirit of God in every age? Whatever may be the motivating forces, what conditions must prevail for a revolution to grow to the proportions that now characterize the global women's movement?

In part I, myths and legends are explored to discover the various ways in which male and female images and relationships have been depicted in cultures as disparate as the Egyptian, Sumerian, Greco-Roman, Japanese, Chinese, Indian and Native American. Questions are raised as to the extent to which myths and legends blend with cultures and religions to create patriarchal social structures, which not only repress women but also seek other peoples to dominate. Over time and varying circumstance these androcentric social pyramids are perceived as the natural order and therefore the "right" and "proper" way of life. Thus, the inertia of the status quo actually prevents revolutions unless discontent becomes widespread among the oppressed. In retrospect, America, France and Iran all seemed ripe for gender revolutions, especially after provoking events that led to new concepts of life resulting in rebellions against the given order. Some researchers believe that it was the spread of liberal philosophies of the Enlightenment around the globe, which gave rise to the global gender revolution and ultimately to the organization of United Nations.

Chapter I

Background of a Revolution

Anne Breneman

Some may question the nature of the global revolution that has rocked every sector of human society during the past century. Yet many of the processes have been underway since the middle of the 18th century, gradually breaking down parochial boundaries, or at the very least, permuting them with new ideas and concepts of life. Besides the socioeconomic, political, religious, geographical, and intellectual boundaries which circumscribed the lives of women in the past there have been mythological ones which are implanted deep within human consciousness and are shared by both females and males in every culture. Some of the myths were friendlier towards women than those that grew out of the agricultural revolution of the Neolithic age[1] Riane Eisler raises the question of why societies based upon the goddess principle turned into what she terms "dominator societies." We begin our discussion with an examination of some of these myths and their implications for gender relationships and values.

Have women and men ever experienced real equality? Was there actually a tribe of Amazonian women in the Brazilian jungles and in the piedmont of South Carolina? Or were these beliefs an expression of masculine fear of the feminine buried deep within the human psyche? A belief in the capacity of women to possess attributes and powers equal to men seems to have existed sporadically in many parts of the world since ancient times.

Buried in the Human Psyche

In her book, *The Chalice and the Blade*, Eisler argues that matriarchal and matrilineal forms of social organization preceded the patriarchal and patrilineal forms that became more prevalent as humans became less nomadic and more sedentary, with the domestication of plants and animals.[2] With division of labor and accumulation of assets to be passed to the next generation, family roles became more prescribed and less flexible, according to this theory. Female deities gave way to androgynous deities such as Re, Zeus, and Shiva.

With the evolution of Hebrew culture came the introduction of one God, Jehovah or Yahweh- "Hear, O Israel! The Lord our God is one!" The religion of Abraham, later etched in stone during the time of Moses, resembling those of Manu in ancient Hinduism, set forth a code of binding laws for human relationships. Further, strong social guidelines and restrictions were exacted by appointed priests. The Mosaic laws prescribed a social structure based upon monotheism, primogeniture and patriarchy. This system spread from the Middle East to Africa during the rule of Solomon. Though Judaic history records some outstanding heroines, such as Esther, Ruth, Deborah and the Queen of Sheba, who began the royal line of Ethiopia's ruling family, there are no matriarchal chapters in these accounts. That is, certain circumstances combined with individual women of outstanding capacity and character to produce situations so unusual that they were considered worthy to record. Yet, these events did not signal a change in the social structure, only an exception to it, something marvelous and extraordinary, the stuff of legends and stories.

On the basis of the larger, stronger male physique, it was not difficult for males to maintain dominance, regardless of the legendary periods of female ascendance. Associated closely with the hunt, even as women were associated intimately with the hearth and childbearing, men often incorporated aspects of animal behavior into their rituals, especially in preparation for war, and perhaps as a ruse for holding women in their places by fear. For example, warriors and hunters of some African and Indian tribes donned ferocious animal masks as an aspect of arousing in themselves the qualities most feared in the bear, the lion, the tiger, the wolf and the snake. These qualities were viewed as aggressive and powerful warrior spirits to be called upon for assistance during the anticipated ordeals.

Bettina Knapp examined myths of ancient civilizations such as Egypt, Sumaria, Greece, Rome, Japan, China and India for evidence of how gender relations developed into perceptions of equality and inequality through male and female archetypes.[3] She found an interesting variety of powerful archetypes for the feminine persona. In some myths, Egyptian, Greek and others, females such as Isis, Athena and Iphigenia became the very epitome of human power, knowledge and efficacy. Isis's strategic intuitive gifts helped her to capture from the god, Re, His unknown name of power, and thus to integrate his powers into her own. That is, she became aware that the power of those who rule, and indeed each individual, is based upon their own secret knowledge of their name of power or secret name. This is not unlike the Biblical story of Delilah, who was encouraged by frustrated military leaders to find out Samson's secret power so that it could be used to defeat him. Apparently Samson's secret name was symbolized by his long unruly hair, which was then shorn in order to render him impotent.[4]

Iphigenia started out as an innocent, unsuspecting girl, who was sacrificed by her father Agamemnon as a ransom to save Helen of Troy from violation by barbarians. During the preparations for the sacrificial ceremony, Iphigenia blossomed into "the paradigm of a profoundly moral force" that "not only nourished and sustained them spiritually [i.e. her community], but was instrumental in their rebirth, and at the root of their ethical development."[5] Though clearly a political pawn in the Trojan wars, Iphigenia became an opportunity for the ancient Greeks to give expression to the sacredness of feminine sacrifice, with its implied qualities of ". . . family commitment and honor, sensitivity toward the suffering of others, strength and courage in the face of death." On the other hand Athena, daughter of Zeus, told Odysseus: "Two of a kind we are, contrivers both. Of all men now alive, you are the best in plots and storytelling. My own fame is for wisdom among the gods-deceptions, too."[6] In this context, Athena assumed the powers of the storyteller, plotter, and contriver—roles more frequently associated with male dominance in ancient Greek society.

In many African cultures, myths depict older women as having power to tell stories, guide, advise, lead, comfort, and obstruct[7] During and after colonialism and slavery, the Big Mama archetype lived on in many African cultures dispersed across the globe. Usually commanding respect from the entire community, Big Mama is depicted as a figure with covert powers covering a wide range of human affairs—spiritual, political, social, economic, and cultural. She may be a mythical descendant of Isis, who combined within herself the powers of male and female after conniving to discover Re's secret name. In America, she is perhaps embodied in such historical figures as Harriet Tubman or Sojourner Truth, whose presence, size, strength, boldness, activism in helping slaves to escape, and oratory were legendary. The following is an excerpt from Truth's impromptu speech delivered at a women's convention in Akron, Ohio in 1851:

> Well, children, where there is so much racket, something must be out of kilter. I think that twixt the Negroes of the South and the women of the North, all talking about rights, the white men will be in a fix soon. But what's all this talking about?
> That man over there (a clergyman) says that women need to be helped into carriages, or over mud puddles, or be given the best place. Nobody ever helps me into carriages, or over mud puddles, or gives me any best place. And a'int I a woman?
> . . . If the first woman God ever made was strong enough to turn the world upside down all alone, these women together ought to be able to turn it back and get it right side up again! And now that they are asking to do it, the men better let them[8]

Truth's boldness and cleverness in assessing and addressing the arguments of several ministers who preceded her on the podium, including her reference to the Eve prototype in Genesis, reminds one of the combined powers of Egyptian deities, Isis and Re. The thundering applause of the entirely white female audience following her address paid tribute to her capacities of oratorical prowess, analysis and insight. Although her speech was laced with metaphor, her argument silenced the three white ministers, who chided the women for demanding rights, which the ministers considered, unsupported by Judeo-Christian scriptures.

Ameratsu, a Japanese sun goddess, also displayed qualities that combined those of male and female: patience, generosity, strength, anger, and the power to mediate between the cosmic and personal, light and shadow. She represents a force of balance between opposites, especially as found in nature.

In East Indian cultures, the mythological figures of Sita and Radha continue to offer Indian women a standard for beauty, grace and wifehood. Sita represents ideals of sacrificial loyalty to one's husband, while Radha, the consort of Krishna, is taken as a symbol of ravishing beauty and loveliness. The Hindu marriage ceremony contains several references to the sacred myths of Rama and Sita, Krishna and Radha, as archetypal unions. Many Indian women in the past have been taught to serve their husbands as gods. Traditional socialization of Indian children bears this out; while both genders were taught to value service to humanity far more than emphasized in western cultures, girls were taught to serve, while boys were taught to expect service. The training of girls for service sometimes included infant marriage and training by a mother-in-law to serve her son from an early age. The mythology transforms this relationship into a romantic one, one in which married love is reciprocal and faithful, even if subservient on the part of the wife.

In some ancient myths women are shown as conniving and dangerous, as "the great whore of Babylon", who strongly resembles Tiamat, a Sumerian primordial mother who turned into a dragon and sea monster—and Delilah, who disempowered Samson through deceit. Cleopatra has been depicted as conniving, while Athena proclaims herself a conniver. Though women have been often depicted mythologically in an idealistic manner, reflecting a deep-seated male fascination with the female images of mother, enchantress and moral compass, women have been often feared because of these same powers, which include sexuality, oratorical skill, conniving and fertility. The ensuing confusion may create something of an avoidance-attraction dilemma for males.

In pre-Confucian Japan, women were preferred as rulers for a time, until patriarchal values transformed what had been a peaceful society into a warmongering one, with Kamikaze and Samurai warriors as the ultimate human weapons. The Americanized story of Mulan, made into an animated film in recent years, appears to combine the classic Ameratsu figure with western ideals of super romantic ideals, which were overtaken gradually by a more patriarchal value system in which girls became the greatest burden a father could possess, to be married off as soon as financially possible to the closest male relative in order to keep wealth within the family. At the height of patriarchal oppression, Indian widows were expected to prove their loyalty to their husbands by throwing themselves on the burning funeral pyres of their husbands, or alternatively, shaving their heads and renouncing a fully human life. Yet, side by side with such denigration, the Sita ideal continues to inspire many Indian girls to attain high standards of service, moral character, intelligence, beauty and wifehood. Such contrasting beliefs may help a society, and particularly women, to reconcile the gap between ideal and everyday gender realities.

Egyptian and Ethiopian female rulers, such as Cleopatra and Sheba, began to disappear with the rise of the Roman Empire, which favored a more patriarchal family type. Yet among North American Indians, an ideal of matrilineal descent prevailed, and has continued more or less to influence the present, in spite of missionary attempts to reorganize the social structure to conform to the dominant early American colonial ideal, i.e. dependent women in the home and independent men in the field and public sphere. The result has been a mixture of values regarding family structure and gender relations, sometimes difficult to reconcile. A Seneca woman wistfully recalled her heritage of a more pronounced matrilineal social structure:

There was cooperation, diversification of roles. . . . There was a certain toughness in the women, who had a tremendous amount of power. Women selected the chiefs, and were consulted in political matters. Women elders were considered special people, with visionary powers. . . . Men and women were equals. Most marriages were long-term relationships. But the women were not dependent on the men—the same yoke was on both their necks. If they separated, it wasn't such a big deal. The woman remained with her clan, the man returned to his mother's home.[9]

This understanding of the role of eastern Indian tribes in North America is reinforced by Joan Jensen's study of Seneca women's pre-colonial agricultural practice.[10] The creation myths of the Seneca began with a woman falling from the sky to give birth to the first woman. Sky Woman then brought earth, seeds, and roots, from which trees, fruits and flowers grew. Domestic plants grew from her grave. Later Corn Maiden, another mythical figure, appeared to teach the women how to plant and prepare corn, dance corn dances and sing songs. From these ancestresses, Seneca women learned to give thanks each season for everything which nature provided and to support one another in the important work of sowing, tilling, weeding, harvesting and preparing food. The women provided more than half of the tribe's subsistence until Quaker missionaries forced the women to weave and the men to farm after General John Sullivan's 1779 invasion and destruction of the Seneca's villages, crops, and farmland in upstate New York. Because the Seneca remained loyal to the British during the Revolution, survivors were treated as prisoners of war by the Patriots.

The Cherokee experienced a similar fate and were driven out of their ancient homelands in the Appalachians to Oklahoma in the 1839 holocaust, known as "The Trail of Tears." In 1787 a Cherokee woman wrote to Benjamin Franklin, pleading for peaceful arrangements between the Cherokee and the European settlers, enclosing a gift of some tobacco for members of the US Congress, "I am in hopes that if you rightly consider that woman is the mother of all, and that woman does not pull children out of trees or stumps, nor out of old dogs, but out of their bodies, so they ought to mind what a woman has to say. "[11]

An Australian-Vietnamese scholar wrote of a time when, during the Chinese rule of Vietnam, two famous sisters, the Trungs, rebelled against Chinese rule in 39 AD, proclaimed themselves queens and ruled three years before being defeated by a powerful Chinese army. Even then, they jumped into the river and drowned themselves, rather than allowing themselves to be captured. The Trung sisters gained legendary status over time; Vietnamese women since have been referred to as "Daughters and Granddaughters of the Trung Sisters."[12]

Similar to both the Japanese experience and that of the Seneca and Cherokee, the spread of Confucianism under the 1000-year Chinese rule gradually modified the tendency toward egalitarianism and matrilinealism found in Vietnam and other Southeast Asian societies. To this day, however, Vietnamese women enjoy a more egalitarian status than traditional Chinese women, according to My-Van Tran, even though French colonial rule tended to reduce the status of women in the process of introducing a wage-based economy and patriarchal concepts of social structure.

Although the ancient myths, histories and archeological records reveal a different status of women than more recent times, when "dominator cultures"[13] ruled by males held sway, there seems to have always been some ambivalence toward the mysterious nature of women. The recognized mythical powers of women often brought fear of the unknown, including a possible threat to manhood. For example, Eve of the Biblical Genesis story received a forbidden apple from the Tree of the Knowledge of Good and Evil from a snake and then offered it to Adam, who succumbed to temptation and partook, leading to their eviction from the Garden of Eden. Eve has been depicted as the classic temptress, similar to the Seirenes, whose singing could lure men forever into their "green mirror" of illusion, or Kirke, who attracted men into her den, to be transformed into swine of lust in Homer's tale of Ulysses.

Male fear of women's potential power has taken many forms, such as attributing witchery or blasphemy to women in Massachusetts for daring to hold unofficial religious gatherings, attended by other women, in one's home, during the 1600s.[14] Male fear was sometimes provoked during experiences peculiar to women, such as menstruation, pregnancy, childbirth, or widowhood, creating segregated genderized cultures. The assaulting of girls and women when alone, mutilating women's genitals, or preventing women from holding positions of overt authority, forbidding speech and occupation of sacred space, "corporeal chastisement"[15] or requiring the wearing of veils to conceal their femininity are common ways in which male fear of women's power has been expressed.[16]

The following description of Anne Hutchinson, who arrived in the Massachusetts Bay Puritan colony from England in 1634, only to be tried in 1638 for her transgression of gender roles, is revealing of the male fear of women provoked in traditional patriarchal societies such as the Puritans:

> One Mistris Hutchinson, the wife of Mr. William Hutchinson of Boston (a very honorable and peaceable man of good estate) and the daughter of Mr. Marbury, sometimes a Preacher in Lincolnshire, after of London, a woman of haughty and fierce carriage, of a nimble wit and active spirit, and a very voluble tongue, more bold than a man, though in understanding and judgment, inferior to many women. . . . then she kept open house for all comers, and set up two Lecture dayes in the week, when they usually met at her house, threescore or fourscore persons, the pretense was to repeate Sermons, but when that was one, she would comment upon the Doctrines, and interpret all passages at her pleasure. . . .[17]

The offense under consideration in the public trial was officially that of "holding unacceptable religious beliefs", but clearly involved a male fear that women who organize, speak out or influence others—whether female and male, and are capable of interpretation and commentary, would be a threat to the social order of patriarchy.

A Philadelphia man wrote in 1848 to a newspaper in response to women's demand for equal rights: "A woman is nobody. A wife is everything. A pretty girl is equal to ten thousand men, and a mother is, next to God, all-powerful. . . . The ladies of Philadelphia, therefore, under the influence of the most serious 'sober second thoughts' are resolved to maintain their rights as Wives, Belles, Virgins, and Mothers, and not as Women."[18] This 1848 declaration pretended to be the sentiment of all women in Philadelphia, particularly the female members of the writer's family. Part of the fear expressed is that of loss of control or ownership of women, with such dangerous powers as to be compared with those of God!

While the myths and legends buried within the consciousness of human beings share many common features, they also reveal some patterned differences. One of the major distinctions is that of societies with distant memories of matrilineal, at times bordering on egalitarian structural arrangements, versus those with memories of only patrilineal and patriarchal structural arrangements and gender values. The latter seem peculiar to those cultures which have a long history of conquest and thus a significant concern with superiority, use of force, military training, maintenance of order, and hierarchies designed to maintain the existing social order of power, authority, and status. Fisherman, nomadic people who follow herds, cooperative farmers and hunter-gatherers who live on a more subsistence basis seem less inclined to value entrenched hierarchies of power and status than those groups of people who have developed settled lives around agriculture, surplus goods, and urban markets.[19]

The Seneca and Cherokee, the Vietnamese, the Malay and Senoi, the Thai, some African tribes, the Shavonti of Brazil, and certain Pacific islanders, are examples of societies which are more cooperative, have overlapping gender roles and often a more fluid and less formal leadership style. The nonhierarchical approach to leadership often values the wishes of the people in decision-making. These are not communities with standing armies or visions of conquest, but in general those who earn a livelihood from the environment in which they live and work together to succeed in providing sustenance. The Western Cherokee elected in recent years their first woman chief, known as Chief Mankiller, an interesting and perhaps humorous recognition of role reversal. The Senoi in Sarawak, Malaysia have been studied by anthropologists, who find them to be among the most peaceful people on earth. The process begins, as one might expect, with the socialization of children by the community. Acts of aggression are strongly sanctioned by shrill sounds uttered in unison by adults. This can be contrasted with American society, which socializes its young males with sports competitions and toy machine guns, weapons of destruction, and monsters that kill with vicious technique. To compete in a patriarchal society such as America, Russia, or the United Kingdom is to engage in a "zero-sum" combat, in which the loser loses all and the winner takes all. On the other hand, the Shavonti of Brazil socializes each cohort of males to work together to overcome obstacles and conquer themselves, as well as to respect women. They are a subsistence culture whose survival depends upon close cooperation of all age groupings.[20]

Another factor to be considered in thinking about myths and legends is how religious belief systems which have been adapted to either patriarchal or matrilineal social structures tend to reinforce them by lending legitimacy to the resulting culture and hierarchy (or lack of hierarchy). Since myths rise over time and take on an aura of sacredness, they cannot be overlooked as significant sources for understanding the inequalities that have been thus inherited and transmitted from one generation to another as habitual, commonplace realities of life that must be learned in order to survive. If we are to dislodge the inherent structures of inequality which are played out in families, among men and women, boys and girls, it is important to consider the possibility of creating new legends and stories which feature more egalitarian relationships between male and female. A neutral search among the older religious teachings, including commentaries and narratives, to identify egalitarian values, examples and relationships which may have been overlooked or dismissed by those upholding and defending patriarchal social structures, may prove to be helpful for this purpose.

Within the more recently revealed religions of the Bábi and Bahá'í Faiths (1844), can be found a teaching suggesting that a Great Reversal must occur in society to signal the birth of a new world order. This reversal is referred to in chapter 2 by the Persian Bábi heroine Tahirih. Gender, race and class are primary structures that can become revolutionized by such changes in status, power and authority. In speaking of these principles on his travels through Europe and America in 1911-1912, Abdu'l Bahá suggested that since the world in the past has been ruled by masculine force, for a time the feminine principles of intuition, compassion and cooperation would be on the ascendancy, until a new egalitarian social structure is established.[21] One of the problems of changing such a primary relationship is the apparent lack of models of equality that are suitable to the diversity of individuals and cultures. An additional problem facing any change in power relations is whether those in possession of patriarchal power are willing to relinquish it for a more cooperative model.

How do we move from the mythological history of gender relations to the social, racial, political and economic relationships that influenced the rise of women's movements? Below we examine the processes that began to cross-fertilize various segments of human society and contributed to the disruption of the dominant social order that held women, along with most nonwhite populations, as subordinates.

Growing Revolutions

As mentioned earlier, the processes, which created women's movements across the world by the 20th century, had their origins as far back as the early 18th century. In awakening from what has been referred to as, "*a nightmare from which I am trying to awake,*"[22] it is useful to examine some of the many factors that stimulated women's movements to begin and to gain momentum during the past century. There seem to have always been women in the mythical past, from every region of the world, who have distinguished themselves through their abilities to twist the hand of fate and—through unusual resourcefulness, intellect, skill, determination, heroism, or beauty—rise above the restrictions of their lives to accomplish memorable deeds that transcended the customary status shared with their sisters. Yet they could, for the most part, be said to have been "born before their time." That is, the circumstances of life, e.g. patriarchal hierarchies, which restricted women in general in their respective lands or cultures were not changed in favor of other women after the demise of these heroines; they were usually dismissed as exceptional. Yet, no doubt, the examples of such women as Cleopatra, Esther, Deborah, Sheba, Joan of Ark, Harriet Tubman, Queen Victoria, the Trung sisters, Yentel, and Sacagawea, served to provide other women with a glimpse of possibilities, something to ponder when trudging through the tedious routines and responsibilities of lives severely limited by the ancient division of labor by gender. Who knows but that such pondering gave rise over time to some of the earliest stirrings at the grass roots to throw off the burden and stigma of sexism and work consciously toward the goal of gender equality?

The point to be made here however, is that these exceptional lives did not in themselves arouse the masses to a consciousness of the general oppression of women, or begin movements of women to throw off the shackles of customary inequalities during their lifetimes. It is too soon to be able to identify all of the social, economic, political and religious forces which intermingled within each region to give rise to what became a social movement, organized, goal-oriented and active, sweeping others into its energy force and idealism, and gaining both public attention and resistance from those representing the established institutions of power and authority. Every country or ethnic group will eventually create comprehensive histories of women's movements that will include a just array of the voices of actors and participants. It is not our purpose to attempt such a task at this time, while the movement is still gaining momentum. Yet, we can begin to search for patterns which characterize the social, political, religious and economic environments, recognizing that the stimulus for women in each region of the world to begin such movements has been varied, according to the prevailing circumstances which often disrupted what had been taken for granted as "the way things are."

Estelle Freedman suggests that it was the rise of capitalism which disrupted the older, more reciprocal relationships within the family in ways that enhanced men's economic opportunities and defined women as dependents, along with the expression of new political theories emphasizing individual rights and representative government, which gave rise to women's movements.[23] That is, the reorganization of human affairs in a manner which further disadvantaged women in capitalist societies and emphasized free markets and wages, combined with fervent public discussions regarding the rights of the common man to have a voice in government, created a stimulus for women to seek equality. The revolution in America against British colonial rule provided opportunities for women to participate in the movement toward democracy and in gaining freedom from oppressive authority.

The efficacy of organized efforts of individuals working together no doubt inspired women to reflect on other applications of the liberating principles. The first of these was the abolition of slavery. European women in England, Germany, France and Italy had already begun to hold salons to discuss slavery and the woman question and to exchange news reports and journals concerning the evils of slavery and the need for women to have access to education so they could speak out more freely in public. Angelina Grimke wrote in 1838, *An Appeal to the Woman of the Nominally Free States*, in which she appealed to American women to not conform to the convention that women stay free of political activity:

> in a country where women are degraded and brutalized, and where their exposed persons bleed under the lash—where they are sold in the shambles of 'Negro brokers'—robbed of their hard earnings—torn from their husbands, and forcibly plundered of their virtue and their offspring, it is very natural to want to know 'the reason why'—especially when these outrages of blood and nameless horror are practiced in violation of the principles of our national Bill of Rights and the Preamble of our Constitution.[24]

By connecting the moral outrages of slavery to those of woman's inequalities, the movement gained momentum and drew sympathizers from South and North and from among male counterparts.

In 1840 Elizabeth Cady Stanton and Lucretia Mott traveled to London to participate in the World Antislavery Convention, but were denied seats on the basis of gender, forced to absorb the proceedings from behind a screen in the gallery of the convention center. The famous 1848 Women's Convention in Seneca Falls was called for the express purpose of demanding suffrage so that women could participate in voting against slavery. Former slave and leading abolitionist Frederick Douglass was among the several men who supported the conference and signed the 1848 *Declaration of Sentiments*, considered as one of the most significant documents for women in the history of the US.[25] This document was couched in the language of the *US Declaration of Independence*, using the abusive power of men in place of that of England and recounting the various injuries and usurpations on the part of man toward woman, while accusing men of being tyrants in relationship to women.

The *Declaration of Sentiments* reveals that there were enough American women who were literate, educated, and familiar with the basic issues and documents of the American Revolution to support a gender revolution based upon the same principles and concepts. It also reveals the assumptions of these women that religion is a moral force that could be appealed to and relied upon to accomplish their purposes. The primary truths upon which the document stands is that there is a Creator who has endowed both man and woman with inalienable rights, making them equal before their Creator, and by extension, before any just government. It is refreshing to note that there are no references to sects or political parties, giving the document a more universal reference. As America has evolved, the recognition of its diversity of religion, race and political values has become increasingly important to development of its capacity to implement its ideals, in spite of its troubled beginnings as a European colony, with an inherited Eurocentric male view of the world and of religion.

With the French Revolution against aristocratic rule in 1789 and the collapse of the most familiar power structures known to the French, women expected that the quest for equal representation would naturally extend to their gender, especially after working women marched to Versailles to demand bread. Olympe de Gouges, a playwright, wrote and circulated *The Declaration of the Rights of*

Women and the Female Citizen but was sent to the guillotine in 1791. Napoleon Bonaparte then forbade all women's organizations and gave formal power to husbands over their wives, a custom which continued until 1944, when women were finally permitted the right to vote. In England, Mary Wollenstonecraft began to agitate for the rights of women and the abolition of aristocratic hierarchies, both in society and within the family. She wrote *A Vindication of the Rights of Man*, followed by *A Vindication of the Rights of Women* in 1792. Later, Harriet Taylor, also an Englishwomen, wrote *Enfranchisement of Women* in 1851. Her husband, John Stuart Mill, continued her work after her untimely death, fighting for women's suffrage in the House of Commons. In 1869 he wrote *The Subjection of Women*, crediting his wife for inspiring his beliefs about gender equality.[26]

Throughout African, Asian and Latin American communities, women had been aroused in response to the yoke of colonialism, which imposed a superficial patriarchal social structure over what had been traditionally matrilineal or agricultural cooperatives. Rebecca Mbuh proposes that women in West African societies such as Cameroon tended to create their own fortresses within male dominant systems, based upon gardening, marketing, food production, childrearing, sewing, crafts, and, in some cases, house building.[27] Through these strategies, some African women were able to maintain a limited measure of power—while many women, particularly in the middle and upper classes within the more dominant European cultures, found themselves imprisoned within their own homes and families, isolated from society and the camaraderie of their female peers as the industrial revolution grew.

Oppressive colonial policies, combined with poverty and the struggle for subsistence, kept many colonized women from focusing on women's equality. Movements focused more on freeing their peoples from the colonial powers or at least surviving and finding means to help their children obtain an education in the missionary schools that appeared throughout the colonies. The mission schools and civil services were hailed by the conquerors as signs of progress and civilization, but they also introduced conflicting values and social hierarchies in comparison with the more traditional and less formal ones.

In the Middle East, restrictions and treatment of women related to traditional interpretations of the practice of Islam played a key role in provoking protest and organization of women in Iran, Afghanistan, India and Egypt beginning in the 19th century.[28] An early example can be found in Iran, the birthplace of the Bahá'í Faith. A young Siyyid referred to as The Báb announced in 1844 that he was the promised Qa'im who had been awaited by the Shiah Muslims since the disappearance of the Twelfth Imam. His teachings and those of his successor, Bahá'u'lláh, emphasized the role of gender equality and racial justice in bringing about a new social order of peace, justice, and cooperation among nations and religions. A consequent religious, political, and social upheaval in Iran resulted in the arrest, torture and execution of over 20,000 men, women and children who were followers of the new religion. The nature of the 19th century religious revolution in Iran and its influence on gender equality is explored further in chapter 2.

In other parts of the Middle East, women were swept into nationalist movements designed to modernize and consolidate political power. According to some

Middle Eastern scholars, women have at times been co-opted into these movements within a party platform, without necessarily having taken part in an initiative by women. Turkey's reforms in the early 20th century by Kewal Attaturk, for example, called for the removal of women's veils and the education of women as an essential feature of its modernization.[29] Similarly, in China Wu Xiaoqun describes in chapter 6 the Chinese Communist Revolution, which required women to abandon home and family to join the work force. A similar convergence of politics and state-mandated gender reform occurred in Russia with the Bolshevik Revolution.

In the United States, facets of the women's movement were provoked by Black women, who organized against the oppressions and abuses of slavery to protest lynching of Black men, and by White women, who organized initially to win the right to speak out and vote against slavery. Both wanted more educational and career choices than were permitted in a patriarchal social structure. The movement grew, in spite of the initial lack of coherence between Black and White women's interests, to one that demanded for all American women full constitutional rights. Women protested the long hours and low pay as factory and domestic workers, devaluation and subordination as mothers and wives, and degradation as sexual objects.

The understanding of the nexus between gender and race was in the beginning more apparent to Black women than White, who participated to some extent in the inherited privileges of color and were less aware of the double burden of inequality experienced by their darker-hued sisters. For many women of color, white women were viewed as the enemy, making it difficult to join forces against the common enemy of sexism.[30] The gap between Black and White women narrowed as the movement collided with the Civil Rights movement 40 years after the women's vote had been achieved in the United States in 1920. Similar to Black women, who were initially concerned primarily with freeing their people from bondage, lynching and demoralization, Native American, Hispanic and Asian American women, though sympathetic, were focused in the beginning of the movement on issues relating to freedom from oppression by the dominant European culture more than on the rise of a pan-American women's movement.[31] Because the oppressor at times included White women, the prospect of joining a movement dominated by White women seemed a formidable one.

How then did the early stages of the movement under consideration gain enough momentum to erupt in the 20th century as a full-blown revolution?

A Cyclical Approach to Change

In examining the nature of these changes, it may be helpful to employ a cyclical approach in appraising both quantitative and qualitative changes from the mid-nineteenth century to the present. Cyclical theory suggests that human life moves forward in a spiral of cycles, repeating basic laws and patterns, with each cycle widening its scope and complexity, building upon gains in human knowledge and experience.[32] For example, currently accepted theory posits that, in general, civilization has moved from small hunting and gathering, nomadic bands in search of food, to settled, intergenerational, and family-based communities, to the city-state with more formal hierarchies, to the nation, with a great complexity of interacting familial, and public sectors, and to what is rapidly growing into a global civilization. There have been many stages between each of these major developments as well as many variations, but the movement is impossible to ignore or deny. That which is simple in nature tends to move towards that which is more complex; that which is small strains to become larger; and disorganization gives way to that which is more integrated and systematic as society grows.

A cyclical theory of human progress, in which human civilization advances and expands in a fairly predictable manner with each cycle, spiraling upward and outward can provide a perspective on the extraordinary 20th century gains in every field of human endeavor. In areas of technology, development and expansion of knowledge the gains have been such as to utterly outstrip all former cycles, constituting an entirely new spiral of human progress. In fact this cycle appears to be laying the foundation for a new way of life on our planet, one characterized by a vast network of human communications based upon new patterns of cooperation and a growing realization of the oneness of all humanity. Such trends were noted by the authors and researchers of *Megatrends 2000,* Patricia Naisbitt and John Aburdene.[33] They identified ten major trends, culled from international teams of scholars who conducted a painstaking study of policies and publications across the global community. One of the reported trends was "women in leadership" described as a rapidly rising phenomenon in the various workplaces and increasingly in high offices. A trend is not a fact, however, but a trajectory into the future based upon an observed pattern of growth in the present. Since 1993, when their work was published, however, most of their expectations have not only been fulfilled but also surpassed.

However, history and experience have shown that such leaps forward come with a high price. That is, as Charles Lemert points out, there is always an underside to progress.[34] In fact, progress may not even be defined as such by different participants. It really depends to a large extent on what role one is playing in a given situation; a villager may experience a program to bring water and sanitation through a new well system as a disaster, if it results in upsetting traditional social patterns. On the other hand, those representing the development agency and perhaps a few in the village who experience some advantage may consider it as progress. Those who represented the colonial powers and discovered lands, peoples and resources formerly unknown to themselves valued their findings as new "discoveries." Women, as well as men, may feel disgruntled by the social pressures that force women out of the domestic sphere into the workplace once dominated by men. Researchers on the condition of children in the 21st century may provoke dismay in readers with their dismal findings on the effects of such disruption of traditional home life on the welfare of children and families in general.

Similarly many criticize the United Nations as pushy, nosy, weak and ineffective and interfering with national sovereignty. However, the formation of the United Nations, after two wars which had engaged most of the world's resources, resulted in the decolonization of the planet—a complete breaking-up of the "*entrenched patterns of conflict*"[35] resulting from centuries of domination of most of the world by several European nations and, more recently, Japan. Not only was empire building brought to an end with the formation of the United Nations, but also the new international laws defined the invasion of one member nation by another as a violation of the Charter. During subsequent years, much of the United Nation's work centered around restoring the balance of justice through programs designed to redistribute ill-gotten wealth to former colonies in Africa, Asia, Latin America and island countries throughout the world. The concept of progress through universal education and human rights, social and economic development projects, and grassroots democracy became widely accepted as the United Nations provided the first universal forum the world has known. While balance of power issues, disarmament, finances, and peacekeeping dominated the headlines, a grassroots revolution occurred throughout the latter years of the 20th century.

Perhaps one of the most significant factors in the transformation of human life in the past century has been the dramatic entry of women onto the world stage. Each country has its own history of how gender relations have been revolutionized during the 20th century, but all of them share in common the fact that changes in the traditional relations between women and men have played a primary role in rearranging the social structure. As long as women were unable to obtain an equal education to their counterparts, whether in the family, primary school, secondary school, or higher education, they were faced with self-sustaining inequality.

A rhetorical question posed in the Qu'ran is: "Are they equal, those who know and those who do not know? . . . Or is the darkness equal with the light?"[36] The same dilemma of inequality has faced millions of illiterate peoples of the world during and after colonization. Equality can only be sustained through access to equal educational opportunities and the means to apply the results. For example, women with professional training, who have been shamed or imprisoned for their efforts to practice their professions, or to organize and participate in a women's movement to gain human rights, may experience more frustration than those with little education. In some Middle Eastern countries, the patriarchal social structure presents a formidable obstacle to changes in the personal status of women and influences the range of opportunities for employment of women.[37] As the poet, Yeats, suggests, "Things fall apart" with the introduction of such new concepts. Nigerian author Chinua Achebe echoes Yeats in his novel with an intentionally matching title. He weaves a story around the experience of former colonies coming out of centuries of internalized oppression, learning how to "push the envelope," how to ask questions and think outside the parameters of prescribed thought and behavior imposed by members of the dominant culture. With such questions and aspirations traditional ways of life begin to become unraveled.[38] Women who are emboldened to take the risk of questioning the status quo are often those who have been exposed to wider domains of knowledge and experience than found in cookbooks, soap-operas, domestic interactions and memorized proverbs concerning appropriate conduct for daughters, wives, sisters and mothers, as well as sons, husbands, brothers and fathers. Many traditional cultures have viewed such women as dangerous and pass laws to return them to the confines of the domestic sphere, veiled and secluded, in an attempt to curtail their influence on the mainstream society.[39]

Investing in Women

Since women constitute approximately 50 percent of the human race, it is not surprising that even small incremental changes such as in the areas of women's literacy and educational attainment have resulted in the transformation of traditional family life. Data reported by the United Nations Development Program reveal that birthrates in any nation tend to decline in direct proportion to the increase of women who attain higher levels of education.[40] At the same time, the greater exercise of female decision-making powers in domestic affairs, economics, education, production, science and technology, design, and government—to name a few—has often led to reconceptualization of theory and practice. According to a statement made by one of the presidents of the World Bank, ". . . *investment in the education of girls is among the most cost-effective development action that countries and international institutions can take."*[41]

Prior to the 20th century, few females in any country were considered important enough to value as an educational investment, compared with the number of males who were trained, tutored or apprenticed to carry out the various functions of society. The role of women was a domestic one and a subordinate one. Social theory itself was written by males and studied by males to perpetuate a social order based upon the qualities in which males excel—competition, aggression, and task orientation. Exceptional males who leaned more toward the arts, compassion, intuition, mental alertness, and nurturance—associated more with feminine nature—were often shunned as effeminate and unworthy of social recognition. Females who achieved in America during the 18th & 19th centuries felt forced to change their names or disguise themselves as males in order to be acceptable in the public sphere.

In China and Russia, peasant revolts and political upheavals in the late 19th and early 20th centuries were accompanied by the movement of women from the home into the workplace to take jobs normally occupied by males. To accommodate the removal of women from their childrearing functions, government-sponsored communal daycares cropped up everywhere, producing generations of children who were reared more by designated government officials than by mothers and grandmothers.[42] Other countries followed suit, as women flocked to new educational and career pressures and opportunities, shaped by the industrial revolution and the world wars.

In this light it becomes essential to understand the nature of the revolution that is sweeping the world. As we trace the awakening of human consciousness to the potential of women in the last century and a half to a small hamlet in 19th century Persia, where oppression of not only women, but all who dared to question the given order, was at its height, we consider the role and implications of patriarchalism in provoking the gender revolution in chapter 2. In part II, we will explore the diverse origins of the women's movement.

Chapter 1 Notes

1. Neolithic refers to a prehistoric turning point when our ancestors began to settle in

communities based upon domestication of animals and plants rather than hunting and gathering.

2. Riane Eisler, *The Chalice and the Blade: Our History, Our Future* (San Francisco: Harper & Row, 1988).

3. Bettina L. Knapp, "Women in Myth" (State University of New York, 1997).

4. Jgs 16 King James Version.

5. Knapp, "Women in Myth," p.85

6. Homer, *Odyssey, t*rans. Robert Fitzgerald, (New York: Doubleday, 1963).

7. Shay Youngblood, *The Big Mama Stories*, (Ithaca, NY: Firebrand Books, 1989).

8. Sojourner Truth, "Ain't I a Woman," in *History of Women's Suffrage*, eds. Elizabeth C Stanton, Susan B Anthony and Matilda J Gage (Rochester: Charles Mann, 1881), 403-404.

9. Laura Wittstock, "We are All Members of One Family," in *Messengers of the Wind: Native American Women Tell Their Stories*, ed. Jane Kantz, (New York: OneWorld Ballantine, 1995), 111-112.

10. Joan M. Jensen, "Native American Women and Agriculture: a Seneca Case Study," in *Unequal Sisters: A Multicultural Reader in US Women's History*, eds. Vicki L Ruiz and Ellen C DuBois (New York: Routledge, 1994).

11. Theda Perdue, "Cherokee Women and the Trail of Tears," in *Unequal Sisters: a Multicultural Reader in US Women's History*, ed. Vicki L Ruiz and Ellen C DuBois (New York: Routledge, 1994), 32-43.

12. My-Van Tran, "The Position of Women in Traditional Vietnam" in *The Role of Women in an Advancing Civilization*, ed. Starih Ala'I and C. Dowes (Australia: Association of Bahá'í Studies, 1989)

13. Eisler, *Chalice and Blade.*

14. Ellen Skinner, ed., "Anne Hutchinson's Trial (1638)," in *Women and the National Experience: Primary Sources in American History*, (New York: Longman-Addison Wesley, 2003), 2-5.

15. Ellen Skinner, ed., "Emily Collins, Reminiscences of the Suffrage Trail (1881)," in *Women and the National Experience; Primary Sources in American History*, (New York: Longman-Addison Wesley, 2003), 79-81.

16. Michelle Z. Rosaldo and L. Lamphere, *Women, Culture and Society* (California: Stanford University Press, 1974)

17. Skinner, "Anne Hutchinson's Trial," 2-5.

18. Elizabeth C Stanton, Susan B Anthony, and Matilda J Gage, eds., "Women of Philadelphia (1848)," from "The Public Ledger and Daily Transcript," in: *History of Women's Suffrage* (Rochester: Charles Mann, 1881), 804-805.

19. George Murdock, Human Relations Area Files (HRAF), Yale University.

20. David Mayberry, ed., *Tribal Millennium*, (Alexandra, VA: Public Broadcasting Services, 1997), TV film.

21. See Appendix C: *Two Wings of a Bird.*

22. from James Joyce's, *Ulysses,* in episode 2 Dedalus refers to "history as the nightmare…"

23. Estelle B Freedman, *No Turning Back: the History of Feminism and the Future of Women,* (New York: Random House-Ballantine, 2002).

24. Angelina Grimke, *An Appeal to the Women of the Nominally Free States, Issued by an Antislavery Convention of American Women,* 2nd ed. (Boston: Isaac Knapp, 1838), 13-2.

25. Elizabeth C. Stanton, Susan B. Anthony, & Matilda J. Gage, eds., "Declaration of Sentiments" in *History of Women's Suffrage* (Rochester: Charles Mann, 1881) 67-94.

26. Freedman, *No Turning Back.*

27. Rebecca Mbuh, "African Women's Challenges in the 21ˢᵗ Century: an Overview," Seoul, Korea, 2002.

28. Azar Tabari and Nahid Yeganeh, eds., *In the Shadow of Islam: the Women's Movement in Iran* (ZED Press: London, 1982).

29. Suad Joseph and Susan Slyomovics, eds., *Women and Power in the Middle East* (Philadelphia: University of Pennsylvania Press, 2001).

30. Stanlie M James & Abena P Abusia, *Theorizing Black Feminisms: the Visionary Pragmatism of Black Women* (New Jersey: Routledge, 1993); Paula Giddings, *When and Where I Enter: the Impact of Black Women on Race and Sex in America* (New York: William Morrow, 1984).

31. Freedman, *No Turning Back;* Ollenburger & Moore, *Sociology of Women;* and Vanaja Dhruvarajan & Jill. Vickers, *Gender, Race and Nation: A Global Perspective* (University of Toronto Press, 2002).

32. See Yeats' Note in the *Collected Poems of WB Yeats*, Richard J. Finneran, ed., (New York: Scribner, 1996); see also *The Cyclic Theory of Abu-Ali Sina* (Avicenna 980-1037 CE).

33. John Naisbitt & Patricia Aburdene, *Megatrends 2000* (New York: Bantam Publishing, 1993).

34. Charles Lemert, ed., Social Theory: the Multicultural and Classic Readings (Boulder, CO: Westview Press, 1999)

35. Universal House of Justice, *The Promise of World Peace* 1985-a statement presented to heads of state and world leaders, calling for a global assembly of leaders to forge a pact of global peace to prevent war.

36. Qur'án 39:12, 13:17.

37. Joseph and Slyomovics, eds, *Women, Power, Middle East.*

38. Chinua Achebe, *Things Fall Apart* (New York: McDowell Obolensky, 1959).

39. e.g. Afghanistan and Iran governments have required all women to completely cover themselves with chadors, dark cloths which are wrapped around a woman, covering all but her eyes. News reports during 1999-2000 from Afghanistan described attacks on women accused of revealing the slightest glimpse of flesh. These included beatings, isolation, rape, imprisonment, and acid attacks.

40. UNDP, *Human Development Report* (Oxford University Press, 1994).

41. James Wolfensohn, *Washington News on Africa*, vol. 22,: no. 2 (1996), 7.

42. Urie Bronfenbrenner, *Two Worlds of Childhood; US and U.S.S.R.* (New York, Russell Sage Foundation, 1970).

PART II

WOMEN AWAKENING

Introduction to Part II:

Women Awakening

What happens when a woman defies the unspoken, but powerfully enforced, rules of patriarchy in a traditional Middle Eastern Society as a disciple of a new religious revelation? Since 1848 the name of Tahirih has become synonymous with gender equality throughout many societies in the Middle East and beyond. But this notoriety came with a high price—her life, and those of others who dared to follow her example.

In the context of western patriarchy, Beatriz Ferreira illustrates through her biographical narrative how the experiences of a Mexican agricultural family, poverty, gender and discrimination intersect in the American southwest. Yet, her story also demonstrates the power of education and social mobility within a democratic society, however jaded by prejudice and classism. Ferreira's story is one of the triumphs of the human spirit against the odds of patriarchy, compounded by abject poverty and discrimination. Sweden and several other Scandinavian countries stand out among the most egalitarian societies of the world. Sweden has allotted more parliamentary seats to women than any other in the world, followed closely by Denmark, Finland and Norway. The Beijing Platform of 1995 called for at least 33 percent by 2000, but Sweden reported 42.7 percent seats, along with 95 percent enrollment of girls in primary education and nearly equal ratios in secondary education as well. Agneta Enermalm shares her journey as a woman and theologian in her native land and how the egalitarian environment in which she grew up influenced her life choices and vision of self in relationship to others.

In western African countries women have carried a lion's share of the economic burden through agricultural, marketing, and domestic work. Multiple wives and offspring provide therefore a solid basis for patriarchal power and prosperity. Males rise in status and wealth according to their wives' abilities to farm and sell the fruits of their labor in local markets. Children also bring status and wealth to male-headed families according to their abilities to succeed in the modern westernized economic structure, whether in Cameroon or abroad. Children thus help to support the family economic unity and in return enjoy the name, status and prosperity attached to the male head of family.

Women's cooperation and skill within the family can be viewed as one of the strengths of traditional Cameroonian women. Yet, without assistance from more liberated family members, the patriarchal value system can become a hindrance to the progress of women who wish to transcend traditional roles to become leaders. Rebecca Mbuh's analysis of gender relations and the progress of women in her homeland provides a case study to which she refers later in her analysis of the pan-African women's movement.

In the last chapter within this part, Wu Xiaoqun provides an insightful historical view of gender relations in China, from within this ancient and powerful patriarchy. Multiple revolutions, some associated with removal of all vestiges of traditional gender relations, have been instigated by various segments of society, most notably the Communist party, over the past century and a half. From the royal patriarchy of Confucian emperors, who could kill anyone who dared to wear the royal color of yellow and prided themselves on as many as a thousand concubines, to colonial patriarchies of Europe and Japan, to a peasant-led Marxist revolution which transferred patriarchal powers to the Communist Party—China maintained its focus on patriarchy. One of the Party's first actions was to force women out of the home and family to join the work force, although no additional provisions were made for reducing the amount of work facing women who worked long hours both outside and inside the home. Rather than led by Chinese women, the laws and policies concerning gender equality emanated from Marxian philosophy, translated into Chinese communist ideology. The question arises as to whether a women's movement conceived within a patriarchal framework, however enlightened, can actually empower women. Can equality be imposed by government or must women share in the conceptualization of such a movement in order for genuine empowerment to occur? Wu Xiaoqun describes the nature of this struggle in her native land, as she sets the stage for the third part of *Women in the New Millennium.*

Chapter 2

A Trumpet Blast: Patriarchies and Women in the Middle East

Anne Breneman

From mid-eighteenth century Persia (Iran) the story of a beautiful gifted poetess from Qazvin named Tahirih spread like wildfire throughout the country and beyond, where the teachings of one called "The Báb", Ali Muhammad, had already begun to stir the masses in 1844 in a dramatic call to a new way of life.[1] Within a brief six years, the Shah and religious leaders of Persia had arisen to stamp out the growing fervor of the new religion by murdering thousands and publicly executing The Báb in Tabriz in 1850. Among the first 19 disciples, referred to as "Letters of the Living" and considered the primary exponents of The Báb's teachings, was a single woman, Tahirih. Tutored by her own curiosity and her father's unusually extensive library, she left her husband to travel across the land giving literacy lessons to women and girls and eloquent expositions on the teachings of The Báb in the homes of upper-class women.

Among her students were awestruck women and men of all classes. Her fame as a poetess of rare beauty and eloquence reached the Shah, who invited her by letter to become one of his royal harem. In a bold gesture, Tahirih turned the letter over and penned an original poem declining the honor and affirming her commitment to the teachings of the Báb and the emancipation of women.

In a famous scene, set in a rented garden in the small hamlet of Badasht, in the early spring of 1848, Tahirih removed her traditional chador (veil) and walked into a tent full of male Bábis, announcing a "trumpet-blast" signaling the long awaited "resurrection" and the opening of a new age. As recorded by a participant:

> when suddenly the figure of Tahirih, adorned and unveiled, appeared before the eyes of the assembled companions. Consternation immediately seized the entire gathering. All stood aghast before this sudden and most unexpected apparition. To behold her face unveiled was to them inconceivable. Even to gaze at her shadow was a thing which they deemed improper, inasmuch as they regarded her as the very incarnation of Fatimih, the noblest emblem of chastity in their eyes.[2]

Shocked and outraged, several Bábis reacted by rushing out of the tent, screaming and cutting their throats, thus turning away both from their newly embraced Faith and the new standards of equality intimated by Tahirih. Her words called forth the imagery of the Qur'án, familiar to all who were gathered, and gave new meaning to the verses quoted to conclude her speech: "*This is the day on which the fetters of the past are burst asunder. Let those who have shared in this great achievement arise and embrace each other.*"[3]

Tahirih's bold actions on behalf of women and her newfound Faith provoked an official sentence to imprisonment and death a few years later, in 1852, at the age of 36. Before being strangled to death with her own scarf, Tahirih is reported to have declared to the witnesses and executioners, "You may take my life, but you cannot stop the emancipation of women!"[4]

The wife of Kalantar, the official in whose home she was placed under house arrest for several months prior to her execution, left an account of what she knew of Tahirih, said to have reached "the high-water mark of her popularity" at the time of her death. Among her concluding observations, was the following:

> I mused over the circumstances of her eventful life, and recalled, with a throb of wonder, her intrepid courage, her zeal, her high sense of duty and unquestioning devotion. I was reminded of her literary attainments, and brooded over the imprisonment, the shame and the calumny which she had faced with a fortitude such as no other women in her land could manifest. . . . The memory of her passionate eloquence warmed my heart, as I repeated to myself the words which had so often dropped from her lips. The consciousness of the vastness of her knowledge, and her mastery of the sacred Scriptures of Islam flashed through my mind with a suddenness that disconcerted me. . . . What could have been the secret, I thought to myself, of the power that tore her away from her home and kindred, which sustained her throughout her stormy career, and eventually carried her to her grave? Could that force, I pondered, be of God?[5]

Her collection of poems and reflections found their way to neighboring countries and beyond to be translated into many languages and read by a host of women still laboring under oppressive conditions of male dominance. In London, the famous actress, Sarah Bernhardt, starred in a theatrical production of early Bábi history featuring Tahirih's unveiling and martyrdom. Martha Root, an American journalist and Bahá'í teacher, traveled through Iran and India in the early twenties and disseminated an English translation of Tahirih's manuscript and her own biography of Tahirih's life. In her travels round the world and throughout most continents, she shared Tahirih's stories and documents, planting seeds of new possibilities wherever she found receptive soil.[6]

We begin this section on the women's movement within the Middle East with the dramatic story of Tahirih, whose given name by her father was "Fatimih," the daughter of the Prophet Muhammad. The Middle East has often been represented as a region of the world with values, beliefs and ideologies that sharply differ from those of the West on the surface of things. The philosophies, political ideologies, economics, religious values and social structures appear in stark contrast with those of western societies, especially with regard to gendered relationships. Therefore, to gain an authentic perspective on the various ways the women's movement has grown in the Middle East it is helpful to review research findings by Middle Eastern scholars. The two representative collections of research reviewed below are nearly two decades apart, 1984 and 2001, and provide multiple perspectives on the progress of the women's movement in countries that fall into the geographic and cultural definition of the Middle East.

Patriarchy and the Family

Scholars such as Joseph and Slyomovics[7] point out that the Middle East cannot be treated in a unitary manner since each nation is situated historically, politically and economically in a unique context. Nonetheless, Slyomovics and Joseph's analysis highlights the pattern of the extended patriarchal family as the core of society in most if not all Middle Eastern and North African societies. This emphasis on the family is based upon its traditional function as a political, economic, social and religious "cell" which is protected by Islamic religious law and reproduced as a "privileged position" throughout the region.

The gender system in the Middle East and North Africa is shaped by and works through the institution of patriarchy, which affects much of the social order. . . . Patriarchy privileges males and elders (including older women in the Arab-Islamic world) and justifies this privilege in kinship terms. For women, these continuities among family, civil society, and state mean that they confront patriarchy in every sphere. Patriarchy is thus reproduced in multiple sites in many Middle Eastern and North African countries—a phenomenon not unique to Arab-Islamic societies. The outcome is that women and juniors must be embedded in familial relationships to make most effective use of the institutions in these spheres and are therefore subject to patriarchal norms and relationships even in public spaces.[8]

Researchers observe that these same countries have assigned family to conservative institutions that are inherently gender-biased, i.e. religious clergy. Whether Muslim, Christian or Jewish, these institutions tend to function on both patriarchal and hierarchical models. Paradoxically, many women activists argue for the retention of these same familial institutions since they have been traditional sources of support as well. Most Islamic societies have no civil law, only religious law, making legal changes that favor changes in women's personal status very difficult. Even those few countries that have civil courts continue to refer issues affecting the family, including personal status, to Islamic courts. When some progress has been achieved, conservative or fundamentalist forces tend to create a backlash of protest, as in Iran, which has caused several governments in the region to retreat from earlier embrace of reforms favoring women's equality and development. In most recent years, Afghanistan and Iran have been often in the news, highlighting clashes between progressive measures to support greater democratic participation and women's advancement against the backdrop of traditional religious movements calling for a return to the more patriarchal, conservative practices of the past. Recently the people of Iran, including women, have taken to the streets to protest the highly patriarchal, authoritarian regime of Iran.

In 1984 a collection of Social Science Research studies by and about women in the Arab world was sponsored and published by the United Nations Economic and Social Commission.[9] In general, the studies and analyses raised questions regarding the operation of patriarchy in Arab-Islamic culture. Rassam concluded that women's status in Islamic society could only be understood in terms of the social organization of power, the ideological and institutional means of controlling women's sexuality, and the sexual division of labor. She posited that the Arab family/household should be considered the logical focus of research, as this is the primary social unit in which all three of these factors intersect. That is, the study of the Islamic/Arab family should not be confined to the assumption that it is simply the domain of women. Underwritten by Arab ideology, the Islamic family can be viewed as a system of structured cross-gender relationships with inherent mechanisms that allow it to both function and reproduce itself from one generation to another. Within this conceptual context, Rassam and other researchers explore how this social unit is influenced by changes in women's involvement in professional or nonprofessional work in the labor market outside of the home. As women earn wages, are they able to negotiate changes in traditional roles and structures of power and authority within the family and state? Do they become more independent as their earning power in the public sector increases?

Pursuing a more Marxian theoretical perspective, Baffoun argues that all social relations of dependence and oppression, including that of gender, have their origins in economic domination. She proposes that in Islamic society and perhaps others as well, ". . . the superstructure plays an important role of camouflaging and whitewashing brought about by those in power [i.e. a social group or the State]."[10] Observing that for the first time in the history of feminist militancy, the women's movement is no longer the exclusive domain of a small group of elites, Baffoun asserts that the movement ". . . is becoming a worldwide phenomenon, making it one of the most significant forces of our time." She believes that there is a correlation between the number of women employed in the public sector in those regions of the world where industrialization has altered the traditional means of production, and the ascendancy of women's movements in societies with patriarchal and class structures. Baffoun's comprehensive survey of research on women in the Maghreb includes the nations of Morocco, Tunisia, Algeria, Mauritania, Libya and Arab Jamahiriya. She calls for further research on peasant and rural women, such as Bedouins, as well as the rethinking of concepts of development, progress, evolution, and women's liberation. She also raises the question of whether biological differences are the only basis for sexual images and double moral standards, given the complexity of male economic domination and female dependency.

Religion or Culture?

Kader approaches the issues of gender inequality and oppression from a religious perspective, affirming that the Qur'án teaches that all believers, male and female, are to be treated as equals before God. She points out that although polygamy is considered degrading to the status of Muslim women, all of the prophets of the Judeo-Christian tradition had more than one wife; therefore, Islam cannot be accurately viewed as creating the practice of polygamy. Rather,

Muhammad limited the number of wives a man may have to four and provided legal protection of their rights to social status, inheritance and property. Kader argues that the status of Muslim women can be attributed to "extra-Islamic conditions" which have resulted in misinterpretation and distortion of the Qur'án and Islamic law, including the customs of veiling and secluding women.[11]

In their more recent survey of women's progress in the Middle East and North Africa, Joseph and Slyomovics reaffirm and elaborate on the centrality of the patriarchal family in Islamic and Middle Eastern societies, which officially designate the family as the basic unit of society. In response to issues raised in the 1984 UNESCO research on women regarding the genderized social structures that obstruct women's empowerment and quest for equality, the authors affirm in 2001:

> The family lies at the core of Middle Eastern and North African society—in political, economic, social and religious terms. This privileged position is enshrined in the constitutions of many Arab or Muslim states and is reproduced at almost every level of political life. Economic (institutions) recognize the centrality of the family in many ways. . . . Religious institutions consider themselves the guardians of family integrity and hold families responsible for safeguarding religious sanctity. People are keenly aware of each other's family memberships, identities, and status. Access to institutions, jobs and government services is often through family connections. The centrality of family to social, economic, political, and religious life has profound implications for gender relations.[12]

While each Middle Eastern society is unique, the religious and legal framework of Islam provides a common denominator in which the patriarchal family is primary. Elder males within each family hold privileged positions of power and influence, with males in general valued above females. The traditional status of women is embedded within such family relationships; a woman is defined by her father, husband, and son's status within the family and society. Joseph and Slyomovics emphasize that in such societies, political, economic and social negotiations are likely to occur among elder males without input from women.

Power and Family Honor

Middle Eastern women scholars have recognized that within the family certain values prevail throughout the Middle East and North Africa, regardless of their diversity of history and culture, which constrain women's sexuality, role and decision-making power. These include family honor and pride, avoidance of direct conflict, domestic largess, strict gender boundaries, and dependence upon male negotiations in the public arena. The value of honor creates a power structure, according to researchers, which requires women to acquiesce to males in all aspects of the daily routine of life and beyond. To not do so is to undermine or even threaten a family's honor.

On the surface, these values may seem commendable and innocent. The problem comes in how these are applied within the patriarchal and hierarchical systems of power. Since women are lower in status and are embedded within the family, rather than viewed as individual agents, much of what is considered a family's "honor" focuses around women's sexuality. According to Joseph and Slyomovics, "The notion of family honor reinforces patriarchal power by circumscribing women's sexuality, movement in social arenas, and to some degree, economic opportunities. It enhances the power of fathers, grandfathers, uncles, brothers, and male cousins over women."[13]

News stories of Iranian-American grooms' frustrations have found their way into Western media. Trying to impose Middle Eastern honor codes on Persian brides within a society that encourages women to exercise a greater measure of decision-making power within the family and society has produced domestic crises that may include violence. American women are encouraged to develop more self-determination or personhood than experienced in Islamic societies. Hoda Mahmoudi, an Iranian-American sociologist, commented: "More conservative Iranian men are willing to go all the way to Iran to find traditional stay-at-home wives. . . . They think women in Los Angeles have become too selfish, that they are not as loving, sacrificing and giving, and that a woman from Iran will be more obedient. Many of them are in for a rude awakening. The minute the women come to the United States and see the opportunities, everything changes."[14] One Iranian-American California businessman admitted, "You bring a woman here and at first it's like helping a blind person to see. Then all of a sudden the women see the opportunities, and they want the freedom and they get out. [I.e. of the marriage]."[15] However, exposure to new standards of gender relationships outside of the social structures of traditional patriarchal power can change male perspectives as well. The same businessman affirmed that he would not resort to returning to Iran for a traditional bride, "I don't think I can go back to that: I'm on another frequency now." His wife has become a bank president and he reluctantly admires Iranian women who are taking advantage of new opportunities to pursue higher education and careers. Caught between traditional and modern perspectives on gender, this Iranian male is concerned about how such dramatic departures from the ancient codes of honor and gender relationship will impact the family: "In the next millennium, men are going to have a lot of problems with women. I don't blame them for wanting equality, but they have to know where to draw the line. It's ruining the family."

Other Iranian families living in the US who continue to base their values on the traditional patriarchal honor codes may go so far as to have reconstructive surgery on their daughters when a mistake leading to loss of virginity threatens her marriage opportunities. Parents often fear their daughters will be stigmatized if they live alone, without legitimate male protection by a father, brother, or husband. One 16-year old Persian-American stood up at an Iranian-American community meeting and boldly complained of the unfairness she believed she and other Iranian teenage girls growing up in America had experienced. It is unlikely that she would have spoken in public of her discontent in Iran, outside of Bahá'í community circles and only cautiously in these.

A divorced Iranian-American therapist commented that few Persian women would willingly return to Iran to marry and live: "If you're a Persian woman back home, you'd marry the devil himself if he got you out. Once they're here, it's like when Columbus sank the Santa Maria. It's do or die. Women have to make it. What do they have to go back to? Men would survive there; women would not." Another young woman born in Iran, told a researcher of her tortuous life which began with her marriage at 16 to a man unknown to her prior to marriage. When she bore no children, he married a second woman and divorced her at the age of 28. In Iran, as in many Arab societies, a divorced woman is under extreme social pressure and suspicion of being a "loose woman." Such women are sometimes executed by male relatives to preserve a family's honor. She married an Iranian living in America and was subjected to severe psychological and physical abuse. When her brother-in-law took her into his household, she learned that her husband had taken photos of her while bathing and sent them home to further degrade and defame her. She knew of another divorced Iranian woman whose husband had sent similar photos of her home; when she arrived home for a visit, she was publicly beaten by a religious committee, which met her at the airport.

Pride and Violence

The heinous nature of the domestic violence experienced by many Iranian women at home and abroad has resulted in a network of Iranian and American female lawyers, committees and NGOs, which in the US specialize in defending their rights under the 1994 Violence Against Women Act. According to one such lawyer, Daliah Setareh, "Domestic violence is still a hush-hush issue in the Middle East. Women who come forward and speak out against their husbands are seen as violating the sanctity of the family. That's why many would rather suffer in silence at home."[16]

It is one thing to pursue equality in a nation that protects freedom of speech and other rights of the individual person. However, in those Middle Eastern countries, where organizations such as the "Iranian Foundation for Islamic Protection and Guidance," work with the Justice Department to administer homes for "runaway girls," pursuing justice and gender-sensitive legal codes is quite a different matter. In 2001 government officials, mullahs (Muslim religious leaders), and members of the State Security Forces were found running a center in Karaj, said to be one of a large network of similar centers. Girls who were either abandoned when their parents were arrested as political prisoners, or who ran away from abusive families, were transferred to one of the notorious centers, run by some of the most influential leaders of the country. Under the pretext of *"protection and guidance,"* the girls are sexually exploited for *"temporary marriages,"*[17] prepared for this form of prostitution by older women working for the government. In a society in which family honor codes center around girl's virginity and innocence, it is not surprising that suicide rates can be extremely high in Iran (3,472 in 1994) of which as many as 81 percent are women and girls.[18]

Not only have helpless female children been exploited and trafficked, but also thousands of women prisoners were reported to have experienced sexual torture and rape. One report described "residential units" of women prisoners in which Revolutionary Guards, torturers and regime leaders are given free reign to rape the prisoners as often as they wish, similar to the reported "rape rooms" of the recently toppled Iraqi regime.

The United Nations Human Rights Commissioner's Special Report on the Situation of Human Rights in Iran reported to the UN General Assembly in October 2000 that there had been little if any change in the systematic discrimination that Iranian women had been facing. Earlier, in the Beijing +5 UN Women's Conference held in Manhattan in June, the official delegation of women appointed by the government was challenged by a group of Iranian women who accused the government of denying representation of women at the UN Conference by sending women who were cooperating with the official party line to cover up the numerous human rights abuses against women in Iran since the 1979 revolution. The Shah, who had confirmed the removal of the women's chador,[19] had been exiled in order to reinstate a fundamentalist regime led by Muslim clergy.

In a dramatic act of self-empowerment a small unofficial group of women from several particularly oppressive Middle Eastern nations, such as Iran, Afghanistan and Iraq, convened an ad hoc gathering during the UN Conference, requesting that UN security guards bar government officials, reporters and cameras. Their intent was to unveil the deception of governments which not only continued to permit and condone severe abuse of women's rights, but which also attempted to create a false impression of the advancement of women's rights within their respective countries. Some governments even resorted to the fabrication of evidence in reports and exhibits featuring the "progress of women." The act of presenting to the conference and the United Nations the unofficial reports of human rights abuses, witnessed by the authors, required unusual courage on the part of the women who participated in "blowing the cover," revealing the deceptive schemes of their governments. Some may have paid for this act of bravery with their lives, or those of family members.

Facing the Opposition

Aside from the dire consequences for many Middle Eastern women who dare to remove the veil, pursue education or a career, or relinquish family support to challenge the system, women must also face male clerics and male representatives of the legal system in most Islamic societies. All members of the clergy are male, as are mujtahids, who are the Islamic interpreters of Quránic law. In most Middle Eastern countries, the entire code of laws is derived from the Qur'án and Islamic jurisprudence, though Egypt has created a civil court for citizens who are not Muslim. Mounira Charrad compares Tunisian, Algerian and Moroccan state formation and the consequences for family policy on such matters as marriage, divorce, child custody and inheritance. She considers family law policy as one of the most critical for gender politics. Tunisia, like Egypt, is one of the few Middle Eastern/North African countries with a civil family code that is not under Islamic religious codes and courts. This may be an advantage for women who seek new avenues for legal protection from male abuse and equal rights in the work place. Female lawyers are unlikely to be accepted in the traditional Islamic system of jurisprudence in which patriarchy is the cherished norm.[20]

Gruenbaum examined the rise of the National Islamic Front (NIF) in the Sudan and how it has influenced Sudanese women's progress toward equality and empowerment.[21] She found that the NIF emphasizes socialization into what "a proper Muslim woman" should be. In this case, Islamic beliefs may contribute to the empowerment of women within a culturally constructed gender identity. On the other hand, other researchers propose that nationalist and religious fundamentalist movements in the Middle East may inspire and even legitimize women's activism, but not necessarily the reconstruction of gender relations toward equality.[22]

Gruenbaum's examples include Palestinian women in Libya, the Gaza Strip and West Bank, where women's activism goes back to the British mandate period. As the domestic sphere of family became invaded by soldier confrontations and violence, women were forced to participate in a struggle with militant women's groups having to face the new Palestinian National Authority, which was itself under constant pressure from Israel. The focus on warfare and conflict did not necessarily lead to transformation of women's role in the family, workplace, or in leadership. Traditional cultures, in general, have acted as constraints on women's empowerment; political revolutions often reinforce the traditional roles of women. There have been important exceptions where changes in the status of women have been integral to the ideology of a revolution.[23] As noted by Giacaman et al, nationalist movements may inspire and even legitimize women's movements, but not necessarily the reconstruction of egalitarian gender roles and relationships.[24]

Owning the Movement

For many women in the Middle East and Northern Africa there is some danger to use of the more western label of "feminism" in speaking of the women's movement. The label "feminist" is described by Graham-Brown as "provocative, imported from the West, unsuitable, and dangerous" for the Middle Eastern women's movement.[25] When any ideology in Middle Eastern society becomes associated with the West, it is likely to meet with powerful opposition from the patriarchal and religious order. Each national women's movement has sought its own definition, voice and path of action toward empowerment and equality.

Among the earliest of grassroots women's movements was that which erupted in Iran in the mid-nineteenth century, followed by those in Egypt and Turkey during the first decade of the twentieth century. In Iran, Bahá'í communities founded girl's schools and hospitals, where female doctors were introduced into the villages to serve the needs of women for the first time.[26] Movements to discard the chador and the seclusion of women grew in urban areas and spread to villages. This movement, after its violent beginning in Iran, gained momentum after the fall of traditional autocratic regimes in 1906 and 1908 in Iran and Turkey, with women participating in what began as a somewhat liberalized social democracy, however limited and short-lived.

Following World War I, nationalist governments emerged in both Iran and Turkey that co-opted the grassroots women's movements and their organizations. They became official symbols, icons of modernization, as defined by each government, and therefore subject to political manipulation.[27] In Turkey, Attaturk's reforms dramatically secularized the nation, reconstituted the traditional legal codes and discouraged veiling and seclusion of women. In Iran, Reza Shah forcibly abolished veiling in the 1930s and reinforced the movement toward universal education of both genders in a curriculum that included standard academic subjects and technology. Prior to this reform, only boys from upper-class families were sent to Madrisih schools to learn to recite the Qur'án and sometimes become a Muslim clergyman or scholar. Members of the upper classes concerned with providing their children with higher education sent them outside of the country to western schools and colleges. Illiteracy rates were high, especially among women, who were considered lacking any need for formal education.

As a nation under British colonial rule, Egypt came in contact with both Middle Eastern revolutionary thought and Western movements toward gender reform. The former spread throughout the Middle East as persecuted members of the Bahá'í Faith in Iran fled from their persecutors during the late 19th and early 20th centuries. Because gender equality was one of the central teachings of Bahá'u'lláh,[28] the fledgling Bahá'í Community was obligated to elect women as well as men to leadership in their communities and to use consultation as a primary form of decision-making within families and communities. Consent of not only both parents to marriage, but also both daughters and sons were required. That is, Bahá'í principles of gender equality made it unlawful for a marriage to occur without proof of consent of all parties. These teachings were often met with opposition by societies in which patriarchal policies had ruled without question for millennia.[29]

Within Egypt, as in the West, the women's movement began primarily in the upper classes, confined mostly to issues of education, charity and intellectual debate. As Egypt began its independence movement, activists Huda Shaarawi and Nalsawiyyih Musa made contact with women of other nations and rallied women of all classes to protest colonial rule, confront soldiers and demand women's political rights. In 1911 Egyptian writer Malek Narif stood up in the all-male Congress and recommended that women have the right to be educated to whatever degree they desire.[30] While Egyptian women now have greater access to education and career opportunities than many women in Middle Eastern countries, and enjoy some progress regarding their rights under the law regarding personal status, their struggle continues within the family and nation as to who should control women's lives. That is, the patriarchal ideology still prevails and creates conflicts and obstacles to women's progress, especially since the revolutionary spirit of the early 20th century waned considerably after Independence in Egypt.

In general, Middle Eastern women have not pursued enfranchisement to the same extent as Western women. Perhaps part of their reluctance is caused by the State's insistence on controlling women's organizations in many nations of the Maghreb. Exceptions are Turkey, where women won the right to vote in 1934, and Egypt, where a woman's group called Daughters of the Nile, led by Duriyya Shafiq, succeeded in achieving the enfranchisement in 1956. Among the Gulf nations Kuwait is the only nation, as of 1999, which granted women the right to vote. Holding seats in Parliament is still difficult, though Egypt has enacted a law that sets a quota for parliamentary seats to be held by women. Some critics are concerned that in nations in which women have been granted voting rights without any significant efforts to raise women's consciousness, they are becoming "ballot fodder" for unscrupulous political parties, whether religious or secular. Without personal liberty, women may feel obligated or forced to vote according to the values of male family members.

In cases of violent or prolonged national movements, many women have been imprisoned, tortured or raped, making it very difficult for them to resume a normal life without the stigma of sexual promiscuity or violation of family honor. Algerian women who participated in the national independence movement struggled with life-threatening insinuations of honor violations. Not until 1984 were Algerian women permitted educational or employment opportunities.[31]

The struggle for rights of equal participation in democratic electoral and decision-making processes has yet to be won in most Middle Eastern nations. As it stands, only a few of these nations permit women to organize without State direction and censorship, such as the Daughters of the Nile in Egypt.

Struggling for Personal Freedom within the Family

Apart from rights as citizens, women in the Middle East are concerned with issues of male control of women's sexuality and personal lives. Moroccan sociologist, Fatima Mernissi, has especially challenged the double standards in male and female sexual norms and privilege and the role of Islam in re-enforcing male authority, sexual purity, and the seclusion of women.[32] To challenge the norms and traditions of Middle Eastern and North African societies involves great risks. Mernissi argues that Arab identity has been conceived in such a way that any social change is a threat to the moral order, an attitude that becomes a significant impediment to both democracy and the emancipation of women.

The same bias creates a boogieman out of the West, making it an easy scapegoat for the intense economic dislocations, moral corruption, and social, political and cultural identity crises underway in many if not all of these nations. On the other hand, some Middle Eastern women scholars take issue with what are considered the Western criteria for progress, given the primacy of family, religion and patriarchy throughout the Middle East and North Africa, and, indeed, many other societies as well. Whether liberal feminism, which seeks to gain privileges and rights accorded exclusively to males within civil society, or Marxist feminism, which seeks to reverse gendered, racial and class-based structures so that those who are disenfranchised, i.e. women and minorities, become managers and owners—both approaches to women's equality assume that citizens are contract-making individuals and property owners, rather than integral parts of a social unit, the family. Pateman argues that the contemporary Western State is a fraternal patriarchy with its dominant idiom brothers—free men constituting a kind of civil fraternity. The traditional social contract of Western political philosophy then assumes that those who are neither property owners, voters, nor contract-makers are to be excluded from the fraternity, not the sorority, of civil society.

Regardless of which perspective is to be used to analyze the similarities and differences between women of the Maghreb, the United Nations has created a global forum of decision-making women who have identified certain universal measures of women's progress and empowerment. Among these are gender equality in education, percentage of seats held by women in national parliamentary bodies and administrative and managerial positions, ratio of women's salaries to men's in the same categories of work, and the extent to which health care is accessible, affordable and appropriate to women and children.

With a goal of at least 30 percent national parliamentary seats for women by 2000, the nations of the Middle East and North Africa are among the lowest, ranging from 0 percent in Morocco, Yemen, Kuwait, and United Arab Republic to 11.5 percent in Tunisia as of January of 2000. This must be compared with Sweden that had the highest percentage of women in parliament, 42.7, 100 female to male ratio per secondary school enrollment, and 51 percent women's share of paid employment in industry and service.

Another measure used to track the progress of women in each nation is one that compares each nation with its own achievement in these categories from the mid-eighties to the late nineties. In Northern Africa, both Egypt and Tunisia showed progress in most of the measures, though Egypt regressed in parliamentary representation. Algeria, Egypt and Tunisia showed gains in the area of income equality. Within the Middle East, Turkey showed the greatest progress in education, parliamentary representation and per capita income. It must be borne in mind that these countries did not meet the targeted goals, but showed progress during the period under examination.[33] If other, more qualitative measures, are to be used to evaluate the progress of women in this region on their own terms, then these criteria must be defined by the "national machinery" each nation has committed to setting up for the achievement of targeted goals related to the advancement of women.

Chapter 2: Notes

1. E.G. Browne, trans, *A Traveler's Narrative*, (Cambridge: University Press, 1891).

2. Shoghi Effendi, trans & ed, *The Dawnbreakers: Nabil's Narrative* (Wilmette, IL: Bahá'í Publishing, 1932, 1970), 295.

3. Shoghi Effendi, *The Dawnbreakers*, 296 and TK Cheyne's, *The Reconciliation of Races and Religions* (London: Adam & Charles Black, 1914).

4. Martha L Root, *Tahirih the Pure*, rev. ed. (Los Angeles: Kalimat Press, 1981), 98.

5. See *Journal of the Royal Asiatic Society*, article 6, (1889), 492.

6. Martha Root, *Tahirih*.

7. Joseph & Slyomovics, *Women, Power, Middle East*.

8. Ibid., 2, 5.

9. Frances Pinter, , *Social Science Research and Women in the Arab World*, (London: UNESCO, 1984).

10. Alya Baffoun, "Research in the Social Sciences on North African Women: Problems, Trends and Needs," in *Social Science Research and Women in the Arab World* (Paris, UNESCO, 1984), 41.

11. Soha Abdel Kader, Ibid., 139-175

12. Joseph & Slyomovics, *Women, Power, Middle East*, 2.

13. Ibid., 6.

14. Anna Marie O'Connor, "New Lives for Women From Iran," *Los Angeles Times*, 10 December 1998, p.1, col.1.

15. Ibid.

16. Ibid.

17. See Lord Curzon, Persia and the Persian Question, 1892, quoted in the Dawnbreakers: Nabil's Narrative, trans, Shoghi Effendi, (Wilmette, IL: Bahá'í Publishing Trust), p xvii: According to ancient custom pilgrims to the holy shrines"… in recognition of the long journey which they have made, of the hardships they have sustained, and of the distances by which they are severed from family and home, they are permitted, with the connivance of the ecclesiastical law and its officers, to contract temporary marriages during their sojourn in the city… a gigantic system of prostitution, under the sanction of the Church, prevails in Mashad…"

18. O'Connor, *LATimes*, p 1.

19. The "chador," known by other names in various Islamic countries, is a dark, heavy cloth designed to cover a woman's entire face & body, usually worn over other clothing when in public.

20. Mounira Charrad, "State & Gender in the Maghrib," in *Women and Power in the Middle East*, eds. Joseph Suad and Susan Slyomovics (Philadelphia: University of Pennsylvania Press, 2001).

21. Ellen Gruenbaum, "Sudanese Women & the Islamist State," Ibid.

22. Rita Giacamon, Islah Jad, & Penny Johnson, "For the Common Good? Gender & Social Citizenship in Palestine", Ibid.

23. See Wu Xiaoqun's article in this manuscript on "Chinese Women's Emancipation". See Latin America's independence movements that have usually incorporated an expanded control by women of the means of production.

24. Giacamon, Jad and Johnson, "For the Common Good?" *Women, Power, and the Middle East,* ed. Joseph and Slyomovics.

25. Sarah Graham-Brown, "Women's Activism in the Middle East and North Africa," Ibid.

26. Marzeih Gail, rev., *Tahirih the Pure*, by, Martha Root (US: Kalimat Press, 1981) orig., *Tahirih the Pure: Iran's Greatest Woman* (Karachi: Bahá'í Publishing, 1938).

27. Graham-Brown, "Women's Activism."

28. Bahá'u'lláh was born in 1817 in Persia, imprisoned in 1853 for His teachings and exiled to Baghdad, Constantinople (Istanbul), Adrianople (Aderne), & Acca, where he died in 1892. The Bahá'í Faith traces its beginnings to his predecessor, The Bab, born in 1819, executed in 1850. The Bab's teachings were reported by European consuls and scholars as causing a national upheaval of the religious community and a bloodbath involving over 20,000 followers of The Bab and Bahá'u'lláh by the end of the 19th century. The Bábi and Bahá'í movements were viewed by the existing monarchy and Muslim clergy as a threat to the entire socio-religious and political order of the country. Thus, the execution of The Bab, the exile of Bahá'u'lláh, and the genocide campaign targeting their followers were part of an effort to stamp out and block the progress of the religious movement. See John Hatcher, "The Emergence of a Global Religion," Edward G Browne & Moojan Momen.

29. Moojan Momen, ed., *The Bábi's and the Bahá'í Faith, 1844-1944* (Oxford: George Ronald, 1981).

30. Graham-Brown, "Women's Activism."

31. Ibid.

32. Joseph and Slyomovics, *Women, Power and the Middle East.*

33. UNIFEM, "Progress of Women Scoreboard," *Progress of the World's Women 2000*, Biennial Report, 83, Table 3.5.

Chapter 3

Equality, Justice, and Prosperity: Hispanic Migrant Worker to Human Rights Lawyer

Beatriz Ferreira

Like millions of other women, I am a product of the twentieth century. That which distinguishes us is our beginnings and our journeys. As a woman, daughter, wife, mother, educator, entrepreneur, attorney, mediator, and commissioner of human rights and domestic violence court, I have experienced the entire scope of equality, justice and prosperity or lack thereof. Though born into a segment of society that has been described as one of the most impoverished and one of the most discriminated against in the United States, I fortunately have tasted the sweetness of equality, justice and prosperity, both spiritually and materially. Though others thought of me as poor, like my college classmate who used my home as an example of poverty in her slide presentation for our social work course, I knew I had been gifted with a sense of richness that I would discover early in life. Thereafter, when asked about my status, I described it as "having been rich since the day I was born."

In a span of forty years I went from a little farm worker girl sitting on a wooden crate in a railway box car eating my beans and tortillas to sitting in a plush chair adorned with lace in the magnificent chandeliered room of the Great Hall of the People, sipping tea in a matching cup and saucer. As I waited to meet with the Minister of Justice in Beijing, China and some of China's top lawyers, both men and women, I flashed back to that metal box I called home during one whole harvest season in Colorado. But, having humbly received great blessings spanning the many experiences that life deposits on our paths, I can easily envision a 21st century with unlimited possibilities for women throughout the world and humanity in general to enjoy equal opportunities and savor a more peaceful, progressive and united global society.

The focus of my discussion is the role of women in equality, justice and prosperity in the 21st century. To reflect on the prospects regarding these issues, I believe that a personal reflection of my own childhood, youth and womanhood, and my evolving professional experiences with equality, justice and prosperity in the 20th century is appropriate. I will share a portion of my 20th century life experience to illustrate how we, as women of the new millennium, regardless of our beginnings or where life's journey has taken us, can choose, regardless of the difficult challenges we face, to have equality, justice and prosperity, and ultimately peace in our lives.

Reflections on the Twentieth Century

My life began in June 1947, in Nebraska. Some would regard it a most unlikely place for a child of Mexican descent to be born, as most think of Mexicans living closer to the United States/Mexico border in such states as Texas, New Mexico, Arizona and California. However, as evidenced in my birth certificate, I was recorded as Mexican. I learned early on that the only reason I was born a "corn husker" was because my newlywed parents and my father's family, all migrant farm workers, happened to be in Nebraska picking red potatoes and sugar beets.

Many Mexican citizens found themselves north of the border, forced to leave their homes and all of their belongings during the Mexican Revolution of 1910-1920, predominantly fought in my maternal grandparent's home state of Chihuahua, Mexico. In 1919, after years of struggling to survive the effects of the Revolution, my mother's family crossed the border at El Paso, Texas. Following several years of working the cotton fields in Texas and New Mexico, my maternal grandmother migrated to and settled in Greeley, Colorado, after she lost her twenty-year old son to lightening in the cotton fields outside of Lubbock, Texas and her husband a year later, at age forty-two. My grandfather was said to have died of depression and sadness for the loss of his beloved son. The Revolution, prejudice and poverty created circumstances under which my grandparents, parents and many thousands more people of Mexican descent were deprived of equality, justice and material prosperity, both in Mexico and in the United States.

Though neither men nor women in my parents' families were formally educated, it was the women who faced greater consequences from both gender discrimination and lack of economic opportunities. The men would eventually leave the fields to learn such vocations as carpentry, electronics, mechanics or masonry. Generally, the women who sought to leave the fields were limited to seeking housekeeping jobs. They busied themselves cleaning the toilets and kitchens of farmers and more affluent citizens of whatever town the migrant stream happened to drop them in. Unlike the men, women were many times subjected to sexual harassment.

Housekeeping and Sexual Harassment

Housekeeping might keep women out of the weathering elements faced in the fields and pay her a little more, but the emotional price was costly. Often in the midst of their chores they found themselves followed and tormented by the "man of the house," the boss, who believed and exercised his belief that the maid was "his for the taking." More than once I witnessed my mother crying after she had fought off the "boss man" during one of her cleaning days. Though my presence was disregarded by the boss because I was considered too young to remember, a child who witnesses the fear in her mother's eyes does not forget. When I was older my mother would confirm my memory of these incidents as she warned me about the potential negative encounters I might experience with men in pursuit of my own livelihood. Little did my protective mother realize then that I would become a sexual discrimination attorney and defend many women from all walks of life. Or, those twenty years later I would be the judge of similar men caught in similar incidents with the power to pass sentence and divert their activities. Such incidents of sexual harassment suffered by my mother and many of the women in her day would become the foundation and the reason for pursuing my career as a human rights lawyer and domestic violence hearing officer. My own experiences with discrimination and violence would never discourage me but would serve to strengthen my own determination to pursue the cause of human rights and implement drastic changes in our own judicial system and attitudes about the treatment of women.

Like many incidents involving men sexually attacking women, these incidents were never discussed or disclosed to my father or any of the male family members. Women maintained this code of silence for years to come. Though my Father can be described as a loving and protective father, the general attitude adopted by the men of my childhood, including my father, was that a man would sexually attack a woman only if she teased him. As a young woman, looking back, I concluded that the real reason men held such an attitude was to save face, because acknowledging that a man had improperly attacked a woman would require a revengeful act to restore honor to the affected family. By ignoring the truth, the reason for honor was never addressed. This, of course, was my theory, and not necessarily that of others.

Traditional Gender Roles

It is assumed by my family that my father's parents also crossed the border, only further south, in the citrus valley of Texas. No one knew where my paternal grandmother had been born, or where she had lived as a child. I asked her once. She replied that she did not know. I persisted, wanting to know why she did not know. Her answer was simply that, "No one ever told me and I never asked." When further questioned as to why she did not ask, she explained that women just did not ask those questions. According to one story, my paternal grandfather, as a teenager, had been adopted and raised by an Anglo rancher in south Texas. Having extremely light skin, the thought crossed my mind many times that perhaps my grandfather had been the fruit of the rancher and one of his Mexican women workers. I have always believed that this rancher gave the child a Spanish surname, then created the adoption story to save face with his wife and his neighbors.

By the time I was one year old, both of my grandmothers were widows. My mother lost her father several years prior to my birth and within one year of my birth, my father also lost his father. My grandmothers remained widows for the remainder of their lives. As was the general custom in those days, women mourned for a very long time. Once my paternal grandfather was buried, my Catholic grandmother never mentioned him again. My Protestant grandmother, on the other hand, constantly reminisced about the past; of the day she had met my grandfather while on his horse, how he had blocked her path and would not allow her to cross to the other side until she promised to see him again. After widowhood, neither grandmother spoke of aspirations for a future relationship. Marriage for a second time was not an option. Everyone understood this and no one ever raised the question of whether these widows would ever meet another man and fall in love again.

Two of my father's sisters, who were either abandoned by their husbands or left widows, suffered the same fate. To this date, now in their seventies and eighties, they are alone. The women were expected to continue taking care of their children, grandchildren and great grandchildren without the assistance of a partner. A man, on the other hand, often had more than one woman, not including his wife. This was almost always discovered when letters from the "other" woman were intercepted. Arguments or silence would follow, lasting several days, until the man convinced his wife that his weakness had taken the best of him and his wife accepted his gift of reconciliation, usually a lamp or a new iron, or in resignation eventually set the matter aside.

In my father's family, it was the men who were the visible decision-makers. My paternal grandmother, Elena, was for the most part the cook and washwoman. The women were not consulted, nor did they ask questions or provide advice on family matters. Throughout my migrating childhood years, I cannot recall a time when the women were invited or encouraged to participate in any form of discussion that would result in a decision affecting the family. The women were either in the kitchen with the children, or washing a pile of clothes. That is how I remember it.

My mother's family, though also initially dependent on the seasonal harvests, early on resolved to seek other methods of employment to support themselves. After the death of my grandfather, it was my Grandmother Rafaela, later earning the nickname "Tuffy" for her tough ideology on religion, raising children and decision-making, who managed the family. After burying her husband, she had chosen not to be bound to the fields. She had been self-sustaining in Mexico, and she was determined to do the same in the United States.

To begin, she decided to settle in Greeley, Colorado. She purchased a spacious home on a large piece of land. The two-story Midwestern style home was set back from the street. Visitors were welcomed into a large enclosed front porch that led into the living or parlor area. French doors draped with lace curtains adorned her front parlor and led into several other rooms. In one corner of the parlor a dark upright piano captured the attention of family and visitors. My mother and all of her sisters played the piano. It was here that visitors, usually women from her church, would come after Sunday school to play the piano and sing church songs. Coffee was served to everyone except the children.

The women in the family spent many hours preparing food for the winter months. The cellar was always filled with preserved fruits and corn and green beans, and the coal bin was always well stocked.

Though she had several intelligent and capable sons, it was Tuffy who provided the guidance and ultimately decided what direction the family would take. She was not easily intimidated nor did she seem to doubt her own capabilities. I clearly remember walking into her home in Colorado and being made immediately aware that if any item was to change its assigned spot, we had better consult with her or face the consequences. She ruled in her house. Her Pentecostal religion provided the policies and procedures that she implemented to control all activity in her home, as well as all social activity affecting her children outside the home, especially those which contradicted the precepts of her religion.

Religion was practiced daily. In her home all family members were expected to be in church every Sunday morning. Sins were clearly defined and listed, with constant reminders of what they were and what the consequences would be for ignoring them. I still sense the pain in my small fingers when Tuffy, noticing that my fingernails had been painted with red polish by one of my Catholic aunts, took a sharp kitchen knife and scraped off every bit of nail polish. The entire time she was doing this, she lectured me on how I would be condemned to hell for eternity if I allowed this to happen again. It didn't happen again during her lifetime.

While the women in my father's family were seen predominantly in field-worker clothes, worn-out shoes, and handmade bonnets to protect them from the scorching sun, there are several pictures of the women in my mother's family revealing well tailored lace blouses, long ruffled skirts of fine fabric and nice black patent leather shoes. Years later I learned that my mother's mother had been a landowner in Mexico and together with my grandfather had worked to earn a reputation which disqualified them from the "poverty class." Ownership of this land continued for many years, more due to my grandmother's refusal to abandon her Mexican citizenship, than because of the inherent value of the land.

My father proclaimed to be raised Catholic, although other than my paternal grandmother's exhibition of a small altar with candles and saints, I never witnessed any member of his family attending church, speaking of confession, or crossing themselves when passing a Catholic church, as was the custom.

My mother, on the other hand, practiced her evangelical Protestantism to the point that every conceivable act of life had the potential of becoming a mortal sin, which could condemn one to hell for eternity. In her church there was no concept of Catholic "purgatory," a kind of holding station where surviving members of a family could pray for forgiveness of a soul's earthly misdeeds until he or she gained admission to heaven. In my mind my mother's religion seemed fanatical and extreme. For many years I struggled silently with the rigidity of the religious rules forced upon me, until my parents began to mellow in their later years, to the point of even encouraging healthy debate on certain religious doctrines.

This growing flexibility on my parents' part, particularly my father's openness as he aged, opened a family forum on such questions as the creation of Adam and Eve. My mother began to raise questions as well, wondering how Adam and Eve's sons could possibly find wives if they were the only two people in the world. I began searching beyond the traditional religious formulae for answers. Eventually, at the age of 51, I became a member of the Bahá'í Faith, which allowed me to embrace the truths of all of the world's religions, leaving behind the man-made doctrines, which had become so life crushing and limiting.

Life On the Road

Living accommodations during my early childhood years ranged from a railroad boxcar in Colorado, to a barn in the Texas panhandle, to tents on the roadsides of California, to dilapidated labor camps made from scrap lumber and old wooden crates. Sometimes a farmer might go so far as to furnish the skeleton of a house—four walls, floor, hollowed out holes for windows and doors to be installed. However, there were no windows, doors, plumbing, toilets, electricity, or running water. At one housing site, I watched my father and uncles struggling to pump water into an empty well that was left wide open and was deep, dark, and hazardously close to the house. Children could easily fall to their deaths, and perhaps some had, but my mother, aunts and grandmother watched over us closely. Unclean water invited intestinal disease to run rampant among all family members, especially children.

Generally when a farmer provided a house, more than one family was expected to share it. I still remember my father building and attaching wooden steps under a window to allow us access to the part of the house we were to call "home" along with two other families during one bean-picking season in Colorado. In California, we lived in what was referred to as "colonies." These were communities that were purposely located in inconvenient distances from a parent community, making it difficult for each to associate with the other. The intentional segregation of colonies required the building of separate schools and forced its residents to live apart, work apart, pray apart and worship apart. Discrimination and references to Mexicans as inferior beings was common. We were only there for one season.

During that difficult summer I experienced my first incidents of domestic violence involving the public beatings and humiliation of children and women. No one interfered. Those present either chose to watch or look away. One case in particular left a lasting impression on me, which still haunts me. At age nine, I watched as the man next door grabbed his two children and held them down and whipped them with a piece of rubber water hose. The woman who was apparently the mother stood by and cried silent tears. The memory of all of the screams and red swollen gashes on the children's small legs remains quite vivid, even today. No one helped. All I could do was cry. Alternating emotions of anger and fear haunted me for days.

I learned of my paternal grandfather and his violent history from listening to all the stories told by my aunts, his daughters. On payday, after the family had worked the fields all week, he collected everyone's earnings and disappeared for two or three days, returning intoxicated, only after he had exhausted all the money. The sons were allowed to keep some of their wages, provided they accompanied him on his drinking binges. The women were never allowed to keep their earnings and hoped only that grandfather was feeling generous enough to release a few dollars for their needs. My father shared a few stories of his father with me, all relating to my grandfather's temper, his violent conduct toward my grandmother and his daughters. At times, because he was my grandfather's favorite child, my young father would be assigned by Grandmother the task of searching for Grandfather and hopefully retrieving some of the weekly wages for food.

Living in the "colonies" proved to be an eye-opening experience.

My father, however, decided that such an environment and the types of lessons it offered were not for his family. He moved us away. Constantly moving was not a hardship, nor did I relate it to the contemporary condition known as "stress." Uprooting ourselves was a way of life, like the potatoes and cucumbers we picked. No complaints were heard. Harvesting locations sometimes changed on a weekly basis and with short notice.

When this happened everyone pitched in with the packing and readying the groups for the next field waiting to be stripped of its harvest. We traveled in a cluster that included my grandmother, aunts, uncles and lots of cousins. Children and women were sometimes crammed into the back of the trucks used to transport crops to the "bodegas" or storage areas, along with bedding consisting of mattresses laid flat on the truck bed. Kitchen and cooking ware were packed last to make it easily accessible for the women to remove and set up at a moment's notice. It was their job to prepare food for the entire group.

The men did all the driving and performed all the maintenance on the vehicles. The women cared for the children, constantly watching that they not get too close to the backdrop of the truck while the vehicles were moving, lest they fall on to the road, never to be seen again alive. This is what we children were told. No one ever got close to the backdrop of the truck. No one ever fell from the back of the truck.

Sadly, during one of the harvest seasons in Colorado, my ten-year old cousin, Daniel, was accidentally run over by one of the trucks used in the field. The result was fatal; Daniel died of internal bleeding in my grandmother's arms in the back seat of the old 1949 Chevrolet that overheated on the way to the hospital. It was the saddest day of my five-year old life. My paternal grandmother was devastated. My uncle cried for months. This was my first experience with death. I still cry today when the image of his small limp body, his arms and legs like tree branches in the wind, floats across my mind. He was like a brother to me.

As was the custom then, no radios were played for at least a year. No one could be happy. It was not allowed. It was the tradition. After Daniel died, the adults watched us like mother hens watch their newborn chicks. During overnight stops along a busy road or under a bridge near a river, the voices of women were constantly heard calling to the children to stay close to the camp and avoid getting too close to the nearby streams or roads for fear of falling into the rushing waters or being hit by a passing vehicle.

Storytelling was the primary entertainment in the evenings. Secondly, was the music. Storytelling was left up to the aunts or older female cousins. The men either played guitars or accordions and they all seemed to have a knack for singing old ballads about revolution or men driven to drinking by women who broke their hearts.

Myth, Culture and Gender

Superstitions, tales of witchcraft and other evil people who preyed on children were the dominant themes of our bedtime stories. By the time I laid down to sleep, I struggled to keep my eyes open, terrified by the possibility that if I closed my eyes one of those horrible characters would appear and take me away. Evil versus good spirits was the central theme of each story. Each story contained a warning and sometimes methods on how to keep from being caught in the web of evil. Most of the warnings were directed at the women and girls. We were warned not to allow any stranger, especially a man, to touch any part of our bodies, take a piece of our hair or look into our eyes too long. If we were careless, a spell could easily be cast without our knowledge and we would be under their control forever. Catching the "evil eye" was common in those days. The only one who could cure you from the "evil eye" was my paternal grandmother Elena, who was a "curandera," a healing woman. Each time I watched my grandmother work one of her remedies for evil eye or some other malady, it worked.

Women were kept in line and in their place with such superstitions. Men on the other hand were never the focus of these stories. Apparently, men were exempt from all those evil consequences that awaited "loose" women. On Friday and Saturday nights my uncles and older male cousins headed into town for "a good time." The women, my father and younger male cousins remained at the home site. A woman's social life was limited to sitting around a fire or tin tub, cooking, caring for children, washing dishes and clothes or telling stories. I have no memories of my grandmother or my aunts ever dancing. As for my mother, I understand exactly why she never danced, it was against her religion. The Pentecostal Church prohibited women from cutting their hair, painting their nails, wearing pants, or dancing. As I grew older in this same religion, I concluded that it was just some man's idea of a conspiracy against women amusing themselves. Years later, when I left home to attend college, I left the beliefs behind and decided to pack instead some of the forbidden acts, such as dancing and wearing pants.

Other than my maternal grandmother, who was clearly visible and outspoken on the rules of her house and her religion, all the other women in my early childhood years were like shadows in corners, not to be heard. They seemed to emerge only to do their chores and then silently retire back into their shadowy spaces. The women in my father's family took care of everyone's needs: cooking, sewing, setting up the camp fires and creating a cooking stove by starting and placing hot coals or burning wood into a tin tub. Here pots could be placed for cooking and the "comal" or hot iron plate for making tortillas could be balanced long enough to cook several dozen tortillas to feed the entire traveling group and whoever else might stop by.

While on the move, the migrating farm worker was faced with the challenge of getting food on the table. Food was obtained in different ways. Some food in the form of fish, e.g. crawfish, came directly from the rivers. Rabbits, doves, or flying squirrels many times provided our only meat source. Men did the hunting. Women never accompanied the men on their hunts. My father usually brought seven or eight rabbits that had to be skinned and cleaned. I, being his oldest child and one of three daughters, was appointed to assist with the skinning of the animals. My job was to hold the poor dead animal by its hind legs and hang it head first over a tin tub while my father, with an extremely sharp knife, cut through its intestinal cavity and removed all the organs. The smell of raw blood and the sight of fresh body organs piling up in the tub nauseated my stomach. The feat was never accomplished without distorted looks all over my face and sounds of disgust throughout the entire butchering process. This, however, never discouraged me from scooping up several spoonfuls of the seasoned and cooked meat into a freshly cooked tortilla to treat myself to a "taco," or what is referred to today as a "burrito."

Father was careful never to shoot the rabbits in the head to prevent damage to the skull. The rabbit heads were boiled in salted water. Once cooked, my sister and I would crack the small skulls and make a hole sufficiently large to allow our index finger in to be used as a scoop. After salting it further to our liking, we scuffed out the seasoned brains and ate them. My two younger sisters who did not experience the migrant life could not stomach this practice of eating rabbit brains, and today can't even bear listening to the stories.

Becoming a Mi'jo

Occasionally, my father allowed me to go with him to the river while the men fished, but only to watch. The water current was too strong and I could easily be washed away. Yet, the male cousins, my size or smaller, were allowed to participate. It was a man's job to provide food and a woman's job to prepare it, serve it and clean up afterwards. In my adolescent years, however, after failing two more times to have a son, my father accepted his fate of having five daughters and would eventually call me his "mi'jo," an abbreviated version of "mi hijo," my son. This realization would broaden the learning opportunities for my sisters and me. We would learn carpentry, masonry, and auto mechanics jumping into many rivers with him.

My mother's role, however, would not change. There was indeed a double standard in our home that was enforced for many years. She would remain the shadow in the corner for twenty-seven years and then, after experiencing her own realization that equality could never be possible in that relationship, would make the painful choice of leaving, but not before she accomplished her work of helping to raise five talented and well-educated women.

My childhood memories are filled with visions of my evanescent lifestyle that continues to this day. I can recall passing through many towns and cities and never getting to know them because our stay might last only a few days or perhaps two weeks. However, my geography and cultural awareness improved considerably. Not just resulting from my "gypsy" lifestyle, but because I had parents who, though caught in the web of society's expectations for farm workers and women somehow understood and cherished the value of education. Whether they were aware of it or not, their decisions in those early years of my life contributed considerably to the development of my intellectual awareness of the world. Whether my father knew it or not at the age of eighteen when he fathered me, his curiosity of the world would influence my own view of and love of the world. For example, at the age of about four or five, my father took me and my sister, eleven months younger, to visit the Museum of Natural History in Denver, Colorado where I remember being startled and frightened by the monstrous bones of giant pre-historic animals. It would be years before I would appreciate their signifi-cance in my world. I don't recall my mother being there.

Rising above Prejudice and Discrimination

Despite the unkind and sometimes vicious treatment I endured as a child by those members of society who viewed themselves to be superior and more power-ful than a dark-skinned child of poor parents, I chose, with encouragement from my father and love from my mother, to develop, nurture and maintain an optimis-tic view of the world and humanity. I truly believe in the divine gift of will power and the power of choice. That is to say that I believe that with proper guidance, shared in a loving and caring environment, humanity will exercise its free will and choose to live in peace. Likewise it will choose to open widely the doors of equality, justice and prosperity to all the members of its family.

Equality, justice and prosperity were not common words in our vocabulary during my young migrating years, at least not in the English language. My father, who possessed a broad view of the world, I suspect, understood the meaning of these words in his own language. He was outwardly inclusive of all the people we encountered. I owe my first meeting with an African-American boy-child to my father who in midday stopped and publicly greeted a man about my father's age and of African descent with a handshake. This occurred in a Texas Panhandle town where many of the white inhabitants were known to our family by experi-ence with their racist remarks and discriminatory treatment. A small boy clasped his father's dark-skinned hand just as I clasped my father's hand. We stared at each other. We probably wondered about the same question, "Where do you go to school?"

It was my father who responded to my curiosity filled question of where this Black child attended school, because I had never seen him in my school. Children of African descent were not allowed to attend the same school as those consid-ered to be "white," my father explained. Buses would come everyday to some-where in the country. That day, the word "injusticia" became real. That day my stomach twisted itself into a knot. I knew this was not right. I felt an unbearable anger and I wanted to cry. Though not fully aware of what it was called, on that day I learned about the outward and legal discrimination of people merely be-cause of their skin color. I was approximately seven or eight years old. I later witnessed the bussing of black children who were ordered to attend school far away from their homes and far away from me. This was prejudice, racism and discrimination at work.

Reflecting back on my childhood years, it was characteristic of my positive attitude that I recall being happy despite the treatment I received in my first two years of elementary school, of which both were spent in the first grade. I was constantly spanked by teachers for speaking Spanish and not English. I was spanked daily. Sometimes the punishment resulted from lack of understanding di-rections and going right instead of left. Years later, with the help of my father, I realized that the incompetence of those teachers who lacked the skill or the desire to communicate effectively with an entire class of students, contributed to my be-ing punished.

Dreaming: Escape and Empowerment

My father had a gift for creating hope and generating a positive vision of the future. My mother was gifted with her gentle nurturing of the dreams I had. And I had many that she quietly encouraged. I loved daydreaming about the world. I clearly recall early in my life laying flat on my back on the ground and using the clouds against the blue sky as my drawing board. There was a time when I found the perfect spot to lie down just on the edge of dirt road where an occasional car passed stirring up clouds of dust and forcing me to tightly shut my eyes. Looking at the clouds was my favorite activity. Laying there on a hot summer day created the perfect environment for a wonderful daydream. For a few moments, I was in full control of my destiny and my feelings. The fact that I was a girl child became irrelevant. Daydreams were my mode of travel and I went where I pleased.

I was only about eleven years old. At the time I dreamed more vividly than usual. We were living in Texas, but my parents were making plans to move to New Mexico, my mother's birthplace. Moving added excitement to my traveling daydream. Today, I thought, I will travel to China. In my head, I had already been to France, England, Spain and most of Europe. But I had not yet journeyed to the Far East. So as I lay there in the dirt, blocking my eyes against the brightness of the sun, I searched diligently for a cloud resembling the shape of China. As I gazed across the sky, I saw a great body of water, a deep blue color, high in the sky. I spotted the giant country floating directly above me, and I was on my way. It was fluffy white with great indentations that represented valleys and mountains. I could see lakes and rivers. I visualized myself getting off a boat, swaying on the rough waters of the coast, and on to a wagon with many other people who spoke a language I could not understand. I promised myself I would learn that language. We were all ageless. There was laughter and playful jesting among us. And then a car drove by raising the dust on my face and making me cough. My wonderful vision was gone. But the memories of another wonderful adventure I had created were imprinted on my mind forever. Only death, perhaps, would erase them. Later in life, when in Beijing, in the Great Hall of China sipping tea with distinguished Chinese women lawyers from a delicate china cup and saucer, I recalled my childhood vision with wonder.

Education and Escape from Oppression

My childhood interactions with the society of those years were not so pleasant. As a member of a family involuntarily caught in the farm-worker migrant stream, I experienced the treatment of inequality of women and female children early on. Unequal treatment was alive and readily imposed on me because I was "Mexican." "Greaser," though heard in other Southwestern states, was the term more frequently used in the daily vocabulary of Texans who intended to insult and create hostility for their Mexican neighbors. I was one of those Mexican neighbors. The word *greaser* and "dirty Mexican" were terms to be heard on the way to and from whatever school I might be attending in Texas. I was called a dirty Mexican many times.

At the age of twelve, my family established a home base in Roswell, New Mexico. Though somewhat more settled, the family still worked in the fields in the surrounding areas and migrated out of state during the summer months. The move, however, did not prove to be an escape from the prejudices and displays of hatred toward people of Mexican descent. Though the years had passed and car models and telephones had evolved, neither the attitudes not treatment had changed much toward Mexicans or other people of color. To some people all Mexicans were greasers and unfit associates for the white man.

Without education or economic power, my parents had to work the fields during my childhood and adolescence. With poverty comes lack of choices. Housing was not a choice. We were forced to live in boxcars, barns, and tents and in ram-shackle labor camps, with unclean outhouses and without running water or electricity. Those who lived in "real" houses—with running water, indoor toilets and electricity—could not be seen with us.

To me, my father and mother had a great amount of education, though none of it was acquired in formal institutions of instruction. Their knowledge was acquired from common sense, experience and the wisdom of my grandmothers. For example, they were both musicians who never studied a note of music. My father played the guitar. My mother played the piano completely by ear and was asked in several churches to accompany the congregational devotional music pieces. Both of them taught me what they knew. All my sisters took up musical instruments, including flute, piano, guitar, saxophone and clarinet.

Though not formally educated, both taught themselves to read English, though neither ever learned to write it well. My father explained early on that those children deprived of an opportunity to education had no other choice during their young lives but to jump into that migrant stream of people who planted and harvested the crops. Although there was also a certain degree of pride in the knowledge that without the thousands of migrant farm workers picking the fruits and vegetables, millions of people in this country would not get fed, education for their five daughters became a focused goal and priority for my parents.

The mere fact that one was a farm-worker in the 1940s and 1950s introduced immediate expectations of unequal treatment by those members of society who deemed themselves to be of the "better" class. Unfortunately for many people of color, discrimination was a way of life in this democratic country. And I, as a female child, would experience unequal treatment in three arenas—gender, color and class—though not forever.

Though discrimination was part of my childhood experience, education was the key to jumping and staying out of the migrant farm worker stream. With education new dreams were possible. The ability to read opened up new possibilities. I could learn about new countries with interestingly strange cultures and languages. More so, it was the love of reading about real people who had sacrificed their lives to change the world for the better that began to have a real impact on the choices I would make in my own life.

Professional Discrimination

Little did I realize as a child that I would grow up to become a human rights lawyer and a businesswoman. At the age of twelve, my mind could not conceive of the notion that someday I would serve as the chair of the New Mexico Human

Rights Commission or that my portrait would hang in the New Mexico Women's Hall of Fame for my work in women's rights. I never dreamed that in 1987 I would be dining with some of Hong Kong's most prestigious women lawyers representing both British Hong Kong and Mainland China. As a child I dreamed only of travel. Yet it would be that dream of traveling the world that would fire my inspiration to continue my education, one degree after another.

Of course the challenges presented by unequal treatment were not absent during my work as a teacher, education administrator, businesswoman, or in my career as lawyer. Owning and operating my own law firm—the Fereirra Law Firm, P.A—for almost fifteen years, did not automatically shield me from the prejudicial attitudes, comments and actions asserted by certain members of that male dominated occupation. Being a dark-skinned Mexican woman lawyer raised eyebrows at times and instigated chauvinistic comments.

Prejudicial assumptions were heard even from people I least expected to possess such attitudes. One of my first federal criminal hearings in the United States District Court is one such example. While wandering about the federal building searching for the appropriate courtroom where my defendant-client was to appear, I was approached by an extremely tall, dark-skinned African American man dressed in the uniform of a US Marshall. As I entered the appropriate courtroom, he asked me, "Are you the interpreter?" "No," I responded. "Are you one of the judge's clerks?" "No," I responded again. And I added jokingly, "You only get three strikes and then you're out!" He paused, realizing that I was referring to the game of baseball. "So you're somebody's secretary?" "Well," I said to him, "You've had three strikes, so now you're out!" Just then, my client was being brought into the courtroom in shackles and handcuffs. As I directed my eyes toward my client I asked the Marshall, "Do you see that man who is being brought into the courtroom?" The Marshall nodded in the affirmative. "Well," I said, "Today I am his lawyer and I will be representing him at this hearing." The Marshall chuckled and looked at me saying, "You're a lawyer?" And before I could answer he added with another chuckle, "You are the cutest little lawyer I have ever met." I stand only four feet, eleven inches in height. So, I smiled at him and responded, "And you are the tallest, darkest African American Marshall I have ever met. In fact, I have never met an African American Marshall before in my entire life!" We both laughed, but I could not help but feel there was still so much work to do in the issue of equalizing humanity. I recall thinking an unspoken comment to the Marshall: "You of all people should know better than to stereotype people." But then I thought to myself: Perhaps I am stereotyping as well by assuming that the mere fact that he is an African American would qualify him to know and understand the history of that particular group of people. Looking back, I think we both grew a little more that day. We spoke of prejudicial assumptions into which we all get trapped in this society. And we became friends.

Emerging from the Shadows

Far from my childhood mind was the future in which I would find myself as an attorney, a "guardian ad litem," representing children who had been the victims of child neglect or abuse, some resulting in death. I would cry for them, as I cried hot tears of anger and frustration when I was a child witness to these acts of violence and injustice. Further still was the notion that far in the future I would be appointed to serve as a Special Commissioner for Domestic Violence for the New Mexico State Court to adjudicate similar cases. The same anger would return, but accompanied by a fierce determination that I would do all that was humanly possible to prevent harm to children, women and other helpless people.

During the 20th century, my life as a Mexican and as a woman changed dramatically. Why? Credit must go to the movement of the Sixties. Such laws as the Equal Pay Act of 1963 and Title VII of the Civil Rights Act of 1964 offered women a new avenue and the tools they needed to address serious inequality issues that they had been facing for many years. In March of 1965 the Voting Rights Act of 1965 was signed into law, following Martin Luther King's historic march from Selma to Montgomery, Alabama. This is the same law that I would rely upon later in my career to file a class action voting rights case in New Mexico that would go all the way to the US Supreme Court.

The Equal Opportunity Act was also passed in 1965, one year before I graduated from Roswell High School in New Mexico and began my first non-farm worker job as an office assistant with the government War on Poverty sponsored program, Home Education Livelihood Program (HELP).

There were those individuals who had their own limited concept of women's capabilities. I ran into my share of those all the way from high school to my years spent working in Germany. However, I learned to listen to my own inner guidance for direction. I remember the words of one of my male supervisors when I informed him that I was resigning my GS-9 civil service job in Germany to go to law school. His response was, "You? A lawyer? What is it with you women? What makes you think you can be a lawyer?" Those words, meant to be discouraging, only fueled my determination to move back to the United States, without a job waiting for me, reestablish my residency in New Mexico, apply and get admitted to law school and, as a single parent with a six-year old son, attend three straight years of law school to receive my law degree and license to practice.

Just as Mahatma Gandhi laid the foundation for Dr. King's struggle for human rights in the United States against all odds, so had reading and learning about the lives of women like Harriet Tubman, Golda Meir and Rosa Parks fed my sense of accomplishment and determination to continue on my path. Clearly education and awareness of the existence of legally protected women's rights, along with moral support, encouraged some of the women in my culture to assertively change the direction of their personal and professional lives. The women around me changed, first in spirit, followed by attitude, then in choices and decisions to change their emotional, intellectual and physical conditions.

The older women in my life began to emerge from the shadows. They began to share their dreams with each other and their daughters. Some went to adult education night classes to learn English and pass their high school equivalency exams. For example, at the age of fifty, my Tia (aunt) Maria decided to earn her high school degree at the Adult Learning Center at New Mexico State University where, years later, I would find myself as the acting Adult Education Coordinator after returning from Germany to attend law school. She continued her education and obtained an associate degree, eventually studying art and producing numerous oil paintings, which have been displayed and admired at various art exhibits. By this time her husband had obtained a degree in engineering and both of her children had earned Masters degrees. She had worked the fields most of her life, but had made a conscious choice not to be left behind.

From Dream to Action

In her 60s my mother discovered her "inner artist" and began producing most unusual pieces of pottery, painted chairs, and framed art decor using combinations of discarded shoes, jewelry and assorted fabrics. Art collectors acclaimed her work as unique and aesthetically pleasing. My mother's journey from a migrant farm worker to a housekeeper, to a successful artist who was able to sell most of her work at her first public exhibit, is symbolic of the changes I witnessed among women, particularly in my culture and family.

It was my good fortune to come of age as the civil rights movement was underway, creating so many changes in American society, which in turn opened the door for both migrant workers and women to pursue dreams which in the past would have remained drifting clouds in the sky. Yet dreaming was more than an escape from the harsh realities of my childhood in a Mexican migrant farm worker family. Knowledge of others who had struggled to overcome the odds in their lives—and their determination to make changes which would help all helpless people, especially women and children, to live happier lives without prejudice and discrimination based upon color, culture or gender—was enhanced by my power to dream beyond the restrictive circumstances in which I grew up. I became able to both dream and develop the knowledge, faith and skills required to fulfill my dreams.

Chapter 4

With Two Wings: Growing up Female in Sweden

Agneta Enermalm

My native country is Sweden. I now live in South Carolina, U.S.A. I have traveled to other continents, mostly to attend conferences within my field, theological education (Christian). Traveling means encountering. Among the most meaningful encounters I have made are those with women from other cultures. My travels to Asia do not include the Beijing conference. The reflections that follow are triggered by limited readings of the documents from the conference and above all by my long-time involvement in women's issues. This involvement I have pursued on more than one level. Most profoundly it is a matter of identity, of finding a sustainable understanding of self-in-relationship.

In feminist theology, from its first development in the 1970s, the notion of experience has been pivotal. I can therefore say that I find myself on firm feminist ground when I choose to begin my reflections by recounting an experience. I will use the story as a metaphor with a bearing on the topic of discussion. From the experience I will pull one main train of thought to pursue: finding connections. I will argue that tradition can be a helpful tool in finding connections for strength and renewal. I will also point to the importance of women's history in this regard, since to a considerable degree finding a past relevant for women is searching for counter-traditions. These are likely to be related to the predominant mainstream traditions, but they are distinctly different. Awareness of such counter-traditions is likely to strengthen our sense of identity as women and could ultimately lead to cultural transformation.

Finally, I will venture a look toward the future from a spiritual perspective. The choice of perspective is personal, but not outside the horizon of the subject of discussion. While equality is predominantly a political issue, it does involve other arenas as well; philosophy is obviously one of those arenas but religion is too. Equality, according to most people, involves the affirmation of equal worth of every human being.[1] Many, like myself, would also make the claim that every person has capacity for a spiritual life, for relating to a transcendent reality whatever its definition. Within that framework, equality would be a matter of whether women and men are given the same or at least equally valuable possibilities to develop that relationship.

In Search of Connections

This said, I want to make it clear that I understand equality basically as an issue of justice, particularly economic and political justice: "Wealth certainly does not guarantee equality, but it increases the possibilities of women to get education and a job, so that they can make demands on the organization of society."[2] The last statement applies to organized religion as well. Religious beliefs can serve as a call to action, with other people of goodwill, for bringing about such justice. I agree with Sandra Schneiders' statement, "Unless Christianity can make a substantive contribution to the project of universal justice; the tradition has outlived its usefulness."[3] Equality between women and men entails the right to the same quality of life: that is, access to basic and continued education and to the richness of one's culture. On a personal and social level, equality denotes right relationship between women and men, respecting differences without framing them hierarchically.[4]

I was born during the Second World War. According to my mother, one of the first regular sounds that I seemingly made an effort to interpret was the rumbling noise of German airplanes on their way to Finland, a German ally at the time against Russia. My father, a mining engineer by profession, had volunteered to go to Finland to drill underground shelters for the civic population. I loved to hear him tell stories about how he had struggled to make himself understood using the few Finnish words he knew. Having no similarity to Swedish at all, the words were a mouthful with their many and long vowels. My mother, a music teacher, told me that Finnish is a very melodious language. In retrospect, I find in my reaction to the sound and the subsequent explanations by my parents an embryonic fascination with foreign cultures which later in life would be influential.

On a deeper level it was a search for connections beyond boundaries. The ties between the Nordic countries Finland and Sweden date centuries back. They include a union of two countries into one nation, followed by the surrender of Finland to Russia in 1809, with Finnish independence gained in 1917, just before the end of the First World War. Connections are still obvious today through the existence of a Swedish-speaking population in Finland nurturing a unique Swedish-Finnish culture which is most notable in the literature. Connections became acts of solidarity during the war. My father constructed shelters in Finland; our family welcomed a young girl from Helsinki to stay with us during the hard times of war and the first years of recovery. Maybe this experience helped me intuitively to understand that life exists only in relationship.[5] There I was, connected without choice to my parents and through them to the wider world. As I reached adulthood and stepped into the public sphere as a single woman, a student and then a professor, I in more conscious ways came to see that interaction with others, through exchange and in reciprocity, is of prime importance for personal growth and also for learning to be accountable.[6]

During my years at the University of Uppsala, I felt most secure, because most connected, as I participated in the discussions at the Center for Women Researchers and Research on Women, established in 1978. The Center served women from all disciplines of the Academy. There was a sharing of experiences of being "first" within one's discipline, there was a critique of male-dominated language within different areas of study, the use of military metaphors within the fields of economics and natural science for example, and advice about how to counter the derogatory jesting about women. But there was also the realization that women can reach new avenues of knowledge by trusting our own way of perceiving things and combining facts.

A lecturer at Uppsala pointed to how one particular scientific problem, which had remained unresolved by male researchers approaching it in an exclusively analytical, separative kind of way, was solved by a female scientist who looked at the problem from the point of view of connection rather than separation. Discussing Sandra Harding's book, *The Science Question in Feminism*, we realized that the society at large was built on a conceptual scheme of dichotomy, fixedly distinguishing for instance between leisure and work.[7] Some of us, if not all, realized that we preferred to see things whole. In this context, then, I was invited to take my own experiences positively as material for study. Furthermore, I received some tools for coherently interpreting these experiences. As philosopher Hannah Arendt said, experience must be embraced by thinking.[8] And I would add, we need to talk about our experiences with the openness of true dialog, with willingness to accept an interpretation differing from our own.

From Philosophy to Equality

The sensed connectedness and the increased awareness attained at the Center empowered me to work actively for greater equality between women and men at my work place, the Faculty of Theology at Uppsala University. We formed a committee of women and men: professors, students and staff. The political climate in the early 1980s was all for it: the governing Swedish Social Democratic Party had adopted a radical equality policy already in 1968, including equal pay and balanced employment, that is preferential hiring of women for jobs where they were under-represented and vice versa for men.[9] The policy entailed a generous parental leave at the birth of a child, mildly pushing the fathers to take time off from work too; it later included the right to shortened work days for those caring for small children and directly applicable to the Faculty of Theology, part of a state university, was a requirement for annual reporting to the government about the status of equality at the institution. Thus one can say that at my educational institution, the 25th article of the Beijing declaration was put into practice: "Encourage men to participate fully in all actions towards equality." "*Fully*," however, was not the degree to which this work had been accomplished when I left in 1987. It probably remains a goal, and an important one: without the qualifier "*fully*" that appeals to our wholeness as human beings, our will and not the least our empathy, equality is in danger of being just a formal principle. The committee made efforts to increase the number of women enrolling in post-graduate programs at the theological faculties in Sweden and had some success. In 1998 out of 342 students enrolled at theological faculties, 135 were women, or 39 percent, while the total number of female post-graduate students of all faculties together amounted to 41 percent.[10] The very fact that efforts were made, including the participation of thesis advisors in seminars on how to mentor women students, the conversations on an official level about teaching women and men with their different relationship to knowledge effectively, and the informal talks about asymmetrical realities of daily life, such as the habits of addressing male professors by their last name but me by my first, all this made it possible to work there without feeling excluded.

Historical Perspectives

I feel proud in knowing that my alma mater, the University of Uppsala, was inaugurated in 1477 with the hope that the Academy might prosper through the intercession of Saint Birgitta, a prophet and a theologian, whose vision of a dual monastic order, including women and men, became a reality shortly after her death in 1377.[11] How ironic, though, that women were allowed to enroll at the University no earlier than in the 1870s; as late as 1909 a theological degree was first awarded to a female student, Emilia Fogelklou. It is interesting to read her story about her struggles to make sense of the seminars in New Testament studies that she attended. Her "inner experiences" forced her to seek more knowledge. That is why she was there. She wanted to *"be and think with life"* as the harbinger of thought and "not the other way around. "[12] Not happy with the dogmatic strictures enforced by professors and students alike (all male); Emilia Fogelklou has become for me a foremother of feminist theology. She would have agreed with the definition of feminist theology proposed by Lutheran theologian Mary Pellauer: by nature ecumenical, but also critical and experiential.[13]

The Evangelical-Lutheran Church of Sweden, to which about 84 percent of the population belongs at least formally, is served by a clergy of which 35 percent are women.[14] The presence of so many female pastors is indeed a change to celebrate - until 1958 no women were ordained at all. The Christian tradition has been, and in many ways still is, more foe than friend to women. There is, however, underneath "the iceberg", if we speak of the Christian tradition in such terms based on our alienation from it, sources of fresh and living water for us to draw from.[15] There are stories in the Christian Bible that have become such sources of renewal and hope for women of faith. The encounter between Jesus and the Samaritan woman at the well, told in the fourth chapter of the Gospel of John, is such a story. It includes Jesus' promise to those who drink of the water he gives that it *"will become in them a spring of water gushing up to eternal life."* Positively, a religious tradition provides us with a language in which we can express our experiences, interpret them, evaluate them, and share them with others.[16] Every tradition calls for revision, if it is true tradition and not only convention, fossilized understandings of life and typecast behavior. Thomas Merton distinguishes between tradition and convention in these words:

> Tradition is living and active, but convention is passive and dead. Tradition does not form us automatically: we have to work to understand it. Convention is accepted passively, as a matter of routine. . . . Tradition really teaches us to live and shows us how to take full responsibility for our own lives. Thus tradition is often flatly opposed to what is ordinary, to what is mere routine. [17]

I accept the Judeo-Christian tradition as a tool that helps me live responsibly. As a woman theologian, I have the task to interpret responsibly not only my own individual experience but also a particular historical experience, the one of Swedish women. A statement by historian Gerda Lerner convincingly conveys how important knowing the past to which one relates is for finding connections and building identity in relation to others. According to Lerner, we acquire stability and gain a basis for community by grounding our identity in some "collectivity with a shared past."[18] For me, in a historical perspective, two collectivities apply: the history of women, particularly of Swedish women, and the history of the Christian community through the ages. My primary interest lies in the interface between the two.

Since I made the choice to leave my country to sojourn in another, the United States of America, and since I am constantly looking for means solidly to relate to both, I find myself looking back to a time of connections between cultures, the time of the Vikings, ca 800-1050 CE. Admittedly this is very long ago, but given the appearance of "millennium" in the title of this book, it might not be totally out of place. If we think in terms of generations instead of centuries, the distance narrows. Counting an average of four generations per century we are down to about forty generations between the women of that time and us. You can without too much difficulty picture the course of time as a chain, one link attached to another.[19] Since I am convinced that my personal identity is related to a "collectivity with a shared past" this is a very powerful image. The time of the Vikings was one of creative cultural activity and of ample contacts between the Scandinavian countries and other parts of the world. The Vikings reached as far as Byzantium on their eastward journeys and the North American continent going west. While it was a time of connections, it was also a time of confrontation. Worldviews and ethical values collided as Nordic religion and Christianity encountered each other. In Sweden, the last Scandinavian region to be converted, the old faith died hard. Mission attempts in the 9th century had very limited success. When the public sacrificial rituals at the Old Uppsala shrine ended in the early 11th century, Christianity had won a decisive victory. This did not prevent blending of elements from both religions to be prevalent for at least a couple of centuries. Christians and pagans lived alongside each other and were buried in proximity of each other as the co-existence of Christian rune-stones and pagan burials show.[20]

Were women the ones to make the shift more easily than men? Evidence indicates that women outnumbered men among the early converts. Else Roesdahl notices that women were not part of the félag associations which were important fellowships of mutual obligations formed to promote trade, shipping or warfare.[21] Thus one can imagine that the possibility of being a member of a community larger than family, in this case a Christian community, would have been attractive to women. Historians intimate that the new faith gave more importance to people as individuals rather than addressing them as members of clans and families. More than one memorial raised to honor deceased parents includes a prayer for the soul of the mother but not the correspondent petition for the father. Among names inscribed on bridges supposedly built to promote the mission travels of the church, more are female than male. This all suggests a greater interest among women in the Christian faith. Ann-Sofie Olander theorizes that women were builders of bridges also in a metaphorical sense, that is, between paganism and Christianity.[22] Looking at this period of history from my professional lens, Biblical Studies, I remember women "at the borders," such as Ruth, the Moabite, of the Hebrew Bible, and the Syro-Phoenician woman in the New Testament who challenged Jesus with her audacious wit (Mark 7:24-30). This "dangerous" remembrance, so called in recent feminist theological thinking, of women who transcended ethnic and faith boundaries, is for me a continuous incentive to find connections beyond boundaries.

Both my deliberate journeying back to the time of the Vikings and the quick path back to my professional arena are, I think, expressions of a will to discover "feminine culture, a kind of historical heritage consisting of body and social practice. . . an archeology of that culture in which all women participate to a greater or lesser degree."[23] A consciousness of historical heritage can only be a strength useful in implementing full participation of women in cultural development, a goal stated in Beijing, Strategic Objective # 220. We need women *"strong of memory, will and judgment,"*[24] to empower us for the next millennium, whether they come to us from a particular past or speak to us now, from around the globe.

Women and Spirituality

The search for a collective past is a possible way of finding connections. Other resources are religious traditions whose life-enhancing potential the Beijing declaration affirms (Article 12). Spirituality is a term used across different religious traditions. It has to do with search for meaning in life, by "centering, building up, connecting, weaving threads."[25] Spirituality, as I understand it, is a process toward realizing the full potential of human life, negotiating the particularity of the situation, its pain and suffering. It is, however, also a calling, to the extent that we see spirituality as linked to a fuller reality that surrounds us and beckons us to actions for the good of others. Dr. Ursula King, professor of Religious Studies, highlights particular manifestations of spirituality among women from around the globe: in Africa community-building, in Asia reverence for life, and in Latin America struggle for justice and peace, fighting poverty and the aggression of militarism.[26] I can add some data about my own country.

Sweden is a secularized country where only 15 percent in a 1995 poll survey claim a faith in a personal God, compared to the average percentage for Europe of 38 percent. Of Swedes in the same survey 69 percent rather believe that there is a Spirit, a life force; an average of only 10 percent Europeans shares that belief. When women and men in Sweden are compared with one another in terms of their world view, there is an interesting discrepancy: 40 percent of surveyed men repudiated the given statement, "Human beings consist only of body and matter," whereas 70 percent of the polled women disagreed with the statement. While very few Swedes are churchgoers and only a limited number acknowledge that they pray with any regularity, a considerable group finds comfort in an "inner dialog with nature." Apparently many find deep connections to nature: trees, flowers, waterfalls. A majority of Swedes are convinced that human beings and animals have the same value, thus "equality" is for them not only a value pertaining to the relation between women and men, but to the relation between animals and human beings as well. Swedish legislation regarding domestic and wild animals is radical by international comparison. What is somewhat puzzling in this picture, however, is that 90 percent of surveyed adults value as most important what derives from the private sphere: good health and happy family life.[27] Will such an attitude be conducive to necessary social transformation? I am afraid it might not. Pouring from my own Christian tradition I agree with feminist Catholic theologian, Sandra Schneiders, that we, and that is both women and men, need to explore how faithfully to mediate the tension between self-sacrifice for the good of others and of the whole on the one hand and self-assertion for the good of self and of society on the other.[28]

Peace, Violence and Theology

I was born during World War II. The rumbling noise of military airplanes awakened my awareness of the wider world. I was privileged not to become a victim of war due to the political stance of the government and simply due to circumstances. I do not know to what extent women's voices directly contributed to the decision of the Swedish government to stay with its policy of neutrality and non-interference. I do know, however, that the struggle for women's rights early in the 20th century often included a deep concern for peace; so also in Sweden. Author Elin Wägner (1882-1949) even claimed that the few who genuinely think in a feminine way are the women "who are prepared to enter the public sphere, emphasize the importance of peace and take responsibility for translating the idea of peace into action." She added that such women do not accept the passive role society has ascribed to them.[29] Others after her became very active for peace, notably Alva Myrdal, who relentlessly participated in international disarmament negotiations for many years and was awarded the Nobel Prize for her efforts in 1982. The first ever, collective peace initiative on a European basis was the meeting of over two thousand women in The Hague in 1915. What developed out of this meeting was the Women's International League for Peace and Freedom.[30] The Beijing declaration rightly recognizes the leading role that women have played in the peace movement (Article 28). This is a legacy we ought not to forget. We should rather let it speak critically to us as we examine our goals for the future.

I live in South Carolina currently. In the United States, South Carolina ranks 50th in the number of women in elected office. In the nation, the state is number one when it comes to homicide against women. These numerical facts are hardly unrelated. I rejoice at the actions being taken as I write on the initiative of women in the state to improve on both issues. Domestic violence is a plague of our time. Unfortunately, it was a plague in times past as well, although hidden. There are, however, examples of women who resisted the violence and created communities of peaceful coexistence. We do not usually look at the monasteries in this connection, but research has found that they were a refuge for women. In the 6th century, Merovingian Queen Radegund, against her will one of King Clothar's six wives, fled from her royal court and founded, by divine inspiration, a convent that functioned as a shelter for abused women. She believed that destructive power could be put to flight only by an alternative, positive and life-affirming power.[31] It is logical that the Beijing declaration addresses violence against women and girls immediately after the article on peace and disarmament. A recent European ecumenical statement of April 2001, Charta Oecumenica, bespeaks the issue of equal rights of women under the heading "Reconciling peoples and cultures." A war ravages our homes and intimate relationships. Conjoined efforts are needed through education, legislation, declarations from international bodies, and I would add, prophetic proclamation. I was pleased to see that the 8th Assembly of the World Council of Churches, Harare 1998, when called to adopt the United Nations' Beijing Platform for Action, chose to name violence against women "a sin."[32] Unfortunately, churches have themselves participated in this violence. Naming it in traditional theological terms equals recognition of the seriousness of the matter. Hopefully this recognition will promote honesty, repentance and change.

I experienced how even in the midst of war relationships were built and nourished. Previous suffering of domestic violence did not pull St. Radegund away from building community, from relating to others in acceptance and trust. In our time, social isolation is suggested as one factor in the spread of violence. Understanding ourselves as always in relationship, let us continue to defend the equal rights of women for the welfare of all.

Chapter 4 Notes

1. B Wistrand, *Swedish Women On the Move* (Stockholm: The Swedish Institute, 1981), 7.

2. E. Hedlund, Kvinnornas Europa/ The Europe of Women (Stockholm: Dagens Nyheter, 1993), 94.

3. S. M. Schneiders, *With Oil in Their Lamps: Faith, Feminism and the Future* (New York & Mahwah, NJ: Paulist, 2000), 95.

4. R.D. De Oliveira, *In Praise of Difference: The Emergence of Global Feminism* (New Brunswick, NJ: Rutgers University Press,1998), 62.

5. E. Moltmann-Wendel, *I An My Body* (New York: Continuum, 1995), 13.

6. De Oliveira, *In Praise of Difference*, 41.

7. S. Harding, *The Science Question in Feminism* (Ithaca & London: Cornell University Press, 1986), 88.

8. M.A.Hill, ed., Hannah Arendt: *The Recovery of the Public World* (New York: St. Martin's, 1979), XIII.

9. T. Skard and E. Haavio-Mannila, A Equality between the Sexes: Myth or Reality in Norden?@ Daedalus 113:1 (1984): 141-167

10. Statistical Yearbook of Sweden (Örebro: Statistics, 2000), 470-71.

11. S. Göransson, ed., *Birgitta och hennes tid/Birgitta and Her Time* (Uppsala: Almqvist & Wiksell, 1973).

12. M. Jarlstrom, "Emilia Fogelklou-teologen/Emilia Fogelklou-the Theologian," Kvinnovetenskaplig tidskrift 2 (1989): 80-81.

13. M.D. Pellauer, "Feminist Theology: Challenges and Consolations for Lutherans," Dialog 24 (1985):19-25.

14. Svenska Kyrkan: Matrikel/Directory of the Church of Sweden (Stockholm: Verbum, 2000), 371.

15. M. Grey, "Have the Wellsprings Run Dry? Re-Sourcing Tradition in Feminist Theology," *Feminist Theology* 3 (1993): 38-52.

16. E. Stuart, "Experience and Tradition: Just Good Friends," in *Sources and Resources of Feminist Theologies* (ed. D.A. Hartlieb and C. Methuen; Kampen: Kok Pharos, 1997), 49-71.

17. T. Merton, *No Man Is an Island* (San Diego & New York: Harcourt Brace, 1955), 150.

18. G. Lerner, *Why History Matters* (New York & Oxford: Oxford University Press, 1997), 118.

19. A. Olander and B. Stromberg, *Tusen svenska kvinnoar: Svensk Kvinnohistoria Fran Vikingatid till nutid! A Thousand Years of Swedish Women's History from the Time of the Vikings until Today* (Stockholm: Raben & Prisma, 1996), 11.

20. B. Sawyer and P. Sawyer, *Medieval Scandinavia: From Conversion to Reformation, circa 800-1500* (The Nordic Series 17; Minneapolis & London: University of Minnesota Press, 1993), 104.

21. E. Roesdahl, *The Vikings* (London: Allen Lane & Penguin, 1987), 58-60.

22. Olander and Stromberg, *Tusen*, 14-16.

23. De Oliveira, *In Praise of Difference*, 57.

24. U. King, "Spirituality for Life," in *Women Resisting Violence: Spirituality for Life* (ed. M.J. Mananzan et al., Mary Knoll, NY : Orbis, 1996), 155.

25. Ibid., 154

26. Ibid., 156

27. C. R. Brakenhielm, "Christianity and Swedish Culture: A Case Study," International Review of Mission 84 (1995): 91-105

28. Schneider, *With Oil in Their Lamps*, 93.

29. H.Forsas, Elin Wagner, *Vad tanker du mansklighet?/ What Do You Think, Humankind?* (Stockholm: Norstedt, 1999), 31.

30. King, "Spirituality," 156-157.

31. M.A. Mayeski, "Reclaiming an Ancient Story: Baudonivia's Life of St. Radegund," in *Women Saints in World Religions* (ed. A. Sharma; Albany: State University of New York Press, 2000), 71-88.

32. World Council of Churches (8th Assembly, Harare, Zimbabwe, 3-14 December 1998, Document No. DE 8), 1998.

Chapter 5

African Women's Quest for Equality: The Case of Cameroon

Rebecca Mbuh

Women in Cameroon have been plagued by unequal and discriminatory treatment at all levels, partly because of the country's tradition of male domination and women's complacency. Some Cameroonian women continue to cling to traditions that exclude them from making significant contributions to the immediate society. However, following the country's independence in 1960, more women have made substantial gains in education, politics, and economics. Since Cameroonian women have united to confront an oppressive society, government officials can no longer ignore them. Because of their advocacy and persistence, women have now achieved certain rights such as owning property, participation in cooperative farming and petty marketing, legal affairs and politics. It has been through influential grass roots women's organizations that professional fields have been opened to women. A major challenge that lies ahead is how to improve organizational skills among women leaders in order to fully involve the continued participation of women in the development of the country.

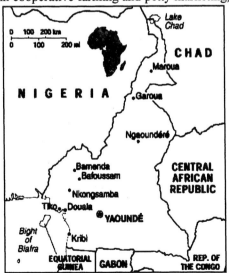

Source: www.cia.gov

Introduction

This chapter centers on the role of the Cameroonian women in education, national economic development, and politics. Suggestions are given for empowering modern Cameroonian women to become more fully organized as leaders at all levels of a male dominated society at the dawn of the new millennium. More than 30,000 women from all over the world gathered in China in September 1995 to plan the future of women everywhere. This was the third of such meetings, which began in 1975. For the first time in modern history, the World Conference of the International Women's Year was held in Mexico City in 1975. At the forefront was women's role in political, social, and global developmental issues. Women from all walks of life were mobilizing to present a unified voice on issues specifically related to the well-being of women. Because of the awareness aroused by the Mexico City conference, it was acknowledged that women were becoming a powerful force in the world and could no longer be ignored. The 1980 World Conference of the United Nations Decade for Women at Copenhagen that followed the 1975 Conference in Mexico City confirmed that women play a significant role in the well being of humankind. In 1985 at the Nairobi Conference women were established as full participants in world development progress. Although the United Nations charter declares equal rights of men and women, as do the constitutions of all nations, in practice women have always been regarded in many cultures as unequal and therefore second-class citizens.

Many scholars on African women put too much emphasis on the pre-colonial and colonial era. In this discussion a different direction is chosen in order to bring the Cameroonian woman and African women into focus within the global community. Here we will examine the era from independence to the present and the role of the Cameroonian women in education, politics, and economic development.

In African countries women comprise more than half of the population. Should it not therefore follow that under the principles of equality women ought to represent half of all political and ministerial positions, own or manage some of the country's large corporations, and play significantly major roles in the administrative and policy development and implementation of decisions guiding the national education of the nation? Sivard surveyed women around the world and found that in the mid-1980s, women represented a mere six percent of national legislative members in Africa.[1] According to Parpart, the limited access of women to higher education and wage employment offers some explanation for the insignificant presence of women at the top.[2] Colonization also contributed to the inequality between men and women. Clignet observes that the inequalities between men and women depend on past and present cultural models and stereotypes.

> Colonial officials had an interest in stabilizing domestic relations and strengthening accumulation processes; they solidified male authority to realize their aims. The stage was thereby set to subsidize men through mal-distribution of state resources. . . . Men occupied positions of political authority in overwhelming numbers. . . . While men used this patriarchal cooperation to wrest power from women, gender struggle was an ongoing, fluid process, and had to be won each day anew.[3]

Unfortunately, modern day society continues to impose these myths, particularly to advance male dominance, which is evident in their reluctance to share power with their competent counterparts. These patriarchal inclinations continue to manipulate the gender division of labor in favor of men, reasoning that men are "providers and supporters" of the family while women are dependents and mere caregivers. Research findings suggest that the reverse is true. Many African women, including Cameroonian women, are the backbones of their families in this new era of globalization. This is evident in the many long hours they put into each day's activities at home, on the fields and in the workplaces, mainly in the informal section.

Cameroonian Women and Education

The population of Cameroon is estimated at 15 million in 2001[4] and about 52 percent of the population is females. Although women constitute more than half of the world's population—and the same is true for Cameroon—Momsen estimated that 80 million fewer females than males are enrolled in school[5] Though Cameroon has one of the highest literacy rates in Africa, and school attendance has increased dramatically since the country's independence in 1961,[6] the disparity between education of men and women is troubling. In 2001, 75 percent of men and 52 percent of women are literate as noted by Africare, a Washington, D.C.-based NGO specializing in aid to Africa.[7]

Although formal education began in the early 1800s under the initiative of mission institutions, notably Protestant and Catholic missions, each had a different approach to educating females. The Protestant mission stressed academic achievement and taught both sexes to read, write and count. On the other hand, the Catholic Mission concentrated on home science training for girls and academic training for boys.[8] The vast majority of educational activities in Cameroon, controlled by the missionaries from America and Europe, were under the supervision of the German missionaries. By 1913 more than 40,000 Cameroonians were studying in about 631 mission schools.[9]

While it is well documented that formal education was brought to Africa during colonial times, it should be noted, however, that the purpose was not to benefit or improve Africans. The objective was self-serving as the focus was mainly to train workers to work in Colonial offices. Davidson notes that while schools during the colonial era focused on teaching colonial values to Africans they were of substandard educational quality.[10] Furthermore, Miriam Goheen notes, "The inequalities based on gender were exacerbated under colonial rule and increased after independence."[11]

During the colonial era, school attendance was generally low. In 1940, the attendance rate for females was 15 percent. This rate doubled (30 percent) by independence in 1961. The year 1940 therefore marked the beginning of school expansion to include facilities specifically for girls. This trend towards increased female enrollment has continued since then, though the rate has slowed down at times, notably at the advanced levels of education.

Education is compulsory for all sexes between the ages of 6 and 14. A study published by the U. S. Department of State, Bureau of African Affairs in 2002, indicated that school attendance in Cameroon was 65 percent, and the literacy rate was 75 percent in 1999.[12] At the primary school level, girls now represent almost half of the pupils. Unfortunately, women are significantly underrepresented at the higher levels of education, as the statistics show. Net primary school enrollment/attendance for both males and females between 1995 and 2001 was 74 percent. For the years 1992 to 2001, net primary school attendance for males was 76 percent and 71 percent for females. During 1990, 72 percent of males were literate compared to 53 percent females.[13]

Many researchers conclude that early marriage for girls and the high value placed on fertility,[14] socioeconomic status, sex, and parents' social status[15] have contributed to the decrease in females at the higher levels of education. Unfortunately, these customs are as prevalent now as they were in the 1960s. My family managed to avoid this through the foresight of my parents. Their first two children are girls (the author is the second), which meant that under normal custom these children could not receive an education. My parents defied the criticisms of my uncles and male neighbors to send my sister and me to college. Some of my relatives and my father's close friends lamented the fact that my father was "wasting" his money to educate girls instead of saving for the education of his male children. Their advice was to marry us off as quickly as possible. Because my parents listened to their conscience, our family is one of the few in the village of Pinyin that educate all children.

Additionally, "beliefs, mental attitudes, traditions, and inadequate means of information, as well as the idea that women have about their own role and status in contemporary society"[16] are other factors contributing to the exclusion of women from fully exploiting the various levels of educational opportunities available to them. These socio-cultural norms account for the majority of women terminating their educational pursuits after only primary education. Moreover, parents are responsible for buying uniforms and books, and paying fees in some cases for primary school, and because tuition and other fees for secondary education remain even more costly, education remains unaffordable for many children. Several social and cultural obstacles continue to prevent girls from going to school; for example, the minimum legal age for marriage is 15 for women and 18 for men; forced marriages of women 14 years old or younger are still practiced in some rural parts of the country and many of these women are forced into polygamous homes.

A 2000 study by ACDI found that an estimated 50 percent of girls aged 16 are pregnant. Worldwide studies indicate that children born to mothers below age 18 are 1.5 times more likely to die before age five than those born to mothers age 20-34. Yet three of every four teenage girls in Africa are mothers, and 40 percent of births there are to women under 17.[17] This is the very group of women who badly need basic education in order to better take care of their children, especially when administering prescription pills. How can these young adolescents possibly be expected to read and understand the doctors' or nurses' directions for giving drugs to their children when they can neither read nor write? A greater danger is posed to the society as a whole when one important subgroup is deprived of basic education that is needed for day-to-day functioning.

Ironically, studies by Bryson found that in the village of Batanga, the first school started by the missionaries in 1879 enrolled twelve students who were all females.[18] Another school established in 1881 had equal numbers of boys and girls. In 1943, the first high school established solely for the education of women in Cameroon was opened in Douala enrolling a total of nine girls. Seven years later, the school enrolled twenty-eight girls in the first form. Overall, by 1968, 67 percent of primary school aged children attended school. Between 1938 and 1970, out of 17 secondary schools founded, 8 were co-ed, 6 were for boys, and only 3 were for girls.

Cameroonian women are aware of their indispensability as a valuable human resource in the development of their country. This awareness was earlier enhanced by governmental legislation prohibiting discrimination based on sex in education, vocational training, or employment opportunities. The first president of Cameroon since independence, Ahmadou Ahidjo, declared in a speech at the Cameroon Union Congress in 1962, In addition to a program designed to teach women domestic science, reading, language, arithmetic, writing, and mixed farming, emphasis will be laid on a family-oriented social and civic education program which will help the African woman to play her true role in contemporary society. . . ."[19] While this is an indication of some progress for women, although still emphasizing the society's view of women's role, this declaration by no means includes women in the mainstream of equal education or gives them access to prominent leadership positions in the country.

Education is essential for improving women's living standards and enabling them to exercise greater "voice" in decision-making in the family, the community, the workplace, and the public arena of politics. Literacy and other basic skills are absolutely vital to women's empowerment, and without the skills acquired in secondary education, women cannot obtain better paid employment.[20]

Education of pupils at the primary level is compulsory, and the government is responsible for providing education at all levels. Until the mid-70s, an impressive increase in the levels of education was observed in Cameroon. Between 1976 and 1987, the illiteracy rate among children 11 years and older fell from 53 percent to 41 percent, while the school attendance rate in the 6 to 14 year age group rose from 67 percent to 73 percent. This rise in school attendance contributed to a reduction in both the disparities between men and women and between rural areas and urban areas, even if marked differences remain.[21] Customs continue to promote education for boys but not for girls, who are destined for early or forced marriage.[22]

The 2000 National Assembly session passed what they termed a huge budget bill increasing spending on national education by 49 percent. Despite this significant step on the part of the assembly, the total education spending during the 1999 and 2000 fiscal year was only approximately 2 percent of Gross Domestic Product (GDP).

Generally, higher education affects only a small proportion of Cameroonians of both genders. Higher education is significant today, as in the past, because the possession of a university degree allows access to higher-level bureaucratic positions, which became available to native Cameroonians after independence. The demand for university-educated Cameroonians led to the establishment of the Federal University in Yaoundé in 1961 and has come to be regarded as a symbol of reunification of the country.

The number of female students at the university and other professional institutions of higher learning has steadily increased since the establishment of the University of Yaoundé in 1961. A presidential decree issued in 1962 placed all other institutions of higher learning, including future ones, under the control of the University of Yaoundé. The decree also allowed for other special branches of the university to be located in the provinces. Today, university branches and professional schools are scattered around the country and include ten establishments, with four campuses at Nchang in Western Province for agriculture; Ngaoundere in Northern Province for animal husbandry; Douala in Littoral Province for commerce; and Buea in South-West Province for languages. University and professional education have expanded considerably and the number of females reaching these levels is slowly but steadily increasing. Ejedepang—Koge observed in 1985 that an extraordinary expansion in the number of schools and students has taken place at all levels of education in both private and public sectors.

In 1970/1971 academic years, there were 50,510 female students enrolled in primary school from level 1 through 7 in both private and public schools. This number accounted for 21 percent of the total enrollment for both males and females. However, by 1976 females accounted for 44 percent of total primary school enrollment. Table 5.1 presents the enrollment of females in academic and technical public institutions from 1966 to 1970.

Table 5.1: Female Enrollment in Public Institutions: 1965-1970

Year	Academic Institutions		Technical Institutions	
	Total	% Girls	Total	% Girls
1965-66	7,324	32	26,308	21
1966-67	8,186	36	28,632	22
1967-68	9,685	35	33,448	23
1968-69	11,272	38	37,237	24
1969-70	13,698	39	43,339	25

Source: MINEDUC, 1975

Table 5.2 shows the enrollment of females from the primary school level to university in 1976. There is a significant drop in enrollment from primary school to the secondary school level. This is due to the enormous pressure female students encounter from society and family to get married or drop out to assist their mothers in taking care of the family, as previously explained.

Table 5.2: Female Enrollment at all Levels of Education in 1976

Level	Total	Females	Percentage
Primary	1,219,579	573,650	44 %
Secondary	113,295	34,216	30%
Technical	33,302	12,001	36%
Higher	10,100	2,001	20

Source: Bryson, 1979, p.71 (modified)

As the level of education increases the number of females at each level decreases. Table 5.3 shows that in 1986 women possessing a higher education comprised a mere .3 percent of the total population with higher education. This is a big decline from 37.3 percent of females with a primary education during the same period.

Table 5.3: 1986 Level of Education in Cameroon (in percentage)

Level	Women Age 15 and Older	All Women	All Men
Illiterate	---	53.4	---
With Primary Education	67.6	37.3	39.2
With Secondary Education	31.3	8.9	44.9
With Higher Education	1.1	.3	14.6

Source: 1987: Second Census General of the population of the inhabitants of Cameroon

Table 5.4 shows female participation in education at the various levels. The data clearly magnifies the widening gap between males and females as they navigate the different levels. Of special interest are the ratio of male to female teachers and the concentration of female teachers at the lower levels, nursery, primary and secondary levels.

Table 5.4
Female Enrollment in Education at Various Levels in 1985-1986

Sector		Students			Teachers	
		M	F	T	M	F
Nursery	Public	21,320	20,808	42,125	--	1,711
	Private	16,408	14,970	31,375	10	733
	Total	37,728	35,778	73,506	10	2,444
Primary	Public	627,840	500,719	1,128,559	24,433	6,376
	Private	229,658	277,101	576,760	4,828	2,617
	Total	927,499	777,101	1,705,319	24,605	8,993
Secondary	Public	86,710	45,013	131,723	3,420	1066
	Private	73,716	51,014	124,730	2,519	505
	Total	160,426	96,027	256,453	5,939	1,571
Technical	Public	14,995	7,592	22,587	1,022	488
	Private	33,671	26,961	60,632	1,252	362
	Total	48,666	34,553	83,219	2,274	810
Teacher Training	Public	2,267	1,591	3,858	372	112
	Private	99	101	200	15	3
	Total	2,366	1,692	4,058	387	115

Source: National Ministry of Education, Yaounde' 1989/90. (Modified)

Table 5.5 Certificates Awarded to Women by Level and Area of Study 1990 and 1991

Level	1990				1991			
Area	Men	Pass %	Women	Pass %	Men	Pass %	Women	Pass %
FSLC/ CEPE	47,870	38.20	34,966	35.20	50,281	39.10	39,607	36.30
BEPC (a)	15,053	31.70	10,035	26.30	26,194	32.50	13,724	28.10
CAP2 (b)/ Industry	2,812	23.00	1,402	36.00	3,464	27.00	1,410	38.10
Commercial	1448	18.00	926	14.20	1,979	26.00	1,375	22.00
BAC3(c)/ Arts	2,810	36.30	1,147	34.10	3,670	42.00	1,648	40.30
Science	3,233	36.00	1,320	31.00	4,319	41.00	1,939	38.00
Industry	323	35.00	35	33.00	382	32.20	43	31.00
Commercial	635	27.00	585	23.10	741	26.00	683	25.00
BA/Letter- Humanities	846	62.00	362	61.30	1,100	64.00	517	63.10
Equivalent Law/ Economics	1,429	30.00	379	64.10	1,188	63.60	336	61.20
Science	693	52.10	141	53.60	632	54.50	139	55.40
Technology	140	93.10	19	96.20	111	94.30	17	97.00
Masters & Letters	81	90.20	16	93.10	114	94.30	17	97.00
Above or Law/ Eco- nomics	142	91.00	24	93.60	108	92.50	18	93.10
Equivalent Sciences	90	92.00	10	95.40	93	91.10	10	94.30
Technology	30	95.10	7	97.10	71	96.20	6	98.10

Source: Ministry of Social and Women's Affairs, 1995

FSLC: First School Leaving Certificate obtained after primary education
(a) Certificate obtained after 4 years of general secondary education
(b) Certificate obtained after 4 years of technical and commercial secondary education.
(c) Equivalent of GCE Advanced Level

During the 1968-1969 academic years, ninety-three females out of a total of 1779 students were enrolled in institutions of higher education. In the 1975-76 academic year, out of 7,169 students enrolled at the University of Yaoundé, there were 6,125 males and 1,004 females. Females accounted for only 15% of total enrollment during that academic year. More recent data shows an improvement in the educational attainment of women in Cameroon. In the 2000/2001 academic year, of the 63,135 students enrolled in the nation's six universities 40,128 were males and 23,007 or 36% were females. Overall there was an increase of 6.5% in students at the university level from 59,280 students enrolled in 1999/2000 academic years in Cameroon;[23] Table 5.6 on the following page presents a summary of the distribution of students by university and gender.

Table 5.6:
Distribution of Students by University and Gender: 2000/2001

University	Male	Female	Total
Buea	3,111	3,001	6,112
Douala	6,853	3,933	10,786
Dschang	8,242	3,049	11,291
Ngaoundere	3,493	1,202	4,695
Yaounde I	12,498	7,669	20,167
Yaounde' II	5,931	4,153	10,084
Total	39,773	22,783	63,135

*Source: Annual Statistics of the Universities of Cameroon, 2001**

At the postsecondary university or higher education level of educators teaching, women are also disproportionately represented. Table 5.7 shows the number of females at various academic ranks at the six state universities in the 2000/2001 academic years. Comparing the numbers to that of males, females are lagging behind at all levels at each of the institutions. At the full professor level there were only 5 females compared to 75 males. Regarding university administration, women have made some gains. One out of the six vice chancellors is a woman, roughly a 17 percent representation.

Table 5.7
*Staff Distribution by Qualification and Gender 2000/2001

Category	PRO		MC		CC		AS		Monitor		Total
UNIV/ SEX	M	F	M	F	M	F	M	F	M	F	
Buea	5	2	13	2	44	8	102	38	8	1	223
Douala		4	0	12	3	92	10	171	48		340
Dschange	5	1	22	0	103	8	164	33	34	0	370
Yaounde I	46	2	111	8	339	47	180	40	18	5	801
Yaounde II	13	0	28	2	115	15	66	22	25	3	261
Ngaoundere	2	0	9	0	49	4	107	13	18	5	207
Total	75	5	195	15	742	92	790	194	85	9	2202
Total M + F	80		210		834		984		94		2202

Source: Annual Statistics of the Universities of Cameroon, 2001

PRO = Professor MC=Assoc. Professor CC= Sr. Lecturer AS = Lecturer Assist
Monitor = Graduate/Lab Assistant
* *These figures do not include data from private institutions of higher education.*

Fatunwa and Aisiku propose that higher education is the means to increased economic production and the transformation of the society through the training of high-level and intermediate labor force.[24] Therefore providing Cameroonian women with equal access to obtaining higher education will be a positive step towards maximizing the total labor force of the country. It is the natural step to embrace since women already account for more than half the population and contribute significantly to cash crop production.

United Nations statistics show that although girls and young women do not have equal access to education, those who manage to get into schools tend to stay—unlike their male colleagues who drop away as the years go by.[25] Educated women in Cameroon have amounted to a critical mass that the government officials and traditional figures cannot simply ignore. What does the future hold for these women? What role will they play and how? When? As women take the initiative to discuss and plan their role in future national development, one thing is for sure, the men will listen, lighten up, and recognize that women must be reckoned with as equals in all respects because they have shown that their contribution is vital to the success of the nation. Group effort has helped in the past to achieve certain rights for women such as owning property, cooperative farming and marketing, exercising legal rights, and making political gains. Group effort again will help women keep what gains they have made and expand their influence.

Figure 5.2 indicates the gross enrollment ratios by level of education. According to UNESCO, the gross enrollment rate is the total enrollment in primary and secondary education, regardless of age, divided by the population of the age group, which officially corresponds to primary or secondary schooling (the ratios include the number of children who repeat a school year). In Cameroon, the African Girls' Education Initiative, a program sponsored by the United Nations Children's Fund (UNICEF), succeeded in increasing the enrollment of girls at the tertiary level by 8 percent between 1997 and 1998. During the same period, the dropout rate for girls decreased from 9 to 6 percent.

Figure 5.2

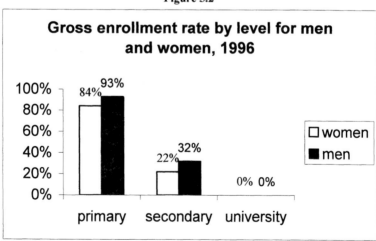

Source: UNESCO

The data in Figure 5.3 from the Ministry of Women's Condition summarize the breakdown of the percentage of female enrollment in the different fields of study at the tertiary level national schools for the academic year 1998/1999. The study of law drew the largest percentage of 30 followed by medicine and administration at 20 percent respectively. As we shall see in the section discussing women and politics, the Cameroon Association of Female Jurists (ACAFEJ) has capitalized on the rapidly increasing female enrollments in the field and has engaged in a number of change initiatives that promote gender equality and improves quality of life for women and the society as a whole.

Women's participation in higher education in Cameroon has increased very quickly since independence. However, women continue to achieve lower levels of education than men because of their domestic role (defined by tradition and society) and the preference for marriage imposed on them over education coupled with general societal prejudice against education of women.

Figure 5.3

Percentage of Girls in National Universities in Cameroon, 1998/1999

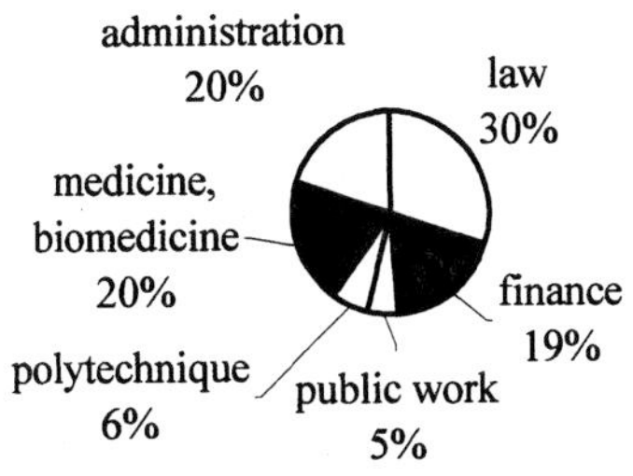

administration 20%
law 30%
medicine, biomedicine 20%
finance 19%
polytechnique 6%
public work 5%

Source: Annual Statistics of the Position of Women in Cameroon, 2001

The educational levels of men and women affect many political, social, economic options. The trend in education gains for women has steadily been increasing but the gap between men and women is till a big one. In order for women to attain parity with men in political, social and economic fields, this disparity must be addressed. Furthermore, women's illiteracy is more easily ignored than men's, resulting in underestimating the situation. Most parents in Cameroon seek education for their children of both sexes as the best means of improving their income-earning potential and ensuring that the children experience a better standard of living than the parents. But many mothers who are over-burdened with the many demands placed on them are forced to withdraw daughters from school to help with farming, trading, collecting firewood and water (in rural areas), caring for the elderly and sick family members, raising young siblings, and other household demands. A girl's education is also constrained by a number of factors besides socio-economic status and sex. Koenig indicates that other variables such as parents' social status play a significant role in determining how much education a child will receive; both boys and girls who come from upper class homes are more likely to get good education.[26] In addition, sex plays a universal role since boys of all sub-samples show a tendency to be more educated then girls. Sexual ascription is more important in constraining educational choice in families with scarce financial resources. In these circumstances women are expected to conform more closely to the traditional role of wife and mother. While this trend still holds true in many parts of the country, many women (educated and non-educated) are beginning to view the situation differently. Partly due to the western influence and partly to the support given them by their mothers, many women are choosing to remain single and raise their children in their parents' compounds rather than work as laborers for their husbands while sacrificing their ambitions and dreams. These women are determined to accomplish something for themselves on their own terms and at their own pace. According to Miriam Goheen, "there is clearly emerging in Cameroon a new group of professional women whose aim is not to abandon the role of being women, but rather to assert the power of being female."[27]

Cameroonian Women and Politics

Cameroonian women were granted voting rights at the same time as the men, but after independence, women found themselves lagging behind when it came to political affairs. It was the popularly accepted perception that women's role in politics was in direct conflict with their role as wives and mothers. Though it seemed that women were doomed, to continual subordination, they did not succumb to the unwritten understanding that should have sealed their fate. They were determined to serve their country beyond the confines of their domestic life.

It was this strong sense of duty to serve that led the first Cameroonian woman in 1955 to run for an elected office. This bold attempt drew numerous vicious criticisms from men, who also used her failure to justify that women should stay out of politics. The women viewed the situation differently, though. Women mobilized at all levels and regions and in 1960 a woman was elected to the National Assembly. The political party at the time, Cameroon National Union, (CNU) created a wing for women. By 1965 three women had been elected to the different assemblies as well as to town councils in many prominent areas of the country. Emmanuel Konde has identified three venues for political participation for women in Cameroon. The direct mode included sovereign queenships, co-chieftains with men, and queen mothers, the indirect methods included power behind the throne reserved for favorite and most trusted wives and titled senior wives, and participation through women's societies. The indirect methods meant that women married to powerful men of any stratum of society relied on the counsel of one of his wives in order to be successful. This approach is very similar to modern day western societies saying, "Behind every successful politician or head of state is a wise woman."

The unification of east and west Cameroon that produced the United Republic of Cameroon in 1960 gave women the power to participate more fully in politics. "In the first United Republic elections, seven women were elected to parliament. Two provinces, the North and the East, which up to 2000 have never returned a woman to the Parliament, are now represented by them. The presence in this assembly of a woman from the North, an all-Moslem area, is for us a true revolution."[28]

In modern day Cameroon, gender issues, mainly inequalities, are becoming increasingly politicized at both the grassroots and the national levels. According to one of the newspapers, several opposition parties are highlighting gender inequalities on their political platforms. For example, the Social Democratic Front, one of the main opposition parties, now put women's issues at the top of their agendas calling for reforms that give women equal access to education, agricultural credit, and high-ranking positions in government offices.[29.]

Although women are slowly gaining representation in the education sector, their participation in politics seems to be declining. Between 1984 and 1992, women elected to the National Assembly showed a positive thrust (See Table 5.8).

Table 5.8. Women in Ministerial Positions Between 1984 and 1992

Year	Government Agencies	Women	Total No. of Ministers and Vice Ministers	% of Women
1984	Social Affairs, Education, Women's Affairs, Public Health	5	43	11.6
1985	Social Affairs, Women's Affairs, Plan & Regional Education Development, Public Health	5	40	12.2
1988	Social and Women's Affairs, Plan & Regional Development	2		
1992	Social Affairs, Education	2	44	4.5

Source: Ministry of Social Affairs, 1993

The trend between 1984 and 1992 was a steady decrease in the number of women in leadership at the ministerial level. Cameroon has highly qualified women who are willing and able to serve their country but are not afforded the opportunity. The government's decision to combine the ministries of Social Affairs and Women's Affairs in 1988 robbed women of one position that was traditionally designated a woman's domain.

The Ministry of Social and Women's Affairs is responsible for formulating and implementing policies to facilitate the equal participation of women in all sectors of the government. These policies include: the social protection and assistance policy, the social advancement of the individual and the family, the respect of women's rights, women's advancement in a society free of any form of discrimination and within which equal rights are guaranteed in the political, economic, social and cultural activities. If the Ministry of Social and Women's Affairs is the main national advocate for women's integration in development, one questions what significant advances women have gained since 1988. Is the ministry being used as a mere token by the government to placate women?

Are the women themselves passive? The statistics indicate that the situation for women in top leadership positions must be revised to reflect women's representation in schools at all levels if the integration of women into political and governmental leadership is indeed to be attained. The challenge remains: Cameroonian women need to awaken, regroup and redefine their roles as leaders. Several women's organizations exist at both professional and nonprofessional levels. All have registered some gains in advocating women's issues over the years. However, an intensive effort is still needed to advance women's issues and involve women in the process.

In other key positions in government women's representation is on the rise. For example, the number of female lawyers increased from 12 in 1980 to 59 in 1990. The Cameroon Association of Female Jurists (ACAFEJ)[30] has been disseminating information and promoting awareness regarding the respect of women's rights as well as encouraging more women to enter the profession. The fruits of these activities are quite noticeable. In 1994, Cameroon had 79 female magistrates.[31]

Further, the Cameroon Association of Female Jurists' other main purpose is to fight discrimination, and to disseminate information regarding women's legal rights, primarily to draw attention to the increased violence against women. In this sphere they advocate affirmative action, an end to job discrimination, better childcare and scholarships for women at the national universities. The association further argues that women are "natural democrats" and that "women work for all people and not just for themselves."

Although the Cameroonian woman has made significant progress in the areas of education and politics, more integration is still desired. Early on, women were oriented in selected areas of education for the fulfillment of various purposes designed by a male-dominated society. It is therefore not surprising that the majority of women in positions of authority, besides the agricultural sector, are in the educational field. Women are well represented as teachers in primary, secondary, technical and high schools, as we noted earlier. At the university and professional levels, their numbers are quite insignificant, but there is hope for more numbers in the future. As more and more girls take advantage of the equal opportunity in education their involvement in leadership and government is inevitable.

One of the university branches in Cameroon, the University of Buea, is headed by a female, Dr. Dorothy Njeuma, who is also the vice chancellor of the University System in Cameroon. This leader is a mother, wife, and counselor, role model to many females, women's rights advocate, civil servant, and one of the few African women to hold such a position. Prior to being appointed Vice Chancellor, Dr. Njeuma was Vice Minister of National Education. Under her leadership, the enrollment at the University of Buea increased from 800 students during the 1992 to 1993 academic year to 1,700 in 1994.[32]

The representation of women in government at the higher levels has seen a sharp decline since 1992. Between 1982 and 1987 there were 27 women participants within the 180 members of the National Assembly. Between 1992 and 1997, the number dropped to 23 women and by 2001; there were only 10 women representatives in the National Assembly. Ninety one percent of the 3000 candidates were men.[33] Currently there are only two women mayors of the 336 municipal regions in the republic. These data fall short of the recommendation by the United Nations Economic and Social Council, which states that women should hold 30 percent of decision-making positions if a country is a member of the United Nations. As of 2000, Cameroon had achieved only 5.6 percent and judging from the current situation, still has a steep hill to climb.[34] There were 8 women in ministerial positions during the years 2000 and 2002.[35] Following is a chronology of women in ministerial positions since independence:

Table 5.9 Cameroonian Women in the Government since 1970

Year	Position	Name
1970-75	Deputy Minister of Health and Public Welfare	Delphine Zanga Tsogo
1975-84	Minister of Social Affairs	
1964-85	President of the National Council of Women	
1972-82	Deputy Minister of Education	Dr. Dorothy Limunga Njeuma
1982-84	Junior Minister of Education	
1983-88	Deputy Minister for Planning and Industries	Elisabeth Tankeu
1988-92	Minister for Planning and Territorial Development	
1984-88	Minister of Social Affairs	Rose Zang Nguele
1984-2000	Minister of Women's Affairs	Aissatou Boubakari Yaou(Yaou Aissatoou)
1988-97	Minister of Social Affairs	
1981-85	Deputy Director of Finance	
1984-87	Secretary of State for Health	Isabelle Bassang-Akouma-Manneyeng
1987-89	Minister of Health	
1985-93	Secretary of State of National Education	Christine Ngomba=Eko
1992-93	Sec. of State for Ind.-Regional and Commercial Dev.	Louise-Marie Tokpanou Nec Atchou
1993-97	Secretary of State of Education	Isabelle-Marie Tokpanou Nec Atchou
1997-2000	Minister of Health	Marie Madeleine Fouda
2000-02	Minister of Social Affairs	
1997-2001	Minister-Delegate in the Presidency for Superior State Controls	Lucy Gwanmessia
2000-01	Minister of Women	Julienne Ngo Sonu
2000-01	Secretary of State of Transport	Dr. Nana Aboubakar

2000-01	Secretary of State of MINEDVC	Diallo
2001-	Secretary of State of Education	Haman Adamana nee Halimatou Mahonde
2001-	Minister of Women' Affairs	Catherine Bekang Mbock
2001-	Minister of State of Supreme State Audit	Mama Njiemoum
2002-	Minister of Social Affairs	Cecile Bomba Nkolo

Source: *Ministry of Social Affairs*

Economic Development

According to World Bank reports, women account for 90 percent of the production of staple foodstuff in the country. Another study found that women are responsible for the production of more than half of the food grown locally in developing countries and account for more than 80 percent in the continent of Africa.[36] Margaret Snyder and Mary Tadesse reported evidence of African women's participation in economic life could be seen throughout the continent. "The burden of food production generally fell to women. . . besides agriculture, women engaged in commercial activity locally and with European merchants."[37] Kofie Daddieh argues that though African women do not receive credit due them, they have been central to the progress of social reproduction of the labor pool as women supply low cost staples and supplement family income from various trading activities.

Cameroonian Women's Economic Traditions

The 1995 World Bank report indicates that 87.3 percent of Cameroonian women are engaged in cash crop production and hunting. In Cameroon, only 1.1 percent of females are in the professional and technical economic activities. Several studies credit Cameroonian women's successes in this area and point to the cooperative organizations of women as the main catalyst.[38] These cooperatives concentrate on efficient marketing, purchasing, distribution, and the education of members on modern ways of increasing the levels of productivity. In 1995 a study by the United Nations found that in the Cameroon economy, women represented 64 percent of workers in the agriculture sector, 32 percent in the service sector and 4 percent in the industry sector. Yet women and children are at greater risk of poverty and malnourishment in the country. In 1999, 33.4 percent of the population lived on less than $1.00 a day, 64.4 percent lived on less than $2.00 a day and an estimated 50 percent of the population was below the poverty line.[39] These data are particularly alarming because most women struggle to feed their families first while placing themselves last on the list.

Many studies indicate NGOs have played a major role in the status awareness of women all over the world. This is also true in the case of Cameroonian women. Generally, the role of the NGO's in Cameroon is to improve women's situations in areas such as the provision of more food via efficient farming techniques, health, and water or the decreasing/narrowing of the inequality gap! Most Cameroonian and African women are responsible for managing the household but not the income. Most do not participate in decisions regarding the welfare of their own families. It is safe to generalize that Cameroonian/African women are subjected to (an unfortunate culmination of customary and colonial practices) the functions of reproduction, production, trading, caring, giving, feeding, farming, cooking, and cleaning, for families.[40] Engagement in such activities is usually time consuming and stressful. Preoccupied with their primary responsibility to their families and society, women find little time to indulge in activities such as education, training, and securing good jobs. This partially explains the absence of women in top levels of politics and corporations.

The NGO's and grassroots women's societies have been successful in empowering women in many venues. Women are more mobilized and speak in a common voice, thus establishing a coherent and unified presence that commands the attention of government officials.

Cameroonian women's unrelenting struggles have yielded some noticeable responses from the government over the years. The Ministry of Women's Affairs, established in 1997, is charged with the duty of empowering women. Through the creation of Women's Empowerment Centers throughout the country, women receive vocational training in the areas of income generating activities, family planning, hygiene and sanitation, and management of the home.[41] Other positive changes from the government include the establishment of a department of Women and Gender Studies at the University of Buea by the Ministry of Higher Education. This department is special because it is the only one of its kind in West Africa that trains African women to be gender experts.

One of the most popular forms of women empowerment groups is the "Njangi," called different names in other parts of Cameroon but bearing the same principle and practice. Njangi is a generic term used to describe a group of women and their activities in either cash savings and borrowing or cultivating members' land. The Njangi is a very common form of support and empowerment for women in the North West Province. These particular activities have been in existence since the pre-colonial era and are now widely practiced in many parts of Cameroon in Africa. While conducting research on Cameroonian women in general and focusing on women in North West Province during my sabbatical leave, it became clear after interviews with several NGO's that the Njangis provided a springboard for many NGO's activities. Because women were already organized with set rules in one form or other, the work of the NGO's was facilitated since traditional women's groups are always seeking new ways to improve themselves.

Njangis are for both men and women though they serve different purposes for each gender. For example, most men in Pinyin clan* belong to several Njangis that mainly serve as a bank. Members contribute a certain amount each month and a portion is given to one person. This process continues until all members have had their turn. Many young men use their share to start businesses or marry and begin a family. Many older men invest in education for their children, marry additional wives (polygamy is widely practiced in Cameroon and other parts of Africa), buy land or expand coffee farms.

My mother belongs to several Njangis. This is typical of most women in

Pinyin. Some of my mother's money from the Njangi is given to my father for the education of their children. (My parents did not acquire formal education but, as mentioned earlier, have been pioneers in Pinyin in the education of both sexes of their children).

Accompanying my mother and aunts to several of the Njangis, I discovered some of the deeper meanings of the long-standing importance of such groups. There are three types:

1. A "rotating account" provides a lump sum of money to each member in a rotating manner until all members are served.

2. In the "savings account," members contribute a certain amount each time that is then given as loans with little interest to needy members who must repay the loan amount plus interest at the agreed upon time.

3. The "trouble account" is savings for unexpected problems or unplanned for events such as illness, funerals or "born house"—celebration of the birth of a new child where family and friends feast with lots of food and drinks.

The savings and trouble accounts are usually "broken" or distributed to members at the end of a year of a specified time frame.[42]

For decades many women have invested in Njangis and other groups for financial and spiritual support for it is in such places that they can lament openly and freely about the inequalities they experience. It is my contention that the success of the activities of many NGO's and government agencies is partly due to these well established practices and also to the open-mindedness of women to embrace new ways of improving their financial, social, and economic standing as well as participating in the building of a stronger, more equal nation.

Joyce Endeley, senior lecturer and Head of the Department of Women and Gender Studies at the University of Buea, sees Cameroonian women's poverty, lack of leadership and participation in decision-making and lack of control over assets as attributable to personal factors which include low literacy, skills, self-esteem, financial security and level of awareness of their rights.[43]

During the 1990s economic crisis, women's activities expanded from the traditional to more creative ones such as smuggling. Usually marginalized economically, some Cameroonian women resorted to the smuggling of cigarettes, etc. to support themselves and their children, make up the deficit in household budget, and attain respect in the society.[44]

Women's organizations have helped to advance the active participation of women in economic development at the grass root levels.[45] In addition to cooperatives, these organizations take the form of savings groups to amass capital for individual and small group businesses. The benefits of these organizations include providing mutual aid for farming work (where a group of women rotate work on farms of members) and provide support in times of sickness and death. All women's organizations whether at the village or city level serve as a focal point for development activities.

A study by Walker found religious beliefs to play an important role in limiting Cameroonian women's participation in economic development since women were limited to minimal education and consequently to limited involvement in economic activities. Walker's study of the Fulbe women of the Mbororo tribe in

Northern Cameroon found that prior to Islamization, the question of which sex was superior was not posed since the roles of each were necessary and complementary for the survival of the group. Female inferiority was introduced with the coming of Islam. This idea was further promoted by the European influence. Traditionally, males and females were given equal education, but the Europeans were the first to interfere with tradition and establish schools only for boys. Therefore, the first Europeans schools among the Fulbe people were for boys, and only the sons of chiefs.[46]

Among the Fulbe people, education is seen as the instrument that will re-establish the traditional complementary balance of the roles of men and women, thus allowing all to contribute equally to the building of a strong society. This microscopic example epitomizes the direction the rest of the country must follow if Cameroon is to advance to the higher level of equality for all sexes. The national well-being of all citizens depends on the extent to which women are allowed to contribute to the development of the nation.

According to Cameroon's general population census conducted in 1987, of 1,271,135 women who had been working for eleven years and more, only 397,315 knew how to read or write in English or French. This represents only about one-third of economically active women in professional jobs. In the urban areas, however, the literacy rate is higher. About 60 percent of women who had worked for eleven years or more read and write in English or French. The low levels of literacy and education among women is reflected in the workforce as well. Consequently, the majority of women find themselves in jobs requiring the least qualifications and lowest level of education. The following chart shows the distribution of women in various employment sectors for 1990.

Figure 5.4

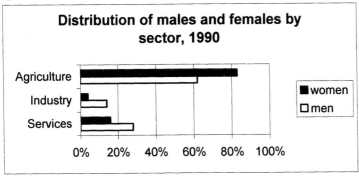

Source: Genderstats, World Bank

The agriculture sector was heavily dominated by women, constituting 80 percent of the workers in 1990.

In 1980, eighty-seven percent of all members of the female labor force in low-income African countries were in the agriculture sector,[47] Although Cameroonian women still suffer traditional and legal discrimination in all aspects of economic development, they are beginning to receive the recognition they deserve. They and other women in Africa are the main agricultural producers. More than 90 percent of these women depend on land for farming, cattle rearing, and fishing for daily survival. In the rural areas of Cameroon, women are the main cultivators of food for feeding their families and also for sale in the cities. Dankelman and Davidson, observe that women in rural areas of Third World countries play a major role in the management of natural resources.[48] Women's tasks in agriculture and animal husbandry, as well as in the household, make them the daily managers of the living environment. It was therefore an understatement when President Ibrahim Babangida of Nigeria declared at the United Nations sponsored conference on the priorities of women in Africa, "*No national development will be meaningful without the full involvement of women in the development process.*"[49] It is well documented that women around the world have not benefited from development efforts as much as men. This situation too applies to women in Cameroon, but they have taken advantage of their majority to unite in order to help each other locally as well as nationally to influence national planning efforts to include them.

In the modern sector of the economy, relatively very few women are employed because women have been involved in the labor force for a shorter period than men. However, Joekes found that the proportion of women joining the labor force has risen in both developed and developing countries since 1950. Statistics from the Fourth Five-Year Economic, Social and Cultural Development Plan for 1976 to 1981 indicate that 82.7 percent of women employees had earned less than six years of seniority compared with 66.5 percent of men. The situation resulted more from lack of qualifications by women which is also a result of having less education than from discrimination by employers.[50] Koenig conducted doctoral research to determine to what extent educational and occupational decisions of modern Cameroonian women were constrained by their sex and to what extent by their place in the social structure. Specifically, Koenig surveyed the relationship between sex, education, and employment at the blue collar, clerical, and elite levels. The analysis indicated that the employment of men and women in the bank and insurance firms was based on their educational levels, and both groups seemed to be given the same employment opportunities. Koenig concluded that in the area of wage employment the situation of women could be expected to improve as the number of women with education and training increases. This assessment is supported by the Cameroonian labor law, which specifies that workers in similar work, with the same qualifications and levels of output will receive the same pay. The law also grants special benefits and privileges with respect to maternity leave and nursing breaks. A wage-earning woman employed in the public or private sector is entitled to fourteen weeks of maternity leave, which may be extended for an additional six weeks if a medical certificate is produced, indicating that she is still ill from the effects of the pregnancy or confinement. During this extended period the National Social Insurance Fund pays the equivalent of the woman's wages.

In 1998, 30 percent of women holding the professional aptitude certificate (CAP) or the professional diploma (BP) were unemployed compared to 12 percent of their male counterparts with the same qualifications.[51] The Ministry of

Work, Employment and Social Security reported that in 1997 the unemployment rate was about 32 percent for women and 15 percent for men. During 1995-2000, the adult (15 years and older) economic activity rate was 48 percent for women and 86 percent for men.[52]

These gains for the working Cameroonian woman, which are not enjoyed by women in western and many developing countries, include a guaranteed employment after fourteen weeks of maternity leave, family allowance, paid maternity leave, and a feeding room on the job. Though relatively few women qualify, this important initiative of the Ministry of Social Affairs under the 1967 Labor Code provides an incentive to the many young women in school. But these gains are limited to a very few women fortunate to work in public and private sectors that respect the labor code in these matters.

Table 5.10 indicates that in 1995, more than 90 percent of the women's primary activities were in the primary sector and only about 5 percent in the tertiary sector. Though this information pertains only to the teaching field, it is an indication of the reduced importance awarded women in Cameroonian society.

Table 5.10: Population of Women Teachers by Sector of Activity and Residence

Sector of Activity	Sector of Residence		
	Urban	Rural	Total Cameroonian
Primary	61.3%	97.2%	92.1%
Secondary	11.7%	1.0%	2.6%
Tertiary	27.0%	1.8%	5.3%

Source: Ministry of Social and Women's Affairs, 1995, p.26

Lack of adequate education is a hindrance to women's participation in the economic activities of the country. A 1996 report on the distribution of economically active women by level of education sheds light on the importance of educating all of a country's citizens. The findings are reported in the following chart:

Figure 5.5

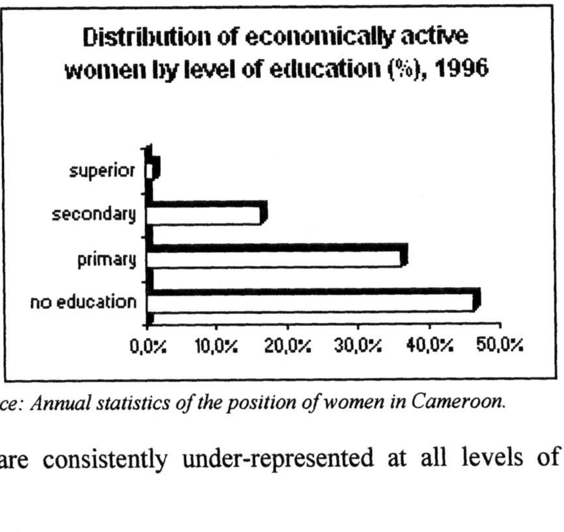

Source: Annual statistics of the position of women in Cameroon.

Women are consistently under-represented at all levels of the economy compared to their male counterparts. During 1987, in the areas of transportation and banking, women comprised less than 2 percent of the workers; less than 10 percent in legislative and superior staff/public administration; about 25 percent in scientific and technical professions; about 30 percent in hotels and services; about 40 percent in commerce and trade personnel and slightly more than 30 percent in administrative personnel.[53]

During 1996, women were mainly present in the informal sectors of the economy. The percent of their representation is summarized in Table 5.11:

Table 5.11: 1996 Distribution of the Labor Force by Sector and Gender (%)

Sector	Total	Male	Female
Formal	14.8%	23.7%	5.4 %
Informal	85.2%	76.3 %	94.6 %
Total	100%	100%	100 %

Source: Annual statistics of the position of Women in Cameroon

A report by World Bank indicated that of 100 working women, 92 are in the agricultural sector.[54] Agriculture related activities account for the country's position as one of the few African countries that maintains food sufficiency status. In spite of women's dedicated role in this sector, little effort has been made to improve the working conditions of women in the agricultural sector. In 1985, the secondary sector employed 35,952 women compared with 27,045 in 1976. The 2.6 percent of women employed in this sector is due to lack of qualification, but indicates a positive trend. During the same period, women accounted for 5.6 percent of salaried employment in the tertiary sector.

Though Act No. 92/007 passed on August 14, 1992 provides for complete freedom to enter into employment contracts, women are still noticeably discriminated against. The reality is that women with equal skills and qualifications are hired for the same jobs as their male counterparts but are paid less. The patriarchal ideology of male superiority in the society is once again being used to marginalize women. Moreover, even with equal skills, seniority, type of employment, and length of work, women's wages remain inferior to men's by 17 percent.[55]

Conclusion

Joseph E. Stiglitz, winner of the 2001 Nobel Prize in Economics, while noting that the world has become increasingly complex, observes that each group of people in society focuses on a part of the reality that affects it the most. Therefore Cameroonian women (and women in general) must take initiative to ask and then answer a few questions pertaining to their well-being and that of their nation. For example, in a society that is so heavily reliant on myths and other socio-cultural values to promote the oppression of women by subjugating them to lower class status as citizens and servants, the question must be asked, whose interests are served by traditional customs that dictate who should be educated, when a girl-child should get married, how many children they should have and other basic rights regarding their bodies? What are the implications to the future of the nation if society clings stubbornly to these notions of women being a "tool," or "property?"

This chapter has pointed out the disadvantages of Cameroon women in education, politics and economic development, while acknowledging some areas of progress. In today's modern globalized world, the participation of women at all levels of society is necessary if the country is to compete with other nations. Education of all citizens is the only means of ensuring that all of the country's human resources are maximized. There is no excuse for neglecting this important opportunity that is responsible for the well-being of the family and the progress of the nation.

In the past women were not included in the leadership circles of the country because there were few highly educated women, few or no women in positions of authority, and because of a reluctance to recognize the valuable contributions and potential of women to contribute to a better future. Today, that stance is changing rapidly. It is well documented that women's economic contribution, through involvement in agricultural, industrial and educational activities, as well as in the home, is vital for national development and must now be acknowledged. The era of simply regarding women as homemakers and child-bearers is long gone, so also is the myth that a woman's place is exclusively in the home.

The planned and unplanned schemes to exclude women from fully participating in political, economic, and educational endeavors has helped to bond women together to share views and act collectively to bring awareness to their predicament as well as to improve themselves as a whole. Thriving associations have been organized such as cooperatives, professional groups and strong alliance with the Ministry of Women and Social Affairs. A few gains have been documented and as women realize the benefits of self-organization as a means of continuous empowerment, the future can be looked to with enthusiasm. Though still affected by traditional beliefs and discrimination, women are beginning to receive recognition as Cameroon's (as well as Africa's) primary producers and caregivers. According to the United Nations, "nearly 80 percent of countries have taken specific measures to enhance the role of women in development."[56] Cameroonian women are assured of their participation through the Ministry of Women and Social Affairs.

The cost of excluding or limiting women in national development are numerous: uncontrolled population growth, ineffective agriculture, a divided country, high infant and child mortality, a weakened economy, a deteriorating environment, a poorer life for all. Therefore, "not developing the full potential of women who constitute over 50 percent of potential human resources translates to sub-optimization of a pool of human resources needed for national and sustainable development.[57] I submit that women know and understand their needs, the barriers to achieving those needs, their role and impact in nation-building, and their contribution to the economic, political and social structures better than anyone else.

I further submit that Cameroonian women and women all over the world also hold the solutions to their own frustrations. It is therefore imperative that women prescribe the solutions to their problems, develop plans for implementing them and make recommendations to the governing authorities. By organizing themselves and empowering each other in the form of associations and cooperatives, they present a force that must be seen and heard. A time frame for action must be included in the recommendations for action to allow for an accurate evaluation. By the next United Nations World Conference on Women, a strategic plan by women evaluating the progress and status of Cameroonian women should be the focus of discussion.

Women's groups should first organize to identify those areas they ascertain as being blatantly discriminatory. Setting priority goals while stipulating the means for achieving them will guide them to achieving and experiencing equality. The impact of a popular Cameroonian women's saying *"Woman's will is God's will"* has finally come to light and must be accepted and respected by all. The final action that women's groups must address collectively is the confrontation of those traditional values, beliefs and customs that have for so long kept them from achieving decision-making positions both in the family and the society. The platform for changing the society's cultural values must be launched by women and led by women in order to bear fruit.

Despite the small gains by women in the areas of education, politics and economy, there is still more, which can be done to narrow or even bridge the gap between the sexes in reality and in governmental policies. Women must continue to assume responsibility for their well-being and that of their children. Through complementary actions of women's NGOs (at home and internationally) and government agencies, policies regarding women's health, education, employment, political ambitions and participation and issues of equity should be formulated and implemented. The strength of a country depends on the development of all of its citizens.

Chapter 5 Notes

1. R. Sivard, *Women: A World Survey* (Washington, DC: World Priorities, 1985).
2. J L Parpart and K A Stuadt eds., *Women and the State in Africa* (Boulder and London: Lynne Rienner Publishers, 1989).
3. Remi Clignet, "Social Change and Patterns of Sexual Differentiation in Two African Countries," *Signs* (1977).
4. UNESCO, "Africa Development Indicators, 2002" (Statistical Yearbook, 2000)
5. J H Momsen, *Women and Development in the Third World* (London: Routledge, 1991).
6. Data for 1999 is provided at:
http://www.tulane.edu/~internut/Countries/Cameroon/cameroonxx.html
7. To get comparable data on other African countries visit:
http://www.africare.org/about/where-we-work/where-we-work.html
8. Joseph Mboui, Deputy of the National Assembly, President of the Commission for education, Professional Training and Youth, UNESCO, 2003-2007; and J C Bryson, "Women and Economic Development in Cameroon," (Prepared under contract No RDO 78/8 with USAID, Yaounde, 1979).
9. T E Mbuagbow, R. Brain & R Palmer, *A History of Cameroon* (London: Essex: Group Ltd., 1987).

10. B. Davidson, *Modern Africa* (London: Longman, 1983).
11. Miriam Goheen, *Men Own the Fields, Women Own the Crops: Gender and Power in the Cameroon Grassfields*. (Madison, WI: The University of Wisconsin Press, 1996).
12. For a comprehensive report visit: http://www.state.gov/r/pa/ei/bgn/26431.htm.
13. For a comprehensive report visit: http://www.unicef.org/files/Table5.pdf
14. Bryson, "Women in Cameroon."
15. Clignet, "Social Change African" and D E Koenig, "Sex, Work, and Social Class in Cameroon" (Ann Arbor and London: University Microfilms International, 1977).
16. OFUNC, "The Face of Women in Cameroon" (Yaounde, Cameroon: AGRACAM, n.d.) 67.
17. Alan Guttmacher Institute, *Issues in Brief: Family Planning Improves Child Survival and Health (*Washington, DC: Alan Guttmacher Institute, 1997).
18. Bryson, "Women in Cameroon."
19. OFUNC, "Face of Women," 65.
20. Progress of the World's Women 2000: A New Biennial Report: http://www.unifem. undp.org/progressww/2000/
21. For more information visit: http://www.acdi-cida_ind.nsf/3f70680bd2c2e2ff8525664200403dad/ 04fc5f588f92ca385256bfe0068cf25?OpenDocument
22. For a complete summary visit: Cameroon Association of Female Jurists (ACAFE) http://www.crlp.org/pdf/SRCameroon00en.pdf
23. For more information refer to endnote 21.
24. A Babs Fafunwa and J U Aisiku eds., *Education in Africa: a Comparative Study* (London: George Allen and Unwin, 1982).
25. Pamela McCorduck and Nancy Ramsey, *The Futures of Women-Scenarios for the 21st Century* (Reading, MA: Addison-Wesley, 1996).
26. Koenig, "Sex, Work, Social Class."
27. Goheen, *Gender and Power in Cameroon*, 181.
28. Mrs. Keutcha Julienne, member of the political Bureau and Former Member of Parliament, quoted in OFUNC, 86.
29. Le Combattant, No. 439 (Monday, October 1990), 10.
30. For a list of Cameroon women's organizations visit: http://www.distel.ca/womlist /countries/cameroon.html
31. Ministry of Social and Women's Affairs, "Evaluation of the Implementation of the Nairobi Forward-Looking Strategies for the Advancement of Women and the Abuja Declaration on Participatory Development" (Republic of Cameroon, September 1995).
32. The Buea University Newsletter, vol 1, no 3 (January 1994), 12.
33. Ministry of Social and Women's Affairs.
34. Gender Equality Makes Headway: UNIFEM: http://english.people.com.cn/200007/20/eng20000720_45966.html
35. For additional personal information on women and other positions held visit: http://www.guide2womenleaders.com/Cameroon_heads.htm
36. Momsen, *Women in the Third World.*
37. M C Snyder and M Tadesse, *African Women and Development: A History* (London: Zed Books Ltd., 1995) 21.
38. Bryson, "Women in Cameroon"; L M Matt, "A Report on Women's Cooperatives in the Northwest and Southwest Provinces." (1979); M DeLancey, "Women's Cooperatives in Cameroon," in *African Studies Review,* 1987, vol. 30, 1, 1-8; V DeLancey., "Agricul-

tural Expansion for Women in Cameroon" (paper presented at the annual meeting of the African Studies Association, Los Angeles, October, 1984); M A McCarthy, "Report on Women's Cooperative Groups Activities for 981; Kom Area women's Cooperative (Peace Corps Volunteer, 1982); J A Mope Simo, "The Political Economy of Cameroon: Historical Perspectives" (paper prepared for the African Studies Center-Cameroon Conference, Leiden, The Netherlands, June 1-4, 1988); C Sterling, "Special report for the Development of Women's Cooperatives in the Southwest Province" (Submitted to the Director of Cooperation, 1979); N P Sullivan, "Mid-Service Report: Women's Cooperatives (Southwest Province, Meme Division, 1981).

39. CIA, "World Bank", *CIA World Factbook* (Washington, DC: Potomac Books, 2002).

40. Goheen, *Gender and Power in Cameroon;* Snyder & Tadesse, *African Women.*

41. L FonJong, "Fostering Women's Participation in Development through Non-governmental Efforts in Cameroon" *The Geographical Journal,* vol 167, No. 3, September 2001, 223-224.

42. In 2001 the author received a Fulbright grant to conduct research and in 2003 a follow-up study was carried on in the same field of study. Preliminary findings were published in *Asian Women 2002 Vol. 15* and in *Research Institute of Asian Women (RIAW) 2002, Program 2002-06.*

43. J Endeley, "Conceptualizing Women's Empowerment in Societies in Cameroon: How Does Money Fit In?" *Gender and Development,* vol. 9, No. 1, March 2001.

44. M Niger-Thomas, "Women and the Arts of Smuggling" *African Studies Review,* Sept. 2001, vol. 44 i2, 43.

45. An in-depth study of Cameroon Women's associations entitled: *Women's Associations in Cameroon: the immediate Post-colonial and Contemporary Eras Compared* by Melinda Adams describes the different associations and traces their development and progress from post-colonial period. This paper was presented at the Annual Meeting of the Midwest Political Science Association, Chicago in April 2003. For more information visit: http://www.mwpsa.org

46. S Walker, "Walled Women and Women Without Walls Among the Fulbe of Northern Cameroon in *Sage, 7* (1990) 13-17.

47. Susan P Joekes, "Women in the World Economy: An INSTRAW Study" New York: Oxford University Press, 1987), 63.

48. I Dankelman and J Davidson, "Women and Environment in the Third World: Alliance for the Future" (London: Earthscan Publications Ltd., 1989).

49. Women's Feature Service ed., *The Power to Change: Women in the Third World Redefine their Environment* (London: Zed Books Ltd., 1993), 43-44.

50. Bryson, "Women in Cameroon."

51. S Tetchiada, "Cameroon Women's Unemployment: A Great Injustice (ANB-BIA Supplement, Issue/Edition Nr. 433, 2002).

52. For more comprehensive UN statistics visit: http://unstats.un.org/unsd/demographic/products/indwm/indwm2.htm.

53. INC, 2002

54. World Bank Report No. 8894 (November, 1990).

55. Ministry of Social and Women's' Affairs

56. Women's Feature Service ed., *The Power to Change: Women in the Third World Redefine their Environment* (London: Zed Books Ltd., 1993), 44.

57. The Buea University Newsletter, vol. 1, no. 3, (January 1994), 12.

Chapter 6

Chinese Woman's Emancipation: Historical Considerations and Future Prospects

Wu Xiaoqun

Men's viewpoints have traditionally dominated historical narratives. However, women compose one-half of humanity and, like men, create and shape civilization. In modern times, people have begun to seriously examine women's issues. Scholars now study women's traditional roles, their current level of emancipation, and increasingly problematic relationships with men. This new relationship at once constitutes an important advance in the history of civilization and is itself made possible by specific cultural and technological changes in twentieth century civilization. The very recognition of women's issues demonstrates humanity's self-reflective capabilities, which are the precondition for all cultural and technological change. Women's issues, that is, not only define a new cultural movement and present a revisionist view of traditional civilization; they reveal a new and essential set of questions, which will inform the social vocabulary of future civilizations.

I would like to examine the history of Chinese women's emancipation and by so doing suggest some possibilities in women's development in the coming century.

Historical Processes Leading to Emancipation

Chinese women began to be "noticed" by Chinese society at large only at the end of the nineteenth century. Before this, there had of course been Empresses (such as Wu Zetian), Empress Dowagers (such as Ci Xi), and even female generals (such as Liang Hongyu), but these cases were not typical.[1] The condition of Chinese women was deplorable; they suffered the day to day degradations and humiliations inflicted by an entrenched Patriarchy. Moreover, they, themselves, lacked the self-awareness necessary to understand their own oppression. They made sense out of their lives through their fathers, husbands, and sons. Confucianism, the cultural standard of ancient Chinese society, provided the rules and even the language which defined woman's place in society. Thus the observation: it is only women and villains who are very difficult to feed was unfortunately typical of the broader language of Confucian discourse concerning women.

During the Eastern Han Dynasty, Ban Zhao, the historian Ban Gu's sister, wrote *Women of Commandments (Nu Jie)*. This book established concrete codes of conduct based on male supremacy. The Confucian idealist philosophy of the Song Dynasty established chastity as the moral norm for women. Along with the gradual development of Confucianism in succeeding dynasties, chastity occupied an increasingly dominant position in Chinese ideology for women. Finally, it came to permeate all of society and to thoroughly normalize women's oppression. By the time of the Ming and Qing Dynasties, feet binding[2] and enforced chastity[3] had become normative and the status of ancient Chinese women reached its nadir through the destruction of their bodies in both a physical and symbolic sense. Moreover, for the last two thousand years, women for the most part remained silent. Indeed most not only endured silently, but also accepted the idea of male superiority and passed it on to their children.

After the Opium War of 1840, Chinese society, faced with the invasion of foreigners, changed politically, economically, and culturally. Because of these changes, women's issues again became important, and from that point on the Chinese women's movement became entangled with all other kinds of political and social movements, always, however, as a subsidiary part.

During the period of the Taiping Heavenly Kingdom (1851-1864), the largest peasant uprising in Chinese history until the 20th century, teaching equality between men and women, reforming the system of marriage, and abolishing the most pernicious forms of discrimination, helped emancipate women. These reforms aroused enthusiasm and thousands of women came out of their homes and joined the army. For the first time Chinese society recognized women's social potential. However, since it was a peasant revolution, and such revolutions often have conservative agendas, the Movement of the Taiping Heavenly Kingdom focused on land and ignored the necessity of women's emancipation.

The Reform Movement of 1898[4] concerned constitutional reform and modernization. Kang Youwei, Liang Qichao, Tan Sitong and others were influenced by the Western ideas, and they introduced western notions of rights and change into China. Specifically, Rousseau's theory of natural rights and Darwin's theory of evolution became popular in China's intellectual circles. Many therefore opposed the Qing government's obstinate view that "ancestral laws can't be changed." One of those changes had to do with women, but again it was not a principle concern. However, it was something not to be ignored. It enlightened Chinese society bound by Confucianism for thousand of years. In 1884, Kang Youwei and his brother Kang Guangren had founded "The Organization of Untwining Feet" in their hometown of Nan Hai, Guangdong province, and people began to follow their example in many places. "The Movement against Binding Women's Feet" sprang up all over China. Meanwhile, the reformers took vigorous action to raise money for founding women's schools, women's institutes and women's newspapers. The first Chinese women's newspaper appeared at this time. In the spring of 1898, the first Chinese women's school opened in Shanghai; over a period of time many other women's institutes opened.

But in this movement, as others before it, women took second place. Women were given attention because the reformers thought that tradition-bound Chinese women hampered prosperity and weakened the nation. The purpose of emancipating women was for creating healthy women to bear sturdy children (especially boys), who could compete in emerging international struggles. It was therefore clear that training the new type of good wife-and-mother was the true purpose in the movement of women during that time. So-called women's emancipation was useful only for preserving the male society and its values.

During the Revolution of 1911 led by Dr. Sun Yatsen, women were once again important participants. Jin Tianhe wrote a famous book, *Alarm Clock for Women (Nu Jie Zhong), which* for the first time proposed a Chinese feminism. Many women's organizations and newspapers appeared in China. There were about 35 women's organizations and 41 newspapers during the Revolution of 1911[5.] These organizations and newspapers argued for the freedom of marriage, monogamy, economic independence, and the right to participate and comment in government and political affairs. They opposed binding women's feet and male supremacy in the family. For the first time, they combined the idea of women's emancipation with the notion of building a democratic republic.

However, during the revolution, it became impossible for women to pay attention only to women's issues. As I have tried to suggest, women's issues were always connected to some larger national and political issues. The movement of women became once again subordinate to the revolution. Nevertheless it left its mark. The so-called new types of women at this time were revolutionary women and even some man-like women. They took part in all kinds of revolutionary activities including assassinations, bombings, arms trading, and instigating uprisings. People such as Qiu Jin, Cheng Xiefen, and Zhang Zhujun were typical female revolutionaries at that time. What they did helped greatly in bringing the issue of women's rights out of the private domain and into the public square. However, feminism could exist only under the cloak of nationalism, since it was nationalism not feminism that in the end was driving social change in China. And so feminists were in a sense swallowed up by the revolution. This movement of women was doomed to influence just a small number of women and really did not succeed in improving women's status and perceived social worth. But it did provide the seed for much that followed.

The May 4th Movement of 1919[6] was an epochal event in Chinese history. It was not only anti-imperialist and anti-traditionalist; it was also the most transforming event in modern Chinese history.

By 1919 women's issues covered a wide range of problems: women's education, marriage and family, economic independence, employment, children's education, prostitution and female servitude, birth control, and much more. Furthermore, by 1919, women's issues were distinct from national and revolutionary issues and were viewed as crucial in their own right. The May 4th Movement of 1919 is therefore properly regarded as the true starting point of Chinese women's emancipation. Women for the first time became aware of themselves as women, and scholars began to ponder the status and condition of women. They targeted orthodox Confucianism as the principle historical and philosophical justification for women's traditional depersonalization.[7] This broader women's movement also offered the possibility of mutual cooperation between men and women. That is, it began to argue that women's emancipation was a necessary condition for any broader movement of emancipation. Once again, however, the women's movement was pre-empted by the broader movement for cultural emancipation; Chinese women were forced to step back. The movement had become purely decorative.[8]

The Kuomintang(KMT) dominated Chinese politics from 1927 to 1949. The KMT's declared policy affirmed the equality of men and women in law, in the economy, and in society. The party aimed to promote the dignity of women. This policy was significant even though it was not enforced, if only because it established for the first time sexual equality in law. And there was a notable presence of organizations within the KMT such as "the Movement of Women Resisting Japan and Saving the Nation," the "Movement of Women's New Life." These groups, however, never really impacted the lives of poor women—their activities were limited to the middle and upper class. In those areas controlled by the Chinese Communist Party, the situation was quite different. The woman-worker became a fresh force in all kinds of social issues because of the Communist Party's extensive education program and its land reform. But again the pattern of events was sadly repetitive; Chinese women's emancipation melted into the generalized patriotic fervor of the War of Resistance against Japan and later the Civil War. There were some women soldiers and women revolutionaries, but the mass of Chinese women stayed home. As in the 1840s, given conditions of domestic unrest and foreign invasion, the women's question could not become a focal point of Chinese society or even a burning question for women themselves.

Chinese Women in the 20th-21st Centuries

From 1949 until the present, women's lives followed different paths in Mainland China, Taiwan, and Hong Kong. I want only to consider women's status in Mainland China. I want to argue that Chinese Socialism has radically altered the lives of women in the last fifty years.

The Chinese Communist Party promulgated the New Marriage Law in 1950. It abolished child brides and arranged marriages. Moreover, it rigorously enforced monogamy. It permitted women to divorce their husbands. This is all to say that the marriage law freed women from the oppression of the traditional marriage and concubine system. From 1954 to 1990, China promulgated four Constitutions, each of which reaffirmed women's equality in politics, the economy, culture, education and social life. The Chinese government promulgated the Secure Law of Women's Rights and Interests in 1992. There are a whole series of national laws concerning marriage, suffrage, criminal and civil behavior, working conditions and property rights, as well as more than 40 regional and local regulations which now guarantee women's rights.

After 1949, Chinese women's working conditions vastly improved. (1) The number of employed women has increased. Working women accounted for 0.22 percent of the population before 1949 and 7.5 percent of the working population. The Chinese government has taken vigorous action to promote employment opportunities for women since then. There were 40,930,000 women workers in

1982—36.3 percent of the work force. By 1992 that number had risen to 55,000,000 or 38 percent of the total work force.[9] (2) In general the principle of equal pay for equal work has been implemented. In 1955, Mao Zedong argued the necessity for women to have equal opportunity to work in all fields and re-ceive the same wages as men.[10] (3) Women's jobs have remained stable. Women's careers do not end with marriage or childbirth, since the government stipulates that no enterprise can discharge any married women or pregnant women. After childbirth women enjoy a two-month vacation and their promo-tions and salary increases remain unaffected. Women who receive the "Certifi-cate of One Child" have six months time off to raise their babies while the family has similarly improved.

Since 1949, Chinese women's status in the family has improved. For 2000 years, Chinese women always depended on someone else. "The three obediences and four virtues,"[11] "the three cardinal guides and the five constant virtues"[12] and other Confucian ideas made sure that Chinese women were subject to the author-ity of fathers and the authority of husbands. After the KMT Revolution, the status of women in the family improved, but the old system of family relationship did not completely change. Since 1949, China has applied political and educational means to abolish this kind of discrimination against women, and has protected the rights and interests of women by law. These laws seem to work. In the "Chinese Women's Issues" investigative report of 1995, 68.8 percent of women surveyed thought they had a fair say in important family affairs; 66 percent of the women asked felt they were treated respectfully at home; 62.1 percent of women felt they had a fair say in household financial management. In large cities this figure was even higher. In Beijing, for example, it was 73.8 percent. This report concluded that 47.6 percent of married women had married on their own, 31.5 percent had discussed their marriage with their parents, and only 17.7 percent of marriages were arranged by parents.[13]

Educational opportunity for women has increased, and more women go on to universities. During the mid-fifties, 30,000,000 illiterate women were educated through the literacy program and the nationwide movement for education. School entrance rates for girls have increased 90 percent.[14]

But even beyond these major areas of improvement, the increased participa-tion of women in the nation's life is palpable in other areas. For example, 90 per-cent of women vote; 20 percent of the delegates to the people's congress are women.[15] From 1980 to 1990 the percentage of women workers in government organizations rose from 12 to 16 percent.[16] According to the Third National Cen-sus in 1982, 31.6 percent of all scientific workers were women. Women com-posed 35.34 percent of workers in cultural and educational fields and 50 percent in health related institutions.[17] In short, the last 50 years have seen a profound change in the life of the ordinary woman in China; one could even argue that it has been they who have reaped the greatest benefits of the policies of the post 1949 regime.

Equality without a Women's Movement

I want to stress one point particularly. These changes are the result of deep changes in the structure of the Chinese economy and society. They are not the result of what in the West is called "Feminism." While there have been, as I have suggested, feminist moments in Chinese history, women's freedom has come without what western feminists would call "self-awakening" or "self-awareness." Because of this, Chinese women feel closely dependent on the post—1949 regime. There is something troubling about this. Once again someone else gives women rights, only now it is the government, rather than a father or a husband, since under it the nominal equality of men and women has become more and more a reality.

On the one hand, a large number of women have joined the work force. They have entered a world previously occupied exclusively by men. Given the deeply rooted idea of male superiority, female inferiority, this newfound approval by society invigorated women, and they have by and large supported the Chinese Communist Party. Women played a great role in the reforms initiated after 1949, reforms such as land redistribution and the cooperative movement. On the other hand, using the slogan "Women Can Do Everything Men Can Do", some women have demanded an eccentric form of equality—even imitating men in appearance. For a while it was fashionable to wear men's suits, to have male hairstyles, even to use men's names. The whole society, including women, ignored women's biological characteristics and so-called femininity. Unfortunately these problems were not corrected early and were ignored, and then became hidden during the Cultural Revolution (1966-76), a movement so broad and ambitious that it temporarily trumped all other agendas including women's issues.

The Genuine Chinese Women's Movement Begins

Since 1978 women's issues have surfaced again. The market-oriented policies that succeeded the ideologically driven ones have not always benefited women, and there has been a revival of traditional prejudices that has created problems for women, who thought these to have been solved in 1949. There has been an increase in the proportion of women leaving school early. Unemployment among women has increased and there has been a rise in job discrimination against women. Sadly, female babies are often forsaken. In short, there has been something of a revival of male chauvinism.

On the whole, however, the market reforms of the late 70s were imperative and these reforms benefited all of China including Chinese women. But it cannot be denied that these reforms reopened old wounds and created some new ones. Half a century ago Chinese women gained social and political emancipation. Today this emancipation has become more problematic, and it seems that the task of the women's movement is not yet complete.[18]

Chapter Six Notes

1. Lee Lilyxiao, ed, *Biographical Dictionary of Chinese Women: the Qing Period 1644-1911*, Vol I, (Armonk, NY: ME Sharpe Inc., 1998).
2. Howard S. Levy, *Chinese Footbinding: the History of a Curious Erotic Custom*, (Lon-

don: Kegan Paul International Limited: 1966, 2001).

3. Fan Hong, *Footbinding, Feminism: the Liberation of Women's Bodies in Modern China*, (Essex, UK: Frank Cass Publishers, 1997). See also Tien Ju Kang, *Male Anxiety and Female Chastity: a Comparative Study of Chinese Ethical Values in Ming-Ching Times*. (Boston: US: Brill Academic Publications, 1988).

4. Ono Kazuko, *Chinese Women in a Century of Revolution, 1850-1950*, (Stanford, CA: Stanford University Press, 1989).

5. Esther S. Leeyao, *Chinese Women: Past and Present*, (Irving, TX: Ide House, Inc; 1983).

6. Elizabeth Croll, *Changing Identities of Chinese Women: Rhetoric, Experience and Self Precept in 20th Century China*, (Atlantic Highlands, NJ: Humanities Press Int'l, 1995). See also Li Yu-Ning, ed, *Chinese Women through Chinese Eyes*, (Armonk, NY: ME Sharpe, Inc., 1992).

7. Patricia B. Ebry, *Confucianism and Family Rituals in Imperial China: a social history of Writing about Rites*, (Princeton, NJ: Princeton University Press, 1991).

8. Christine Gilmartin; Hershatter, Gail; Rofel, Lisa; White, Tyrene, Cambridge: *Engendering China: Women, Culture and the State*, (Cambridge, MA: Harvard University Press, 1994).

9. Barbara Entwisle; Henderson, Gail, *Redrawing Boundaries: Work, Household and Gender in China*. (Berkeley: University of California Press).

10. Elizabeth Croll, *Chinese Women since Mao*, (Armonk, NY: ME Sharpe, 1984). See also Sha Jicai: Liu Qiming, *Women's Status in Contemporary China*, (International Scholar's Press, 1996).

11. Harriet Zumdorfer, ed, *Chinese Women in the Imperial Past: New Perspectives*, (Boston: Brill Academic Publishers, 1996.)

12. Ibid.

13. All China Women's Federation (ACWF) & National Bureau of Statistics (NBS), The Survey: Women's Status in Transformation.

14. Department of Economic and Social Affairs, UN, "The World's Women: Trends and Statistics," (New York: UN Publishing, 2000).

15. ACWF & NBS, Survey: Women's Status ACWF: Beijing 1990.

16. Ibid.

17. National Bureau of Statistics: Third National Census in 1982, Beijing 1983.

18. See Chapter 12 for further discussion of the new directions anticipated for the Chinese women's movement.

PART III

WOMEN ARISING

Introduction to Part III:
Women Arising

In the last section of Women in the New Millennium we examined an international variety of approaches to the awakening of women to both their oppression as unequal partners and their potential as fully developed human beings. In chapter 7 we review the women's movement as it transcends its national origins and enters the global arena of organization, implementation, and institutionalization. By the end of World War II women in many countries had been compelled by the absence of man power to provide "woman power" in maintaining their families and the economic sector. Yet the return of men, however welcome, from the wars signaled women's reluctant return to second-class citizenry. Once the proverbial Pandora's Box was opened, and all of the new possibilities released, whether good or evil, women were no longer as willing to continue as passive participants in the patriarchal structures, which favored maleness and devalued that which was associated with femininity. The "gender box" could no longer be closed with all of its contents intact. The gender box is a symbol of the sort of gender relations prescribed by social norms and maintained intergenerationally through systems of reward and sanction.

The founding of the United Nations in 1945 opened a new era for human rights, including those of women. The UN's growth and development became synonymous with the growth and development of an international women's movement, one which gradually both included and encouraged the multiple women's movements and "feminisms" percolating within the regional and national communities of the world. As Rebecca Mbuh points out in the second article in this section, African women across the continent, however diverse, not only picked up the torch from the first UN Women's Conference in Mexico and carried it to Nairobi for the second decade women's conference in 1985, but passed it on to the women of China in Beijing in 1995. What are the implications of these events for the progress of African women? This then is the focus of Mbuh's analysis in chapter 8.

Chapter 7

Women and the United Nations

Anne Breneman

Would the women's movement have become a global one without the support and initiative of the United Nations? In this chapter we examine the influence of the United Nations on the emergence of a global women's movement.

A distinction must be made in this context between "international" and "global." Throughout world history, from the beginning of nation formation, one can discover innumerable examples of relationships between two or more nations, whether for trade, exploration, conquest, exploitation, cooperation, collaboration or missionary purposes. Therefore, internationalism carries with it a great deal of ambivalence as to its ultimate value to those involved. An international women's movement could refer to an event attended by members of several European nations, or one attended by representatives of all nations. Often it has carried with it an unequal connotation, as in the "balance of power" concept of traditional international relations theories, in which international relations are based upon unequal configurations of economic and military power and the resulting tensions.[1] On the other hand, "global" implies something inclusive and potentially involves not only every nation, but also every people, though it may be used in more limited ways by those who simply fancy the term or wish to gain prestige by doing so. In this discussion it will be used to imply inclusiveness and universality.

Before the United Nations

It may be instructive to consider an attempt to create an international coordinating body prior to 1945, when the UN was formed. By the 19th century, power arrangements among nations were almost completely organized to the advantage and assumed superiority of colonial powers. That is, the countries, kingdoms, tribes, islands, and territories of the world had been explored and settled by a few European countries and eventually Japan. Motives for colonization or conquest were mixed—mercenary, missionary, exploitation of resources, assumptions of a superior, industrialized civilization, and need for land to support overpopulated homelands. Japan, an island nation, shared similar motives, including a sense of "manifest destiny." A common assumption was that those who were subjugated were in need of those aspects of culture, religion and technology developed during the industrialization process in Europe and Japan. Although touted as an instrument of international peace, the League of Nations was designed to support and maintain this configuration of power and privilege.[2] Its ability to function even on this basis was, however, severely limited by competition and power struggles among its members. It was, in effect, an exclusive country club for conquering nations and limited to European male delegates. Neither Japan nor the United States were members of this elite club. The League of Nations, therefore, was rendered powerless to prevent the conflagration, which erupted into World War II.

As wives, daughters, sisters and mothers, European and Japanese women acted as both victims and perpetrators of an international hierarchy based upon military, economic and industrial power. In books and films, such as *Passage to India, Out of Africa,* and *Gone with the Wind,*[3] both women and men are depicted as living lives based upon assumptions of white European superiority and privilege, while Indians, Kenyans, and African slaves position themselves as inferiors to their colonial conquerors. In the United States and Latin America this pattern was imposed by subjugating the Native American populations and importing captured African slaves to perpetrate the feudal systems of Europe in the Americas, where large landholdings held by the ruling class were known as *"plantations"* and *"haciendas."*

As in Europe, land grants and large purchases allowed the few to create serfdoms or kingdoms. Through a combination of patriarchy and primogeniture a small number of European men passed their land and slaves to their sons or nephews. Some of these land holdings were doubled or tripled through intermarriages with paternal cousins.[4] The often extravagant lifestyle, which resulted among planter families, resembled those of lords and princes in Europe and contrasted sharply with the lives of deprivation, hardship and long hours of labor by the enslaved population. Although far more European settlers owned neither large estates nor slaves, nonetheless the patriarchal hierarchy created a socioeconomic and political structure, which privileged those who did. In such a pyramidal context it is common for those in lower stratum to emulate, value and envy the manners, attitudes, behaviors and lifestyles of the ruling class.

Without power, influence, education or means, those at the lower base of the social pyramid were the silent majority, half of whom were women, whether slave or free. While women were also half of those in the ruling class, they were forced to submit to their husbands, fathers, clergy and other men of the ruling class. Yet, in relation to both men and women of the lower classes, and most particularly slaves, who were without legal or human rights, some women of the ruling classes were reputed as domineering. This system was buffered somewhat by the growth of a middle class as industrialization expanded.

A Paradigm Shift

The purpose of reviewing the colonial social order, which was widespread by the middle of the eighteenth century, is to set the conceptual stage for the drama that began with the formation of the United Nations in 1945. From a quasi-medieval social order to one which suddenly demanded that all colonies be prepared for independence, self-determination, democracy and the participation of women and all classes in voting and representation—was more than a revolution. It was a paradigm shift, which has taken over half a century to comprehend. Other than complaints about parking tickets and foreigners along the Avenue of the Americas in Manhattan, many Americans, including members of the government, seemed to be unaware that choice land in the heart of New York City had been granted to an entity which did not belong to any nation, was not to be controlled by any national interest, and was mandated to enact policies in the interests of the peoples of the world, "civil society." This same entity held within its charter the capacity to derange the existing world order.

The discovery of how to explode an atom, which led to the horrific bombing of Japan at the end of the Second World War, seems an apt metaphor for the consequent explosion of the existing social order, which the implementation of the United Nations Charter set in motion. Those liberation movements, which began in the eighteenth, and nineteenth centuries, described in earlier chapters, were imbued with exponential powers. These included the formation of a global regulatory body that included all nations and required all former colonies to be prepared for independence and self-determination as nations. The UN's commitment to world peace through universal representation, literacy, education, improvements of standards of living, human rights, and the development of women were made concrete by the formation of organizations, committees, and strategic planning over specified time periods. Though initially only 50 nations were prepared to join as charter members, and only five were awarded the "veto power" on the decision-making body, the Security Council, the General Assembly provided ample space in its chambers to accommodate 150 new delegations, as colonies gained independence and recognition as "sovereign nations" by the UN Security Council.[5]

As the UN assisted nations with plans to bring electricity, plumbing, sanitary water, immunization, schools, colleges, hospitals, transportation and communication, technology and improved agricultural methods, quiet revolutions began to occur throughout the country sides of the world. The major beneficiaries of these changes were children, women and those who had been oppressed under colonial or Fascist rule—the rank and file of humanity. At the UN headquarters in Manhattan and its outposts scattered throughout the world, humanity in all of its diversity poured through its gates as delegates, officials, staff, and workers. Unlike its predecessor, the UN represented all of the nations of the world and included a growing number of women in its offices, committees and functions.

Within several decades, the UN focus on universal education and literacy reaped a rich harvest of diversity at all levels of its organization. Among these was an international cadre of educated women who worked together on committees, NGOs, task forces, and staff, sometimes in leadership roles, representing African and Asian nations, as well as the Americas, Europe and the island nations. For the first time in world history, women, along with all the peoples of the world, had a voice and a forum in which to express concerns, ideas, and proposals regarding issues which affected their lives and those of other women of the world. This constituted a global revolution—often underestimated in its power to transform the world as it has been conceived and lived for many millennia.

The process of universal empowerment is a work in progress, as it will take centuries to free humanity from the chains and habits of internalized oppression, as well as dominance. Nonetheless its fruits are already beginning to appear. One of these is the global woman's movement, with multiple facets and diverse voices.

Raising New Voices

As former First Lady of the United States, Hillary Clinton, said in a recent address to women of Uruguay and other Latin American countries:

> Today, more than at any other time in history, women have the opportunity and the responsibility not only to raise our own voices but to empower others to raise theirs as well. The women gathered here, we, are among the blessed. Even though many have suffered, the spirit was not broken. And you are here as testimony to resilience and determination.[6]

The spirit and ideal of Hillary Clinton's words as First Lady addressing a Latin American conference hearkens back to that of the first UN International Women's Conference, called in 1975 in Mexico City. By the seventies, three decades after the founding of the UN, it had become apparent that development projects that excluded, ignored, or devalued the roles of women in their families and communities could not succeed in their aims. The increased presence of international women at the UN helped to create an ongoing discourse on the evidence that was beginning to accrue through the first quarter century of experience at the grass roots. The new voices were multicultural, fresh and persuasive. As Mary Ann Tetreault points out in her compilation on women and revolution throughout the world: "As primary producers, women are essential for a sustained challenge to the state to be successful."[7] Tetreault views the state as an expression of patriarchy which must be undermined in order for a new system, more just and caring, to arise.

Yet another observation made by Tetreault is that revolutions are traditionally treated as events that transform political relations rather than products of a flawed social order, which inherently embody many of the flaws. The growing numbers of national women's movements are often such products, as they are limited by the host nation's flaws of vision, tradition, philosophy and historical interpretation of religion and culture. It is at the global level, then, that the women's movement can raise consciousness above national attempts ". . . to guide the process of political change along a preferred path of system transformation."[8]

That is, through communication, dialogue, and strategic planning supported by the United Nations, with input from the regional and local levels, women are being enabled to conceptualize and define universal standards for progress toward complete gender equality. It is then left to the NGOs and national governments to negotiate a process of implementation within specific cultural contexts and report to the United Nations the progress made toward the achievement of these goals. During conferences, summits, and meetings of delegates and task forces, the results are reviewed, evaluated and used as a launching pad for further goal-setting.

As women become increasingly involved in decision-making as equals, certain issues tend to appear on the table more frequently: issues of inclusiveness, caring, organization, children, fairness, health, democracy, spirituality and diversity, to name some of the more common. Concerns regarding authority and power among social classes, races, groups and nations tend to resemble very closely those between women and men. Each can be viewed as a metaphor for the other; both involve assumptions of superiority and strength on the part of the dominant and inferiority and weakness on the part of the subordinate. Vanaja Dhruvarajan explains:

> Once we understand how privileges are accrued, maintained and reproduced, we can transform those processes to stem the tide of oppression and domination. . . . Once we organize social life to respond to the needs and concerns of all people and to treat all people as equally deserving of a good life, we will not have these 'problems.' We will all be involved in finding solutions by examining how we live and how our lives affect other people.[9]

It is revealing that once the women's movement emerged on the world stage, supported by the United Nations, it grew exponentially in strength, organization and public interest, as the historical development of the world women's conferences and platforms illustrates.

Globalizing the Women's Movement

The 1975 "World Conference of the International Women's Year" in Mexico City was conceived initially as a culmination of a one-year period designated by the United Nations as "International Women's Year." This was consistent with the pattern which had been established by the UN of identifying a pressing international development issue as a theme for each year and hence as a priority for allocation of development resources among the UN projects scattered throughout the developing world.

When the UN General Assembly passed Resolution #3276 designating 1975 as International Women's year, it also passed Resolution #3277 establishing a Committee for the Conference for International Women's Year, a Secretary General for the year to lead the Committee, and a mandate for both to prepare an international plan of action to be finalized by the Mexican conference delegates.[10] Hence the concept of moving issues to plans of action was built into the first UN women's conference and remained as an integral part of the conference's continuity.

It is noteworthy, too, that UNGA Resolution #3276 included a sweeping mandate called "Status and Role of Women in Society, with special reference to the need for achieving equal rights for women and to women's contribution to the attainment of the goals of the Second UN Development Decade, to the struggle against colonialism, racism, and racial discrimination and to the strengthening of international peace and cooperation between States."

In planning the conference, the UN Economic and Social Council requested that the Secretary-General of International Women's Year and of the women's conference, Helvi L. Sipila, focus on two major issues: (1) the evaluation of current trends and changes in the roles of women and men in political, social, economic, family and cultural life, including the sharing of responsibilities and decision-making; (2) the examination of major obstacles which hinder the contribution of women and men as full partners in the total development efforts and in sharing its benefits in both rural and urban areas.

In preparation for the conference in Mexico, regional women's meetings and consultations were held throughout 1974 and early 1975. Among these were the following: *(a)* International Forum on the Role of Women in Population and Development, *(b)* Regional Consultation for Asia and the Far East in Integration of Women in Development, *(c)* Regional Consultation for Africa on Integration of Women in Development, *(d)* UN Interregional Seminar on National Machinery to Accelerate the Integration of Women in Development and to Eliminate Discrimination on Grounds of Sex, and *(e)* Regional Consultation for Latin America on the Integration of Women in Development. The regional and international gatherings helped to garner interest in the first global conference solely about women, thus assuring widespread participation and engagement in the attending issues. The gatherings helped to define more specifically what kinds of women's issues were significant to specific cultures and experiences. The generic language which emerges on a global platform can assist in creating the power of shared concerns by abstracting them from the situations in which they arise and providing a common indicator for surveys and reports, such as women in decision-making, women and violence or women in development. However, without the opportunity for coalition building from the grassroots communities in which girls and women are situated, such generic terms become meaningless and too abstract to create a strategic plan to drive the plans forward and assess their effectiveness. Coalition-building between local, regional, national and international agencies helped to create a healthy decision-making climate for strengthening and advancing women's position in society.

The strategy of consulting with women at national and regional levels had the additional value of engaging increasing numbers of women from the grassroots level in the conference and platform planning process. This action resulted in the presence in Mexico of 114 nongovernmental organizations (NGOs), addressing a wide variety of issues facing women in the home, family, community, workplace and within the social, political, economic and cultural structures in which women are embedded. However, one of the goals of the conference was to *"break through"* the notion that the problems facing women are independent of those facing society in general. That is, what women face as obstacles to their equality, dignity and effectiveness are usually the result of "entrenched patterns of conflict,"[11] some of which surface in every society as ignorance, tradition and prejudice.

Mexico—a New Beginning

When the 1975 conference opened with greetings from Mexican President Luis Escheverria Alvarez, the enthusiastic participants elected "by acclamation"

Mexican Attorney General Mr. Pedro O. Paulladai as the Conference President. He made an opening remark that the conference was the first intergovernmental meeting the agenda of which was devoted solely to the situation of women in society. He also noted that the conference was the first of which women formed a part of every delegation. Vice-presidents from each region of the world were elected to assist in the mobilization of women: eleven from the African continent, ten from the Asian continent, six from Eastern Europe, nine from Latin America, and ten from Western countries. Chairwomen were elected from Guinea and Iran to lead two main committees with advising and coordinating functions in relationship to the regional and national levels of women's organization.

What resulted at the Mexican conference was a first World Plan of Action, known as the "Declaration of Mexico," a commitment to a United Nations Decade for Women on the theme of Equality, Development and Peace, and a decision to hold such conferences at five year intervals to assess national and regional progress towards achievement of women's equality. The areas to be assessed were still somewhat vague and general in that the indicators of progress were yet to be addressed in a language that could fit every national situation.

Nonetheless, the Mexican Conference was an official beginning for the globalization of the Women's Movement. With the conference participants' determination to create an action plan by which member nations could be assessed for gender equality and women's development, the movement was transformed from scattered national movements to one that included all nations and peoples. The world conferences which began with Mexico addressed consistently these issues and demonstrated mounting evidence of the embeddedness of women and their struggles for equality within the issues which faced decolonized nations and subordinated peoples throughout the developing world, as well as within Western societies, where racial and class prejudice had been rampant, vicious and insidious.

For the first time, women of the world, working together across cultures, political barriers, economic systems, religious identities, and geographic locations, had the means to hold nations, organizations, individuals and themselves accountable for removing obstacles to their progress and development toward full equality. Further, the road toward equality became intimately and officially linked with the struggle to free the entire human race from the blight of racism and colonialism.

Human Rights and Accountability

Although the Universal Declaration of Human Rights, adopted in 1948, created standards of human dignity and well being for all of the peoples of the world, and UN committees were formed to oversee the implementation of each standard, the Convention on the Elimination of All Forms of Discrimination against Women (CEDAW) did not come into force until 1981, two years after its adoption. No doubt the Mexican Women's Conference provided a catalyst for the ratification of CEDAW and a minimal administrative structure to maintain focus while building momentum for its implementation within the human rights framework. It is within such a framework that the global women's movement has developed its texture and vision.

Women have played a significant role in developing each of the human rights instruments into covenants and conventions. The executive director of the United Nations Development Fund (UNDP) commented, "If globalization is to be pro-women and pro-poor people, it must be steered and shaped in accord with international human rights conventions and the development consensus and targets reached at various UN conventions." Heyzer also points out that policies to implement various "targets" of UN development programs, such as women's health and reproductive rights or elimination of racial discrimination, must be implemented in a manner that enhances protection and enjoyment of women's rights equally to those of men. Consistent with UNIFEM's mandate "to provide financial and technical assistance to innovative programs and strategies that promote women's human rights, political participation, and economic security,"[12] UNIFEM works with other institutions within and without the UN to create gender-sensitive strategies, assessments of progress and budgets, assuring that each policy in favor of women is also provided a budget to implement it, something often overlooked. Too often gender related policies, like many other well-meaning ideas, had been left with the status of "unfunded mandates," without the financial means to carry through on real actions.

An example of UNIFEM's contributions to moving the women's movement forward is its partnership with women in the Caribbean and a regional chapter of the International Labor Organization to produce a handbook informing women of their rights in the workplace and suggesting various litigation strategies for obtaining more gender-sensitive employment policies. The inspiration for the manual was the recognition of a gap between official ratification by Caribbean countries of CEDAW and the actual legal systems in the area that fail to incorporate the rights of women, resulting in many human rights abuses against unprotected women workers.

Even more developed countries such as the United States have been held accountable by UN women's organizations. Reports revealed in 1999 that its privatized health care system caters to a minority of wealthier Americans, while denying affordable, quality heath care to the poor, the majority of whom are women and children. This placed the US government in violation of its commitment to the Beijing Platform for Action, which calls for national plans to: "increase women's access throughout the life cycle to appropriate, affordable and quality heath care, information and related services." An example of positive action recorded by the United States State Department refers to the CEDAW Platform:

G.1. Take measures to ensure women's equal access to and full participation in power structures and decision-making.[13]

The organization under examination was that of the Small Business Administration and Women in High Positions. The report indicated that during the five years following the Beijing Women's conference, the agency had promoted 2,207 people to higher positions, of which 71 percent were women. In 2000 the agency also reported that 56 percent of middle management, and 36 percent of senior-level positions were held by women, bringing their entire management percentages above the minimum goal of 30 percent.

Yet another initiative to assist women's progress in achieving greater measures of decision-making power has been the "Vital Voices: Women in Democracy," an international project involving women leaders initially from the U.S., Eastern and Western Europe in *"exploring ways to strengthen women as democracy builders through three tracks of workshops: law and leadership, politics and public life, and economics and business."*[14] This initiative expanded in 1997 to a Vital Voices of the Americas Conference in Uruguay, including women from the entire hemisphere, and to the Caribbean and Iceland in 1999.

A Global Women in Politics program began soon after the Beijing conference, sponsored by the US Agency for International Development, but supporting women and women's organizations in 15 countries within the regions of Asia, Middle East, Africa and Latin America. At the U. S. Department of Agriculture, an additional 228 women were reported to be in high-level positions, from 1995 to 2000, with the "most outstanding improvements" occurring at the highest level positions. Out of seven Under Secretaries, three women had been appointed since Beijing. In addition this agency had created a new full-time position, Director of Women's Programs, to work on issues affecting women.

The United States Department of Transportation reported that 42 percent of the 85 agency presidential appointees were women. Other governmental agencies, such as the CIA, seemed to mince the wording of their reports to skirt around the percentages of women among employees and management but nonetheless were compelled to note some progress:

> The executive leadership of the Agency includes a number of women, each integral in decision-making processes for the crucial issues of intelligence analysis to U.S. policy makers. Intelligence analysis periodically examines the changing role and status of women, particularly in Muslim countries, where they have experienced both advances and setbacks, depending on the countries observed.[15]

The purpose of this brief discussion then has been to track the subtle evolution from separate national women's movements to what has become a revolutionizing force for social, economic, and political change across national boundaries. Without much contention, and regardless of their enormous diversity, women around the planet have identified common standards for establishing universal human rights for women. Further, through the agency of the United Nations, they have begun to succeed in holding governments accountable for achieving reasonable progress toward the set goals and standards. How has such a far-reaching revolution happened in such a short time?

Building Momentum for Empowering Women

From the first UN Women's Conference in Mexico 1975, a series of world women's conferences followed, through 2000. The second conference, originally to be hosted by Iran in 1980 was moved to Copenhagen, Denmark, when it became clear that Iran's revolution was far from a women-friendly one. The third, hosted by Kenya in 1985, was held to assess the results of the decade long World Plan of Action created in Mexico. The Fourth World Women's Conference was hosted by China and continued assessing the progress of women towards equality, using the instruments created by various organizations of the UN. The World Action Plan was updated to the Beijing Platform for Action and included new measures and concerns, among which was the concept of the empowerment of women.

The concept was given teeth through "targets" which identified concrete goals, timeframes and indicators that could be assessed in the areas of leadership and decision-making, primary and secondary education, and wage income. In 2000, a fifth World Women's Conference was held in Manhattan, NY, Beijing +5. Its purpose was to use the Beijing Platform for Action and the various measures developed to assess the progress of nations toward fulfilling commitments made in Beijing, particularly those with targeted dates of 2000. Much of the data used in this book are derived from the 2000 assessments of progress.

In addition to the above specific World Women's Conferences, eleven other international conferences were sponsored by the United Nations during the nineties to address related human rights issues:

—World Summit for Children 1990,
—UN Conference on Environment & Development 1992,
—World Conference on Human Rights 1993,
—International Conference on Population and Development 1994,
—UN Global Conference on Sustainable Development,
—World Conference on National Disaster Reduction 1994,
—World Summit for Social Development 1995,
—9th UN Conference on Prevention of Crime & Treatment of Offenders 1995,
—Ninth UN Conference on Trade & Development,
—Second UN Conference re Human Settlements 1996 and
—World Food Summit 1996.[16]

Each of these conferences provided opportunities to highlight and advance awareness of how women have been impacted by policies on these issues within each nation. The primary instrument for creating gender awareness during these occasions was the formation of a Women's Caucus, organized by former U.S. Congresswoman, Bella Abzug, and the Women's Environment and Development Organization (WEDO). The Caucus held daily briefings to review conference proceedings, prepare amendments, and develop strategies for gender sensitive actions, resulting in the incorporation of hundreds of recommendations advancing the equality and empowerment of women in the final conference agreements.

By 1993 a worldwide coalition of groups and individuals, coordinated by the Center for Women's Global Leadership, mounted a "Global Campaign for Women's Human Rights," just prior to the UN Conference on Human Rights in Vienna, Austria. They gathered over half a million signatures from 124 countries for a petition under the slogan, "Women's Rights Are Human Rights." The petition brought attention to gender violence as ". . . a universal phenomenon which takes many forms across culture, race and class" and ". . . as a violation of human rights requiring immediate action." The Vienna Declaration, which resulted, recognized for the first time that violence against women constitutes a human rights abuse. The victories of the Vienna Conference on Human Rights were incorporated into the Beijing Platform for Action in 1995 and fueled another global campaign to "Celebrate and Demand Women's Human Rights" in 1998.

This step added an even greater power of accountability as the Vienna Declaration requested both a report from the UN on the implementation of the human rights commitments made in Vienna and their incorporation into the Beijing Platform for Action. Including 6 chapters and 12 areas of critical concern, the Platform was adopted unanimously September 4-15, 1995 by delegates from 189 countries, and called on member nations to strengthen or establish "national machineries" as well as support these with both human and financial resources. That is, the Platform called for specific actions to be taken by designated dates—2000, 2005, 2010 or 2015—to remove targeted obstacles to women's equality and empowerment and to ensure a "gender-sensitive" perspective in all policies and programs.

As the various measures of CEDAW are interpreted into specific social, economic and political structures, and legislative actions taken to ratify and implement this United Nations treaty, new concepts of gender relations become inevitable, first out of necessity to comply with a law or policy, and gradually through the restructuring of values, relationships and beliefs. This process then becomes something more than a political rebellion with uncertain outcomes. Transformations of the most primary structures of society, including the family, are inevitable when girls and women are both protected and empowered by law and policy within a framework of strategic planning. Transformations within the family gradually are replicated in the school, the community and workplace, widening over time to the nation and ultimately international relations, creating a process of continuous revolution, a plowing up of the soil to plant new seeds, rather than a recycling of the same plants.

What Women Want

The Beijing Platform for Action sought to reverse the negative impact on women of widespread economic recession, political instability, heavy military spending and increased violence against women. By 2000 the New York Beijing +5 Women's Conference served as an international accounting of progress made since 1995 in fulfilling government commitments as well as in actual indications of progress from country to country in advancing gender equality. What governments had agreed to, in general, by 2000, included:

—30 percent of decision-making positions to be held by women,
—Each country to specify a date for the eradication of absolute poverty
  among women and children,
—Universal access to basic education by at least 80 percent primary school-aged
  children,

—100 percent gender equality of children enrolled in primary school, with
increase in gender equality in secondary school,
—Average life expectancy raised to minimum of 60 years for all nations,
—Mortality rates of children under 5 reduced to 1/3 of 1990 levels,
—Maternal mortality rates reduced to 1/2 of 1990 levels,
—Malnutrition of children under 5 reduced to 1/2 of 1990 levels,
—Primary healthcare for all,
—Eradication or control of major diseases, including HIV/AIDS and
—Greater availability of affordable, adequate shelter to all.

Each government was charged with the responsibility of creating national machineries so that the agreements could be implemented, evaluated, and reported to
the Secretary General of the UN. In order to determine progress towards these
goals a number of organizations, including those within the UN family, developed instruments for assessing progress by 1996.

Measuring Progress

In order to hold governments accountable for keeping the agreements made
in the Copenhagen and Beijing conferences, an organization, Social Watch, was
established in Uruguay for the express purpose of overseeing compliance of governments, UN agencies and corporations to the Copenhagen, Vienna and Beijing
agreements regarding women. In 1999 Social Watch reported: *"While the goals
targeted are feasible, many countries have failed to make a sufficient effort."*[17]
Using a different approach to assessment, a UN Research Institute for Social Development study compared resources available to women in each country, and the
personal agency they are able to exercise, with resulting achievements, as a
measure of women's empowerment.

UNIFEM researchers noted the difficulties of assessing such qualitative evi-
dences of women's empowerment as self-esteem, autonomy, and personal
agency. Therefore, their assessment focused on obstacles to women's autonomy,
exercise of human rights and to what extent such obstacles are increasing or decreasing. For example, rather than reporting only birth and death rates in each
country, these are also reported by gender, as are statistics concerning numbers of
primary school-aged children actually enrolled in schools.[18] Other reports with
indicators for assessing UN conference commitments include: OECD[19] Development Indicators, UN Common Country Indicators and UNIFEM Regional Initiatives to Monitor Beijing Platform for Action. In the OECD instrument only 2
out of 24 indicators break out to measure gender equality and empowerment of
women, both related to education. The UN Common Country Assessment identifies 40 indicators, created in cooperation with nations with development projects
underway. All 40 of the indicators measure progress toward the equality and empowerment of women, whether directly or indirectly, through gender aggregated
data collection.

The UNIFEM 2000 report addresses three key indicators used in the UN
Common Country assessment relating to economic empowerment of women:
gender ratios in secondary education, parliamentary representation and paid em-

ployment from 1985 to 1997. The use of 1997 as the end-date for reporting commitments made by nations for 2000 will necessarily create a somewhat distorted understanding of where nations actually are in their efforts to complete their commitments, as 1997 was only two years into the five-year period of the targeted goals. However, the collection of data on the Platform objectives for the equality and empowerment of women is a dynamic process. Updated reports appear regularly on the UN websites and those of cooperating national and regional women's organizations.

Holding Governments Accountable

Among such updated reports is the UN's Economic and Social Council's report card on international compliance with the Beijing Platform for Action. Overall, the progress reported from 1985 was notable throughout the world—116 member nations had submitted action plans by January 2000, 120 by 2002. Unusual cooperation among governmental and nongovernmental organizations had been exercised in preparing the plans. The areas of the Platform, which the plans focused on as priorities, were *education, empowerment through leadership and decision-making, health and violence against women.* To create such plans on a national level is a highly desirable step towards identifying areas of the social, economic, and political structure which undermine the progress of women toward achieving equality. When such plans are formulated by authorized groups of women serving on a nationally appointed committee, which is empowered to propose methods for the removal of obstacles, the planning process itself becomes part of a solution. However, the national plans submitted to the UN Secretary General often lacked provisions for indicators of achievement within a specified timeframe, and most plans lacked a budget to implement them effectively. Planning effectively is a learned skill, one that requires some training and monitoring, particularly by those whose best interests are at stake, in this case women representatives within each country.

Government accountability is a ticklish concept in a world of nations in which each is quick to defend its sovereignty. Yet, fueling the global revolution, which is a primary subject of our interest, is the growing ability of the UN to create "report cards" of government compliance with the Beijing Platform as well as the Millennium Forum Declaration of May 2000 and other "Global Action Plans" created during the 1990s.[20] The latter integrates aspects of the Beijing Platform in its vision of a world in which poverty has been eradicated. Among those issues, which tend to affect women disproportionately is that of poverty.

Globalization has continued to increase income gaps, both among and within nations, creating greater disparities between rich and poor than ever, with women and children counted disproportionately as victims, particularly in developing countries. Only 39 out of 130 countries surveyed by UN agencies in 2000 had set targets for the eradication of poverty among women and children.

At least part of the problem seemed to be a lack of connection between agreed upon causes of the feminization of poverty and the solutions recommended to remedy or eliminate abject poverty. Conceptualization of the problem tended to be macroeconomic, while the proposed solutions tended to be micro-economic in nature. For example, if globalization, growth of multinational corporate power in western nations, and loss of family farms to such corporations and wealthy landowners are considered obstacles to eradicating abject poverty, then proposing more access to micro credit for women may not resolve the actual causes of growing poverty in the world community. Can increased national economic growth result in increased prosperity for those who are poor? The assumption is that there will be a trickle-down effect of wealth to the middle and lower classes from the increased wealth of the upper classes. Instead, homelessness has increased throughout the world, and women and children comprise a disproportionate percentage of the homeless, making them more vulnerable to violence, disease and malnutrition.

International and civil conflict also takes a heavy toll on women and children. Forced migration and placement in unstable refuge camps has greatly increased the numbers of women and children living in abject poverty. A recently published news photo depicted a desperate young woman being beaten by Liberian soldiers for trying to obtain grain. The pain and hunger on her face and body contrasted sharply with the smirks of derision on the soldiers' faces.[21]

Reneging on national commitments to women's equality and empowerment occurred in at least 27 countries, including nations as diverse as Afghanistan, Bosnia, N Korea, Liberia, Micronesia, Saudi Arabia, Somalia and Turkmenistan. These are nations that lacked national machineries, national action plans, national responses to the UN Secretary General's Questionnaire re national commitments, signatures on the optional protocol of the Beijing Platform for Action and ratification of the optional protocol. In many of these countries armed conflicts and violence have been factors disrupting the social order, while in others a lack of sympathy towards the Women's Movement, or the UN may prevail in the cultural belief systems. In still others, lack of reporting skill or technology may account for not submitting a plan of action or creating national machinery, which could assess progress and prepare reports to the UN Secretary General. Climates of frankness may not exist in some governments, which may be more concerned with "keeping face" than with creating structures to implement their agreements concerning the Beijing Platform for Action.

Some nations, which registered little or no official support for the women's movement on this measure, nonetheless have active nongovernmental organizations, which are pursuing the targeted goals of women's equality and empowerment at the regional or grassroots level. For example, the Bahamas had put into place a national machinery for pursuing the goals of the Beijing Platform, but was not in compliance with the other five indicators of legal infrastructure for the advancement of gender equality in 2000.[22] As will be seen below, however, the Bahamas had scored rather high in measures of women's empowerment in education ratios and percent of parliamentary seats held by women. In addition, as mentioned earlier, a manual for working women in the Caribbean had been developed by a women's organization, which includes strategies for litigation when women's rights are violated in the workplace.

The gap between national machinery creation and progress in other measures, found in many countries, may indicate that little national budgeting had occurred to implement verbal and written commitments to women's progress. This has been a common problem, especially since economic recession has been a global phenomenon in recent years. However, UN Secretary-General Kofi Anan issued a report on the implementation of the Copenhagen Social Programme of Action, after gathering data from 74 countries and other agencies. The report noted the gaps between policy agreements and provision of the financial means to accomplish them in many nations. A process for assisting governments with the creation of national action plans and matching budgets was created by some NGOs, supported by UNIFEM and WEDO.[23] UNIFEM reported that "in early 2000, gender-sensitive budget initiatives were underway in 20 countries in four regions."[24]

Prioritizing Women's Progress

Priority measures of women's progress include ratios of girls enrolled in primary and secondary education compared with boys, proportion of parliamentary seats occupied by women, comparable salaries of women and men employed in similar work and provision of affordable, appropriate and accessible health care for all. We begin with assessing progress in girl's education compared with that of boys.

Women and Education. In some regions of the world there has been some decline of secondary enrollment ratios between girls and boys, creating an increased gender gap, while others exceeded the 100 percent mark. However, the most recent measurement of this variable was 1996, making the period of assessment too small a window to extrapolate a reliable trend. The other caveat is that the ratios report only those boys and girls who are in school, not those who have never entered school.

Overall, sub-Saharan Africa reported a highly variable ratio of girls to boys in secondary education: from a high of 122 percent in Lesotho, a median enrollment ratio of 77 percent in Cameroon, to the lowest enrollment ratio of 31 percent in Guinea. In the Latin American/Caribbean region a high ratio of 130 percent was reported in the Bahamas, with the lowest ratio of 83 percent in Guatemala. The lowest ratio of girls to boys in secondary education in western nations was 92 percent in Switzerland and the highest ratio in Canada, 108 percent. Asia and the Pacific reported the highest gender ratio in Malaysia, 132 percent, and the lowest ratio in the region in two countries- Bangladesh and Nepal-58 percent.

Another approach to measuring gains in female secondary education enrollment is to compare from 1985 to 1997, in those nations in which data is available. However, it has been pointed out by researchers that this is a limited indication of women's progress since the data collection instrument only measures numbers of girls and boys enrolled in school, rather than how many actually complete an entire program of study equivalent to a secondary school diploma. No goal was set for women's progress in achieving post-secondary school degrees within the Beijing Platform, but the UN Millennium Development Goals (MDG) program has targeted gender disparity in education, eliminating all disparities in primary and secondary education by 2005 and in all levels of education by 2015.

Targeting Government Seats for Women. A significant measure of women's empowerment is related to decision-making in the family, community, workplace and government. The Interparliamentary Union developed an instrument for examining women's share of seats in national parliamentary bodies since 1992. Not all nations existed at that time, had representative governments, or kept gender-aggregated databases. Therefore the reports referred to in these analyses were limited in accuracy of trends in representation of women compared with men. Some nations have upper and lower houses within their parliamentary bodies, while others have only one or the other. The database included only those nations with parliamentary assemblies elected by direct suffrage. Nonetheless the results of this comparative measurement are invaluable in examining the extent to which women are being valued as equally capable leaders at the highest levels within each nation within a given period of time. The data was current as of 2002.

With a target of 30 percent seats of government and administration occupied by women by 2000, some nations created quotas for candidate lists for elections, with a 20-30 percent quota adopted by more than 25 countries. These countries were scattered across the regions of the world. France in 1999 passed a constitutional amendment requiring political parties to nominate equal numbers of women and men. The quota system of promoting women's empowerment in government resulted in an increase overall of women to higher ratios, especially in lower houses, but was rejected by some nations as leading to nepotism and favoritism in choosing women to run for office, as in some communist states. Once the Communist Party lost favor in Eastern Europe and the former USSR, women's representation also declined. However, Australia actually targeted, rather than created a quota, 35 percent winnable seats in state and federal elections to be allocated to women by 2002.

On the global report card of women's empowerment, the Scandinavian countries scored the highest in achieving seats: Sweden 42.7 percent, Denmark 37.4 percent, Finland 36.5 percent, Norway 36.4 percent, Netherlands 36 percent and Iceland 34.9 percent. However four other nations achieved the minimum as well: Germany 30.9 percent, New Zealand 30.8 percent and Mozambique 30 percent. South Africa achieved 29.8 percent in the Lower House and 32.1 percent in the Upper. Not only did women obtain at least 30 percent of parliamentary seats by 2000, but these countries also had relatively high ratios of girl to boy enrollment in primary and secondary education and at least 95 percent net enrollments of girls in primary education. These are considered significant indicators of the empowerment of women, suggesting that case studies, interviews and other more qualitative data need to be collected in these countries and others which achieved the minimum women's seats in the upper houses rather than the lower ones. Qualitative data, if consistent with the above findings, will increase validity of such measurements as true indicators of women's empowerment.

Using percentages of women to men in the upper rather than the lower houses, the six nations which achieved the targeted goal of 30 percent women seats are a little different than those which achieved the goal for the lower houses of parliament: Belize 37 percent, Barbados 33.3 percent, Canada 32.4 percent, South Africa 32.1 percent, Bahamas 31.3 percent and Australia 30.3 percent.

The United States ranked 44th among the 178 nations surveyed, as of 2001, with a low representation of 14 percent women's seats in the House of Representatives and 13 percent in the Senate. The goal of 30 percent has yet to be achieved by the US and a majority of nations. However, the Beijing Platform for Action, in targeting parliamentary representation of women as a goal for which governments are being held accountable, has accelerated the process of the political empowerment of women by creating international dialogue, fact-gathering, and public pressure on the issue of women in decision-making at the highest levels.

Women, Wages, and Unpaid Work. While no targets have yet been established for women and employment across nations, UN Common Country indicators measure what ratio of salary exists of women to men employed within the same job categories within nations, what portion of women's compared with men's work is salaried or unpaid and women's share of administrative and managerial positions. These issues have frequently arisen within national women's movements and particularly within the context of global women's conferences, such as Nairobi 1985, where comparisons revealed the universal tendency to reward men with higher salaries than women, regardless of equal credentials and qualifications for specific positions. Although the numbers of women who entered the workplace throughout the world during the twentieth century was unprecedented, questions have been raised as to whether they have received fair opportunities for employment, fair wages, and remuneration for their labor. Using combined data from several sources in 63 countries, UNIFEM found that between 1998 and 1999, the average percentage of women's wages to those of men in both industry/services and manufacturing was from 75 to 78 percent.[25]

Similarly across the world, women have been found to carry as much as 2/3 more than men of the share of "unpaid work" associated with the domestic arena, often in addition to full or part-time jobs outside of the home. Some of the work of women outside of the home has also been unpaid, though recorded data is difficult to accurately track in either national or international databases.

The *unpaid care work* is often expected of girls and women, though unacknowledged and undervalued, creating inequalities and injustices which can lead to lowered self-esteem, domestic conflict and ill health.[26] The assessment compares the hours of unpaid care work of women with that of men, finding that women average 70 percent of their working time in unpaid care work within the family compared with men, who average 30 percent.[27] This must be compared with average percent of hours per day spent by women in formal work time, which is 54 percent for women, compared with 45 percent for men. There was little variation from the formal to the informal sector in this comparison. The collection of more data on women's unpaid labor was again stressed at the Beijing Conference in 1995, leading some nations to devise time-use surveys as tools for engaging women and men, girls and boys, in reflections and dialogues about fair shares of unpaid work for families and communities. This is an issue that weighs heavily in the negotiation of true equality between women and men. Efforts to advance equality and empowerment of women must take into consideration the need for consciousness-raising on this issue as women begin to approach the same employment levels as men in an increasing number of countries.

The question of fair shares of unpaid work for both genders is one of the areas of the women's movement of which it can be said, "This is where the rubber meets the road," to use a common American proverb that speaks to the relationship between theory and actual practice. How can the number of formal work hours continue to increase for women while the percentage of unpaid care work remains the same? This may be a formula for family dysfunction if not addressed more effectively within families and communities across the world, whether urban or rural.

Women as Leaders. Another aspect of women and work, which is used as a measure of women's progress, is that which records changes in women's share of administrative and managerial positions from the mid eighties to the mid nineties. In order to determine to what extent governments have lived up to their commitments to have at least 30 percent of such positions occupied by women, statistics are collected from member nations by the International Labour Office, which tracks numbers occupying managerial, administrative, professional and technical positions in each country by gender and by women's share of decision-making positions. Data are available from the mid-eighties to the mid-nineties, though it is unlikely that quantitative indicators alone can discriminate between lower level and higher level decision-making positions that women may occupy. However, the changes in women's share of administrative and managerial positions during the ten-year period ending in 1995 are nonetheless instructive.

Among the countries which seem to have reached the targeted goal of 30 percent of administration and management positions held by women by the mid-nineties were: the Philippines, Bulgaria, the Bahamas, Barbados, Belize, Colombia, Costa Rica, Canada, New Zealand, Norway, Portugal, Spain, the United Kingdom and the United States.

Some countries made no progress or even lost what had been gained, such as Botswana, Ethiopia, Syria, Iran, N Korea, Singapore, Estonia, and Haiti had gained nearly 40 percent of the required target, but slid back to around 25 percent, whereas Iran and N Korea never moved past 2 and 3 percent respectively. Haiti, however, began and ended the period above the target, at around 35 percent. Estonia began at a high of 40 percent but slipped back to about 32 percent, but still a little higher than the targeted goal of 30 percent. Much effort by both women and men will be needed in each country to achieve the goal of at least 1/3 of women in administrative and management positions, even more to sustain it, as it implies a transformation of the underlying social structure of each country and society.

Leading by Example: Within the United Nations system, comprising 24 organizations, programs and funds, an analysis was made of changes in gender parity, from 1991 to 1996, in three different categories of positions, geographical, non-geographical and project posts. The percentage of women working in the first category changed from 22 to 27 percent, with the percentage of women in the second category changing from 30 to 34 percent. Within the third category, "*project posts*," the share of positions occupied by women rose more dramatically, from a low of 13 percent to 24 percent, yet fell short of the 50 percent target. The latter are short-term, specific assignments, usually to developing countries, lasting five years or less.

The great majority of women employees at the UN, 60 percent, work in support functions: administration, language interpretation, and library-related fields. Only 20 percent of the geographical posts involving senior management were occupied by women, with only 1 percent change during the period under consideration.

The UN General Assembly requested that the UN system achieve gender parity (50/50) by 2000. As the sponsoring body of the global women's conferences, the example of the UN and its agencies in making efforts to improve gender equality and empowerment is an essential step in creating incentives for member nations to do the same.

Women and health care. The fourth prioritized measure of women's progress in the Beijing Platform is that of women's right to enjoy "the highest attainable standard of physical and mental health . . . throughout their whole life cycle in equality with men."[28] The Platform specifies equal relationships in matters of sexual relations and reproduction as those involving mutual respect, consent, shared responsibility, freedom to decide whether to have children, how many and when, and the freedom to obtain information and make such decisions without discrimination, coercion or violence. Health care for women is also one of the *"priority issues"* to be included in national action plans and reported to the UN Secretary General.

During the first three decades after the formation of the United Nations, attention had been given in many development plans to improving health care through providing more clinics, hospitals, doctors, nurses, and immunizations in under-served areas of the world. The UN Declaration of Human Rights prioritized to some extent the care of children and pregnant or breast-feeding women. However, the simultaneous growth of multinational corporations, which in some countries controlled the economies of developing countries, tended to undermine breast-feeding by aggressively marketing canned baby formula and bottle-feeding methods. Many young women came to believe that breast-feeding was *"old-fashioned"* and undesirable, leading to higher rates of infant mortality in populations marginalized by natural environmental disasters or armed conflict.

The health of women and the health of children are very closely connected. Since women are enmeshed within social, economic and political forces which impact their health and well-being and those of their children, programs to increase clinics, hospitals, doctors and nurses alone could not address the growing need for affordable, appropriate and accessible health care for all. Such well-meaning programs, though helpful, have been inadequate to prevent or treat, for example, the scourge of HIV/AIDS throughout the continent of Africa. As devastating as HIV infection has become in the past two decades, there are yet other significant factors that influence women's and girls' health and well-being.

The Gender and Women's Health Department of WHO has developed reports on the impact of gender inequality on a variety of health issues, including aging, nutrition, diseases such as tuberculosis and malaria, female genital mutilation (FGM), maternal and newborn health, mental health, and violence against women. The issues of FGM and sexual trafficking will be addressed in chapter

10.

Various health issues affecting women are tracked by specific departments of WHO, such as the Department of Reproductive Health and Research (RHR), which has identified "skilled attendants at delivery" as "the single most important factor in keeping women healthy and safe in pregnancy."[29] Currently 62 percent of births are attended by a skilled health worker, with a low of 33.9 percent in Eastern Africa, higher levels in Latin America and the Caribbean of 81.3 percent, and the highest in Australia and New Zealand of 100 percent. Western Europe reported 99.1 percent and Northern America reported 98.9 percent births with a skilled attendant.

As can be seen, the health of women is complex and involves the health of children and the entire family. Resolution of the issues touched upon in this section is not easily achieved since each is interlocked with elements of custom, social structure, economic factors and assumptions regarding the value and roles of women and girls within each cultural context. Yet, as a member of the Beijing Conference Planning Committee quipped at the opening ceremony in 1995, "Most women of the world understand that what is difficult to accomplish can usually be done right away, while that which is impossible just takes a little more time." The support of the UN in providing both an international forum to identify the issues which threaten women's health and well-being and the means to design and implement programs of action with the grassroots has an encouraging effect on national governments and NGOs to follow suit with trained workers, projects and funds. Local and regional individuals and agencies are becoming empowered to both assist and manage such projects in local communities which are concerned with infant mortality rates, pre- and post-natal care, immunization, family clinics, prevention of FGM and HIV/AIDS, and protection from exploitation and violence.

Supporting the Revolution:

The critical areas for measuring women's progress are linked with the means for women to become empowered as women and men achieve greater levels of parity in education, leadership, work and health. The national women's movements, some of which are discussed in Section II, may never have blossomed into a full blown global revolution without the institutionalization of each movement's goals within the UN's CEDAW and Beijing Platform, among other UN policy development during the nineties. The UN has accomplished what seemed difficult or impossible for each society steeped in its own customs and norms for gender relationships. This process has evolved over time, through trial and error, input from delegates of each member nation and many NGOs, and of particular importance, accountability of each member state to the UN regarding its progress toward achieving the goals set at each UN conference.

It is interesting to note that while the United Nations holds all 191 governments of the world accountable for a National Plan of Action, national machinery to implement the plan, and annual progress reports, more than 5000 local and national NGOs, registered with the UN, work within communities throughout the world to rally and organize women and girls to become empowered to take actions consistent with the Beijing Platform and within their own lives. The same forces which have enhanced such negative developments as sexual trafficking have also lent power and agency to a global women's movement. A momentum is certainly building within and among nations to move women toward equality, regardless of, and with respect to, the enormous variety of cultural issues facing the movement. Clearly, the formation and development of the United Nations and its capacity to organize human beings and nations toward levels of cooperation and empowerment never before dreamed possible has played a primary role in catapulting the women's movement from national battlefields to an arena of global possibilities.

In the next chapter Mbuh explores the progress of African women since the first United Nations women's conference and particularly since the United Nations conference held in Nairobi in 1985 to celebrate the first decade of women and development.

Chapter 7 Notes

1. Hans Morganthau, *Politics Among Nations: the Struggle for Power and Peace*, 5th ed revised, (NY: Knopf 1978).
2. Ibid, and League of Nations, "Statistical and Disarmament Document Collection," (Evanston, IL: Northwestern University Library).
3. E M Forster, *Passage to India* (1924, reprint Orlando, FL: Harcourt/Harvest Books, 1965); Isak Dinesen, *Out of Africa* (1937 reprint New York: Random House, 1992); Margaret Mitchell, *Gone With the Wind* (1936, reprint New York: Scribner 1964).
4. e.g. William James Ball in Edward Ball's, *Slaves in the Family*, (New York, Toronto: Ballantine Books, 1998).
5. United Nations Office & Dept. of Public Information, *Everyman's United Nations*. (New York: UN Publications, annual).
6. Hillary Rodham Clinton, "Keynote Address to the Vital Voices of the Americas Conference," (Uruguay: US State Department Archives, 10/1998).
7. Mary Ann Tetreault, ed., *Women and Revolution in Africa, Asia and the New World* (Columbia, SC: USC Press, 1994) 8.
8. Ibid
9. Dhruvarajan & Vickers, *Gender, Race and Nation*, 306.
10. See Report of the World Conference of the UN International Women's Year, Mexico City, 19 June-2 July 1975: Equality, Development and Peace, E/Conf.66/34.
11. See The Promise of World Peace, International Bahá'í Community, 1985, III.
12. UNIFEM, *Progress of the World's Women*,(New York: UNIFEM HQ, 2000) inside cover.
13. See http://secretary.state.gov/www/picw/2000commitment/americas_commitment.pdf for 2000 Report on Women in Power and Decision-Making.
14. Ibid, 2/14/01, 4.
15. Central Intelligence Agency Report 2000, ibid.
16."The World Conferences: Developing Priorities for the 21st Century," *UN Briefing Papers* (New York: UN Dept of Pub Info, 1997).
17. Ibid, also Social Watch '99, Montevido, Uruguay: Instituto de Tercer Mundo in Progress of World's Women.
18. Division for the Advancement of Women, UN Department for Feminine and Social

Affairs, UN: NY.

19. Organization for Economic Cooperation & Development, see http://www.oecd.org/dataoecd/30/28/2754929.pdf

20. The New Millennium Forum Declaration: an Agenda of 'We the Peoples... Millennium Forum—the UN for the 21st Century, Draft: 18 May 2000, p 3, http://www .un.org/millennium/declaration.htm.

21. A rebel soldier uses electrical cord to whip a woman trying to loot grain from the port of Monrovia," is the photo caption: Richmond Times Dispatch, p.1, AP, 8/14/03.

22. See Implementation of the Beijing Platform for Action & Compliance with International Legal Instruments on Women as of 8/8/02, UN Dept for Economic & Social Affairs, http://www.un.org/womenwatch/daw/.

23. World Environment and Development Organization.

24. UNIFEM, *Progress of the World's Women,* 113.

25. Ibid, 92.

26. For example see Roberta Cantow's Emmy Award winning film documentary, "Clotheslines"

27. See UN 1995a, Table 4.8 and Mexico: UNIFEM/CONMUJER 1999:65; Bangladesh: Zohir 1998.

28. See Appendix E: Beijing Platform

29. Department of Reproductive Health and Research (RHR, WHO, visit http://www.who.int/reproductive-health/mpr/attendants.

Chapter 8

African Women since Nairobi

Rebecca Mbuh

This chapter is a direct result of the original thoughts that evolved from the book manuscript idea and the Beijing +5 Conference. With this backdrop, the focus of this discussion is on the challenges facing African women since they hosted the Nairobi UN Conference in 1985 and the prospects for their future. Africa is a continent of many countries and diverse peoples with literally thousands of languages and identities. In such an environment of diversity we also find great diversity in the situation of women. However, in spite of this diversity there are many common challenges faced by women throughout the continent. Some of these may be peculiar to Africa while others are problems common to women throughout the world. What are the specific issues pertaining to African women in the 21st Century? What steps are African women, individual countries or regions employing to advance their course? What does the future hold for African women? What equality, if any, has been achieved to date?

Background

African women were the first to create a regional office for a centralized approach to women's issues prior to the 1975 United Nations Women's Conference. This institution was known as the African Training and Research Center for Women (ATRCW), now referred to as African Center for Women (ACW). It should be noted that the first United Nations Women's Conference in Mexico was preceded in 1960 by the first United Nations Decade for Development. Margaret Snyder and Mary Tadesse pointed out that the policies and programs that appeared to offer economic security to the newly independent countries (mainly in Africa) of the world failed and only a few of the expected benefits reached communities or individuals in Africa or elsewhere.[1] Though the expectations fell short, many important lessons emerged from this experience. For example, there was the need for an evaluation of what went wrong and to formulate new relevant, practical policies that would directly impact on the people:

> the people are the heart and foundation of the African society. All during that decade, under the aegis of the Economic Commission for Africa and of the UN itself, governments and women's groups had been consulted and data collected and analyzed. What added strength to the discussions and arguments on behave

of a change in direction was the lack of positive results during the First Decade for Development, together with the hard proof that had been amassed of the importance of women to economic life. More and more evidence built up to indicate that women played central roles in the economy and that their participation at all levels was essential if development was to succeed."[2]

Many researchers of womanist, feminist, or gender issues emphasize equality or lack of equality of women and men. While women all over the globe share commonalities first as humans, they are also regarded by most societies dating from pre-colonial times to the 21st century as mothers, wives, caretakers, neighbors, friends, counselors and sisters. Though in recent decades, the women's movement has gained some equality in many aspects, the majority of women in developing countries are still struggling for basic human rights, daily survival and equality. In most of these societies, especially African societies, women are still less equal to their male counterparts and are treated markedly different. As African women's struggle to achieve equality and certain basic human rights continues, there is documentation of their contributions to economic development, nation building, education, social welfare and politics. In many countries the historical contexts of women and their contributions have been examined, dissected and debated, social and moral perspectives have been x-rayed and conclusions pointing to the value of women in global survival. Yet African women still fall behind men in many regards. Women earn less than men with the same qualifications and experience; women are less represented in politics and leadership positions in governments, in educational institutions of higher learning, in the corporate world and in information technology. The situation for African women is very sad and will be presented in summary form in this paper. Though the complexities of women's issues and struggles as a collective class would probably never be fully comprehended, the picture for African women is somewhat different and unique. Therefore a piece meal approach is needed to examine issues by continent yet keeping the global perspective.

In many societies, class, location, age, marital status and society's changing expectations of women have all had direct impact on what was expected of them, what they did, and how they did it.[3] African women are victims of these factors and in addition are plagued by the burden of customary roles and expectations.[4] In many African cultures, women are to be seen and not heard thus rendering them conveniently invisible. It is impossible to ignore a subpopulation that constitutes more than half of the continent's inhabitants. Some African countries have women as the majority of the population. This is the case in countries where civil war and famine have significantly reduced the male population thus leaving women to take control. Yet, African women learned early on to make their voices heard by applying various methods including protests. Diduk argues that the women's movements of the grass-fields of North West Province, Cameroon are related to the *"moral economy"* of subsistence farming. Diduk conducted extensive research in this area between 1981 and 1996 by interviewing numerous men and women about protests and disciplinary action. She concludes that "women's mobilizations occur in order to draw attention to the violation of rights, including unreasonable physical maltreatment of children, women or young men, the failure of local institutions to perform rituals that safeguard women's fertility, the imprisonment of local citizens for unsubstantiated reasons, and corrupt decision-making by political authorities."[5] Of the reasons cited, many have also been articulated by scholars of other African countries.[6]

In 1975, the challenges facing African women were classified into two categories as barriers to progress, namely, traditional and imported values and practices. Reducing or eliminating such barriers would require: "literacy, formal and non-formal education, vocational and technical training, wage employment and money-earning opportunities, decision-making and community, time and labor-saving technology, time to give early education to their children, leisure, participation in social and community activities, access to loans and credit, and participation in national planning."[7] After three decades the major concerns of African women are still quite similar. While some of these barriers have been lessened, we shall see in the following text that some new challenges have been brought to the forefront to be addressed.

Major Challenges in the New Millennium

The World Bank, UNICEF, United Nations, international and African NGO's and other independent researchers/organizations have conducted studies of African women and women in other developing countries throughout the world and arrived at the same disturbing conclusions. The result is that the state of affairs for African women is alarming and demands immediate attention, particularly because these studies focused on women's education, health care and economic integration. According to John Toye, Director of the Center for the Study of African Economies at the University of Oxford, "poverty is a multi-dimensional condition that cannot be understood by focusing only on low levels of material consumption, . . . to be poor is to be subject to many distresses—to risks that greatly affect one's own and one's children's life chances, to fear and anxiety about how to cope with those risks, and to humiliation and loss of status and dignity when coping is no longer possible."

The challenges currently faced by African women will be addressed in two categories: general societal problems and specific women's problems. General problems include: poverty, illiteracy, HIV/AIDS, child labor, community violence, civil conflicts, unemployment, malnutrition, health care and infant mortality. Problems specific to women include: female genital mutilation (FGM), early marriages, early pregnancies, rape, violence, HIV/AIDS, political participation, and prostitution.

General Societal Problems

Of the 20 countries identified by the Human Development Report 2001 as suffering setbacks in the human development index, 12 are African countries, mostly Africa south of the Sahara. Though all regions have made progress in human development and have advanced at different paces and achieving at very different levels, African countries in general clearly lag behind the rest of the world. For example, the literacy rate for adults in Africa is 60 percent, well below the developing country average of 73 percent.

Life expectancy at birth in Sub Sahara Africa is still only 48.8 years compared with more than 60 years in all other regions of the world. Generally, women live longer than men in many countries including the continent of Africa. With less education, few or no employable skills, women and children in most of Africa are among the number of the world's people living on less than $1.00 a day. This rate has reached an alarming high of 46 percent in Sub Sahara Africa compared with only 15 percent in East Asia and the Pacific and in Latin American countries.[8] World Bank and UN officials have unanimously recommended that increasing the level of human development in general and that of African women in particular is a worthy investment to ensure continuation of a healthy people. Since human development is about creating an environment in which all people can develop their full potential and lead productive, creative lives in accord with their needs and interests, promoting and supporting such projects should be a source of national pride for all governments. After all, many politicians, as well as academicians, agree that a nation's people are the true and very valuable wealth of the country. Africans and African women in particular desire to lead long and healthy lives for them and their families, and women desire to be knowledgeable, to have access to the resources needed for a decent standard of living and to be able to participate in the life of the community. Women's groups, from the local grass roots to the national forum, stress these basic needs in their campaign to be a part of the decision-making process for national well-being and development that affects their lives.

Poverty

Of the many issues facing humankind all over the world, none has the potential to affect humans with greater force and consequences like poverty. Poverty impacts the lives of children and adults, women and men, without regard to race or religion. The UN Secretary General, Kofi Annan, denounced poverty as a threat to human security.

> On this International Day for the Eradication of Poverty, let us recognize that extreme poverty anywhere is a threat to human security everywhere. Let us recall that poverty is a denial of human rights. For the first time in history in this age of unprecedented wealth and technical prowess, we have the power to save humanity from this shameful scourge. Let us summon the will to do it.[9]

Due to natural and human caused disasters, many countries in Africa are plagued with alarming rates of poverty. According to World Bank statistics in 2001, the proportion of people in Africa living under US$1 a day in 1994 to1997 ranges from 1 percent in Morocco to 88 percent in Guinea Bissau. During the same time period the national poverty headcount as percentage of population ranged from 11 percent in Mauritius to 86 percent in Zambia. The percentage of household income spent on food in 1991 to 1997 in all of Africa was 64 percent with a range from 39 percent in Ghana to 75 percent in Mali.

Illiteracy

Of the more than 4.6 billion people in developing countries, more than 850 million are illiterate. Nearly 325 million school aged boys and girls are out of school. Education is one universal human right that is a luxury in many African countries. In many African countries, parents still prefer to send boys to school, seeing little need for education for girls. In addition, factors such as adolescent pregnancy, early marriage and girls' greater burden of household labor take precedence over education in order to fulfill short-term needs. At school the curriculum is gender biased, guiding girls into stereotypical "feminine" jobs in teaching, nursing and clerical work. Few women are found in scientific or technical education where they could develop better skills to secure better paying jobs.[10] The teaching profession shows a similar level of female participation. In 1993, women accounted for 30 percent or less of primary teaching staff in 13 African countries, while their proportions in secondary schools remained at 33 percent in sub-Saharan Africa between 1985 and 1994. Women are largely underrepresented in technical fields, with the exception of home economics and secretarial courses, depriving girls of needed role models.

Numerous studies by World Bank, UNICEF, and NGO's have shown that a woman's education beyond primary school is a reliable route to economic empowerment and long-term change in the status quo, as well as a determinant of a family's health and nutrition. Yet many governments continue to reduce spending on education. The advantages of education of both girls and boys to the national development of any country cannot be overemphasized. Education beyond ten or more years of school is also a reliable predictor of lower fertility, improved infant survival, reduced maternal mortality and enhanced levels of infant and child development and educational attainment.

A UNICEF special report titled, "Education for All, No Excuses," summarizes the importance of education as follows:

> Educating children opens an infinity of possibilities for them that would otherwise be denied: a better chance to lead healthy and productive lives, to build strong and nurturing families, to participate fully in the civic affairs of their communities, molding mores and values, creating culture and shaping history. When a nation strives to educate all its young people- girls as well as boys, the poor and the disadvantaged child as well as any other- then that nation lays a solid foundation for progress and sustainable development, catalyzing freedom and democracy within its borders and extending its reach as an agent of international peace and security. Education plays a crucial role in solving the most complex problems facing any country: child labor, HIV/AIDS, poverty and disparity, community violence and civil conflict, and the devaluing of girls and women. Education's obvious usefulness to individuals and countries, while a strong argument in support of its value, is secondary to the more fundamental reason why it demands our attention. In truth, the world has no choice but to pay heed and ensure a basic education of good quality to all children. Such is their due as one of their inherent human rights. Ensuring children their right to education ensures their other rights as well, including the rights to survival, development and participation. And by ensuring girls their right to education, we take the critical first step towards dismantling the gender discrimination that threatens

all other rights.[11]

At the World Conference on "Education for All" in 1990 in Thailand, dele-gates from more than 155 governments established six key goals and an action plan for Education for All (EFD) by the year 2000, with partnerships led by UNESCO, UNICEF, the World Bank, UNDP and UNFPA. Several African coun-tries were represented at this conference and took part in developing an action plan to include ensuring children their right to education and other rights as well, including the rights to survival, development, and participation. The action plan called for the reduction of illiteracy rates by 50 percent in the year 2000. Today several countries have closed the gap, but many others, especially African coun-tries, are still in the process of achieving this goal.

According to World Bank statistics, the percentage of population 15 years of age and above that was illiterate in 1985 was 58 percent for all of Africa. For Sub Sahara Africa the percentage was 56. During the same year the percentage of male population that was illiterate was 45, while that of females was 66 percent. The country with the highest illiteracy rate was Niger, with a total population of 90 percent that could not read or write, 84 percent male and 96 percent female. South Africa had the lowest illiteracy rate with a total of 21 percent for the popu-lation, 20 percent for males and 22 percent for females.

Table 8.1: Selected African States: Literacy Rates by Gender, 1999

Country	Female Rate (% age 15+) 1999	Female Rate as % of male rate 1999	Female Rate (% age 15-24) 1999	Female Rate as % of male rate 1999
Mauritius	80.0	92	94.3	101
South Africa	84.2	98	91.0	100
Algeria	55.7	72	83.8	91
Egypt	42.8	65	61.7	81
Namibia	80.4	98	93.0	104
Zimbabwe	83.8	91	95.5	97
Ghana	61.5	77	87.3	94
Lesotho	93.3	130	98.4	120
Kenya	74.8	85	93.7	98
Cameroon	68.6	84	93.1	99
Madagascar	58.8	81	75.6	91
Nigeria	54.2	76	82.5	93
Sudan	44.9	65	70	67
Tanzania	65.7	78	87.8	94
Senegal	26.7	57	40.7	69
Rwanda	59.1	81	80.5	95
Mali	32.7	69	58.1	82
Mozambique	27.9	47	44.8	60
Ethiopia	31.8	74	51.8	97
Niger	7.9	34	13.2	42

Source : World Bank 2000

By 1998 some progress to reduce illiteracy across the continent had been achieved. Table 8.1 on the preceding page summarizes gender inequality in education as of 1999. The percentage of population 15 years of age and above that was illiterate in 1998 was 41 percent for all of Africa. During the same year the percentage of male population for all of Africa that was illiterate was 32 percent, while that of females was 50 percent. The country with the highest illiteracy rate was Niger with a total population of 85 percent that could not read or write; 78 percent were male, while 93 percent were female. South Africa had the lowest illiteracy rate with a total of 15 percent for the population, 15 percent for males and 16 percent for females.

Child Malnutrition, Survival Prospects and Child labor

According to a report by the UN Food and Agriculture Organization, more than one third of Africans are undernourished. In 1998 about 186 million Africans south of the Sahara or 34 percent of the total population, compared to 38 percent in 1979. Somalia was the most malnourished country in the world with 75 percent of the population suffering chronic undernourishment in 1998. Afghanistan was second with 70 percent, followed by Burundi, Eritrea, and Haiti; 19 of the 24 countries with malnutrition rates higher than 35 percent are in Africa.[12]

It is universally understood that the future leadership of any country depends on the youth. In many African countries youths are regarded not only as a source of prestige but are held in great esteem because they ensure the continuity of family lineage, therefore the nation. But judging from the conditions in which they live we must conclude that this is not the case. According to the World Bank in 2001 the majority of the world's children suffering from malnutrition, engaging in child labor and with greater danger of dying before the age of five are on the African continent. The burden for taking care of these children falls on the women, who act as caretakers for the whole family, the sick, the old, and the young. Because of the large number of children involved women must make sacrifices and trade-offs between fending for the family and attending to the pearls of their country. Worldwide, eleven million children under age five die each year from preventable causes, equivalent to more than 30,000 a day. In 1990 to 1997 child malnutrition rates for African countries were as follows: Exclusively breastfed (0-3 months) was 32 percent, breastfed plus other food (6-9 months) was 59 percent and still breastfeeding (20-23 months) 45 percent. The percentage of infants with low birth weights in 1993 to 1997 ranged from 4 percent to 21 percent while the percentage of under-five in 1990 to 1997 suffering from moderate to severe malnutrition was as follows: underweight percentage range was from 5 percent to 50 percent, wasting range was from 2 percent to 23 percent and stunting range was from 10 percent to 64 percent.

Life expectancy in most African countries is the lowest compared to the rest of the world. Several reasons can be attributed to this situation. The lack of adequate health care facilities, poor sanitary conditions, poverty, war, and natural disasters are a few of the reasons. Due to the high death rates at birth many African families in the past resorted to having many children with the hopes that a few would survive the first critical years. Although current living conditions have improved somewhat, many African children are dying from preventable diseases.

In 1992 life expectancy at birth (years) in Africa was 50; in 1998 it rose to 54. The life expectancy range in 1992 ranged from ages 35 to 69. The range for 1998 rose slightly to 37 to 72. Infant mortality continues to be a challenge. In 1992 the overall infant mortality rate was 109 infants out of every one thousand births. In 1998 the rate was 86 infants out of every one thousand births. The mortality of children under 5 years (per thousand) in 1998 was 140. Maternal mortality per 100,000 live births in 1998 was 50 to 1800 deaths across the African continent.

During the past twenty years child labor has reached the attention of the international community. This phenomenon has been confined mainly to the poorer and developing countries. In Asia, the Middle East and South America the governments have yielded to pressures from international groups and proponents of children's rights to begin addressing the problem. Though Africa has the highest incidence of child labor in the world, most African countries still lag behind and are slow in admitting that child labor is a problem, thus delaying plans to put an end to the practice. Recent disclosures of severe child labor trafficking in some West African countries have finally brought international pressure on the leadership of these countries. As a result, the African branch of the International Federation of Transport Workers in June 2001 urged its affiliated road, port and sea worker's unions to be on the alert for trafficking activities.

According to Harsch,[13] there are about 80 million child workers in Africa. More than 51% of children in Burkina between the ages of 10 and 14 work. Dr. Rima Salah, UNICEF regional director for West and Central Africa, cites numerous reasons for this problem: poverty, inadequate educational opportunities, ignorance among families and children about the risks of trafficking, migration of adults from village to urban slums, high demand among employers for cheap and submissive labor, ease of travel across regional borders, the desire of young people to travel and explore, and inadequate political commitment, legislation and judicial mechanisms to deal with child trafficking. Trafficked children generally work from 10 to 20 hours a day. In Nigeria one out of five children trafficked in that country died of illness or accidents while others contracted sexually transmitted diseases, including HIV/AIDS. Child labor begins slowly as a small contribution to house chores and then escalates into abuse. Often the result is that children drop out of school to assist their mothers (mostly girls), are sent to live with relatives in the cities to "help out" in the house in exchange for an education, or taken forcefully from their homes and put to work for long hours with little food and no pay. Children 14 and under (10 to 14) reported as working in the labor force as a percentage of the population was 31.4 percent in 1970, 30.9 percent in 1980, 28 percent in 1990 and 25.8 percent in 1998. The country with the highest percentage of children under 14 years working as a part of the labor force in 1998 was Burundi with 48.7 percent. Tunisia was the only African country that did not have children under 14 years working.

Violence, War and Child Soldiers

Civil conflicts and war in many African countries have resulted in serious atrocities against women and children. For many African women and children these on and off conflicts have become a way of life. Unfortunately, they are also the group most affected in times of civil unrest resulting in mass migration, being forced to join the army, or suffer from starvation and diseases. The worst part for women is watching their children die in a cause they do not understand. In countries such as Angola, Sudan, Somalia, Sierra Leone, Liberia, Congo, Rwanda, Burundi, Uganda, Mozambique and Central African Republic, where most children have rarely experienced a normal day, the long term effects can be devastating for the future if these conflicts do not end.

According to Africa Recovery, about one third of the world's child soldiers are in Africa. It is estimated that about 300,000 child soldiers between the ages of seven and fourteen are actively fighting in 41 countries, with more than 120,000 of them in Africa. Here also poverty, hunger, economic, social, political pressures, illiteracy, and ignorance play a significant role in involving children in these conflicts. A senior adviser to the UN Children's Fund (UNICEF) states "you find that some of them just volunteer to get a meal a day. Many of the children are being promised access to education."[14]

Health care

The economic, social and political vitality of a nation is dependent on its health care facilities. According to popular slogans, healthy people are happy people and a happy worker is a productive employee. Generally, health care facilities in many African countries can be classified as inadequate and substandard compared to western countries. From 1990 to 1994, Libya was the only African country to boast of having 100 percent of the population with access to health services. Angola was the worst with only 24 percent of the population having access to health services. From 1990 to 1995, Mauritius had 91 percent of births attended by trained health personnel while Somalia had only 2 percent. Total public health expenditure as a percentage of Gross Domestic Product (GDP) in all African countries between 1990 and 1997 was 14 percent compared to 26 percent in the private sector.

The percentage of population with access to sanitation facilities is distributed as follows: In 1990, Mauritius had the highest percentage with 100 percent of the inhabitants in urban and rural areas with access to sanitation facilities while Seychelles had the highest percentage from 1993 to 1997 (98 percent total population and 99 percent of the rural population). Sudan had the lowest percentage with 5 percent of the total population (20 percent in urban and 1 percent in rural areas). From 1993 to 1997, Ethiopia and Lesotho were the countries with the lowest percentage with 8 percent each of the total population with access to sanitation facilities. Lesotho had 7 percent of the rural population with access to sanitation facilities.

The quality of life in every country is also determined by access to safe water. Many African countries lag behind most western countries in this area. From 1993 to 1997 in Sub-Saharan Africa, 100 percent of the population of Seychelles had access to safe water, while 100 percent of urban Botswanians and 100 percent of rural Equatorial Guineans had access to safe water. During the same period 7 percent of the population of Eritrea, 14 percent of the urban population of Lesotho and 8 percent of the rural population of Liberia and Republic of Congo had access to safe water.[15]

HIV/AIDS

AIDS is the world's fourth largest cause of death. According to a recent United Nations study, more than 28 million Africans are currently living with the disease, with some countries having over 30 percent adult populations infected. The short and long term effects on the economy and national security are devastating since governments are unable to plan for effective development. Dr. Peter Piot, executive director of UNAIDS states, "The devastating impact of AIDS is rolling back decades of development progress in Africa. Every element of African society, from teachers to soldiers to farmers, everybody is under attack by AIDS."[16] The study reveals that HIV had rapidly weakened the economic stability, national security, agricultural output and the capacity of governments to serve their citizens, which are pre-requisites for effective development. According to the report, the rate of economic growth in Sub-Saharan Africa had already fallen by as much as 4 percent due to AIDS. With fewer people available to do agricultural work, the nutritional status and hunger are the ever-threatening order of the day, the report said. All sectors of the population are vulnerable to the disease. Among the hardest hit are the armed forces, especially the upper cadres, with some countries recording prevalence rates of between 20 to 60 percent. In Kenya, AIDS accounts for up to three out of every four deaths in the police force.

United Nations officials now estimate that AIDS will kill 70 million people over the next 20 years unless rich nations step up their efforts to curb the disease. AIDS killed a record 3 million people last year—2.2 million in Africa alone—and HIV infected another 5 million worldwide. The disease, which has killed 20 million since its discovery in 1981, has so far created 14 million orphans. Three million of the 40 million people now infected are children under 15 years of age. Nine percent of adults between the ages of 15 to 49 in Sub-Saharan Africa are now infected, the report said, up from 8.6 percent at the end of 1999. In Zimbabwe, one-third of adults are infected, up from one-quarter two years ago.

A new United Nations report predicts AIDS will kill 65 million people between now and 2020. This number is three times more than in the two decades since the epidemic began. The findings shatter the widespread belief that AIDS had peaked.[17] Countries in Sub-Saharan Africa have the most new cases. Unfortunately these countries also are the least equipped to treat the sick and head off new infections. The epidemic continues to spread, mostly by heterosexual contact. Only tiny proportions of the infected millions receive useful treatment.

Women and AIDS

According to Stephen Lewis, special envoy of the Secretary-General for HIV/AIDS in Africa, African women and girls are two to three times more likely to contract AIDS than men. Two current UN studies warn of a pandemic among females in sub-Saharan Africa. Of the 26 million people in sub-Saharan Africa infected with AIDS/HIV, 58 percent are female, according to a report from UNAIDS. A UNICEF study concluded 8.6 million cases—almost one-third of that 26 million—are between the ages of 15 and 24. Of those 8.6 million who have HIV, two-thirds are young women. In Botswana, 45 percent of women have AIDS, compared to 19 percent of men; in Lesotho, 51 percent women to 23 percent men; South Africa, 31 percent to 13 percent; Swaziland, 47 to 18 percent; Zambia, 25 to 10 percent; Zimbabwe 40 to 15 percent; Namibia 25 percent to 8 percent; Malawi 18 percent to 8 percent; Cameroon 15 percent to 6 percent; Central African Republic, 16 percent to 7 percent, and Rwanda, 13 percent to 6 percent. The UNICEF report blamed the widespread lack of knowledge about AIDS and transmission, prevention and sexuality among the young people.

In some countries, up to 95 percent of young women surveyed said they were at little or no risk of contracting the virus and almost two-thirds of young men said they did not use condoms during their last sexual encounter. This response is in keeping with the attitudes of many African men that AIDS is a "Whiteman's invention" and that it is a means to control the population.

Economic Opportunities and Unemployment

The economic development of Africa depends on the development of women who have provided the unfaltering backbone of the rural economy in most of Sub-Saharan Africa. About 80 percent of the economically active female labor force is employed in agriculture, and women comprise about 47 percent of the total agricultural labor force. Abala, reports that most African countries lag behind the world in economic planning and that the position for African women in meaningful contributions to national growth is constricted. The report cited inadequate education, training and government support as some of the reasons for the current situation of African women.[18]

Food production is the major activity of rural women; their responsibilities and labor inputs often exceed those of men in most areas in Africa. Women also provide much of the labor for men's cultivation of export crops, from which women derive little direct benefit. It is estimated that women work on the average 13 to 16 hours more than men. In many rural areas, women contribute unpaid labor to the household's agricultural production and spend up to 50 hours a week on domestic labor and subsistence food production, with little sharing of tasks by spouses or sons in the household.

FAO found, in a survey of nine African countries in 1996, that women's contribution to the production of food crops ranges from 30 percent in Sudan to 80 percent in the Republic of Congo, with estimates for other countries tending toward the higher end of the scale. World Bank data further demonstrate that women are responsible for 70 percent of food production, 50 percent of domestic food storage, 100 percent of food processing, 50 percent of animal husbandry and 60 percent of agricultural marketing. African women account for the majority of the unpaid family workers as a share of the population's active workers. The percentage of women in the unpaid workers' category ranges from zero to 41.8 percent compared to men's range of zero to 36 percent.[19] Economic opportunities for women are limited to agriculture as captured in the book title *Men Own the Fields, Women Own the Crops* by Miriam Goheen. A study of nine countries (Benin, Burkina Faso, Congo, Mauritania, Morocco, Namibia, Sudan, Tanzania and Zimbabwe) showed that women rarely own land and when they do, their holdings tend to be smaller and less fertile than those of men. In the late 1990s, the Ugandan government began taking bold steps to make sweeping reforms allowing women and girl children to inherit or buy land.[20]

While women are the majority in agricultural sectors, their numbers reduce significantly in the industry and service sectors. In 1995 women were 67 percent of the economically active population compared to 5 percent in industry and 22 percent in service jobs. Overall, 42 percent of the total labor force in Sub-Saharan Africa in 1998 was women. The female/male ratio of participation in economic activities in 1995 was 87 percent. Female as a percentage of male in administration and managerial positions was 13 percent, and female as percentage of male professional and technical domains was 41 percent. Data from the ILO and other sources suggest that women's formal sector participation rates dropped from 57 percent in 1970 to 53 percent in 1990, with 2.5 million women losing their jobs between 1985 and 1990. In Benin, to cite just one example, women accounted for 26 percent of retrenched workers, although they were only 6 percent of formal sector workers; women had predominated in the lower echelons of the social services sector, which faced the heaviest budget cuts. Many of such retrenched women have relocated to the informal sector.

Specific Problems of Women

Every ten years the UN hosts a world conference to discuss important issues related to women. In 1995 the 4th world conference on women was held in Beijing. Here the Beijing Declaration and Platform for Action was produced, building upon other UN Human rights documents affecting women. The Platform for Action identified 12 critical areas of concern including health, education, poverty, human rights and the girl-child. Many consider the Platform for Action to be a universal document on how to achieve gender equality as well as the advancement of women. In fact 185 governments of the world agreed to put it into action. The Beijing conference in 1995, followed by the United Nations sponsored Beijing +5 Conference in New York in 2000, stressed the empowerment of women as one of the central development goals of the 21st century. Women from all over the world gathered to share stories of gender discrimination. Women's organizations, UN delegates and NGOs presented a unified platform for action to the member countries of the UN. Among these were delegations of African women who presented a list of specific issues facing women including early marriages, early pregnancies, female genital mutilation, incest, illiteracy, prostitution, war, health services, a lack of participation in political and economic decision making, poverty, child labor, child soldier and violence.

On March 15, 2000 about 90 people gathered for a panel session about the realities of young women's lives, organized by Youth for Women's Rights. Young women from all the regions in the world presented problems they and others are facing and moved the audience with their accounts. From Latin America to Eastern Europe, from Africa to Asia, young women face specific problems but also have a lot in common. The African accounts were very much related to what affects some traditions and cultures have on the girls and young women. From Senegal were narrations of forced marriages at early ages, the dangers of early pregnancy and the fact that women have no say in whether or when to become pregnant. From Nigeria, the realities of incest, unwanted pregnancy and forced silence were reported.[21] Female Genital Mutilation is common as a traditional for of female circumcision in many African countries.

Female Genital Mutilation (FGM)

An estimated 132 million women and girls experience genital mutilation each year in 28 African countries, according to the World Health Organization. Of the numerous challenges African women encounter none is so personal and inhumane than what has come to be known as "FGM." The brutal conditions under which such surgery is conducted are very unhygienic and painful. Each year, over 80 per cent of women in Sudan, Somalia, Djibouti, Ethiopia and Sierra Leone undergo various forms of FGM. Besides the immediate pain and trauma FGM inflicts on its victims, it can result in infertility, incontinence, painful sexual intercourse and obstructed labor, in addition to severe psychological trauma. Groups such as Mali's Association pour le Progrès et la Défense des Femmes, and others in Sierra Leone and Niger, have carried out intensive campaigns in cities and villages against the practice of female excision. Many women turn to traditional women's groups for comfort and protection against their violators. Women's organizations have acted often as parallel authority structures to those of men. Some of these include, women's courts, market authorities, secret societies, and age-grade institutions that allow men and women to exercise authority over their own sex and activities.[22.]

In some parts of Africa, girls as young as five-years old have fallen victim to these cruel practices. The psychological and physiological effects have a long lasting impact on the individuals and the society. From Kenya to Mali women's cries to governments for an end to this practice have gone largely unnoticed, thus forcing women to take matters into their own hands. Local communities mobilize to change indigenous practices which have posed constraint to the social well being of a local community; such movements have quickly spread throughout other communities, such as Senegal where rural women mobilized to abolish female circumcision in their community.[23]

By informing themselves on practices elsewhere and on the effects of circumcision on girls' health and sexual life, these Senegalese women developed an arsenal of arguments and eventually convinced the village council to abolish the practice officially. They helped to mobilize and help women in other parts of the country to speak out against such practices. The move quickly gained national and international attention when Abdou Diouf, President of Senegal, proposed the "Oath of Malicounda" as a model for national adoption.[24] Those who committed themselves to the oath agreed to help prevent the practice of FGM in their families and communities.

Early Marriage and Early Pregnancies

About 50 percent of women in Africa are married by age 18, and one in three women are in a polygamous marriage. Marriage which was once seen as the only option for women, has taken on a new meaning, thus changing the status quo. Once considered a taboo in many African countries to have children outside marriage, today's women are challenging these societal beliefs, and more are choosing to remain single, have children, reside in their parents compounds rather than marry husbands who cannot offer them anything, yet expect everything from them. Most young women prefer not to marry and work as laborers for their husbands. This trend is particular popular with educated females who want to pursue careers. As Miriam Goheen puts it, women labor is not only the backbone of the rural African economy but is also crucial in developing the national welfare for the benefit of all citizens.

Research indicates that children born to mothers below age 18 are 1.5 times more likely to die before age 5 than those born to older mothers. Yet three out of four teenage girls in Africa are mothers, and 40 percent of births are to women under 17.[25] With very little or no education the prospects of a good job elude them, yet the family health and general survival is entrusted in their care. By her mid twenties the average woman in many African countries has at least five children. Estimates of average total fertility rates in Africa were 5.7 children per woman in 1995, although some Southern African countries, as well as Kenya and Mauritius, have begun to see declines. High fertility arises from the economic value of children, high infant mortality and low levels of contraceptive use. Children's labor is crucial inside and outside the home as they are needed to help their mothers care for the sick, old, infants and the husbands. The current economic crisis has added justification for informally employing child labor rather than to educate them. Also, in many African societies a mother's security is determined by the number of children, particularly males, and justifies her claims in her marital home to her husband's assets.

Girls' associations all over the world are organizing and mobilizing support for the governments to make policy changes to protect children. These young women believe strongly that they have some valuable contributions to make for the benefit of mankind. At the Beijing +5 Conference in New York, youth from all over the world gathered to lend support to these and other issues affecting women. In March 2000 the Beijing +5 Youth Caucus managed to lobby successfully on the need for wider youth participation in the Beijing process and to promote an image of 'youth for women's rights' working for the platform for action. According to Catherine Kamau, a youth volunteer from the Family Planning Association of Kenya "there are more than 800 million young women in the world and this needs to be reflected in decision-making bodies."[26]

Rape, Violence and Prostitution

Rape, sexual assault and domestic violence, once discussed only by women because of lack of support from their governments, are beginning to receive due attention in discussions of women's health. Violence to women includes physical beatings, acid throwing, honor killings, and lack of access to medical care. Such violence cuts across culture, class, education, income, ethnicity, and age throughout the world. A UNICEF report on the global epidemic of domestic violence states that 20 percent to 50 percent of girls and women have experienced physical violence from a family member or partner, and between 40 percent and 60 percent of known sexual assaults occur within the family and are committed against girls under 16 years old.

In August 1999, 250 survivors of gender violence from all over Africa testified before the newly established African Court of Women. Rwandan and Somali women told of gang rapes in the refugee camps, Ethiopian women told of forced child marriages and a Kenyan woman described in vivid detail of being raped by a religious minister when she was 13 years old.[27] In many countries women were blamed for such acts against them. Officials argue that if victims were not behaving badly they would not attract men to them. Unfortunately in some African societies, it is believed that if a man does not beat his wife or wives it means he does not love her. Thus physical abuse against women is an indication of their husband's love for them. With this attitude still accepted it will take a long time to convince women in this position that such acts are a crime and a violation.

In many African countries, women's groups and NGO's are compiling data on the prevalence of violence against women. In Namibia and South Africa, women's groups are organizing around the issue of rape and demanding that offenders be prosecuted to the full extent of the law. In 1999 the government of Tanzania enacted a Sexual Offences Provisions act that would impose the maximum penalty for any one found guilty of such violations. While progress to stop unwarranted violations of women's rights is being made in one part of the continent, in some parts, for example, Nigeria, the Islamic "Sharai" laws punish victims of rape to death. Recent events in that country have drawn international attention forcing the government to consider lesser punishments.

In situations of conflict, refugees and displaced women and girls often have been sexually assaulted. In Liberia and Rwanda, rape and torture were used as weapons of war. During the long war in Mozambique, women and girls faced extreme violence, including exposure to landmines and the severe dismemberment that resulted. Some women in refugee camps have been pushed into prostitution, while the conditions in and around camps have contributed to the spread of AIDS and tuberculosis. UNICEF reports indicate that the percentage of girls between the ages of 9 and 14 engaged in prostitution is on the rise.

Political Participation

DeLancey & Russell conducted a comprehensive study of African women in 1998 at the ministerial levels, and the results were very disappointing. Women were grossly underrepresented at that rank, and in some countries women at the cabinet level were appointed by the presidents. Sivard surveyed women around the world and found that in the mid-1980's, women represented a mere 6 percent of national legislative members in Africa.[28] According to Parpart, the limited access of women to higher education and wage employment offers some explanation for the insignificant presence of women at the top.[29] African traditional practices, beliefs and attitudes toward women have carried over into public life. Colonization also contributed to the inequality between men and women. Goheen indicated that it was boys, not girls, who were educated in the government and mission schools so that they could assume roles, first in colonial and later in national political establishments. In Cameroon as in many African countries, women have taken on a different line of approach to reach governments. Goheen concludes that,

> women's protests have multiple voices and various forms. Women have called for equal access to jobs, to land, and to credit within national party platforms. They have demonstrated against male appropriation of farmland and the destruction of their farms by cattle on the village level. They have published protests in national magazines and newspapers against what they perceive to be men's inability or unwillingness to contribute to the household, and have labeled the economic crisis, rightly or wrong, a direct result of men's mismanagement of the economy."[30]

Table 8.2 shows a summary of women's political participation in Africa.

Table 8.2 Women's Political Participation in Africa, 1998

Country	% of Women in Gov'ment at Admin. Level	% Lower House or Single House	% Upper House or Senate
Libyan Arab Jamahiriya	12.5		
Mauritius	9.1	5.7	
Cape Verde	35.0	11.1	
South Africa	38.1	29.8	31.5
Algeria	0.0	3.4	5.6
Namibia	16.3	25.0	7.7
Botswana	26.7	17.0	
Zimbabwe	36.0	9.3	
Ghana	8.6	9.0	
Lesotho		3.8	27.3
Kenya	1.4	3.6	
Cameroon	5.8	5.6	
Congo		12.0	
Madagascar	12.5	8.0	
Nigeria	22.6	3.4	2.8
Sudan	5.1	9.7	
Mauritania	13.6	3.8	1.8
Tanzania		22.2	
Uganda	27.1	17.8	
Zambia	6.2	10.1	
Senegal	15.6	12.1	18.3
Angola	14.7	15.5	
Eritrea	11.8	14.7	
Guinea	11.1	8.8	
Rwanda	13.0	25.7	
Mali	33.3	12.2	

Source: World Bank, 1999

Women are grossly under-represented in government at high levels and in positions of decision-making that impact their lives and the well being of the nation. Average female representation in parliaments is less than 8 percent and many of the women are nominated, not elected. In only two countries, the Seychelles and South Africa, are women more than 25 percent of elected members in parliament or in ministerial positions, thus approaching the 30 percent minimum threshold in decision-making for women recommended in the UNDP's 1995 Human Development Report. Although they are active in community affairs, women also are not adequately represented in regional and local structures, except where conscious efforts have been made to guarantee a quota for them, as in Uganda, Ghana and Namibia. Despite the presence of a few women in judicial and parliamentary systems and in top ministerial and decision-making positions, their low numbers hamper their effectiveness in initiating change for women and the social health of the country.

South Africa has the highest percentage of women representation in government at the administrative level at 38.1 percent while Algeria has no female representation. At the lower house, or single house Mozambique has the highest percentage of women representatives at 30 percent while Djibouti has none. At the upper house, or senate, for countries reporting, Lesotho has the highest percentage of women representation at 27.3 percent, while the lowest is Morocco with 0.7 percent.

Table 8.3 presents a summary of the history of political participation for African women. The first African country to grant women the right to vote and to stand for election was Kenya in 1919, followed by South Africa in 1930. Namibia was the last country to grant women voting rights in 1989. However it was not until 1933 that the first African woman was elected or appointed to parliament. South Africa again set the pace. In 1994, Eritrea appointed the first female to parliament.

Table 8.3: History of Women's Political Participation in Africa

Country	Year Women Received the Right to Vote	Year Women Received Right to Stand for Election	Year First Woman Elected (E or Appointed (A) to Parliament
Libyan Arab Jamahiriya	1964	1964	
Mauritius	1956	1956	1976E
Cape Verde	1975	1975	1975E
South Africa	1930, 1994	1930, 1994	1933E
Algeria	1962	1962	1962A
Namibia	1989	1989	1989E
Botswana	1965	1965	1972E
Zimbabwe	1957	1978	1980E + A
Ghana	1954	1954	1960A
Lesotho	1965	1965	1965A
Kenya	1919, 1963	1919, 1963	1969E + A
Cameroon	1946	1946	1960E
Congo	1963	1963	1963E
Madagascar	1959	1959	1965E

Nigeria	1958	1958	
Sudan	1964	1964	1964E
Mauritania	1961	1961	1975E
Tanzania	1959	1959	
Uganda	1962	1962	1962A
Zambia	1962	1962	1964E + A
Senegal	1945	1945	1963E
Angola	1975	1975	1980E
Eritrea	1955	1955	1994E
Guinea	1958	1958	1963E
Rwanda	1961	1961	1965I
Mali	1956	1956	1964E

Source: World Bank, 1999

Looking to the Future

Throughout the history of African women's struggles, women have always found strength in women's societies and organizations. These avenues provided financial assistance, moral support, and lobbied local and national authorities on behalf of women, children and girls. Women's organizations have strongly established their roots in their communities. The introduction by the United Nations of conferences specifically designed to address women's issues gave these grassroots operations more visibility and power. Today many such organizations link with NGOs at the national and international levels to advance their cause.

The 1990s saw an increase in the role of women's associations as many more were formed or revitalized in response to international dictates. For the first time since their formation, the quality of their work has improved significantly since the 1995 Beijing Conference and the 2000 Beijing +5 follow up. Operating at both grassroots and national levels, these groups have taken advantage of new political openings in many countries to raise issues in new ways and to form alliances with other civil society groups to advance women's rights. While many of the associations receive external funding, a number seek to stress internal responsibility, African agenda-setting, and the development of organizational potential. African women and gender studies programs also have been set up in many universities, both to teach and to engage in fundamental and applied research to improve the conditions of women in Africa. Many international donors now tie in the provision to include women in decision-making, and government officials are realizing the significance of women in nation building.

Recommendations

African women have the solutions to many of the challenges they encounter daily. They deserve to share these ideas with government authorities for implementation. There are several basic critical areas that African governments must address to ensure improved conditions for women and children. These are education, leadership training and partnership and improved health. It is only when governments develop implementation plans with built-in periodic evaluative and assessment mechanisms and commit to the success of these simple areas that there will be positive change in the future of African women, their children and communities.

Education

Education opens doors and restores hope. Education enables a young woman laden with responsibilities of child bearing to read instructions on medication to save her family. Education increases self-confidence and improves the quality of life. For many decades many African governments have paid only lip service to the education of girls. For the benefit of national development, girls' education should be a priority. It is said that learning begins at birth and continues through adolescence and adulthood. Early childhood care is a critical factor for success in school. Governments must partner with women's NGOs and organizations to provide safe day care facilities for children in urban areas and provide resources for schools and teachers in the rural areas. The greatest emphasis should be placed on primary education in both schools and alternative programs.

The exploration of continuous partnership opportunities among governments, NGOs, and civil society organizations at all levels are necessary, and should be adopted. Many of Africa's children have been abused and need special education. Developing special programs and services for these poor and disadvantaged children with disabilities is essential for the future of the continent. A commitment to reduce adult illiteracy, with emphasis on female illiteracy, and the improvement of dissemination of the knowledge, skills, and values required for better living and sustainable development is critical. In addition to making education of girls and women a national priority, African governments should demonstrate their commitment by increasing education appropriations and setting guidelines for achieving them.

Leadership Training and Partnership

African women have demonstrated their abilities to lead in their communities and at national levels when given the opportunity. They have also assumed positions of leadership in times of national crisis. Developing and implementing training programs for women leadership and organization, facilitating network arrangements with organizations locally and internationally, including men in discussions about gender inequalities, providing regular training in information technology to women, and including women in decision making at the highest levels of governments advances the process of reducing gender inequalities.

It is crucial to train women in new and improved agricultural practices and use of equipment, implement technological advances in food processing and preservation, subsidize loans to women's cooperatives to minimize food spoilage and waste in order to reduce labor time, and free women to embark on continuing education to experience a new quality of life with their families, neighbors, and community. Facilitating partnership arrangements with women's organizations in other countries will expose African women to new ideas in management and, organizational skills, problem identification and resolution techniques. Such partnerships will encourage sharing of information on successful strategies and the development of joint sponsorship of women, girls and youth's programs within member countries and in other regions of the world. Developing programs that encourage women in high positions to monitor young women will help to build self-esteem for teenagers, providing positive role models, and guiding them toward leadership and responsibility in the future.

Improve Health

The most important step in improving women's health is for governments to increase spending on social welfare and especially targeting women and children. Civil war and conflicts, HIV/AIDS, unemployment, illiteracy, rape, refugee abuses, early marriages, female genital mutilation, as well as taking care of the family, inflicts hardships on African women that many women in the developed world can not imagine. The result is a poor quality of life, stress and death. African governments must increase the marriage age for both girls and boys so that all may have the opportunity to attain at least primary education. Governments must encourage family planning and partnership with women's organizations to make sure that all women receive the information they need. Governments should reduce military spending and increase spending on health services to prevent the spread and treatment of HIV/AIDS. They should also provide pipe born water and improve sanitation conditions to rural areas, stop child labor and child trafficking, declare all violations against women, girls and children illegal and impose tough penalties to violators.

Women should be taught to take ownership of their bodies. Governments must also use diplomacy and conflict resolution involving women negotiators with neighboring countries in order to reduce civil strife and war. This would reduce the refugee problems and war crimes against women.

Conclusion

African women face many challenges similar to those of women in many countries worldwide. This chapter had addressed some of these challenges and the author submits that in order for any country to develop in all areas, the input of women most be encouraged, supported and promoted. These challenges did not occur over night; the solutions however are in the hands of women who have done a fantastic job so far in championing their (everyone's) course. Women are the backbone of any country. To ignore or only partially engage them in national development is a gross mistake. Women do not need pity, they deserve opportunities. Women's NGOs and organizations in partnership with governments will make changes in action that directly impact the conditions of women. This is necessary for the survival of the nations and for positioning African countries in competitive positions with the rest of the world in the long run. As I have always emphasized, women have always been a part of any country's development and advancement and will continue to be active. However, being only passively active is not enough. Women most be fully assimilated in to policy development, implementation and evaluation and assessment at all levels. We, as a collective conscious humankind must wakeup and realize that women's issues in every corner of the universe affects men and children everywhere else.

• This chapter was previously presented as a paper 'African Women Challenges in the 21st Century' at the Partnership Building for Asian Women in Development Workshop, Sookmyung Women's University Seoul, Korea on July 11, 2002.

Chapter 8 Notes

1. Snyder & Tadesse, *African Women History.*
2. Ibid, 2.
3. E A Errington, W*ives and Mothers, Schoolmistresses and Scullery Maids: Working Women in Upper Canada, 1790-1840* (Montreal & Kingston: McGill-Queen's University Press, 1995).
4. A A Gordon & D L Gordon, eds., *Understanding Contemporary Africa,* 3rd ed. (Boulder, Colorado: Lynne Rienner Publishers, Inc., 2001).
5. S Diduk, "Moral Guardians and Women's Protests in the Grassfields of Cameroon" (paper presented at the 13th Satterthwaite Colloquium on African Ritual and Religion, Satterthwaite, UK, 1997).
6. P G Clark, "A Gender View of the History of Professionalism in South Africa," in *Africa Development* vol. XXIII, Nos. 3 & 4 (1998); Gordon & Gordon, *Contemporary Africa; A* Mama, "Transformation Thwarted: Gender-Based Violence in Africa's New Democracies," (2000); I Sall, ed. *Women in Academia: Gender and Academic Freedom in Africa.* (Dakar, Senegal: Council for the Development of Social Science in Africa, 2000); C L C E Witcombe, "Women in Egypt: Egyptian Queens and Pharaohs," (Sweet Briar College, 1998); World Bank; 1996.
7. Economic Commission for Africa, "Women of Africa: Today and Tomorrow" (Addis Ababa: ECA, 1975) 22.
8. United Nations Development Program, "Making New Technologies Work for Human Development" *Human Development Report, 2001,* (New York: Oxford University Press, 2001).
9. Habitat for Humanity International, "Habitat World" (Americus, Georgia: February/March 2003) 20.
10. R N Mbuh, "Women in Leadership: The Case of Cameroon" in *The Leadership Journal* (spring 1998).
11. UNICEF, "Education For All: No Excuses," (New York: UNICEF: Division of Communications, 2000) 2-4.
12. Africa Recovery, "210 Million Africans Go Hungry" vol. 12, No. 3 (December 1998).
13. E Harsch, "Child Labour Rooted in Africa's Poverty" vol 15, no. 3 (UN Department of Public Information, October 2001).
14. UNICEF, *The State of the World's Children,* (New York: United Nations Publications, 2000) 10.
15. World Bank, 2001
16. Associated Press, July 2, 2002.
17. USA Today, July 7, 2002.
18. L Abala and C L Morna, "Target Practice: Africa Lags Behind" in *Flamme,* The African Daily Newspaper of "Women 2000:Gender Equality, Development and Peace for the 21st Century," (New York, June 6, 2000).
19. World Bank, 2001
20. Ovonji-Odida, "Do Ugandan Women Have any Good Deal on the Land Reforms?" in *Eastern African Initiatives,* No 1, (Kampala, Uganda 1999) 4.

21. Youth for Women's Rights, *The Realities of Young Women's Lives* (New York, March 17, 2000) 4.

22. Gordon & Gordon, *Understanding Africa*; Diduk, "Women's Protests in Cameroon."

23. P Easton, "Indigenous Knowledge for Development" (University of Florida, Dec. 1998) 4.

24. Senegal Ban on Female Genital Mutilation, University of PA, African Studies Ctr. 01/04/1999 for more information visit: http://www.sas.upenn.edu/African_Studies/ Urgent_Action/apic_1499.html.

25. Guttmacher Institute, *Family Planning*.

26. S A Friedman, "Girls 2000: NGOs Report on Progress Since Beijing, 1995" (New York: The Working Groups on Girls, 2000) 7.

27. Mail and Guardian, March 8, 1999.

28. Sivard, *Women: A World Survey*.

29. Parpart and Stuadt eds., *Women in Africa*.

30. Goheen, *Gender and Power in Cameroon*, 196.

PART IV

HAZARDS OF GROWING UP FEMALE

Introduction to Part IV:

Hazards of Growing up Female

And what is to be said of the alarming rate of the spread of HIV/AIDS in Africa and elsewhere? Mokgadi Moletsane and Mark DeLancey's research and analysis of this epidemic points back to the dangers of gender inequalities in power and privilege. Young girls are being infected with the HIV virus as older males impose their sexual desires on them, both through male privilege and a mistaken belief that sexual relations with virgins will protect them from the HIV virus.

In America, violence toward women and girls, and in some cases, boys, is also on the rise through molestation, sexual abuse and rape. The growth of drug cartels has fed the development of prostitution rings run by pimps who specialize in the exploitation of young girls as prostitutes in most major cities of the US, as well as other cities of the world. The recent revelations of sexual exploitation of young boys by Catholic clergy has expanded the dialogue regarding sexual abuse to include boys. How many seemingly innocent boy-scout camps, monasteries, boarding schools and other all-male programs have inducted young boys into sexual victim hood by older men? Is this too an outgrowth of patriarchy or male privilege and power?

Historically, rape of women has been considered the ultimate weapon and evidence of victory by enemy troops. During war, such as in Germany during WW II and more recently in Bosnia, some violations have gone so far as to rip open the bellies of pregnant women to kill the embryo or to force conquered women and girls into sexual slavery as "comfort women" for the troops. None of these well-documented events are comfortable for academic discourse, more often considered as too lurid in detail to discuss.

Issues connected with male privilege and its perpetration from one generation to another in patriarchal societies throughout the world are addressed by Breneman in chapter 10. Though empowerment of women through education, increased decision-making and greater economic status will contribute toward the resolution of this abhorrent situation, these are inadequate per se without acknowledgment of one of the greatest obstacles in any nation toward the achievement of full equality, from infancy to old age. Traditional male privilege needs to be modified or preferably completely abolished. How can any nation attain true democracy or join the community of civilized societies as long as one half of its population has arbitrary power and privilege, while the other is considered little more than a "ladies auxiliary" for those who hold such power? Are human rights restricted to upper class males or are they the birthright of all human beings? As pointed out in a well-known verse from the Qur'án, "Are they who know and those who do not know equal? Nay, immeasurable is the difference!" Victimhood requires passive, powerless, half-witted cooperation with those who hold the upper hand. Once both parties have equal access to knowledge, power and justice, victim hood can be greatly reduced, if not eliminated.

Chapter 9

HIV/AIDS: A Problem for Africa— A Special Problem for African Women

Mokgadi Moletsane and Mark DeLancey

A study of the HIV/AIDS epidemic in Sub-Saharan Africa indicates the severity of the disease for the continent and highlights the unequal gender distribution of the infection. Although once thought of as a disease of men, in Africa women are now being infected in greater numbers than men. In addition, HIV is becoming a disease of the young, with young women and girls much more frequently infected than young men and boys. Biological differences between women and men offer only a partial explanation for this phenomenon. For a more complete explanation we must look to African economic and political inequalities between genders. Also significant are various cultural practices and beliefs, some of which are widely distributed in the region and some of which are specific to particular locales.

Introduction

At various times in human history significant outbreaks of disease, epidemics and pandemics have significantly affected local and world events[1] Today, the world faces a similar situation. The HIV/AIDS epidemic continues to expand the number of people infected and the geographic scope of its spread. In addition to the terrible personal and family tragedies this involves for millions of people, there are important consequences for the larger community, as well. In Sub-Saharan Africa, the current center of the pandemic, several countries have reached such levels of infection that education, agriculture, business and industry, and even the governments and military forces are being negatively impacted. Social unrest, economic disaster and political instability in some countries—and perhaps in some regions of the continent—are possibilities in the near future.[2]

A brief survey of the HIV/AIDS phenomenon shows the very rapid spread of the epidemic since we first became aware of it, and indicates several themes of significance for our interests in this paper.[3] Prime among these is the tendency of the disease to increasingly attack women in greater numbers than men in Africa. This essay presents a brief introduction to the general situation of HIV/AIDS in Africa and then focuses on the particular situation of women in the epidemic. We will attempt to explain why HIV/AIDS has become a disease of, and a special problem for, African women.

The spread of HIV has been exceedingly rapid. In 1981 the first cases were diagnosed in Great Britain and the USA. In these first years, the disease was thought to be a problem for gay men exclusively. In 1985 WHO received reports of 20,303 cases, including the first case from China. in the next year, 38,401 cases in 85 countries were reported. The vast majority of these, some 31,741 cases, were in the Americas and only 84 cases were reported for Asia and 2,323 in Africa. But only three years later, in 1989, WHO estimated that between five and ten million people were HIV positive; by 1990 the estimate had increased to 8 to 10 million, *with a ratio of five men to three women.* It was no longer seen as a problem only of gay men. By far, the largest number in this estimate was in Africa, with 5,500,000 cases. Asia was estimated to have 500,000 HIV positive, 843 AIDS cases, and 2,000 deaths.

In 1996 the Joint United Nations Program on HIV/AIDS (UNAIDS), the successor to an earlier WHO program, estimated that 23 million were now infected, plus 6.4 million that had already died. However, in the next year UNAIDS revised the estimate, stating that the epidemic was much worse than thought. The estimate of those infected was raised to 30,000,000. In 2000 it was estimated that 36.1 million persons were living with HIV/AIDS, that 5.3 million were infected that year, and that there had been 21.8 million deaths since the start of the epidemic. In a widely quoted statement, it was noted that, "HIV/AIDS levels are more than 50 percent higher than predicted ten years ago."[4]

At the end of 2002 the UNAIDS program reported that 5 million people were newly infected in 2002; of the 4.2 million adults newly infected, 2 million were women. More than 42,000,000 persons were living with HIV or AIDS. Of these, 38.6 million were adults (aged 15 to 49) and 3.2 million were children under 15 years of age. Of the adults, 19.2 million were women. *Almost fifty percent of new and existing adult victims were women.* In 1991 women represented 41 percent of adult cases in the world; by 2000 this figure had increased to 47 percent.[5] This increase in the proportion of women is expected to continue for some years. From men to women, from the Americas to Asia, the gender distribution as well as the geographical distribution have changed radically over the course of the short history of the disease. There were 3,100,000 AIDS deaths in 2002. Sub-Saharan Africa still had the greatest number of cases (29.4 million), but the estimate for Asia had increased to 5,600,000.[6] In addition to the trend toward higher proportions of women being infected, the problem was now a youth problem with about half of new infections worldwide in the 15 to 24 age group.[7]

The data in Table 9.1 suggest that there is a strong relationship between the predominant mode of transmission of HIV infections and the percentage of adult women infected. At this level of generalization, all situations where women are 50 percent or more of the adult cases, the main mode of transmission is heterosexual intercourse. In all instances where heterosexual activity is a major mode of transmission, women account for 20 percent or more of cases. In the location where women represent less than 20 percent of cases, heterosexual transmission is not listed as a major mode of transmission. However, as we will discuss below, there are additional factors that explain the high rates of infection for women in general and in Africa in particular.

Table 9.1. World Distribution of HIV/AIDS, 2001 and 2002*

Region	Total 2001 HIV/ AIDS	Adults HIV-positive 2001 (15-49)	Total 2002 HIV/ AIDS	New Infec-tions Adults & Children 2002	Women as % of HIV adults 2002 (15-49 yrs.)	Main Modes of transmission for HIV adults**
Global Total	40m	37.1m	42m	5m	50%	
Sub-Saharan Africa	28.5m	26m	29.4m	3.5m	58%	Hetero
East Asia and Pacific	1m	970,000	1.2m	270,000	24%	IDU, hetero, MSM
Australia, New Zealand	15,000	14,000	15,000	500	7%	MSM
South and SE Asia	5.6m	5.4m	6.0m	700,000	36%	Hetero, IDU
E. Europe and Central Asia	1m	1m	1.2m	250,000	27%	IDU
W. Europe	550,000	540,000	570,000	30,000	25%	MSM, IDU
N. Africa, Middle East	500,000	460,000	550,000	83,000	55%	Hetero, IDU
N. America	950,000	940,000	980,000	45,000	20%	MSM, IDU, hetero
Caribbean	420,000	400,000	440,000	60,000	50%	Hetero, MSM
Latin America	1.5	1.4m	1.5m	150,000	30%	MSM, IDU, Hetero

**Hetero (heterosexual transmission), IDU (transmission through injecting drug use), MSM (sexual transmission among men who have sex with men).
*UNAIDS. *Report on the Global HIV/AIDS Epidemic*, July 2002, pp. 190-202 found at www.unaids.org and UNAIDS "AIDS Epidemic Update December 2002," on CD *The Global HIV/AIDS Epidemic 2002-2003*. Geneva: UNAIDS, 2003.

HIV/AIDS: An African Problem
Reading the Africa summary of the UNAIDS 2001 report on the worldwide status of the HIV/AIDS epidemic is quite a grim task, in spite of the authors' attempts to find gleams of hope. The most discouraging statement overwhelms the positive ones. Some observers had expressed the hope that the epidemic would reach a "natural limit" in those countries most seriously affected and that there would thus be a leveling off of new infections. The new report dashed that hope:

"Unfortunately, this appears not to be the case as yet. . . . If a natural HIV prevalence limit does exist in these countries, it is considerably higher than previously thought."[8] In Botswana, for example, an infection rate of about 38 percent in 1997 had increased to 44.9 percent in 2001, the highest incidence in the world. Zimbabwe, Namibia and Swaziland, each with among the highest rates in the world, have also seen continuing increases in rates of infection in the past few years.

Of the 44 countries in the Sub-Saharan Africa group, seven have HIV/AIDS infections rates higher than 20 percent (Botswana, Lesotho, Namibia, South Africa, Swaziland, Zambia and Zimbabwe), and an additional five are above 10 percent (Cameroon, Central African Republic, Kenya, Malawi and Mozambique). The states above 20 percent are all in southern Africa, the center of the epidemic at this time, but among those states above 10 percent are central (Cameroon and Central African Republic) and east African (Kenya) countries, a frightening portent of things to come. One West African state, Côte d'Ivoire, is very close to 10 percent and Cameroon, at 11.8 percent, is a borderline central-west African state. "In west and central Africa, there is evidence of recent, rapid HIV spread."[9] In Cameroon the prevalence rates of several adult categories have jumped in the last two years, suggesting that overall steep increases in infection rates may be forthcoming. In this regard, Nigeria, the continent's most populous state, presents a frightening situation. Already 3.5 million persons are infected, but the rate has risen slowly to 5.8 percent in 2001 and some of its constituent states have much higher rates.

Uganda, Zambia, and Senegal are the most positive cases. Uganda has apparently reversed the increase in its very high prevalence rates. This country has frequently been praised for its very active, and seemingly effective, anti-AIDS campaigns and its efforts to provide antiretroviral drugs to those infected. The Zambian campaign seems to be moving toward reversing the expansion of infection. In Senegal, intervention was made at a very early stage of the epidemic and thus the country still maintains a very low rate of infection.[10] Some other countries are trying to emulate these successes, but others are still not making a serious effort. Even those that are taking a strong stand suffer from numerous disadvantages, and, as many of the world's poorest countries are in this region, low levels of funding are a major detriment.

We all accept that the impact of HIV/AIDS at the individual and family level is painful and often disastrous. It is less widely understood or accepted that this syndrome can have powerful negative effects at higher levels of societal organization as well. As adult incidence rates have reached and surpassed 30 percent in a few countries in recent years, leaders and scholars have begun to give serious consideration to the impact that such numbers might have on a society. It is rather too easy to say that such impacts will be negative; examination indicates that the impacts are more widespread than the casual observer might expect. As we approach higher incidence rates and as the death rate from AIDS that follows goes into higher realms, the possibility of societal collapse emerges.

Table 9.2.
Sub-Saharan Africa, HIV/AIDS Incidence by Selected Countries, 2001*

Country	Total Adults and Children 0-49	Adults (15-49)	Adults Infection Rate (%)	Women (15-49) Absolute and as % of adult	Orphans Currently Living 0-14 yrs.	Deaths, Adults and Children, 2001	Total Population 2001 in 000s
Sub-Sah. Africa	28,500,000	26,000,000	9.0%	15,000,000 58%	11,000,000	2,200,000	633,816
Botswana	330,000	300,000	38.8%	170,000 57%	69,000	26,000	1,554
Cameroon	920,000	900,000	11.8%	500,000	210,000	53,000	15,203
Dem Rep of Congo	1,300,000	1,100,000	4.9%	670,000 61%	930,000	129,000	52,522
Ethiopia	2,100,000	1,900,000	6.4%	1,100,000 58%	990,000	160,000	64,459
Ghana	360,000	330,000	3.9%	170,000 52%	200,000	28,000	19,734
Kenya	2,500,000	2,300,000	15.0%	1,400,000 61%	890,000	190,000	31,293
Lesotho	360,000	330,000	31.0%	180,000 55%	73,000	25,000	2,057
Namibia	230,000	200,000	22.5%	110,000 55%	47,000	13,000	1,789
Nigeria	3,500,000	3,000,000	5.8%	1,700,000 57%	1,000,000	170,000	116,929
Senegal	27,000	24,000	0.5%	14,000 58%	15,000	2,500	9,662
South Africa	5,000,000	4,700,000	20.1%	2,700,000 57%	660,000	350,000	43,792
Swaziland	170,000	150,000	33.4%	89,000 59%	35,000	12,000	938
Uganda	600,000	510,000	5.0%	280,000 55%	880,000	84,000	24,023
Zambia	1,200,000	690,000	21.5%	590,000 59%	570,000	120,000	10,649
Zimbabwe	2,300,000	2,000,000	33.7%	1,200,000 60%	780,000	200,000	12,852

Source: *UNAIDS, Report on the Global HIV/AIDS Epidemic, July 2002, p. 190 at www.unaids.org.*

Some examples in Africa indicate the widespread effects of the epidemic. In Côte d'Ivoire one schoolteacher dies of AIDS each day. Fifty percent of in-patients in Zimbabwe's hospitals have AIDS related illnesses. By 2005 over half of Kenya's health budget will go to AIDS patient care. Maize production in Zimbabwe is reduced by 61 percent in farm families with one member ill. Families with an AIDS patient must pay out more for treatment and care, resulting in cuts in funds allocated to food or children's education. Average life expectancy in some countries may be reduced by 10 to 20 years. HIV rates are as high as 20 to 40 percent in some African military forces and reach 50 to 60 percent in those countries where HIV has been present for more than a decade.[11] The Director of UNAIDS, Peter Piot, states that AIDS has become the "greatest obstacle to development" in much of Sub-Saharan Africa.[12]

South Africa: South Africa presently has the largest number of HIV/AIDS cases in the world. As in many countries, young people are the most affected, and women are much more affected than men. AIDS is now the number one cause of death for women. Mining, migrant labor and trucking are significant factors in the spread of the disease. The adult incidence rate is expected to rise to 25 percent by 2010; by which time 2/3s of all deaths will be AIDS related. By 2005 the population will be 16 percent smaller than it would have been in the absence of AIDS; South Africa is one of the few countries that will actually experience a decline in population. Life expectancy in 2010 will be about 45 years, but without AIDS it would be 70 years.[13]

Namibia: This is one of the five worst affected countries in the world, and most of its cases have been reported only in the last two to three years, an indication that much higher rates may be forthcoming. Since 1996, AIDS has been the number one cause of death here, causing a 24-year drop in life expectancy. Among the major problems faced in the AIDS campaign are the stigma surrounding AIDS, cultural/religious attitudes toward the use of condoms, and failure to bring about changes in sexual behavior.[14]

Zimbabwe: HIV/AIDS prevalence has increased from 25 percent in 1999 to 34 percent in 2001. Women account for 60 percent of those affected and children under 5 years old 15 percent. Young women tend to have higher incidence rates than men of the same age, indicating that much transmission is from older men to younger women. Average life expectancy was 66 years in 1997; it is expected to be 35 years in 2010. Gender inequality, the stigma of AIDS, and a lack of change in sexual behavior lead to expectations that the crisis has still to reach a peak.[15]

Kenya: This country was hit heavily early on in the epidemic and from 1990 to 2000 life expectancy dropped from 60 to 40 years. Young women are particularly vulnerable and high age differences between male and female partners are considered a major cause. The burden of AIDS is now beginning to appear in the economy and estimates indicate that in 2005 GDP will be 14.5 percent lower than it would have been without AIDS. A lack of central government commitment and of appropriate education in the schools are major factors in the failure to stem the spread of HIV/AIDS.[16]

Democratic Republic of Congo (DRC): The DRC, previously known as Zaire, has had a long history of violence. Movements of refugees and soldiers; inadequate safeguards in blood transfusions; inadequate counseling, education, treatment, and condom availability; and the disruption of almost continuous wars are factors leading to an increase in prevalence rates. Heterosexual contact accounts for 87 percent of infections, mother-to-child transmission 8 percent, and blood transfusions 5 percent. Violence by soldiers against women, disruption of governing and social systems and poverty are aggravating factors.[17]

Rwanda: This is another country involved in internal conflict and massive population movements. It is among the nine worst HIV/AIDS situations in the world; AIDS is one of the three main causes of death and life expectancy by 2010 is estimated to be 32 years. Poverty, civil strife, multiple sex partners, commercial sex, and resistance to discussing sex and using condoms are suggested by the government as key factors. High illiteracy rates for women and men make the spread of HIV knowledge difficult. Lack of security in the many refugee camps and rape are additional causes. Mother to child transmission (MTCT) is a significant cause of infection, but the government is struggling with this issue.[18]

Nigeria: Infection rates appear to be increasing in this country, a country plagued by poverty, ethnic and religious diversity, and a violent history. Sexual networking practices such as polygamy; lack of treatment for sexually transmitted diseases; poverty, low literacy and the low status of women; stigma attached to AIDS; and the difficulties of disseminating information in a multilingual society are among the factors causing the spread of the infection.[19]

In a recent report, the US National Intelligence Council (NIC) notes that Nigeria is one of five major countries facing a rapid increase in HIV/AIDS problems. The NIC suggests that rather than 3.5 million cases, Nigeria presently has between 4 to 6 million and in 2010 there will 10 to 15 million cases; infection rates by the NIC estimate are currently 6 to 10 percent and by 2010 will be 18 to 26 percent. There are regional variations, with the Muslim north having lower rates than the southern portions of the country. The report concludes that, "The social and economic impact of AIDS in Nigeria and Ethiopia probably will be similar to the hardest hit countries in Africa."[20]

Angola: Although Angola's infection rate was only 5.5 percent, it was increasing rapidly. Sexual intercourse, especially multiple-partner intercourse, was considered the main mode of transmission. In 1999, 14 percent of new infections were due to mother to child transmission. Lack of knowledge about HIV is a major issue; a UNICEF study indicated that only 8 percent of women had adequate knowledge of the disease and its prevention. Civil strife, massive population movements with the end of the civil war, and poverty were contributing factors.[21]

Ethiopia: UNAIDS estimates that at the end of 2001 there were 2.1 million persons infected, but the Ethiopian government estimates that there were 3.2 million. By 2010 life expectancy will be 42 years, without AIDS 55 years. Heterosexual contact is a causal factor in 87 percent of transmissions and perinatal transmission is the second major cause. In 1997 men represented 61 percent of infections, but young women (15-19 years old) had a much higher rate than men of the same age, "due to earlier initiation of sexual activity by women and the fact that their older partners often had more than one sexual partner."[22] By the end of 2001 proportions had reversed and women accounted for 58 percent of total adult infections. Young people are the most vulnerable. Obstacles to efforts to reduce the incidence of HIV/AIDS include lack of power among women and negative attitudes toward condom use by men, religious and cultural barriers, and lack of effective HIV-STD treatment and services.[23] The NIC report notes the limited capacity of government to respond to the situation. Again taking issue with UNAIDS data, the NIC estimates that there are presently between 3 and 5 millions case in Ethiopia and that by 2010 this will increase to 7 to 10 million cases with a current prevalence rate between 10 and 18 percent that will increase to 19 to 27 percent by 2010. HIV becomes AIDS more rapidly here than in many other countries because of the poor quality of health. The long civil war and the recent war with Eritrea have increased the rapidity of the spread of HIV—and the end of the war is having a similar effect as soldiers are demobilized and they and the prostitutes that aggregated near the near camps and bases disperse to their homes and other locations.[24]

HIV/AIDS: An African Women's Problem

If there was no gender difference in the spread of HIV through heterosexual relations, then we would not see more women than men infected in situations where heterosexual relations are the main mode of transmission. But as the numbers show, this is not the case. The World Health Organization (WHO) published a "Fact Sheet" titled "Women and Aids" which asks the question, "Why Are Women More Vulnerable to HIV infection?" WHO presents three categories of explanation: biological, economic and social/cultural.[25] We will discuss these and then consider the additional, special burdens for African women that result from the HIV epidemic.

Biological Factors

Women are more vulnerable to HIV infection than men because of physical differences between the genders. The WHO note lists the following factors:

> Larger mucosal surface; microlesions which can occur during intercourse may be entry points for the virus; very young women even more vulnerable in this respect.
> More virus in sperm than in vaginal secretions.
> As with STIs [sexually transmitted infections], women are at least four times more vulnerable to infection; the presence of untreated STIs is a risk factor for HIV.
> Coerced sex increases risk of microlesions.[26]

As discussed below, the increased risk for very young women and the effects of coerced sex are particularly significant.

Economic Factors

The interdependence or intertwining of factors in the economic, social and cultural categories is so powerful that it is difficult to separate them in discussion. In essence, the wide-spread phenomenon that women are economically, politically, legally and socially in weaker positions than men is a major explanation of the increasing number of women infected by HIV in Africa and elsewhere where heterosexual relations are the main mode of transmission. "Financial or material dependence on men means that women cannot control when, with whom and in what circumstances they have sex."[27] Social and cultural aspects of life in most African societies place women at a serious disadvantage. Poverty adds to this. Poverty may not be a cause of HIV infections in the direct, biological sense, but poverty presents a very hospitable environment for the spread of HIV. Poverty is widespread in Africa, and this places women in a dangerous setting, increasing their vulnerability well beyond the biological aspects. Data in Table 9.3 makes the economic point quite strongly. Whether compared to the USA or to Korea, African states in our sample have very low income per capita (from $100 in Burundi to $2900 in South Africa) and high percentages of persons living below the poverty line (33.4 percent in Senegal to 86.0 percent in Zambia) or on less than one dollar per day (from 11.5 percent in Senegal to 70.2 percent in Nigeria). Indeed, most of the poorest countries of the world are on the African continent. Especially relevant to this report, health expenditures per capita are extremely low in this sample of African states, ranging from $4.00 per person in Ethiopia to $230 per person in South Africa. In the USA the figure is $4,271 and in South Korea $470.

Table 9.3 Country Economic and Social Indicators

Country	Gender-related development index (GDI) (Rank)	Gross National Income (US$ per capita)	Population below poverty line (%)	Population below US$1/day (%)	Health expenditure, private and public (US$ per capita)
	2000	2001	1987-2000	1983-2000	1998
Angola	Nd	500	Nd	Nd	Nd
Botswana	104	3,630	Nd	33.3	127
Burundi	145	100	36.2	Nd	5
Cameroon	115	570	40	33.4	Nd
C.Afr. Rep	139	270	Nd	66.6	9
Cote d'Ivoire	132	630	36.8	12.3	28
DR Congo	131	Nd (1)	Nd	Nd	Nd
Ethiopia	142	100 (3)	Nd	31.3	4
Ghana	108	290	31.4	44.8	19
Kenya	112	340	42	26.5	31
Lesotho	111	550	49.2	43.1	Nd
Malawi	137	170	54	Nd	11
Mozambique	144	210	Nd	37.9	8
Namibia	101	1960	Nd	34.9	142
Nigeria	124	290	34.1	70.2	30
S.Korea	29	9400	Nd	Nd	470 (4)
Rwanda	135	220	51.2	35.7	10
Senegal	130	480	33.4	26.3	23
South Africa	88	2900	Nd	11.5	230
Swaziland	103	1300	40	Nd	46
Uganda	125	280	55	Nd	18
USA	4	34,870	Nd	Nd	4,271 (4)
Zambia	129	320	86	63.7	23
Zimbabwe	107	480	25.5	36	36 (4)

Nd = No data

Source: www.hivinsite.com (See data notes on the following page)

Table 9.3 Data Notes
   1. Estimated to be low income ($755 or less) (2000).
   2. Indicates data that refer to years or periods other than those specified in the column heading, differ from the standard definition or refer to only part of a country.
   3. Data Prior to 1992 include Eritrea for the following categories: national accounts, balance of payments, trade, government finance, monetary indicators, and external debt.
Data refers to 1999.

The Gender-Related Development Index (GDI) is an indication of the relevant economic situation of women in their country. Like the Human Development Index (HDI), the GDI considers life expectancy, education and income but it does so in respect of gender differences. In Table 9.3 we used rank order rather than absolute scores. Thus, as a country's rank approaches #1 this indicates a more equitable distribution between men and women, but it does not suggest gender equality

Unfortunately inadequate African data is available to construct the Gender Equality Measure (GEM), another useful figure for our purposes.[28] The GDI scores do tell us that most African countries rank quite low in economic equality between men and women.[29] This, added to the general low economic conditions, means that often African women are in very difficult economic conditions and that they must look to men for economic support; they are often economically dependent upon men. In turn, this means that women frequently are sexually exploited. "Many women have to exchange sex for material favors, for daily survival. There is formal sex work but there is also this exchange which in many settings, is many women's only way of providing for themselves and their children."[30]

Of course, poverty influences the spread of HIV infection in many other ways. Poorer people tend to have a lower nutritional and overall health status, and due to various aspects of African cultures, this may be greater for poor women than for poor men. Poor nutrition and health make a person more susceptible to HIV infection. Poor people tend to have lower education levels. Again, this is more influential for females due to cultural reasons. Female children tend to be enrolled in school less frequently than males and they tend to be the first withdrawn from school during hard economic times. If not in school, a girl receives less information about HIV and its prevention and she tends to marry and be exposed to sexual exploitation at an earlier age, all factors which increase female vulnerability to HIV infection.

Social and Cultural Factors
   Sub-Saharan Africa is culturally very complex, heterogeneous, and it is difficult to generalize for the entire region. Some of the factors discussed here may exist only in some areas or be of greater or lesser significance in one part of the region than another. Some factors appear to be important throughout the region; the most important of these is the universal lack of equality between women and men in legal, social, economic and other matters. Second is the widespread ten-

dency for younger women to have sexual relations with older men. Third are frequently found customs, practices and beliefs that encourage multiple sexual partners and other risky behaviors.

The influences of African culture, the colonial experiences, and post-independence development activities have placed African women in unenviable economic, political and legal positions of inequality in comparison to men. This topic is introduced well in a chapter by April Gordon in, *"Women and Development."*

> African women have neither the political, legal, educational, nor economic opportunities of their male counterparts. Men in Africa overwhelmingly dominate the institutions of society and have used their positions more often than not to further the control and advantages men have in both the public and domestic arenas.[31]

Symbolic of the weak position of African women is a report on the number of African women holding cabinet positions in African governments. "Typically, women represent a very small proportion of the members of the cabinet and, often, those women holding cabinet positions are relegated to the less significant ministries."[32] At the personal level, this male dominance can play an insidious role in giving men the ability to demand sexual relationships and interactions even though a woman may not wish to have such an involvement. The ability of a woman, and especially a young and poor woman, to say "No" is limited in such a situation, "No" both in respect of having sex and in the conditions of having sex. Thus, many women do not believe they can demand that their partner use a condom, even when they know that this is a major way to protect themselves and when they are aware that their partner is involved in sexual relations with other people. A study of sexually experienced girls in South Africa found that 33 percent of respondents were "afraid of saying no to sex" and 55 percent agreed that "there are times I don't want to have sex but I do because my boyfriend insists."[33]

A man having multiple sex partners is a frequent occurrence in Africa, much less so for women. There is a widely held belief that it is normal, even healthy, for a man to have many partners, whether as a young, unmarried man or later as a married man. The frequent polygamous family is indicative of this belief, although the attitude finds expression in many other ways. A series of twenty HIV/AIDS country briefs prepared by the United States foreign aid agency almost unanimously point to multiple sex partner practices as a main factor in the local HIV situation. Any practice that increases the number of sexual partners for an individual increases the risk of being infected with HIV. Even if a woman has only one partner, her husband, she is exposed to a higher chance of infection through him if he is having intercourse with other partners, and particularly so if he is practicing unsafe sex. A survey in Eritrea indicated that 56 percent of women interviewed knew that their husband or partner had more than one partner.[34] Because of the inability to say no, especially for a married woman, this behavior greatly increases the woman's chance of infection. A survey in Zambia indicated that less than 25 percent of women thought they could refuse to have sex with their husband and only 11 percent believed they could ask their husband to use a condom.[35]

As noted above, younger females are more vulnerable to HIV infection for physiological reasons. They are also more vulnerable because of their even weaker economic and power situations vis-à-vis men. In almost every African country surveyed, girls and young women tend to have higher rates of infection than boys or young men of the same age group. A report from Kenya shows that in the 15-24 year age group, women are twice as likely to be infected as men. In Ethiopia, women 15-19 have a much higher rate of infection than similarly aged men. In Zimbabwe, the rate for women aged 15 to 24 is 2.6 times that of men of the same age. In Mozambique for the 15 to 19 age group, women have double the rate as men and in the 20 to 24 year group women have quadruple the rate of men.[36] This phenomenon occurs because young women are frequently having sex with older men, and older men are more often involved in multiple sexual relationships and thus have a higher chance of HIV infection.

A review of 45 studies of cross-generational and transactional sex relations in Sub-Saharan Africa found that, "Engaging in sexual relations with older partners is the norm for adolescent girls. There is a widespread transactional component for adolescent girls, and in some contexts, large proportions of girls have engaged in this type of relationship." Although there is a bias to underreporting in the studies, it is shown that, "Men have large proportions of adolescent girls as non-marital sexual partners." And, the studies indicate; "Significant relationships between unsafe sexual behaviors, HIV risk, and cross-generational sex" exist.

The main motivation for the girls is receipt of gifts and financial benefits, "ranging from economic survival to desire for status and possessions." Such relationships between older men and younger women are "fundamentally unbalanced" and men control the conditions of sexual intercourse, "including condom and contraceptive use and the use of violence." The risk of HIV infection becomes greater when the age difference is greater and as transaction value increases. In general, for girls to suggest condom use "jeopardizes their goals for the relationship."[37]

It may be almost a universal in sexual behavior that older men seek relationships with younger women, but there are several aspects of the African situation that exacerbate this tendency. Widespread poverty with the existence of a small middle and upper class that is economically very distant from the mass of the people is one factor. It has been noted that those men in the higher economic brackets have more money for risky sexual behavior, usually with younger women and with multiple partners. As suggested above, the "sugar daddy" phenomenon is widely reported in studies of African and especially urban behavior.

African marriage customs in the past and the present have frequently encouraged age differences between the men and women involved. In many parts of Africa a man must pay a dowry to the family of the bride, and it may take some years for a man to earn this dowry, whether in cash or goods. Polygamy, widely practiced in Africa, also favors unions between older men and younger women. While the first marriage may involve a man and woman of relatively similar ages, as the husband grows older and wealthier, he is able to arrange additional marriages, generally with quite young women.

The HIV epidemic appears to have fostered new rationales for older men having sexual relations with younger women. One is the practical argument that a younger woman or a girl is more likely to be a virgin or at least to have had fewer sexual partners than an older woman and thus there is less chance that a younger woman will be HIV infected. However, there are many reports of a second rationale. A myth has developed that having sex with a virgin is a *cure* for HIV/AIDS. Infected men desire to have sex with ever-younger women in the belief that this will rid them of the disease. This may occur through transactional sex, but a man may also resort to violence and/or incest to get the cure he seeks. The net result is an increase in the infection rate for young women. There is no data to show how widespread is this belief and nothing to indicate the frequency in which the myth is merely an excuse to have sex with a girl, but existence of the myth is frequently mentioned in the literature.

Other aspects of various African cultures are also important in the spread of HIV infections in women. Though these customs may have, or have had in the past, positive consequences for society, in the HIV context they have become negative. Polygamy has already been suggested in the context of any practice that encourages multiple sexual partnering. Another such practice is "wife inheritance" or various forms of the levirate. Even today, this may be highly valued by many women for the economic and social security it provides them and their children in a society where women have minimal property and inheritance rights in traditional law and no modern social security or welfare systems are in existence. In essence, a widow is inherited or becomes the wife of a male relative of her deceased husband. The new "husband" may not demand sexual access to the woman, but this is his right and often does occur. Again, this places all of those involved in a multiple partnering situation. The wife inheritance practice is recognized for its role in the spread of HIV and appears to be coming under attack in several locations. Articles published in 2003 in Tanzania, Malawi and Kenya argue for or report on public meetings demanding an end to the practice.[38] There are some reports of a related custom, "sexual cleansing," in which a widow is expected to have sexual intercourse with a chosen member of the family of the deceased husband's family. This is regarded in some areas as a means of freeing the surviving spouse from the ghost of the deceased.

Traditional healers may also play a role in the spread of HIV infections to women and men. There are several reports of such doctors following unhygienic procedures, particularly in respect of using unclean instruments in cutting and surgical procedures. This may affect women and men equally, although research on gender aspects of decisions to use traditional doctors and on gender aspects of techniques used would be useful here. However, one frequently reported technique does directly affect women. As in many societies, women are generally held to be at blame when a couple fails to have children. A common treatment offered by traditional doctors is for the women to have sexual intercourse with the doctor in the belief that when they have sex with their husbands they will become pregnant. Of course, this may lead to the woman becoming pregnant by the doctor, but it also exposes the woman to the possibility of HIV infection. If the doctor has established a reputation for solving fertility problems, he may have had numerous sexual partners and may be HIV positive himself. It has also been suggested that the "sleep with a virgin" cure for men who are HIV positive has been promoted by some traditional doctors.

Female genital mutilation (FGM) is another practice that promotes the spread of HIV infection in women. Male circumcision is also widely practiced in Africa and must be considered as a factor in the spread of infection, but male circumcision is less invasive and has shorter-term harmful problems than FGM. There are numerous negative aspects of this surgery, often performed under unsanitary conditions, and its after effects may leave a woman more vulnerable to all forms of infection, including HIV. FGM is practiced in several of the countries with high rates of HIV infection in women, but it is also practiced in several countries with low rates of infection. Of high infection countries, Ethiopia, Kenya, Nigeria are reported to have high rates of FGM (above 50 percent), but some countries with very high levels of HIV infection also have very low rates of FGM; Uganda and the Democratic Republic of the Congo (Zaire) have estimated FGM levels of only 5 percent. Some countries with high FGM rates, Mali and Sudan, for examples, have FGM rates above 70 percent but have relatively low rates of HIV infection in women.[39] This is a factor in need of further micro level study.

Violence against women is an additional aspect of African life that increases the likelihood of a woman becoming HIV positive. The recent excellent work by December Green, *Gender Violence in Africa: African Women's Responses*, provides a powerful analysis of this situation.[40] Such violence occurs in several settings, frequently in the home and increasingly in situations of civil and international conflict. Thirty-nine percent of sexually experienced girls in South Africa report that they have been forced to have sex.[41] Research in rural Uganda indicated that 70 percent of male and 90 percent of female respondents "viewed beating of a female partner as justified in one or more circumstances,"[42] such as neglecting household chores or disobeying a husband. One factor increasing the risk of such violence is male HIV infection and a woman's perception of her partner's risk of HIV infection. The study concludes that ". . . domestic violence may represent a significant factor in women's vulnerability to HIV acquisition; this raises the possibility that current programs to prevent HIV may be overlooking a key behavioral dimension of HIV transmission."[43] A recent study in Zambia highlights a specific aspect of the HIV epidemic and gender violence:

> Abuse of the human rights of girls, especially sexual violence and other sexual abuse, contribute directly to this disparity [between boys and girls] in infection and mortality....This report shows sexual assault of girls in Zambia in the era of HIV/AIDS to be widespread and complex. It documents several categories of abuse that heighten girls' risk of HIV infection, including (1) sexual assault of girls by family members, particularly the shocking and all too common practice of abuse of orphan girls by men who are their guardians, or by others who are charged with to assist or look after them. . . (2) abuse of girls. . . who are heads of household or otherwise desperately poor and have few options other than trading sex for their and their siblings' survival, and (3) abuse of girls who live

on the street[44]

Of course, HIV/AIDS has increased the number of girl orphans and heads of household and thus increased the number of girls subject to such abuse. The report argues that in Zambia, as in many other countries, the government has provided inadequate protection for orphaned and poverty stricken girls, thus placing them in positions of jeopardy.

Civil and international wars and similar conflict situations in Africa are sadly common and these provide additional settings for violence against women, especially young women. Rape is a frequent occurrence in times of war, as indicated in a note in *The Asian Wall Street Journal*, "Girls as young as six are raped in Burundi by rebels, government troops and militiamen . . . .[45] "Congo's Warring Factions Leave a Trail of Rape," headlines the *New York Times.*[46] The Executive Director of UNIFEM reports that, "Increasingly, warring factions rely on systematic rape to terrorize opposing forces."[47]

The frequent use of children as soldiers and slaves by rebel groups is another aspect of conflict situations that impinges on young women and increases their vulnerability to HIV infection. In Angola, for example, "UNITA combatants sexually abused girls and assigned them as 'wives' to soldiers. Some were also forcibly given as 'comfort women' to visiting guests in UNITA-held areas during the war."[48] Similar reports come from Liberia, northern Uganda, and Sierra Leone. The situation for young women does not seem to be improved in post-war and refugee camp situations where they are highly vulnerable and dependent upon soldiers, peace-keepers, and camp officials.[49]

Recent reports of the enslavement of children to be used as farm laborers, domestic servants, and prostitutes and a growing sex trafficking situation indicate another form of violence that has important implications for the spread of HIV infection for women and girls.[50]

In trying to understand why HIV infection is increasingly becoming a problem for women in Africa, we have seen that biological, economic, social and cultural factors provide explanations. In addition to women being more vulnerable to HIV infection, the epidemic poses additional problems for women and girls.

HIV/AIDS: A Special Burden for Women

. In her frequent role as caregiver in the African family, HIV has brought heavier burdens to women. Hospitals and other institutional care facilities in most African countries are not able to accept the additional burden of large numbers of AIDS patients and thus the care of these persons falls completely to the home— and this usually means to the wife/mother or to one of the daughters. In addition to caring for the patient, the wife or daughter may find work loads increased in other ways. The male/female division of labor disintegrates, and work previously done by the male now falls to the female. As family income declines, costs for medicine are added. Nutrition levels go down and, to save money, daughters are withdrawn from school. The tendency to give precedence to the education of boys is widespread. Once out of school, the girl's chances of HIV infection are greatly increased due to the possibility of earlier marriage or onset of sexual activity, greater chances of sexual violence, and less ability to assert her right to say "no" when demands for sex are made or to control the conditions of sexual activity.

Mother to child transmission (MTCT) is another consideration for women who are HIV-positive. HIV-pregnant women can pass the infection to their unborn child, during delivery, and again through breast-feeding after birth. This places tremendous pressure on a woman and in some cases a psychological burden, a sense of guilt, as well. Although such transmissions can be reduced through the use of proper medication or the use of formula feeding, these are expensive and therefore unavailable options for most African mothers.

Conclusions

Although in the early years of the epidemic, HIV was thought to be a man's problem, in particular a gay man's problem, the virus has increasingly affected women and has reached the point in Africa that women are more affected than men. Biological differences play only a partial role in explaining the greater impact of HIV on women. The relatively weak position of women in society, in the economy, in law and in customs and social practice is a significant factor in this situation.

The purpose of this paper has been to provide an overview of the HIV/AIDS epidemic in Africa and to give a more specific discussion of the ways in which the epidemic is impinging on women and girls, but in closing we wish to indicate some of the directions that must be taken to reduce the effects of the epidemic on women. In the overall struggle against the HIV/AIDS epidemic, there must be a gender-specific component. Special attention must be given to women. In the long term, the best solution is the empowerment of women; the equalization of power is a necessity. Women must be able to say "NO" and have that backed up by law, society and culture. Women must have adequate economic independence to control their lives without being dependent on men.[51] Access to political power is a necessity.[52] But this solution will take much time, and in the interim hundreds of thousands of women will be infected. In the meantime, women must gain better access to education and thus to employment opportunities. Other interventions are needed to attack the problems we have discussed above. For examples, there must be stronger protection for those orphaned and made destitute by the effects of AIDS in their families, and community-based care systems must be devised to assist those families.

In addition to attacking the problem through social and cultural gender imbalances, there must be efforts to correct the biological imbalance. There is a need for widespread education for men and for women on the HIV process and the role safe sex can play in interrupting that process. The condom must become universal and men must be made to understand their role in the spread of this disease.

An important step will be taken when medical science devises the means for women to protect themselves; a prevention method that women can afford and control is a necessity. A protective vaccine would be a wonderful thing, but a microbicide that prevents the spread of HIV would be a very significant improvement over today's situation.

Chapter 9 Notes

1. See R. S. Bray, *Armies of Pestilence: The Impact of Disease on History.* (New York: Barnes and Noble, 1996).
2. See, for example, Ed Stoddard, "History Holds Clues to AIDS Impact on Africa", The Miami Herald, July 29, 2002 at www.miami.com.
3. The following section relies heavily on AVERT, "The History of AIDS", in 5 sections at http://www.avert.org/historyi.htm and AVERT, "So Little Time. . ." At the same address.
4. See UNFPA, "Population Numbers and Trends: HIV/AIDS: Impact and Prevention," at www.unfpa.org.
5. Noeleen Heyzer, "The Challenge to Sustainable Development in Africa: The Gender Dimension of HIV/AIDS, Peace and Economic Security," (presentation to ECOSOC, June 21, 2001). at www.unifem.undp.org/newsroom/speeches/ecosocJune21.html.
6. UNAIDS, "AIDS Epidemic Update, December 2002," p. 6 on CD, The Global HIV/AIDS Epidemic 2002-2003." (UNAIDS, 2003).
7. UNAIDS, "New UNAIDS Report Warns AIDS Epidemic Still in Early Phase and Not Leveling off in Worst Affected Countries," July 2, 2002 at www.unaids.org and Patricia Reaney, "Women Make up 50 Percent of AIDS Sufferers," November 26, 2002, Reuters at http://story.news.yahoo.com.
8. UNAIDS, Report on. . . op. cit., p. 23.
9. Ibid, p. 24.
10. See USAID. "HIV/AIDS in Uganda: A USAID Brief," July 2002", HIV/AIDS in Zambia: A USAID Brief," July 2002, and HIV/AIDS in Senegal: A USAID Brief," July 2002 at www.synergyaids.com.
11. UNAIDS, "UN Releases New Data Highlighting the Devastating Impact of AIDS in Africa," June 25,2002, press release at www.unaids.org; Peter Wehrwein, "AIDS Leaves Africa's Economic Future in Doubt," at www.cnn.com/SPECIALS/2000/aids/stories/ economic.impact; and, "AIDS: The Development Emergency," Africa Recovery, vol. 13, nos. 2/3, September 1999, p.30.
12. Ibid.
13. US. Agency for International Development (USAID). "HIV/AIDS in South Africa: A Country Profile," July 2002 at www.synergyaids.com and Ravi Nessman, "AIDS Main Killer of S. African Women", Associated Press, at cnn.news.com.
14. Ibid, "Namibia".
15. Ibid, "Zimbabwe".
16. Ibid, "Kenya".
17. Ibid, "Democratic Republic of the Congo".
18. Ibid, "Rwanda".
19. Ibid, "Nigeria".
20. US. National Intelligence Council (USNIC), "The Next Wave of HIV/AIDS: Nigeria, Ethiopia, Russia, India, and China," September 2002, pp. 7-23 at http://www.cia.gov.
21. USAID, Ibid, "Angola".
22. Ibid, "Ethiopia".
23. Ibid.
24. Ibid, pp. 7-23.

25. World Health Organization, "Women and Aids: Fact Sheet 242," June 2000 at www. who.int/inf-fs/en/fact242.html.

26. Ibid, 1.

27. Ibid, .1-2.

28. GEM is calculated for many countries in the UNDP, Human Development Report, 2002 available on line at htttp://www.undp.org.

29. HDI, GDI and GEM are described in the useful chapter by Virginia DeLancey, "The Economies of Africa," in April A. Gordon and Donald L. Gordon, Understanding Contemporary Africa, 3rd Ed.(Boulder, CO: Lynne Rienner, 2001) 127-129.

30. Ibid.

31. Ibid, 271-298.

32. Catherine A. Russell and Mark W. DeLancey, "African Women in Cabinet Positions— Too Few, Too Weak: A Research Report," Asian Women, vol.15 (2002), 147.

33. Table "E Young People 2" in UNAIDS, The Global HIV/AIDS Epidemic 2002-2003, CD.

34. USAIDS, Ibid, "Eritrea."

35. Commonwealth Secretariat. Gender Affairs, "HIV AIDS: An Inherent Gender Issue" 2000.

36. USAID. Op.cit, HIV/AIDS briefs for Mozambique, Ethiopia, Tanzania, Zimbabwe, and Kenya.

37. N. Luke and K. Kurz, "Cross-Generational and Transactional Sexual Relations in Sub-Saharan Africa: Prevalence of Behavior and Implications for Negotiating Safer Sexual Practices," 2002, Eldis Dossiers, at www.eldis.org.

38. Imani L Winga, "Why AIDS Takes Heavy Toll on Women," Business Times (Dar Salaam), April 4, 2003; Brian Ligomeka, "Malawi Fights Wife Inheritance," Malawi Standard, April 23, 2003; and Mathias Ringa, "HIV/AIDS: Men Urged to Shun Risky Activities," East African Standard (Nairobi), April 6, 2003 all at www.allAfrica.com.

39. "FGM in Africa: Statistics," at www.fgmnetwork.org/intro/stats.html.

40. December Green, Gender Violence in Africa.(New York: St. Martin's Press, 1999).

41. Table "E-Young People 2 eps," in the CD UNAIDS, The Global HIV/AIDS Epidemic 2002-2003. reporting data from a survey conducted by the Kaiser Family Foundation.

42. Michael A. Koenig et al, "Domestic Violence in Rural Uganda: Evidence from a Community-based Study," Bulletin of the World Health Organization, vol. 81, no. 1 (January 2003), p. 53.

43. Ibid., p. 59.

44. Human Rights Watch, "Suffering in Silence: The Links between Human Rights Abuses and HIV Transmission in Zambia." (London: Human Rights Watch, 2002), 1-2.

45. Asian Wall Street Journal, April 30, 2003, 1.

46. Somini Sengupta, 'Congo's Warring Factions Leave a Trail of Rape," New York Times, June 9, 2003 at www.nytimes.com/2003/06/09/international/africa/09cong.

47. Noleen Heyzer, "Facing the Challenges: Commitments for the Future," June 21, 2001 at www.unifem.undp.org/newsroom/speeched/ecosoc/June01.html.

48. Jim Lobe, "Child Soldiers Abandoned in Angola", Oneworld US, April 29, 2003, found at www.Oneworld.net.

49. UNAIDS, "Gender and HIV", p. 4.

50. See, for example, "SA Sex Trafficking Widespread", (BBC News, April 1, 2003) at http://newsvote.bbc.co.uk.

51. See Kati Marton, "Protect Women, Stop a Disease", *International Herald Tribune*, (March 4, 2003) at www.iht.com/articles/88504.html.
52. See the excellent report by Sheila Smith and Desmond Cohen, "Gender, Development and the HIV Epidemic", October 2000 at www.undp.org/hiv/publications/gender /gendere.htm.

Chapter 10

Girls and Women, Violence and Male Privilege

Anne Breneman

In examining violence against girls and women, one becomes aware of how the victims of male violence are conditioned from infancy to understand the power, privilege and authority which accrue to males from birth in patriarchal societies. Sandra Bem suggests that, it is through experiences and interactions with members of the opposite sex in families and play groups and watching television or movies, playing video games and receiving multiple *"meta-messages"* from the public environment that patriarchy is established as a central organizing principle. However minute such interactions may seem, these can have a powerful influence on how one views oneself in relation to all others. Indeed to become empowered as a woman is to reverse in effect the multitude of disempowering *"meta-messages"* and relationships which have socialized each member of society into a patriarchal, male dominant consciousness.[1]

From a symbolic interactionist perspective,[2] it is at the micro-level of society that individual identity and concepts of personal effectiveness form within one's social group and culture. Through daily interactions within one's primary reference group, the family, and secondary reference groups- peers, school and community- gender values and expectations are conveyed and internalized. A young girl who has been the victim of male sexual privilege within her family and the young boy who witnesses such interactions internalize at an early age a primary patriarchal assumption: women are subordinate to the needs and whims of men. Similarly both female victims of domestic beatings and silent juvenile witnesses are provided with a traumatic lesson of how patriarchy works.[3] When women who act in self-defense are apprehended, imprisoned and sometimes raped by prison guards, the lethal lessons of patriarchy are deeply internalized, both by the victims and those who witness through the process of *"social learning."*[4] Women are viewed as the weaker sex, who deserve ill treatment as inmates to reinforce their awareness of the traditional power configuration.

Objectification of Women

The objectification of women is to a large extent what makes it possible for males, who otherwise may consider themselves to be "decent and respectable" members of society, to become capable of violence towards girls and women. For example, upon hearing a 16 year old male speak of the rape of a 14 year old female classmate by several older high school boys in terms of, "She was asking for it," one can perceive the way such a violent crime is dismissed as not only the fault of the victim, but as a natural and necessary display of the older boys' virility. In this particular case, little more was mentioned in the town's newspaper or in the streets, of the heinous crime, its perpetrators or the victim, so ordinary is such an interaction between privileged males and subordinate females.

When media clips, advertising such mundane products as cars, toothpaste, soap, shampoo, and menstrual pads or tampons, are accompanied by a fanfare of female sexiness, women become objectified as sexual stimulants for the male dominant population, rather than as individuals worthy of dignity and respect. Western advertisements for clothing similarly focus on women's body parts and sexual attraction, creating a "meta-message" that females are indeed little else than playthings, degrading their capacities as intelligent, capable human beings and fellow citizens in a civilized society which presumes to value human rights for all.

Girls growing up in war-ravaged countries, or who are sold by their parents to prostitution ringmasters in poverty-stricken areas, or forced out into the streets by violent, drugged, abusive family members, are among the most vulnerable members of the world community. The way this happens has been reported by diverse groups, from agencies of the UN to Jehovah's Witness and Covenant House advocates- and described poignantly by women writers who have become empowered to share their stories with others. Unfortunately the growing number of female juvenile delinquents entering the criminal justice system can often be traced to abusive homes, according to researcher, Chesney-Lind, who attributes the trend partly to an extensive focus on disadvantaged males by the media. Girls who are victimized by abuse often run away from home only to find more violent treatment in the streets. As in many countries of the world, the criminal justice system is often insensitive to the fact that such girls have entered the system more as victims than criminals. She believes that the detention centers of the U.S. are filling up with girls who should be provided with opportunities for counseling and rehabilitation instead.[5]

In a recent news flash on National Public Radio, the U.S. was reported to have the highest record of sex trafficking in the world.[6] This should not be surprising since sexuality and violence have been the major focus of the great majority of popular shows on television, pornographic videos and many best-selling music cds in the US. The lack of regulation of pornography and hence the wide promotion of it has transmitted the meta-message that in a "free society" any immoral act is one's private business, leaving the victims without protection and the predators free to continue their sordid and often violent activities.

What makes a young girl so vulnerable? It may be a feminine desire to be loved, valued and cherished. When an older male shows interest in her, a girl is likely to respond with a smile and an offer to help him. If the male seems to need her affection, a girl may innocently offer kisses or hugs, arousing sexual desire in the male before the young girl understands that the "*attention*" being shown is not necessarily in her as a person, but in her as a sexual being.[7] The result is often shocking and demeaning to the young girl, who gradually learns that what males want from her is not what she is willing to give and that she has become "unclean" by allowing herself to be used as a sexual object. It would be unusually precocious for a young girl to possess the complexities of consciousness, experience and information required to express to a trusted person what is happening to her, without shame. Therefore it is likely that the great majority of such experiences are not told, even within a family. Yet the damage to a young girl's self-image and psyche can be far-reaching.

Many women growing up in American society and elsewhere have experienced such sexual overtures from older males.[8] These overtures may take the form of extra hand squeezes, touching of personal body parts, offering of promises, money and gifts, asking a girl to sit in his lap or to touch his body, and various forms of sexual stimulation. Because those who request or demand such inappropriate attention are older males with power and authority, young girls quickly learn that they are powerless to protect themselves from such attention, especially when they are threatened with further violence if they report what has happened to a parent or authority figure. One of the major concerns of Black women both during and after slavery was the protection of their daughters and themselves from such unwanted advances, which combined with the advantage of White power, often moved from molestation to rape, regardless of age or marital status.[9]

A Double Standard

In some families older brothers or cousins may molest or rape younger female family members, infants, toddlers, or school girls, with only mild reprimand from adult family members, who are themselves familiar with the pattern of male privilege. Supporting social myths are heard frequently by girls; "Men must have their way," and "Boys must sow their wild oats," or "Boys cannot control themselves." A particularly wrenching case was that of a school teacher whose husband would occasionally find her after work curled in a fetal position in a corner of the house in a catatonic condition. Therapy revealed that as a toddler, she had been used by her older brother and his friends as an introduction to sexual experience, pushed into a closet and repeatedly raped. Further she was threatened to not reveal to her parents the trauma of her experiences. Unfortunately such cases are not uncommon.

In countless ways, some subtle and others more overt, American boys are socialized to believe that they must prove their manhood by successfully and often forcefully thrusting themselves sexually upon girls, whether willing or not.[10] In the past, when virginity was a more common value, boys were encouraged to "sow their wild oats" among girls who were from subordinate cultural groups so as to preserve the sexual purity of those within the marriageable group of young virgins. Married men in America and other societies similarly sought extramarital experiences from subordinate groups of women prostitutes. In a very real sense, the habits of male privilege are linked intimately, and are even dependent upon, racial, ethnic and class inequalities.[11]

In this double standard, practiced in many patriarchal societies, males are not held to religious teachings and cultural standards regarding sexual purity prior to and within marriage. However, they are expected to choose a bride who has adhered to such religious standards. In this value system, those girls who have been the sexual partners of young men "sowing wild oats" are automatically dismissed as marriage partners. The "wild oats" refer to sperm which has been planted without regard for moral standards and for which the owner is hence not responsible. Although many standards regarding sexual purity before marriage have slackened since the Sixties in western countries, a lingering value assumption may contribute to the American problem of male responsibility for offspring born out of wedlock, though there are also divorced fathers who conveniently forget to support their own children.

During America's increasing renunciation of responsibility for moral standards, the birthrate of children born out of wedlock has grown to more than 33 percent, leaving both mothers and children at the greatest risk for poverty and HIV/AIDS infection.[12] As a multicultural society, America has in general taken the position that the exercise of sexuality and morality is a matter of relativity, depending on one's point of view, culture, religion or non-religion. This meta-message has created a receptive social environment for violence toward girls and women, as well as the spread of HIV/AIDS virus.

With the growth of HIV/AIDS virus, such moral ambivalence, whether in America, Europe, Asia or Africa, may have lethal consequences for the hapless participants, who often have no idea how many sexual partners have preceded their own tryst with a current boyfriend. Not surprisingly, those women who are promiscuous also suffer psychologically from chronic bouts with depression, timidity, and low self-esteem. Could this be prevented by high school parenting classes and a greater emphasis on moral standards in sex education for both sexes?

Violence and the Vulnerability of Girl Children

When one considers the nature and logic of human rights, it becomes clear that a child needs support, nurturing and protection not only to survive, but to prosper and develop its full potential. To grow up instead with the knowledge that those who have been appointed to nurture, protect and encourage its well being are in effect condoning and participating in exploitation through force and violence is to guarantee unhappiness, cynicism, and tendency toward self-deprecation and often, suicide.

The vulnerability of all children from infancy has been a concern of the UN since it's founding. However, the women's movement has increased awareness of how traditional gender values in many countries can result in female infanticide, female genital mutilation, molestation, rape, and neglect of nutrition, education, and childhood needs for play and nurturance. In an NGO report on the progress of women since Beijing, the Working Group on Girls (WGG) point out that grouping girls into a monolithic category of ages 0-18 has the effect of blinding policy makers to the very different needs and vulnerabilities of each developmental stage. They recommend a disaggregation of research instruments and findings into at least three stages of the life cycle: infant and preschool girls, school-aged girls, and adolescent girls.[13]

Infant and preschool girls need nurturing and safe environments so that their physical, emotional, social, and cognitive potentials are fully developed without interruption.[14.] They also need protection in many areas of the world from infanticide, a practice which can take the form of abortion, starvation or neglect. In some extreme cases, unwanted female infants have been sold or discarded by parents to unscrupulous agents of prostitution rings, trafficked across borders and drugged, similar to chickens going to a market, to be raised by a pimp for the sexual gratification of wealthy, predatory males fearing HIV/AIDS virus.[15] As horrific as such incidents seem, WGG has found that dangers to girls increase as they move into school ages 6-12. This group, worldwide, is at high risk for AIDS infection, drugs, prostitution and other forms of exploitation. In addition, the freedom and encouragement to develop talents, skills and aspirations in good schools is often disrupted by the imposition of heavy household and childcare responsibilities, unequal to those expected of their brothers.

When reaching adolescence, girls ages 13-19 represent more than 10 percent of all women in the world who are giving birth. According to WGG, adolescent girls. . .

> face a high possibility of developmental and life-threatening dangers: early marriage, early pregnancy and maternal mortality, trafficking, sexual and other interdependent high-risk behaviors. As young females in families incapacitated by HIV/AIDS, girls also face the possibility of being forced to become heads of households while still children.[16]

In examining the situation of girls in diverse societies around the world, NGOs report that it may be difficult for those in industrialized nations to understand how girls who are over 14 are perceived as adults by their societies. Many countries, such as Senegal, the Philippines, Brazil, Peru, China and India, see early entry into the labor market empowering for young girls, as long as the work is not prostitution or domestic employment, which are recognized as among the worst forms of child labor and exploitation. Some of the NGOs in these countries have developed working movements for children which assist them in understanding their rights and in organizing to enforce their rights in various workplaces in relationship to their employers. However, some countries reported an increase of multiple violence against girls, differing from culture to culture, but often having lifelong psychological damage. Listed were: female genital mutilation (FGM), rape, incest , honor killings, acid throwing and prostitution. Among the results are death, HIV/AIDS, low self-esteem, and repetition of patterns of abuse toward girls as brothel owners, employers of domestic servants, or even mothers-in-law. A spokeswoman for WGG suggests that such combinations of violence can force girls into further risky behaviors:

> Stripped of self-respect and disempowered, unprotected and unable to protect themselves, many girls engage in "survival sex", high risk sexual behavior with multiple partners, in return for security such as housing, food, or small sums of

money.[17]

In Search of Solutions

Although there clearly are no easy solutions to the growing number of girls who are becoming objects of male violence, the low levels of education and information about the subject of male privilege and human sexuality creates vulnerability which can be remedied through more effective educational programs for girls as well as boys. Some of these educational programs will only succeed if they have an outreach component which connects the school to the home and family life, assisting families to make structural changes to protect and nurture girl children as equals to their brothers. Fathers, and indeed all males, such as those reported in some South African communities,[18] must be willing to relinquish male sexual privilege over all girl children within their households.

Health care for young girls must go hand in hand with health education. It is insufficient to simply treat girls for the outcomes of their vulnerability. It is essential that from an early age girls learn about their sexuality, their bodies, their human rights, and how to prevent or cope with aggressive male advances and assaults. Rather than continuing to assault and exploit girls, male family members, from boyhood, need formal sex education classes which teach them how to respect, encourage and empower girls as equal partners rather than as "comfort women" and sex objects.

At the governmental level, NGOs are working with policy makers to empower women as leaders and decision-makers through political appointments and training. UNIFEM offers workshops for governments in the development and funding of national plans of action (NPAs) and agencies which work to improve conditions and policies leading to violence against girls and women. As these plans of action are reported to the UN Secretary General and various UN agencies, such as UNIFEM, the outcomes are reviewed by WGG and problems identified for further action.

Often the overseeing process has resulted in highlighting the difference between what is supposed to happen and what actually is happening as a result of lack of funding, cultural lag, political infighting or active resistance to change involving girls. The most effective NPAs are those. . . "that provide substantive and specific Plans of Action relating to girls," according to WGG's review of 120 National Plan of Action summaries for the Beijing +5 Conference in New York. Notably Mynamar addressed sex trafficking of girls, while India created a plan for the reduction of infanticide as part of their respective NPAs.

In general, WGG looked for evidence of each nation's serious commitment to girls through. . .

    (a) a wide coverage of the strategic objectives of the Beijing Platform,

    (b) a holistic approach to eliminating violence against girls,

    (c) or significant and well-developed individual sectorial programs.[19]

Using these measures, WGG found a number of divergent nations which appeared to have more than average concern for the welfare of girls and women Australia, New Zealand, Norway, Palestine, Uganda, and Vietnam. Their NPAs included such objectives as collecting gender specific data on childhood, gender-sensitive teacher training (Palestine), supporting educational programs for girls in difficult circumstances such as refugee camps (Uganda), encouragement of rural families to send their daughters to school (Vietnam), creation of technology to identify pedophiliac networks used to exploit children (Norway), and recognition of the special needs of girls throughout their life cycles in planning (Australia).

From an individual and community standpoint, besides the education of girls and resocialization of boys into an egalitarian relationship with the opposite sex, one can seek to raise the level of discourse on gender violence to the level of spiritual principle. This can become complicated when one is culture bound, seeing religion through a lens which prefers males to females throughout the history of religious practice. At the level of spiritual principle, however, it is possible to see that the advancement of consciousness regarding human relationships is largely the expression of increased levels of understanding of the teachings brought by the great Prophets throughout the ages and the corresponding efforts of followers to put them into practice. Unfortunately such efforts have often been hindered by misguided interpretations of the teachings themselves. Further advancements in civilization, however, have permitted greater measures of implementation of social teachings, such as those concerning marriage, family, education and childrearing. The current awareness and concern for girl children, for example, has been sparked by a greater adherence to principles of education, equality and justice, along with individual human rights and freedoms, all of which have derived ultimately from religious values and beliefs. Throughout traditional societies, prior to the birth of industrialization and material civilization, it has been common to respect women as bearers of children and managers of households, even as marketers, gardeners and traders or bringers of delight as musicians, poets and dancers, however restricted such roles were conceived. Respect is a sentiment which arises from a spiritual consciousness which also values such universal principles as integrity, honor, trustworthiness, friendship, humility and concern for the well being of others. Religion served to cultivate such standards in communities and individuals, creating a certain self-discipline, however male centered.

As religious belief systems have crumbled in the face of industrialization, materialism, individualism, and the pursuit of selfish gratification— objectification of human beings, including those most vulnerable- girl children, has increased exponentially.[20] The same global economy which has produced untold wealth and extravagant lifestyles has also distributed the wealth, privilege and power in such a way that only the most aggressive, greedy and ruthless are encouraged to acquire it and use it for their own selfish gain, with some noteworthy exceptions.[21] The masses of humanity, including girls who are the victims of sexual trafficking and male privilege, continue to work longer hours than ever for enough to provide for their families, and to protect themselves from further violence and indignity.

Has the baby been thrown out with the bathwater? This commonly heard query can be applied to the western model of modernization, which has overvalued material benefits and undervalued spiritual consciousness. But perhaps it is too easy to use the West, or even capitalism, as a scapegoat. While Karl Marx's analysis of the process by which capitalism objectifies and commercializes most, if not all, human life is brilliant and insightful, Marx's remedial proposals in practice have tended to create a similar over valuing of the economic sector. That is, the institutions associated with the State, which ideally were to be the distributors of equal goods and services for all, became the new bourgeoisie or privileged upper crust of society, under the guise of the Communist Party. Marx erred by ignoring the broader picture of society.[22] Nonetheless, social science is somewhat indebted to Marx for his scathing analysis of the process by which raw capitalism, with its seemingly innocent claim to be simply pursuing prosperity, has the effect of transforming even children into objects to be evaluated for their profit-making possibilities, as in sexual trafficking. All that was sacred in traditional societies is reduced to a simplistic evaluation of its financial value, regardless of its aesthetic, social, or human worth. Yet it was in a communist nation, where a busload of infant girls packed in nylon tote bags recently were found by police to be on their way to market. Although the scale of the female infant trade isn't known, China's Justice ministry reported that a three-month crackdown in 2000 resulted in the discovery of 10,000 female infants, who had been "abducted, abandoned or sold by their parents."[23] Clearly neither political ideologies nor economic systems are inherently adequate to resolve the problem of violence against girls and women, or of the tendency for the strong to seek advantage over the weak.

Some Theoretical Perspectives

On the other hand, Max Weber, another social scientist widely touted for his insightful theories of society, though intrigued by Marx's passionate condemnation of the inroads of capitalism with the spread of industrialization, considered his approach too one-dimensional with its myopic focus on the relationship between human society and the means of production. He preferred to look at all of the social forces and sectors of society as operating together to create a certain *zeitgeist*. In this case, violence can best be analyzed within the mesh of operating social, political, economic and religious forces.[24] Within such a complex maze the pathology of violence may become rather difficult to track,

Emile Durkheim tended to use a more functionalist approach in examining how each element of a society operates to maintain a certain equilibrium, engaging in social change only when faced with disruption great enough to force it out of its natural inertia. He contributed the concept of "*anomie*", proposing that rapid changes, such as those brought about through industrialization, could create enough disruption to produce psychological confusion, or anomie, regarding norms, mores and traditional values.[25] Some researchers have pursued the hypothesis that the abnormal violence experienced in the West by women, girls and youth could be related to this anomie or confusion, while others have attributed it to unresolved racism and sexism intrinsic to patriarchal systems.[26]

To make use of Bem's concept of *meta-messages* which assault the subconscious as subliminal messages, patriarchal incentives for violence would need to be counteracted by equally powerful incentives to practice equality and to empower women and girls rather than seek an advantage over them. Such *meta-messages* need to be as consistent as those that disempower members of the female sex and encourage the molestation, rape and exploitation of females as sexual objects. That is, the entire media industry, worldwide and within each nation and community, can be viewed as playing a significant role in marketing women as sex objects and recreational playthings, so powerfully that many girls and women become themselves convinced of their limited worth as human beings.

A less often used perspective in understanding how violence has become so insidiously prevalent against females is that of religion. This is perhaps because more often religion is blamed for the promotion of sexism and patriarchy. And, of course, religions of the past have been thought guilty of watering down spiritual principles with traditional practices, which have been permeated to a great extent with assumptions of male superiority and privilege in relation to women.[27] However, to dismiss the role of religion altogether with its consciousness-raising powers, is to "throw out the baby with the bathwater," as a popular saying suggests. Might we not turn to spiritual principles for some solutions to violence, promiscuity, mistreatment of girls and women, double standards, and the spread of the HIV/AIDS virus?

To look to spiritual solutions is not to ignore the enlightenment brought by well-designed research and adherence to individual human rights and freedoms. Nor is it to suggest that local, regional, and national responsibilities should be ignored. Rather, spiritual approaches to reducing violence against women and children can open the door for the development of greater individual responsibility for the respect and dignity of every human being as well as for a standard of gender equality. In order for the multitude of legal, social and economic approaches to have enduring effects, something within the nature of human consciousness itself must be altered. What other force is adequate to such a need than ethical or spiritual principle which has become internalized?

It must be admitted that the traditional arrangements of many societies, though not all, have simply adhered to a division of labor in which the domestic is separated more or less from the public sphere and often made subordinate to it as well.[28] Quite simplistically assumptions have been made that the role of woman must be singular, one associated with maternity—nurturance, caretaking, food preparation and the like, with various exceptions, such as African farming and marketing and Native American agriculture. Males on the other hand are cultivated as hunters, warriors, chiefs, priests, politicians and athletes in many traditional societies, often quite separately from females. Some of the extremes of these arrangements can result in such rigidity that women or girls who venture alone outside of the women's assigned areas are subject to the worst forms of violence—not only rape, but gang rape.[29] The mind reels at the thought of what kind of meta-messages are emitted to participants and bystanders regarding the consequences of violating gender norms which have been thought of as religiously sanctioned. The cruelty and inhumanity of such actions could be easily transferred to an interpretation of the actions of those clergy in more complex western societies who, in a gesture of patriarchal self indulgence and privilege, have molested children and youth of both genders within their congregational flocks.

Would the presence of a greater proportion of women in religious leadership create a significant alteration of patterns of clerical sexual abuse? That is, could violence be interpreted as an extension and abuse of male power and privilege, or an abuse of power and privilege of any kind? Is a capacity for such violence inherent in the human psyche? If so, could not the opposite be intrinsic to human nature as well, that is, the capacity for peaceful resolution of conflict, control of anger, tolerance of differences, inclusiveness and acceptance of varying viewpoints?

Most of the world's religions have taught some variant of the Golden Rule, that one should treat *others* as one would like to be treated. The problem seems to have arisen in the definition of *"otherness."* That is, if religion is perceived as only addressing men—but not women, or Whites—but not Blacks, or northerners—but not southerners, or one's own countrymen—but not foreigners, or those of one's own clan, tribe or religion—but not strangers, heathen or infidels—then it becomes possible by arbitrary definition to ignore this basic and universal religious rule for harmonious human relations, beginning within the family and spiraling outward to concentric circles of personal relationship and proximity. Who then is responsible for failing to apply the Golden Rule with all of its implications for egalitarian relations to relations both within and without the family and across gender? Could it be leaders of religions, clergy, some of whom are even now inciting exclusive and violent behaviors towards *"others."* Such *others* have included at times women and members of other nations, tribes and religious groups. One is led to wonder whether religion's value lies in its hierarchical ranking of men, in its capacity to conquer and subdue the enemy *other*, to acquire the greatest wealth and numbers of followers, or to perform ancient rituals. However, I would be remiss in omitting the observation that liberal beliefs and trends have influenced some exceptional clerics to lead their flocks toward a more inclusive, egalitarian view of humanity and social structure. Dr Martin Luther King, Jr. is one such cleric, and exceptions can be found in every religion.

It is conceivable that notions of superiority and inferiority have stemmed from this most basic attribution of the inequality of women and men, accepted as fact and confirmed by the speech and behavior of most of the religious communities of the world until recently.[30] Scholars have interpreted this fundamental inequality in religious traditions differently. Bahá'í scholars, Janet and Peter Khan, propose that while the original teachings and examples of the Prophet-Founders of the major world religions in the past have not explicitly advocated gender equality, the followers of these religions have adapted them to their pre-existing cultural preferences, often based more upon a biologically driven division of labor with a Darwinian spin. That is, women have been viewed in many traditional cultures as having the primary sacred function of bearing children, especially sons, and preparing food for the patriarchal family. Judaism, Hinduism and Islam support this concept scripturally, while Buddhism has given rise to more egalitarian family arrangements in Southeast Asian cultures such as Malaysia, Singapore and Thailand. Christ's example and teachings didn't specifically support gender inequality, but the Judaic traditions into which it was interpreted by its early exponents supplied the superior vs. inferior beliefs and practices.[31]

An exception to this pattern can be found in the most recently revealed world religion, the Bahá'í Faith, based upon the teachings of Bahá'u'lláh. His teachings call for the full recognition and practice of gender and racial equality by all members, the prioritization of the education of girls, the abolishment of all priesthood and the full participation of women in all aspects of community life, including election to leadership on administrative bodies. Since these teachings are not adjustments, interpretations and social updates to what has already been established practice, the culture of existing and developing communities throughout the world based upon Bahá'í teachings provide intriguing models of developing egalitarian communities to be studied.

Other Models of Nonviolence

Anthropologists have discovered and studied Malaysian "Orangasli" tribes of aborigines living in the interiors of the Malay Peninsula who raise their children to be peaceful, nonviolent, noncompetitive members of families and communities. In searching earnestly for alternatives to male violence and privilege engendered within patriarchal societies, such examples and possibilities cannot be overlooked and dismissed as insignificant.[32]

Other processes which have proved effective in reducing gender violence and inequality have been community workshops led by trained facilitators under the Oxfam grant program.[33] Participants act out various village authored scenarios which occur within families of their respective cultures, followed by group identification of harmful assumptions, values and habits expressed within intergender relationships. Skits are then performed incorporating new behaviors and assumptions into relationships within the family. Malaysia, Bolivia, Cameroon and Nigeria were among the targeted communities.

The United Nations and its agencies have become key sponsors and advocates of change at both the grassroots and national levels by organizing groups of women and men to identify harmful practices in their own countries and communities, and proposing solutions and resources needed to implement the programs of change. National accountability has become one of the keys to enforcing, funding and following up on the effectiveness of such programs. UN Secretary-General, Koffi Anan utilizes the UN Secretariat to review the progress of national plans to implement commitments to gender equality during specific time frameworks. Other UN agencies sponsor training for government workers and grassroots organizations on how to create gender sensitive policies and budgets to implement them.[34]

An example of how women's empowerment can influence the course of human happiness was featured recently by a newspaper in the U.S. In Shunyi, China, according to a March 2004 article,[35] both criminals and children of criminals have been traditionally considered unworthy of any community or state assistance. Rather the children suffer neglect, abuse, and vulnerability by their communities. Many such children become homeless drifters, victims of crime, prostitutes and criminals. A divorced mother of two children who served as one of China's *"barefoot doctors,"* traveling from village to village to deliver basic health care which often included abortions under China's one-child policy, became concerned about the children of the incarcerated. She opened a private shelter to care for this neglected population of children and expanded it to three such shelters. Children ten years and older work the farm lands to produce fruits and vegetables which help to support approximately 600 children. Her program for the children includes education, prison visits and phone calls, communal chores and clothes washing. Her project arose out of her compassion, as well as from her education and experience. The results are unique in her country, where the government, unaccustomed to nonprofit philanthropies, is likely to offer more financial and legal support as Zhang ShuQin's efforts result in lowered crime and victimization rates among children of those incarcerated.

Michael Penn and Rahel Nardos review the steps taken toward gender equality from the nineteenth to the twenty-first centuries and the role of the United Nations in promoting the full participation of women in developing new standards of human relationship throughout the world.[36] Their research examines the prevalence of structural violence towards women and girls as one of the 12 areas of critical concern in the United Nations 1995 Beijing Platform.[37] Penn and Nardos point out that efforts to eradicate such violence have been mainly focused on international law and human rights, while overlooking the ". . . magnitude of change necessary . . . inasmuch as violence against women and girls is sustained by long-standing, maladaptive practices of thinking and relating, legal strategies, unaccompanied by efforts to address the intrapersonal dimensions of the problem, are likely to prove ineffective."[38]

It is Penn's view that an international moral education project known as the Authenticity Project offers significant approaches to solving problems of gender violence through the cultivation of human consciousness and values associated with authentic relationships with others. He argues that all human qualities can be strengthened or weakened by training and thus aggression and violence should not be accepted as immutable characteristics of being human. Using examples of slavery and women's subordination, he suggests that in the past centuries these were not considered immoral behaviors but rather were widely condoned until the 19th century. Subsequently the capacity and volition of the collective human consciousness has gradually led to a degree of discomfort with the idea of willful subordination of one people, or one individual, to another. This discomfort has been sufficient to spark social movements, change laws, and create new ideals and standards for human relationship based upon a more egalitarian vision.

Each of the aforementioned efforts to understand and tackle the ancient problem of violence against women and girls offers a measure of hope. We find ourselves wanting to believe that the existence of an aboriginal tribe in Malaysia which continues to socialize their children to live in harmony with all others and above all to avoid violent confrontations, the continued work of the United Nations to encourage, support, and organize a global campaign to eradicate violence against women and girls, and the deep analysis of human behavior leading to both violence and peace by the Authenticity Project will ultimately create capacity for progress in this thorny and universal issue. Yet, if we are able to succeed in reducing and eventually eradicating violence toward women and girls, can we not tackle the issue of violence against all humanity?

Ending Violence against All Humanity

As the cofounder of the Singapore women's movement remarked in 1960, "The world's modern yardstick measures the greatness of a country according to the heights to which women have arisen. If women are kept in subjection, then to that extent the country is considered backward."[39] To a great extent, violence against women can be reduced by the empowerment of women through education, equality of opportunity and treatment within the workplace, along with greater participation in leadership and governance. Thus as women play a greater role in decision-making, there will be more emphasis on developing human resources, multiplying opportunities for education and employment, planning creative activities for children, utilizing the energies of youth and reducing official support of violence and conflict as methods of problem-solving.

Within the family unit, where the seeds of violence find their first expression in oppressive, abusive actions towards others, women can learn to educate both sons and daughters in nonviolent approaches to disputes and tolerance of differences, whether of gender, race, nationality or religion. Respect for all human beings everywhere can be taught along with spiritual character. The most enduring changes are those which begin at the roots, within the individual and the family, and spread gradually throughout every branch and twig of human society. In this process, not even one cell is left without the potent nourishment rising from the roots. The social environment, government policies, education, religious community and other external forces can provide the water and light which then nurture and protect the growing sapling from threats to its full development and production of blossoms and fruits. Gradually a culture of nonviolence which not only prevents fearful and paralyzing actions and words, but one which inspires and encourages a culture of human prosperity becomes possible.

Chapter 10 Notes

1. Meta-messages are conveyed pervasively to members of a society through media, social structure, patterned behaviors and relationships. See Sandra Bem, "Enculturated Lens Theory of Gender Formation" in *The Lenses of Gender: Transforming the Debate on Sexual Inequality* (New Haven, CT: Yale University Press, 1993) 139.
2. For further discussion of "symbolic interactionist theory" refer to the works of George Mead, Herbert Cooley & Erving Goffman at the following websites: http://spartan. ac.brocku.ca/%7Elward/Mead/mead_biblio.html; http://spartan.ac.brocku.ca/ %7Elward/ Cooley/cool_bib.html; http://people.brandeis.edu/~teuber/goffmanbio.html;

3. See Chapter 3 Beatriz Ferreira.

4. For more information on Alfred Bandura's, "Social Learning Theory" visit: http://www.mhhe.com/socscience/comm/bandur-s.mhtml.

5. Meda Chesney-Lind, "The Female Offender" cited in *Deviance, Crime and Social Control, Sociology*, 5th ed. (Prentice Hall: NJ: John Farley, 2003) 269.

6. "Fresh Air," National Public Radio, US, January 26, 2004.

7. See, for example, Maya Angelou's, *I Know Why the Caged Bird Sings*. (1968; reissue, New York, Toronto; Random House, 1970).

8. (face to face interviews), Patricia Tjaden and Nancy Thoennes, "Prevalence, Incidence, and Consequences of Violence Against Women" (Washington, DC: National Institute of Justice, 2000); Susan Brownmiller, *Against Our Will* (1975; reprint, New York, Toronto: Ballantine, 1993); Michael Ghiglieri, *The Dark Side of Man*, (New York; Perseus, 1999).

9. Giddings, *When and Where I Enter*.

10. Andrew Hatcher, "The Fragility of Masculinity" in *Mismatch: the Growing Gulf Between Women & Men*, (New York: Scribner, 2003).

11. Note for example recent public discourses in the US regarding a prominent US senator's early sexual involvement with a young servant girl, resulting in and interracial daughter who after a life of secret diplomacy regarding her father's identity, revealed her true identity only after her father's death. Colonialism and militarism have also promoted the concepts of male sexual privilege, particularly in relation to the subdued, conquered or occupied populations, who were at the mercy of the more dominant males.

12. Bureau of the Census, US 2001: "Fertility of American Women."

13. WGG, "Girls 2000: NGOs Report on Progress since Beijing", 6-7.

14. See Girl Interrupted, a book about a young girl whose innocence and girlhood was violated by a male teacher who kissed her on the lips, causing her to drift into what became a psychological disorder that changed the course of her life.

15. Joe McDonald "For Sale: baby girl, unwanted, cheap: illegal trade thrives in China," *Richmond Times Dispatch: Associated Press*, 3/26/2003, A7. (The article reported discovery of 28 baby girls, three months & less, packed in nylon tote bags and being transported on a long-distance bus in southern China. A three-month national crackdown in 2000 resulted in the rescue of 10,000 babies from female infant trafficking).

16. WGG, "Girls 2000":, Beijing +5, June 2000, 7.

17. Ibid.7.

18. See, for example, Chapter 9, Moletsani & Delancey.

19. WGG, "Girls 2000", 21.

20. Al Santoli, "Fighting Child Prostitution" *Freedom Review*, 1994, Vol 25: No 5, 5-8; Christopher Janus, "Slavery Abolished? Only Officially" *Christian Science Monitor*, 5/17/1996.

21. UN Development Program 2000; Jeffrey Kentor, "The Long-Term Effects of Globalization on Income Inequality, Population Growth, & Economic Development." *Social Problems*, Vol 48: 4, 11/2001, 435-55; Cynthia M. Duncan, *Worlds Apart: Why Poverty Persists in Rural America* (New Haven: Yale University Press, 1999).

22. Karl Marx and F. Engels, *The Communist Manifesto* (1848, reprint Mass Market Paperback: Signet Classics, 1995).

23. McDonald, *Richmond Times Dispatch*, A7.

24. Max Weber, *Economy and Society*, orig in German 1922, (New York: Bedminister Press, 1968).

25. Emile Durkheim, *Suicide: a Study in Sociology*, orig in Fr 1897, (Glencoe, IL: Free

Press, 1964).

26. e.g. Bem, "Enculturated Lens Theory."

27. e.g. To what extent is the veiling of women in early Judaism, Christianity and current Muslim practice an adherence to religious principle or the requirement of patriarchal cultures?

28. E.g. see Friedrich Engels, *The Origin of the Family*, Charles Kerr, 1902 (orig. 1884)

29. Andrew Hatcher, *Mismatch: the Growing Gulf Between Women and Men*, (New York: Scribner, 2003); David D. Gilmore, *Misogyny: the Male Malady*, (Philadelphia: University of PA Press, 2001).

30. E.g. David Gilmore, "Scriptures," in *Misogyny*, 79-97.

31. See R Adler, *Engendering Judaism* (New York: Jewish Publication Society, 1997).

32. RK Denton, *The Semai: A Nonviolent People of Malaysia*, Fieldwork, ed. (New York: Holt, Rinehart & Winston, 1979); James Silverberg and Thomas Gregor, eds., "The Rise, Maintenance & Destruction of Peaceable Polity" in *The Anthropology of Peace and Nonviolence* (New York; Oxford University Press, 1992) 214-270.

33. "UNIFEM Bahá'í Project Raises Community Consciousness" in *The Greatness Which Might Be Theirs: Reflections on the Agenda & Platform for Action for the UN Fourth World Conference on Women*, Bahá'í International Community Office of the Advancement of Women, Beijing: 1995, 51-60.

34. See Chapter 7 for discussion of the UN's role in promoting gender equality.

35. "Kids of Disgrace Find Solace in Village," *Daily Press*, Hampton Roads, VA, USA: March 6, 2004, A10.

36. Michael Penn & Rahel Nardos, *Overcoming Violence Against Women and Girls: the International Campaign to Eradicate a Worldwide Problem* (Lanham, MD: Rowman & Littlefield Publisher, Inc., 2003).

37. See Chapter 7, Women and the United Nations.

38. Penn & Nardos, 13-14.

39. Quoted by Phyllis G L Chew, in "The Singapore Council of Women & the Women's Movement," Association of Women for Action & Research: (Singapore University Press, 1999), 29.

PART V

REFLECTIONS AND PROSPECTS

Introduction to Part V:

Reflections and Prospects

In this final section of Women in the New Millennium we examine a diversity of visions for gender relations within a common frame of reference. That is, we raise the question of where the quest for gender equality will take members of a particular society, a new generation or, in some cases, the world community during the 21st century and new millennium. Since the global women's movement, embodied in the Beijing Platform, has gradually narrowed its focus to the empowerment of women, critical areas of concern and the development of national machineries for implementation, opportunities for leadership, initiative and action rest with the local and national communities.

And it is here where, as the well-known western adage suggests, "the rubber hits the road." That is, experience has shown that unless those at the grass roots level of community and family are empowered to tackle the gender issues prevalent in their own communities, such as female genital mutilation, domestic violence, healthcare, leadership and education, little else will be accomplished to relieve the suffering and pain of discrimination and inequality. Similarly, it is perplexing to note that many aspects of patriarchal family life have contributed to family stability, even while perpetuating violence and tyranny. It is instinctual to cling to what is familiar even when it is harmful to ourselves; that is, it is easier to maintain the status quo than to exert energy, placing ourselves and others at risk, to create a more caring and just social order. In fact it takes nothing less than a revolution in human affairs.

Must the family as we know it be completely dismantled in order to empower women as equals to men? Would a completely matriarchal society be any more desirable or beneficial than what we have experienced as patriarchal? Can new systems of gender relationships emerge without males taking some ownership for the empowerment of women, and both women and men creating new possibilities for equal partnerships untainted by patriarchal assumptions of dominance and brutality? Could a more egalitarian world contribute to a more fair and prosperous one?

While Beatriz Ferreira has chosen to work towards gender justice in the U.S. and abroad through human rights legislation and advocacy for women (chapter 3), Wu Xiaoqun has exerted her influence as a scholar, wife, mother and citizen to awaken Chinese women to a greater awareness of their personal roles in the gender revolution begun by a series of social, cultural and political revolutions in

China during the past century and a half.

Bret Breneman wrestles with literary assumptions of manhood and break-throughs in male awareness conceding an exile that gender relations can be a zero-sum conflict, a tango, or a life-enriching experience. He invites males to shed the temptation of relating to females as a potential conqueror and the belief that women want to be rescued, suggesting that males are in search of a new iden-tity, one which emerges as a wing on the bird of humanity, no more essential than the other wing representing females. He reminds readers that the flight is a singu-lar one.

Results of a survey of African women's concerns in Nigeria and Cameroon and an analysis of efforts to reverse African roles and expectations are indicative of the revolution which has been stirring within the mother continent of Africa over the past century. Within the kaleidoscope of visions arising from small numbers of individuals working together to empower women and girls through education and leadership to take control of their bodies, Mbuh presents a world-embracing vision of progress. One begins to perceive that there is enough power in the African continent to guide women and men to new understandings and be-haviors which can transcend older patterns of gender relationships, the habits of which are among the main sources of internalized oppression among women.

Can humanity escape the tyranny of patriarchy without provoking violence and depriving children of their need to be nurtured, loved and trained into good human beings? How central is the role of motherhood to womanhood? Can the functions of mothers, or fathers for that matter, be synthetically replaced without losing some valuable and essential elements in the formation of a child's prepara-tion for a healthy and prosperous life? Are there examples to be gleaned from less patriarchal societies, such as the Senai in Malaysia, which can assist us as we grope our way toward the long awaited egalitarian society?

The imagery of midwifery is explored in proposing that women have a sig-nificant and perhaps critical role to play in the emergence of a world community which values and encourages a prosperous life for all of earth's inhabitants. Without denigrating the value of maleness, Anne Breneman suggests that women may possess the missing key to balancing the aggressive, forceful qualities of men with the more intuitive, compassionate, consultative and life-sustaining qualities associated with women. In order for this formula for peace and prosper-ity to become an established way of life, male qualities may need to be somewhat modified as female qualities are more publicly valued and rewarded, whether manifested by women or men.

And, finally we gather the threads of diverse perspectives and themes and weave them into recommendations for improving the lives of girls and women everywhere. In doing so, we consider both the past century of progress, with both its failures and successes, as we look toward the creation of new paths to bring justice and the end of suffering to victims of violence beginning with infancy. What progress have women made toward their own empowerment, and what ef-forts have been made by men to relinquish some of the power, authority and privilege which have sustained gender injustice throughout the past millennium? To what extent do women themselves envision higher aspirations? How can each society in the world community alter its traditions, relationships, expectations, and values to increase possibilities for building families and communities in which both boys and girls have equal opportunities and protection from those who would prey on their vulnerabilities? How can both girls and boys be given optimum conditions to grow into good, prejudice free human beings with knowledge, skills, talents and volition to contribute to an advancing civilization?

The conclusions of the authors are intended to raise as many questions as answers, thus watering the seeds of a revolution already underway and destined to reverse the fortunes of a world over committed to authoritarian, economic and militaristic approaches to solving problems which originate in the habits of gender inequality and definitions of "otherness." For Mbuh and Breneman are not lacking in conviction that both women and men everywhere in the world are capable of transforming and transcending relationships which have been based more or less upon assumptions of the inherent inequality of the sexes, rather than upon their capacities for mutuality and complementary cooperation. For the authors, multiple national women's movements have spawned a global gender revolution which is as irreversible as the emergence of a butterfly from its cocoon.

Chapter 11

Chinese Women and Men: Future Prospects

Wu Xiaoqun

In looking back over the road of Chinese women's emancipation, one thing stands out: it is not an exclusive feminist movement of the kind one finds in the West. The modern Chinese women's movement is deeply connected with broader currents of change in society and with broader movements of social reform. Women's gradual emancipation has shaken the foundation of traditional Chinese civilization; it has challenged the whole traditional social structure. However, women's emancipation has caused much cultural and social dislocation. These dislocations compel one to reflect on the actual life of women and men and how they have been changed for better or for worse by the new social arrangements which women's emancipation has created.

It must be observed that because women's emancipation has become entangled in all kinds of Chinese social changes, women and men have both gained and lost from these changes.

The task of women's emancipation has always been attached to larger requirements of some age or some movement, and the struggle of women for equal rights isn't generally considered a "movement" in its own right, simply because neither society nor Chinese women conceive of it as such. This suggests that the social rights of Chinese women are the results of common efforts by men and women. Thus Chinese women's attitude toward men is always quite gentle. The Chinese Women's movement lacks the confrontational quality so common to western feminism. With few exceptions, as noted above, Chinese women have always connected social responsibility and family duty, and the gender consciousness has always been minimal.

Reviewing history allows us to face the future with more insight. Especially at the beginning of a new century, it is very necessary, to reflect on the past and to look forward to the future. The history of Chinese women's emancipation over the last one hundred years, its gains and losses, can provide lessons not only for the future development of Chinese women but also for women worldwide. As we enter the twenty- first century, it is not only the end of a century but also the beginning of another new millennium. People must understand that the struggle for women's emancipation isn't some kind of slave revolt. It isn't a fight between classes nor is it a war between men and women. On the contrary, men and women are always mutually dependent. Therefore, women's emancipation does not only demand the self-awakening of women, but also the self-awakening of all humankind. Women's emancipation invites a truly equal partnership between men and women. This partnership can be established between men and women only when people understand women's emancipation as a component of the emancipation. of humankind. This partnership can be established between men and women only when humanity understands that injury to women damages all of society and conversely women's gains benefit all of us.

The establishment of this new partnership is dependent on the common understanding of some basic principles between men and women. First, men and women are different. This difference isn't a cultural or a class construction; it is natural. There are real differences in physiology and psychology between men and women. If people ignore these differences and only stress the similarity between men and women, both men and women become standardized. Women will copy men and take them as their model. Such standardization damages women by distorting their distinctive dignity. The fight for formal equality between men and women has dominated in the 20th century. We hardly realize that it is the distinction between men and women that makes the world rich and colorful, and provokes humankind to improve society. Women's emancipation should not mean the elimination of sexual distinction, but should enlarge the possibility of women's participation in the life of the community. Ideal women's emancipation means giving women the capability of realizing their broadest possibilities.

Second, women bear children. Women have a special dignity as mothers and the first educators of children. We have to reconsider how present social arrangements dictate the notion of "worth" if we want to affirm women's value as mothers and educators. According to the World Women's Conference of the United Nations, today's women do 2/3 of the world's work, but receive only 1/10 the total remuneration. The reason is because much of women's work, including child bearing and attendant housework, isn't considered as wage labor. For a long time, salary and profession have been a principal mark of valuable work. The higher the salary and the more distinguished the profession the more valuable the worker. Thus it is easy to understand the low status of women when women's most important work isn't counted as paid labor. Therefore, it is necessary to re-examine the predicates of social value. A new model should broaden the notion of social contribution; it should take into account not only public society, but also those contributions not recognized or presently rewarded by society.

Third, men and women form our world. To improve the status of women isn't only a women's issue, it is a human issue. Therefore, it is time to invite men and women to work together. This invitation has always existed in the history of Chinese women's movement, but there is more to be done.

Women must be aware of their rights and their capabilities, must desire to improve themselves and realize their potential, and must step forward to play an active role in solving the world's problems. Men must learn how to cooperate with women and encourage their efforts, because it is very hard for women to achieve these goals without the support of men. Thus men must strive to change their attitude and behavior in order to prepare themselves to work as real partners with women. In a word, partnership calls for changes by both women and men.

Finally, some personal reflections: consultation must become an important principle in each family and every society. Review the history; in the past, the world has been ruled by force, and men have dominated women, just because men are more forceful and aggressive both in body and mind. But times change and more and more people understand that force and power cannot bring about well-being and peace. Consultation is the only effective prescription for solving problems. Consultation means defining problems, gathering facts, identifying relevant principles, exploring together with open minds and hearts, ways to apply those principles. Of course, it is not easy to ask men and women to discuss with each other on everything, including family issues and social issues, especially in a traditional country like China. It means a real change, and it is a great challenge. However, I believe that it is the best way to solve problems.

Humankind is like a bird; men and women are just like the two wings of a bird. "So long as these two wings are not equivalent in strength the bird will not fly. Until womankind reaches the same degree as man, until she enjoys the same arena of activity, extraordinary attainment for humanity will not be realized; humanity can not wing its way to heights of real attainment."[1] And today with globalization, humankind is going to enter a new stage of collective life rather like a person who having gone through childhood and puberty is standing at the front door of maturity. The establishment of the New World Civilization must be a collective enterprise. It depends on both men and women.

Chapter 11 Notes

1. Abdu'l-Baha, *Promulgation of Universal Peace*, comp. Howard MacNutt, end ed, (Wilmette, IL: Bahá'í Publishing Trust 1982), 375.

Chapter 12

Commiserating with Kermit and Becoming a Man

Bret Breneman

Remember Kermit the Frog's song, "It isn't easy being green?" It's not so easy being a man these days either, and sometimes the order of difficulty reminds one of Kermit's problems. We are said to be "from Mars," after all—presumably, "the little green men." But no longer the Jolly Green Giant. The concept of manhood as dominant, controlling, and triumphant necessitated a view of woman as an underling rather than an equal, and, as women struggle to gain their rightful places in society and to achieve a sense of identity that accords with the dignity of the human station, the man's superiority is called into question and a painfully glaring light is cast on his splendid isolation.

The novelist and travel writer, Paul Theroux, in fact, writes in an essay entitled "Being a Man:"

> Even the expression "Be a man!" strikes me as insulting and abusive. It means: Be stupid, be unfeeling, obedient, soldierly, and stop thinking. . . . It is a hideous and crippling lie; it not only insists on difference and connives at superiority, it is also by its very nature destructive—emotionally damaging and socially harmful.1

Theroux goes on to maintain that the definition of masculinity as above and separate from women incurs a sense of inadequacy "because it denies men the natural friendship of women." While little girls are trained to be coquettish and seductive and to identify themselves in relation to the opposite sex, little boys "are enjoined to behave like monkeys towards each other" in a kind of gender vacuum.

Tom Sawyer aspires to be Huckleberry Finn, in other words, he feels urged to throw off the confining refinements of Aunt Polly and to strike out for the open spaces of the "territory" where mere survival, not civilized refinement, is the challenge—where the animal (the "monkey") attributes of physical strength and courage, wiliness and aggressiveness will be at a premium. There is a powerful romance to this myth; it is at the heart of the romance of the Wild West. Tom, of course, dreams of winning Becky Thatcher through the outmost extreme of the charisma of wildness—that is, by staging his own funeral. But the world of Huck

Finn is a man's world. He is motherless and his father's violent, drunken presence is suffocating. Events circulate around the male bonding of Huck and Jim, events which feature con men using defined demeanors to disguise their corrupt schemes and the feuding of gentry that "reveals" their classy manners to be mere masks of their animal realities.[2]

Stephen Crane's story, *"The Bride Comes to Yellow Sky,"*[3] turns this romance of splendid male isolation on its head. The sheriff, who has gone "back East" to get married, returns to town with his gentle, rather homely, bride while Scratchy Wilson is in the throes of one of his periodic drunken shooting sprees. These terrifying outbursts by a harmful soul who goes wild when he gets drunk are almost a ritual that dramatizes the essence of the town of Yellow Sky. Scratchy rises up as a kind of parody of a "real man" on these days, sending the town's male dignitaries into discomforted hiding, and challenging "the man" himself, the sheriff. The sheriff always wins by bringing even greater masculine force and prowess to bear on Scratch's blurred state, but it is a "victory" that perpetuates the cycle, planting the seed of the next crazy contest, the pathetic comedy of which is always encompassed by its real terror.

This time the sheriff has no gun when he encounters the raging drunk. But he has his wife beside him. This, however, is a misleading statement. The fact is that the sheriff as a champion gunslinger no longer exists. It is the marriage, the *relationship*, which defeats Scratchy. He slinks off leaving "funnel-shaped" tracks in the dust like some sidewinder sliding back to its hole. One senses that civilization has conquered the animal in human nature. And it is not that the sheriff is diminished in his humbled, softened state. He is enlarged by relationship, as well as by his commitment to a divinely ordained institution.

This story reminds us that the first permanent English colony in America—Jamestown, Virginia—though it began in 1607 did not really take root until 1619 when women arrived—and that was also the year that representative government was established there, a historic coincidence of extreme significance.

Since women and men are the wings of the *one bird* of humanity, it seems that men cannot properly define themselves apart from women. And since each individual, whether man or woman, is a representative of the species, masculinity and femininity must be a matter of emphasis. Such a definition rejects the win-lose paradigm often implied by polarization. The sheriff in Crane's story will not only continue to maintain law and order but upon that foundation he will help to build civil society. Through his wife he *identifies* with refinement and with peaceful solutions to age-old forms of conflict.

A win-lose, dominant-subordinate paradigm has long been at play in gender relations, it seems, to the detriment of both halves of the equation. A late 19th century short story by Charlotte Gilman entitled *"The Yellow Wallpaper"*[4] captures the well—intentional tyranny that has often characterized marriages, where the husband is a kind of parent or even pet-owner. The husband in this story confines his wife to their bedroom to remedy a nervous disorder which his controlling behavior seems largely to have caused. The tattered wallpaper of what amounts to her cage is yellow with age and decay and seems morbidly "alive" with trapped women and their bulbous eyes and with a "creeping fungus" (did the

"Yellow Sky" of Crane's story also refer to age and decay?) The husband's acts of solicitousness are further nails into his wife's mental coffin as she goes steadily insane, until by the end of the story she is creeping on the floor like a fungus herself, carefully crawling over her husband, who has fainted. Her fall, which he has unwittingly orchestrated, precipitates his own, since they are bound in a kind of master-slave relationship.

A poem by Richard Wilbur, "She,"[5] makes even more explicit the view that man's spiritual "fallenness" is reflected in a failure of love that cripples gender relations. Here is the poem:

What was her beauty in our first estate
When Adam's will was whole, and the least thing
Appeared the gift and creature of his king,
How should we guess? Resemblance had to wait

For separation, and in such a place
She so partook of water, light, and trees
As not to look like any one of these.
He woke and gazed into her naked face.

But then she changed, and coming down amid
The flocks of Abel and the fields of Cain,
Clothed in their wish, her Eden graces hid,
A shape of plenty with a mop of grain,

She broke upon the world, in time took on
The look of every labor and its fruits.
Columnar in a robe of pleated lawn
She cupped her patient hand for attributes,

Was radiant captive of the farthest tower
And shed her honor on the fields of war,
Walked in her garden at the evening hour,
Her shadow like a dark ogival door,

Breasted the seas for all the westward ships
And, come to virgin country, changed again—
A moonlike being truest in eclipse,
And subject goddess of the dreams of men.

Tree, temple, valley, prow, gazelle, machine,
More named and nameless than the morning star,
Lovely in every shape, in all unseen,
We dare not wish to find you as you are,

Whose apparition, biding time until
Desire decay and bring the latter-age,
Shall flourish in the ruins of our will
And deck the broken stones with saxifrage.

This richly suggestive poem begins by keying on the word "separation," a word which punningly reminds us of failing marriages even as it refers to the estrangement from the Creator symbolized by Adam's fall. While he gazes on her "naked face" his "will was whole." She was central to the beauty and harmony that was Eden but was not merely one object among others: "She so partook of water, light, and trees/As not to look like any one of these." But as history proceeds woman becomes the "subject goddess of the dreams of men." Wilbur seems to be punning again here, since as "subject" goddess she is being pinned down as an *object* and not allowed to be the *subject* the title "She" implies. Her "Eden graces" are hid, that nakedness of beautiful creation, and she is "clothed" in the wishes of the male. She is Mother Nature in his eyes, the one who "labors" to produce. She becomes the very pretext and reason for warfare. She, like the narrator of "*The Yellow Wallpaper*," becomes imprisoned by the males' very attempts to defend and rescue her—a "radiant captive." But, estranged from the Creator, "We dare not wish to find you as you are."

History, then, that "nightmare" from which James Joyce's character Stephen Daedalus is "trying to awake" and of which the poet Shelley says all people are "weary," is identified here with masculine will and desire. The "latter age"—of some measure of reconciliation and attunement with God's will—will witness the end of self-will and rebellion, and woman's primal beauty will "deck the broken stones like saxiphrage," not as mere adornment or diversion for the male eye, but as a clear sign of the Creator's ineffable presence. "She" as subject, as "thou," will emerge to help guide humanity to a higher Eden.

However accurate or inaccurate the reading of Wilbur's resonant but rather mysterious poem, it does seem clear that masculine will has dominated history and has somewhat painted all of us into a corner, so to speak. The mere will to win, the force of initiative and aggressive, calculated taking of action, while they may advance the space program, cannot, it seems, save our own planet, much less nurture its blossoming into anything like a golden age. The bird cannot fly with only one wing; in fact, as one wing dominates, the creature goes into a tail-spin. Part of the solution is surely for the male to "let go" a bit and start cheering. We are all on the same side, after all, attempting a single flight. We males are still learning to *become* men.

In a recent essay entitled "*The White Man Unburdened*," Norman Mailer writes, "For better or for worse, the women's movement has had its breakthrough successes and the old, easy white male ego has withered in the glare."[6] I think there is some therapy in the process.

It is a sign if effeteness in society, traditionally, for males to exhibit effeminate mannerisms, but it is surely a sign of health for them to so appreciate "la difference" in women, the alterity that they emulate and come to acquire, those virtues of relationship which women so often possess. Emerson[7] quotes Napolean as saying, "Leave sensibility to women; but men should be firm in heart and purpose, or they should have nothing to do with war or government." These are incisive distinctions that capture much about "la difference:" sensibility, on the one hand, firmness of purpose, on the other. But it is not surprising that the one who would insist on these natures remaining separate because unequal should be described as one who "treated women with low familiarity" and who "had the habit of pulling their ears and pinching their cheeks."[8] Napoleon is our anti-model. His ruthless urge to conquer and dominate, his self-deifying posturing, his outright refusal to love even his brothers ("perhaps Joseph a little. . . and Duroc. . . because he is stern and resolute. . . and never shed a tear") should remind all males that defining manhood rigidly in terms of traditionally "masculine" attributes drives us into island exile.

Chapter 12 Notes

1. Paul Theroux, "Being a Man" in, Linda H Peterson , gen.ed., *The Norton Reader: An Anthology of Nonfiction Prose,* (New York: W.W. Norton & Company, 2000).
2. Mark Twain in Elliot, Emory, gen. ed., *American Literature: A Prentice* Peterson *Hall Anthology,* (New Jersey: Prentice Hall, 1991).
3. Stephen Crane in Elliot, Emory, gen.ed., *American Literature: A Prentice Hall Anthology,* (New Jersey: Prentice Hall, 1991).
4. Charlotte Gilman, "The Yellow Wallpaper" (Boston, MA: Small & Maynard, 1899).
5. Richard Wilbur, *New and Collected Poems,* (Harcourt, Brace, Jovanovitch, 1988), p 193.
6. Norman Mailer, "The White Man Unburdened". *The New York review of Books* July 2003: 4-6.
7. Brooks Atkinson, ed. *The Selected Writings of Ralph Waldo Emerson.* (New York: The Modern Library), 1992).
8. Norman Mailer, "The White Man Unburdened. 4-6.

Chapter 13

African Women: Gender Relations and the Redefinition of Roles

Rebecca Mbuh

The social, political and economic inequality among men and women has been a historical contention that is well documented. Throughout the world, women continue to be treated as the second, lower level, subordinate half in all spheres of life. The common string binding women together is not only their gender but the depth and width of their challenges which vary from continent to continent and from country to country. In many African countries these differences vary from region to region and from village to village under the umbrella of the same country. While researchers generally agree that there are huge gaps between the equality of the genders, there is no clear and comprehensive approach to bring about equality. Over the centuries African women have increasingly made important contributions to the political, social and economic activities of their countries. But female participation in any activity ought not to be treated as a privilege; it is a right that African women have been trying to assert for centuries with very little success. Of recent endeavors, international and regional conferences, devoted and dedicated women leadership, groups and inter-group activities and the advent of ever increasing and available technology has increased women's drive towards making their plight known and dealt with throughout the world.

The United Nations International Conferences on Women, which began in 1985, have provided positive support to women who are relentless in their struggle for equality. These conferences and regional follow-up conferences have provided a forum for African women to faithfully pursue their own interests first for the first time in modern African history. As these women recognize that productive economic independence is the fundamental springboard to acquiring self-esteem, this awareness and encouragement has swept through the cities and villages of many African countries. Women's groups have been more motivated to rally openly against traditional patriarchal practices that have for centuries reduced women and girls as mere objects not worthy to be heard. Moreover, the UN Conference held in Beijing, China in 1995 marked the beginning of a new chapter of demand for equality by many African women. It is our assertion that numerous intervening factors arising during the post-Beijing conference positioned these women in a better bargaining position than before. After the women's conferences many governments began responding to resolutions from UN sponsored conferences by pledging to pay more attention to women's issues. Due to pressure from international organizations such as the World Bank, UMIFEM and others, many African governments created special ministries designated for women's welfare, appointed women to high government positions, and increased funding for the education of females.[1] Increased technology facilitated networking opportunities between women's organizations worldwide. At the Beijing +5 Conference sponsored by the UN in 2001, I witnessed firsthand how the sophistication of the latest technologies put women delegates from Africa and other continents in constant touch with their home countries. In addition to using earlier methods such as faxes, delegates used cell phones and the Internet to update members of their groups.

During the last few decades the education of females in many African countries has been a major social reform priority and continues to attract attention. The World Bank, International Monetary Fund (IMF), United Nations, UNIFEM, and private organizations, have made it clear that the education of all children, especially the females, is important for the development of a nation. These conditions appear to be working as statistics indicate the level of illiteracy among African women has dropped and more females are enrolling at higher levels of education beyond primary school. The previous chapters give specific evidence to support this point. As more African women gain access to achieve universal education, the future of women's political, social, and economic participation is expected to increase in spite of the many challenges they must overcome.

Table 13.1 on the following page provides a summary of literacy statistics in Africa from 2000 to 2004 for women and girls 15 to 24 years old in selected countries. The range of literate African women, from 8.1 to 81.5 percent for the age group ages 15+, and from 14.0 percent to 92.2 percent for women ages 15 to 24 suggests that the majority of the main caretakers and bearers of children cannot read or write. What does this tell us about the future leadership of African nations? Education is the key to knowledge and it has been said that *knowledge is power*. This table provides a backdrop from which to conceptualize the gains made in the education area for comparison with the findings of this research.

There still exists a huge gap between the literacy rates of men and women in the two age groups in most African countries. Though many countries did not report data for the age group 25 and above, one can only guess that the information was negative given the trend for these countries.

Table 13.1
Literacy, Selected African Countries, in Percent, by Gender, 2000-2004

COUNTRY	WOMEN AGES 15+	MEN AGES 15+	WOMEN AGES 15-24	MEN AGES 15-24
Algeria	59.6	78.0	85.6	90.4
Benin	25.5	54.8	38.5	72.7
Botswana	81.5	76.1	92.8	85.5
Burkina Faso	8.1	18.5	14.0	25.5
Burundi	51.9	66.8	69.5	75.6
Cameroon	59.8	77.0	N/A	N/A
Central African Republic	33.5	64.8	46.8	70.3
Chad	12.7	40.6	23.1	55.4
Congo	77.1	88.9	97.3	98.8
Democratic Republic of Congo	51.9	79.8	61.1	76.7
Egypt	43.6	67.2	66.9	79.0
Ethiopia	33.8	49.2	51.8	63.0
Ghana	45.7	62.9	N/A	N/A
Kenya	43.6	67.2	66.9	79.0
Libyan Arab Jamohiriya	70.7	91.8	94.0	99.8
Morocco	38.3	63.3	61.3	77.4
Niger	10.6	30.4	15.7	37.2
Nigeria	59.4	74.4	86.5	90.7
Rwanda	28.6	56.1	42.1	62.3
Togo	38.3	68.5	63.3	83.1

Source:http://www.uius.unesco.org/TEMPLATE/html/Exceltables/education/
literacy_National_Sept04.xls. Accessed: January 4, 2005

The chapter "African Women Since Nairobi" gives an in-depth discussion of some of the specific issues African women face. The chapter concluded with practical suggestions directed at governments, NGOs and women's organizations for overcoming these challenges. Most of the suggestions were based on research findings and are very practical. In order to go beyond the scope of what previous research has suggested we decided to solicit the voices of the younger generation of women. We asked African women from several West African countries about their opinions on current and future issues pertaining to women in particular and society in general. Those who participated were literate and had completed at least basic a basic education, though the great majority of the women were university students, 65 percent.

Methodology

This study was conducted on two continents: Africa and the United States. The questionnaire was first administered to African women participants in Nigeria soon after the 1995 Beijing Conference by Fakhereh Mottahed. Another administration of the Mbuh-Breneman interview schedule occurred during the UN Beijing +5 Conference in New York in 2000. Twenty women, mostly delegates, from nine African countries returned their questionnaires with many useful comments. Feedback from the survey was used to refine the survey instrument. Questionnaires and interviews with women in Cameroon and Nigeria were conducted between 2000 and 2003. The interviewees were randomly selected from several women and youth organizations in the Northwest Province of Cameroon and Zaria, Kaduna State, and Nigeria. The participants completed the survey and were also interviewed individually for about one hour at their homes, workplaces, and market locations. Since most of the women could not read, an interpreter was used to relate the questions to these women. Two languages were used: Pidgin English and Hausa.[2] In some cases, youths were interviewed at Internet cafes or on school campuses. In three instances, we conducted small group interviews during lunch break at the University of Yaoundé I, Cameroon and Amadou Bello University (ABU), Zaria, Nigeria.[3] The fifteen question questionnaire was a combination of open-ended questions and fill in the blanks or selections from a list of possible responses. (See Appendix). Our aim was to encourage participants to provide as much information as possible. The main objectives were:

1.   To identify the changes in gender relations over the past century and
2.   To explore what changes are needed in the new millennium to improve these relations, from the standpoint of African women.

Among the numerous challenges constantly encountered by African women, early marriages and illiteracy were identified as fundamental issues that social policy change could rectify for the benefit of the nation. The religious backgrounds of respondents were of great interest to the researchers because certain religious beliefs impact on the way gender relations are affected. Given that all the world's major religions[4] are equally present in or originated in Africa, this religious component sheds light on cultural practices and beliefs. The religious backgrounds of the respondents included: Apostolic, Bahá'í, Baptist, Buddhist, Catholic, Muslim, Presbyterian, Traditional/Ancestral, and Hinduism.

General demographic survey items were included to gain a better understanding of African women's' location within their respective societies. The data collected from interviews and surveys is summarized into categories reflecting the impact of responses on women's lives in the areas of education, political participation, equality, economic involvement or employment and other pressing issues challenging African women. The total number of women who participated in this research was 387. The major delimitation of this research is that the great majority of participants came from western African countries, Nigeria and Cameroon, and they were university students.

FINDINGS
Demographic Background of Respondents
In order to present a comprehensive summary of what were qualitative and quantitative responses, tables have been developed. About seventy one percent of respondents between the age group, 21 to 25, were married and had an average of

1.9 children, compared to the age group 51 to 55 with an average of 5.3 children. Respondents who were less than seventeen years old had an average of 1.1 children. Table 13.2 presents a summary of the respondents' age, marital status and number of children. Only the number of living children was reported. Of the 254 respondents who were full time university students, only seven percent of them were married.

Table 13.2: Respondent's Age, Marital Status and Number of Children

Age Group	Number	Marital Status Percentage Married	Avg. No. of Surviving Children
<17	23	56.2%	1.1
17-20	68	36.75%	1.5
21-25	85	70.59%	1.9
26-30	74	33.78%	2.2
31-35	62	72.58%	3.5
36-40	25	80.00%	4.2
41-45	17	88.24%	4.6
46-50	12	100.00%	4.9
51-55	11	100.00 %	5.3%
56-60	7	71.43%	5.8 %
61 and over	3	100.00%	5.7

Table 13.3: Respondents Education Level and Profession

Education Level	No.	% of Total #	Profession	No.	% per Education Level
Doctorate	2	.52%	University Professor	2	100%
Masters	11	2.33%	Lawyer	2	18.18%
			Lecturer	8	72.72%
			Gov't Worker	1	9.09%
Bachelor of Arts/ Bachelor of Science	80	20.67%	High School Teacher	18	22.50%
			Secondary School Teacher	25	31.25%
			Gov't Worker	12	15.00%
			Businesswoman/Part-time	8	10.00%
			Laborer	6	7.50%
			Housewife	8	10.00%
			Nurse Manager	3	3.75%
University Student	254	65.63%	Full-time Student	254	100%
Associate Degree	25	6.46 %	Primary School Teacher	7	28%
			Nursing Assistant	5	20%
			Businesswoman	8	32%
			Housewife	2	8%
			Housewife/Businesswoman	3	12%
High School Diploma	8	2.07 %	Nursing Assistant	2	25%
			Housewife/Businesswoman	6	75%
<High School Elem School Certificate < 5 yrs. Elem School	2 5 3	.52 % 1.29 % .76%	Housewife/Businesswoman	10	100%

Table 13.3 on the previous page summarizes the education level of our respondents and the professions in which they are engaged. Clearly, our respondents are better educated than African women in general. The majority of the respondents were university educated. But this is also advantageous in that these respondents were more literate and so would be more versed in the problems arising from gender inequality/relations than the less educated who are prone to accepting the ruling status quo. However, further studies need to be done among rural and less educated women to either support or refute this assertion.

The teaching profession attracted the majority of our respondents as shown in the table. The professions of the respondents ranged from university professor to housewife/business woman. While Table 13.1 paints a bleaker picture of the current educational status of African women, the women in our survey revealed they are not resolved to accept this predicament but are actively taking measures to improve themselves and their children. The fact that the majority of our respondents were employed as teachers and students shows the dedication of women to education as they serve as role models for their children and community. In some cases, these women had no choice in selecting a profession. Therefore teaching was the best alternative for them since many African societies are reluctant to allow women to participate in public decision making within the government.

Respondent's Goals

The respondents and interviewees indicated a strong commitment to making long-term and short-term goals for themselves and their children. One woman in her late fifties summed it this way:

> Goals keep me alive. When I retire to bed at night all I think about is how to make life better for myself and my children. I want my children to have more decision making in matters affecting them than I am doing. The only way out of this is to plan, plan and plan because planning gives me hope and the will to face all the odds of basic survival in a male hostile society. While my husband is sleeping at night I usually stay up late thinking of ways to make life better for us and then before I know it, it is time again to get up before everyone and prepare food.

Table 13.4: Goals of Women for the 21st Century

Category	Issue/Number	Percentage
Education	Educate all of my children (215)	55.27%
	Complete primary education, further my education/return to school(262)	67.4%
	Become computer literate(102)	26.22%
Financial	Become financially independent (129)	33.2%
	Own my own business(86)	22.11%
Political	Become active in local government(64)	16.45%
	Work for the government(50)	12.85%
	Become active in national government(47)	12.1%
	Run for office(25)	6.43%

Women's Issues	Work to abolish polygamy, female genital mutilation or circumcision, arranged marriages and early marriages (295) Push for changes in laws in granting and enforcing more rights/equal rights to women in divorce, inheritance, and ownership of property(286) Press government for harsher punishment for those committing violence against women (255) Draw international attention to violence against women including wife beating, marital rape, rape, etc.(198) Attend more conferences on women's welfare(75)	75.84% 73.52% 65.55% 50.90% 19.29&

In order to accomplish any goal no matter how small it may be, planning is essential. Educational planning for both women and their children and financial planning were the most cited types of strategies to ensure that their goals are kept alive. About 54 percent of the respondents indicated their commitment to educating their children while 48 percent cited furthering their own education as their main goal for the 21st Century. (See Table 13.4) Becoming financially independent was the third most popular response for their main goal according to 33.2 percent.

Respondents were asked to list in order of importance the three most critical goals for their future in the new millennium. Therefore the percentages do not total 100 percent but serve as indicators for each category goal. Of the four main goal categories under which the goals are summarized, education and women's issues drew the most response from participants. The goals listed here are part of a growing set of women's issues gaining ground in women's groups especially after the 1995 Beijing Women's Conference. Because women have amassed unprecedented support for their causes at both the national and international levels, a determination to secure a better future for their children propels them to keep on fighting. Thus said one respondent at the University of Yaounde:

> "Here comes Ms. Beijing," I hear my male classmates saying as I approach them. "She thinks she can now wear trousers better than men and do everything better than the men. She says she will only marry when she is ready. When will that be? In the next world?" I shrug and give them a big smile as if I did not hear their sly remarks and in a loud voice tell one of the male students that he can copy my homework before class starts.

As women continue to assert themselves, they face different kinds of challenge such as ridicule, hatred, and resentment. The male students feel threatened that women are determined to go shoulder to shoulder with them into all levels of education, government and the military while continuing to perform household chores. This attitude is not limited to the institutions of higher learning in African countries but a reflection of the societies' views.

Respondents' Role Models

Table 13.5 Role Models of Women

Category	Type/Number	Percentage
Family Member	My mother (110)	28.28%
	My grandmother (100)	25.71%
	My children (16)	4.11%
	My sister (15)	3.86%
	My father (7)	1.80%
Political Leader	Women in government (65)	16.71%
	Hillary Clinton (15)	3.86%
	Margaret Thatcher (5)	1.30%
	Nelson Mandela (3)	0.77%
	Indonesian President (Megwati)(1)	0.26%
Religious Leader	My Pastor/Religious leader (17)	4.37%
Educator	Teacher (35)	9.00%

Many participants accredited their mothers and grandmothers for implanting in them the determination for hard work, endurance, and self-respect. Respondents praised and admired these relatives for their strength in the face of many adversities, their sacrifices and their spiritual leanings. Our respondents stressed that their mothers and grandmothers encouraged them to never give up on their ambitions regardless of the obstacles. Political role models were chosen not so much for their struggles for women's rights, issues and equality but for their symbolism. A symbol to which suppressed women and girls could look up to and hope for better days was highly ranked. In the case of Margaret Thatcher, one college student adamantly stated:

> Mrs. Thatcher may have been the second most powerful and influential woman in the world as Prime Minister of the United Kingdom but she was always referred to by her husband's name. While she acquired the reputation as "Iron Lady" for her political astuteness, at home she was the one who served her husband and nursed her children. Mrs. Thatcher is a role model for serving her country well in a male dominated society, as well as being a housewife, showing us that with support and opportunity any woman anywhere can contribute to the well-being of their country.

Our participants viewed women in government positions as the venue through which women's voices, concerns, suggestions and criticisms could be conveyed to the government authorities. Women in government offices are closely monitored and scrutinized by ordinary women and girls who aspire and are empowered to join their ranks in serving their country.

Although the African continent is comprised of 54 independent countries, women continue to be underrepresented in all elected and appointed offices in governments with few exceptions. These would include, South Africa, Seychelles and Mozambique in 2000.[5] According to recent reports Rwanda tops the list of countries with the highest proportion of women parliamentarians in the world, 49 percent, followed by Sweden with 45 percent, while the average for Africa is a low 15.3 percent.[6] Women represent more than 50 percent of the population, yet the highest ranking government positions ever held by African women are that of interim head of government in Liberia and Vice President in Uganda.[7]

Effects of Changes in Gender Relations

Table 13.6 presents a summary of the views of our respondents as to changes in gender relations that have occurred during the past century and provide a litmus test for measuring what the various governments highlight as advances in addressing gender inequality and what is verifiable through the people.

Table 13.6
Respondent's Views of the Response of Governments to Changes in Gender Relations

Category	Issue/Number	Percentage
Political	Government's response to women's issues such as passing laws abolishing Female Genital Mutilation (96)	24.67%
	The appointment of women in government positions (94)	24.16%
	More women in the army and other military establishments (83)	21.34%
	The establishment of a ministry of women's affairs by many governments (79)	20.31%
Education	Focus on the education of female children by governments (80)	20.57%
Social	Improved communication between husbands and wives (131)	33.68%
	More men helping around the house (127)	32.65%
	More open discussion about women's issues (117)	30.07%
	More independence gained by women (111)	28.53%
	Respect for women by many men (52)	13.37%
Financial	More Businesswomen (240)	61.70%

Four main categories (political, educational, social and financial) summarize the changes in gender relations provided by our participants. While many participants agree that some progress has been made in this area, many more take the position that inadequate progress has been achieved and therefore governments must work actively to address women's and all human issues. These ideologies are reflected in the suggestion/recommendation section giving governments and other influential groups specificities of women's priority checklist.

Personal Life: Many African women tend to view their "second class" status as defined by their personal situations first before generalizing to other groups of women. Many more are reluctant to share very personal and intimate information about their lives. One respondent echoed this position by stating that revealing her personal situation without assurance of assistance is hopeless. It is better to suffer in silence than to "hang your dirty laundry outside for all to see and make a mockery of you," she added. This survey underscored this point; many participants opted not to respond to the questions in this section. Only 22 percent or 86 women responded to the question, "How has this change affected your personal life?" Their responses indicated that some women have gained more self confidence and are also more active in the community.

Family Life: Family life is very important to Africans. Women are seen to be the protectors of the family though they do have limited decision-making roles. Twenty-five percent, or 98, of the respondents to this question indicated closeness of family members, the husbands' support of education for their wives, increases in the number of divorces, and an increase in conflict and violence within families as the most prominent adjustments and evolutions that have occurred as a result of changes in gender relations. Many respondents noted that as more women gain independence and become more self-reliant, they are less likely to tolerate their husbands' brutality. Moreover, women have quickly realized that many NGOs are working to assist women with problems emanating from the traditional influences.

Community Life: Respondents indicated an increased awareness in women's and children's issues, increased support for women in government, increased support for better health for women and children, increased support for longer maternity leave for women, and a general willingness on the part of the older generation of men to listen to women's "complaints" as some of the major changes in gender relations visible at the community level. For example, although Female Genital Mutilation is still widely practiced in many African countries, it is cited as a successful example of how men and women in a community, working together, can see the evils of such practices on young women and together take action to abolish them. Other important issues that have also brought the community closer together (when respondents answered questions on educational and social issues) include awareness and open discussions on previously tabooed matters such as early marriages, forced or arranged marriages, wife inheritance, blaming wives for the death of their husbands, and general violence against women.

In the past decades it seems that African women accepted their oppression under the patriarchal system as directed by God and bore in silence their sufferings. One respondent is currently a member of her village council, which is composed mainly of men. She is a representative of the women though she serves in the observer function. But it is a beginning, and women are ready to accept this since having a woman on the council is seen as revolutionary, paving the way for full participation in the future. This is viewed as a victory for women who for a long time have been oppressed, degraded, and humiliated under the patriarchal system sanctioned by their colonial and postcolonial governments.

The World: Continuous progress in technological advancements has made it easy for women and men all over the world to be constantly updated about new developments. One of the advantages of technology is that information spreads at a faster pace to many people than in the past centuries. One respondent indicated that:

> Cell phones have changed the life of the village woman for life. She can be informed of what goods would fetch the most money for her products in the cities before making the long journey. She is in frequent contact with her main whole-

sale dealer and always delivers fresh, needed vegetables. To her, the availability of the cell phone and her investment in it has already paid off. No spoiled vegetables and fruits to deal with any more.

Though many households in Africa and other parts of the world survive on less than $2.00 a day, many of these people have access to televisions, radios, and other means of communication through their neighbors. In many poor communities, the nightlife usually centers in the house of a neighbor who has a television. CNN, BBC, and many other television networks broadcast live reports that reach millions of people throughout the world. In addition, many major international newspapers also cover topics related to the plight of women in Africa. These media have contributed significantly in facilitating the sharing of information on women's challenges and how to address them. For the increased awareness of the sad situation of African women and children and the international attention drawn to Female Genital Mutilation of African women and girls, violence and girl-child prostitution, rape and other atrocities we must credit the international media for exposing the horrible conditions endured by African women.

Role of Women: The survey findings reveal that the role of women has not changed per se; it has only been redefined. African women's role in African societies and the world continues to be a subject of debate in academia as well as among African women themselves. Most respondents saw themselves as primary caretakers of the elderly, wives, family nurses, mothers, farmers, businesswomen, and role models, physicians, lawyers, dentists, university professors, students, activists, friends to all, and peacemakers. The role of the African woman has been expanded to include leader, manager, and head of household, politician and even decision maker, but with no real power of freedom to defend herself and make decisions about her life and future. However, participants provided an extensive view of what the role of African women should be and how this can be achieved for the benefit of humankind, not just *"womankind."*

During one of the small group discussions participants made two important observations relating to women's roles. First, role assignments in a society afford each gender specific areas of responsibility, and many African societies define those roles in terms of patriarchy. Second, women are overburdened within these traditional social constructions. African women responses to new roles for women within family, workplace, community and world are tabulated in Table 13.7 on the next page. Fifteen women chose "other" to describe what they considered new roles for women, their responses have been grouped under political, economic, social and managerial. A little less than half of the respondents (48.3%) viewed the family as the primary responsibility of women. This is worthy of special attention since the general belief in African societies is that the woman's place belongs in the home and on the farms. It is also important to remember that participants in this study were more educated than most African women. Higher proportions of respondents identified more visible and meaningful roles for women in the community, workplace, and the world respectively (81.1%, 79.8% and 62.3%).

Table 13.7: The New Role of Women

Category	Number responding	Percentage
Family	187	48.3%
Workplace	309	79.8%
Community	314	81.1%
World	241	62.3%
Other: **Political**: Family stabilizer, community stabilizer, children and women's rights advocate, Voiceless in fight against HIV/AIDS and ownership of self, **Economical**: Trading and informal economy, agricultural producers, **Social**: Major wife duties including caretaker of family, health care providers, **Managerial**: Household planner, strategizer and overseer, budgeting and expense tracker.	58	15%

This trend shows younger, educated African women as having been "awakened" from bondage of captivity to a position where they dare challenge patriarchy as a hindrance to not only women's progress, but also to that of society as a whole. In many African countries women bear the burden during times of conflict and war and must be solely responsible for their families during such times as well as in peaceful times. Their contribution to economic, social, and political welfare of the development of the nation is usually marginalized at the most or simply dismissed as insignificant. Such misrepresentation is bound to become, in both social and monetary terms, a family as well as a national economic cost, which naturally under-reports the gross national product of many countries. This approach also represents a tremendous under-utilization of a nation's human resources. A 1995 statement by UNESCO puts the situation in perspective, "Equality, development and peace are inextricably linked. There can be no lasting peace without development and no sustainable development without full equality between men and women."[8] UNESCO goes on to emphasize that a culture of peace aims at:

—transforming values, attitudes and behaviors based on violence to those which promote peace and non-violence;
—empowering people at all levels with skills of dialogue, mediation and peace building;
—democratic participation of peoples in political decision-making;
—equal representation of women in decision-making at all levels;
—the political and economic empowerment of women;
—the free flow of information and transparency and accountability of governing structures;
—the elimination of poverty and sharp inequalities within and between nations;
—the promotion of sustainable human development for all;
—the preservation of the planet and all it's species; and
—advancing understanding, tolerance and respect for diversity among all peoples.[9]

Role of Men: Table 13.8 shows that respondents seek to have male support of women at all levels, from home to the world at large. In Table 13.7, the majority of the respondents signaled a diminishing role for women in the family while Table 13.8 presents summaries of responses calling for greater male support for women in the family, workplace, community and the world. This study shows patterns consistent with the worldwide women's call for equality and increased opportunities for women's participation in governmental, economic and social activities of the society. The United Nations sponsored world women's conferences from 1975 to the present have sought to highlight women's potential and their necessity in the advancement of humanity.

Table 13.8: The New Roles of Men

Category	Number Responding	Percentage
Family: Head and supporter, protector, provider, consult wife in decision-making, education of children, plan for retirement, share household responsibilities	298	76.74%
Workplace: Respect females, share responsibilities, support and advocate equal pay for equal work, empowerment of women in participation, planning and implementation of policies, serve as mentors to women, as managers/directors emphasize training for women, establish daycare facilities for working women	305	78.81%
Community: Involve women in matters affecting the community, include women in leadership positions, appoint/elect women to local boards and councils, spearhead drive for equality of men and women, support women's activities, understand and appreciate women's contributions to the welfare of the community, encourage education for all genders	360	93.02%
World: Support women's organizations, support women's political ambitions, support women's economic and social activities, recognize and support women's struggles for equality, advocate equal education for all genders	158	40.83%

Traditionally, African men have always defined the roles for men and women without consultation or input from women. Women were not expected to negotiate any part of their handed-down functions regardless of how disdainful they felt. In many rural areas the roles are ambiguous by design in order to allow men to change them at will to benefit the males, for the most part. Men are expected to be "the head of household" but in reality, they are only figureheads. Women are more likely to comply out of obligation rather than by choice, and this practice has been observed for many generations. In the wake of the new millennium, questions about male and female roles have been discussed openly by both genders. While the female would like a complete overhaul, the male is still clinging to the traditional way, thus breeding a major source of conflict between the genders. One respondent indicated:

Common sense will dictate that if I am pounding fufu[10] and preparing the soup at the same time, all this after spending the day fetching water, trading, feeding the family, taking food to my in-laws . . . and if the baby is crying my husband should at least show some concern if not for me, at least for the child. My husband is my other child, but unfortunately he does not help like the other children. When I leave in the morning and return late in the afternoon I usually find him lying on the mat with his male friends drinking tea.

For many decades women's roles and status all over the world have been the subject of many international conferences, workshops, seminars, and research. Unfortunately, little attention if any has been devoted to men's roles and positions, making the subject appear "taboo." During the United Nations Fourth World women's conference, the issue of male roles in many aspects of the family was discussed and emphasized strongly in the Beijing Platform for Action and in the UN-ECOSOC meeting in July 1997, and is now more widely understood. Since then greater interest has been generated on the role of men in building and maintaining gender equality.[11]

Summary and Recommendations

Inequality of men/women in employment/salary is wide spread worldwide. Research shows that women are paid 30 to 40 percent less than men for equal work. Furthermore, women are primary victims of economic crisis and unemployment while at the same time often the victims of violence, armed conflict, and cruel and inhumane traditional practices that endanger their lives such as Female Genital Mutilation. To be blunt, women have been deprived of their basic human rights in many African countries since tradition guides lawmakers and law enforcers, predominantly men, to treat women as personal properties rather than as equal partners in society. The World Conference on Human Rights affirmed at a conference held in Vienna June 14-25, 1993 that:

All human rights are universal, indivisible and interdependent and interrelated. The international community must treat human rights globally in a fair and equal manner, on the same footing, and with the same emphasis. While the significance of national and regional particularities and various historical, cultural and religious backgrounds must be borne in mind, it is the duty of States, regardless of their political, economic and cultural systems, to promote and protect all human rights and fundamental freedoms.[12]

Highly respected international organizations have long joined the fight for equality through their policy statements and funding initiatives. Organizations such as the WHO,[13] UNICEF,[14] UNHCR, UNESCO,[15] and ILO, through their missions have sought to empower women.

While WHO, UNHCR, and UNICEF are working to improve the status of women, UNESCO has been and continues to concentrate on the improvement of access to education of women throughout the world with special emphasis on strengthening women's roles in decision making. WHO stresses that women have the right to better living conditions and access to adequate health services.

Several conclusions can be drawn from this study to assist governments, NGOs and international organizations in planning and developing policies that reflect the maximization of the highest potential of all humans. The following suggestions and recommendations are summarized from the findings of this study and are divided in to five categories.

1. Government Accountability

The majority of respondents cited good leadership, transparency in government, elimination of corruption, institution of stricter punishment for embezzlers and bribe seekers/receivers, and inclusion of women in higher positions (by appointment, election—quotas or rotation of leadership positions) as some of the areas that governments can no longer afford to ignore. For several years, perhaps decades, African countries consistently outpaced other nations as the most corrupt nations in the world. Weak and corrupt governments, wide spread acceptance by government officials that such behaviors are the norm, and the only lip service to address these issues continue to plague many African nations. In a survey of 133 countries by the Berlin-based organization Transparency International in 2003, the majority of African countries surveyed scored in the 2+ range out of 10 points, ranking them among the most corrupt nations in the world.[16] It is therefore imperative that a commitment to deal with these issues should begin at the top and filter through all sections of the society.

2. Economic and Agricultural Reform

Without the maximization of a country's human resources, progress is slowed. Women's involvement in the development of African nations has been grossly misunderstood and under appreciated since women's greatest contributions are in the informal sectors. But without women, many African populations will experience even more alarming cases of malnutrition than have already been reported. In order to reform the economy, governments must commit to providing job training for women in all sectors to improve women's employability in both the formal and informal sectors through educating and training women in new farming techniques. The case of Cameroon's North West Province *Mission Pour Le Development du Nord Ouest* (MIDENO),[17] an African Development Bank sponsored Agricultural restructuring program, is a glowing example worth praising and emulating here, even though the real and long term gains from such a program are often slowed by the World Bank Structural Adjustment Program implemented in Cameroun.[18] The acquired skills will enable women (in Phase II of the MIDENO in Cameroon) to improve their farming activities, leading to greater harvests.

Government should prioritize the improvement of farm to market roads; provide grants for the purchase of farm equipment, seeds and fertilizer, and provide loans to farmers. These improvements will reduce the human labor hours that many women currently apply to farming, thus allowing them to spend quality time with their families. Specifically, plans should be implemented to reduce females' dependence on their male counterparts and provide opportunities for networking with other businesswomen and men.

3. Social Reform

The secret to the development of any nation is the quality of its educational programs. Many of the world's illiterates are located in the African continent. Moreover, the majority of these are women and girls. African governments' agendas should be topped by a commitment to gender equality in education. In addition, building more schools, improving the educational system, updating technology, practicing the *"education for all"* philosophy, and adapting a global view of education have the potential of exponentially expanding human resources and capacities for identifying and solving problems from within African countries rather than from external sources.

Promotion of self-reliance and spiritual growth among citizens encourages appreciation and understanding. Improving the healthcare system, empowering women, as well as providing clean and safe shelters for refugees (protection for women and children), developing parks and other recreational facilities for public use, committing to caring for the elderly, fostering religious harmony, banning weapons, reducing crime and enforcing stricter punishments for violators, legalizing abortion, and educating the public on domestic violence are some of the areas needing attention and action from governments.

According to Charles Cobb, Jr., about 70 percent of persons with HIV/AIDS live in sub-Saharan Africa and of the estimated 25 million children who would have lost one or both parents to the disease by the year 2010; 20 million are likely to be living in Africa.[19] Poverty has been directly linked to the spread of HIV/AIDS and women are usually the victims of such conditions.[20] Economic independence for women will help curb the spread of this disease and spare many lives. Thus, this pandemic, if not curtailed now, threatens the work force and the general survival of the societies. Efforts should be intensified in educating people about the disease, facilitating the distribution of medication and focusing on prevention education, not only for the youths but for everyone.

Findings of Cobb's study yielded numerous social reforms for governments and societies to adopt. Specifically, African governments should:

—organize poor rural women and widows and provide support for their children's education.

—provide social security for older men and women and handicapped people through improving healthcare delivery and provision of medications.

—collaborate with local officials and religious leaders for better treatment of women and prevention of domestic violence.

—organize workshops and seminars that focus on discussions between the old and the young and the implications of issues affecting the society such as FGM, polygamy, early marriages, arranged marriages, forced marriages, family planning, education, wife inheritance, bride worth/prize, child labor, slavery and the education of girls.

—promote dialog with men (through discussions of traditional culture in light of modern times).

—protect women and children from sexual violence such as gang rape, sexual torture, and other abuses during tribal, regional or civil conflicts and wars. Reardon[21] described acts such as these as the most severe of all forms of direct, physical violence against women. Laws governing these violations should be strictly enforced.

—improve health for women and children through access to health centers and health education. The introduction of mobile vans to remote areas should be investigated and implemented.

4. Political Reform

Many African nations claim to be democratic, but in reality many governments are dictatorships, authoritarian, or at best have one political party under the pretext of a multi-party system. Political oppression is wide spread, but within this realm, women experience a double standard of oppression/repression. Women continue to lag a far distance from men in being elected/appointed in government positions. With the exception of a few countries such as South Africa, women are still struggling to rise above the clouds even after the Beijing Declaration by world leaders in 1995. A study of 40 African countries conducted by Catherine Russell and Mark DeLancey[22] found that women are highly under-represented in cabinet positions in many African countries. Not only are women's proportions much smaller in comparison with the males, but also "those women holding cabinet positions are relegated to the less significant ministries." Of the 40 countries studied, 35 reported very low (0.9 to 4.9%) and low (5.4 to 8.9%) of women holding ministerial and sub-ministerial positions. With the world average of 9.1% for women ministers, African governments have a challenging task to address.

Political reform should have as its top goal efforts to include women in decision-making positions, not just in the ministries of women's affairs, as is the case in many African countries, but also in other areas of government. Africa today boasts of a growing number of well-educated and talented women who are willing, capable and anxious to serve their nations in various capacities if given the recognition they deserve. The under-utilization or neglect of these resources could be costly.

5. International Awareness

Usually, international attention is drawn to Africa only in times of disaster, war, and conflicts. This image should be changed as Africa has many valuable qualities to offer the world. Better cooperation with and understanding of other countries to reduce conflicts and wars and to share cultures and traditions is needed to facilitate international trade and attract foreign investments. Therefore, improving relations with the international donor community is critical for the development of African nations.

Conclusion

As the African women's struggle to achieve equality and certain basic human rights continues, there is documentation of their contributions to economic development, nation building, education, social welfare, and politics. African women are victims of class, location, age, and gender discrimination; marital status; colonial policies; and modern society's unchanging expectations of women. Additionally, women across the African continent are scrutinized and judged primarily by traditional customs dominated by males. This study revealed interesting issues and points us to the fact that contrary to societal belief and expectations of women, women are ready, capable and willing to participate on equal footing with men in all aspects of the society while still devoted to their families. The recommendations advanced suggest that women also have a rough blue print of strategies to address these issues.

African women aim to use their numbers in an organized manner to gain a share of the power structure which has been traditionally monopolized by men to achieve economic independence and more freedom, in order to improve their status. These gains not only benefit women, but children and families as a whole. But the traditional African man's selfish improvidence threatens this development. There is little doubt that the status of women has risen considerably over the past half century. Many women's organizations and NGOs have fought to get public acceptance of a visible and viable presence of women in positions of power and authority at all levels of government. Through these efforts women have been empowered in many ways. There is heightened interest in the value of universal and higher education for all citizens and demands for the improvement of family living and health conditions, which women see as essential for the survival of the family and nation. Without women's unconditional devotion to health and happiness, their families will be at risk, as will the nation. Women continuously advocate fair and equal treatment of women in the family and community as a practical means of national welfare.

It is the author's conviction that patriarchal tendencies, beliefs and practices continue to prevent African women from fully achieving freedom and equality. Communities must undertake more unified approaches to understanding the African female, which in the long run means understanding the strengths of the female struggle, thus reducing and/or abolishing male oppression for a stronger and better future. According to the *Human Development Report 2003: Millennium Development Goals, A Compact among Nations to End Human Poverty,* the majority of African countries south of the Sahara top the list of low human development countries. Unless the other half of Africa's human resources, women, are fully developed, men will be less able to rise out of the cycle of poverty, disease, war and violence which has become Africa's blight. The new generations of African university educated women are less willing to reproduce traditional societies and gender roles which offer such bleak futures for their children and families. Rather many younger African women are organizing, particularly in Cameroon and Nigeria, to create life affirming opportunities for new generations and to bring to an end customs and traditions, whether colonial or African, which are life-destroying and oppressive to women and girls. The voices of African women are fresh and original but also urgent and compelling.

Chapter 13 Notes

1. See http://www.worldbank.org/gender/prr/ for full report entitled: "Endangered Development Through Gender Equality in Rights, Resources, and Voices." Also see "Women's Participation and Leadership: Vital to Democratic Governance." Presentation by Noeleen Heyser, Executive Director of UNIFEM Summit on the Americas, Monterrey, Mexico, 13 January 2004 at: http://www.unifem.org/speeches.php?f_page_pid=77&f_pritem_pid= 155. Accessed on 18 May 2005.
2. Pidgin English is a form of language spoken in many West African countries to conduct

business. It has a combination of many languages for example, English, French, German, and the local languages. Hausa is the language of many Muslim communities in Africa.

3. These focused sessions provided a forum for participants to discuss freely and honestly while voicing their frustration at the non-congruency between traditional adherence and modern legal settings. Suggestions arising from these sessions provide the majority of the ways to improve gender relations for the future for addressing one of the main objectives of this study.

4. For more information on world religions see: http://www.refdesk.com/factrel.html

5. For more information see: www.femnet.or.ke/documents/csw.asp. Accessed 18 May 2005.

6. See also Women in National Parliaments at: http://www.ipu.org/wmn-e/classif.htm. Accessed 18 May 2005.

7. For more information see: www.femnet.or.ke/documents/csw.asp. Accessed 18 May 2005

8. For a complete report see Statement on Women's Contributions to a Culture of Peace at http://www.unesco.org/cpp/uk/declarations/wcpbei.htm Accessed: 18 May 2005.

9. See Canadian Voice of Women for Peace at http://www.peace.ca/vowunesco.htm. Accessed 18 May 2005.

10. Fufu is a mashed potato-like consistency prepared by pounding cooked yam, cocoyam or plantain.

11. For a complete list of declarations see: "Beijing Declaration and Platform for Action, Fourth world Conference on Women," 15 September 1995, A/CONF.177/20 (1995) and A/CONF.177/20/Add.I (1995) at http://www.un.org/womenwatch/daw/beijing/platform/declar.htm. Last Accessed:18 May, 2005.

12. http://www.unhchr.ch/huridocda/huridoca.nsf/ (Symbol)/A.CONF.157.23.En? Open-Document. Accessed: 18 May, 2005.

13. See specifically The Department of Gender and Women's Health at: http://www. who.int/gender/en/.

14. Visit http://www.unicef.org/whatwedo/index.html for additional information on specific programs.

15. See http://portal.unesco.org/education/en/ev.php-URL_ID=38873&URL_DO=DO_TOPIC&URL_SECTION=201.html for a detailed discussion of UNESCO's goals for the education of girls and women human rights declaration.

16. Details can be found in Transparency International, World Index on Corruption Report, 2003 at http://www.transparency.org.

[4]17. See "Changing Fortunes of Government Policies and its Implications on MIDENO2" at: http://www.njas.helsinki.fi/pdf-files/vol13num1/fonjong.pdf see also Highlights of the Nigerian Livestock Resources Report," at: http://www.odi.org.uk/pdf/papers/35d.pdf; and Mbuh, J. (2005) CHAPTER 5, "Redressing a Mismanaged Economy," at: http://docs.indymedia.org/twi/pub/Main/JusticeMbuh/ICCPC5.doc;see also "Recent Interights Commonwealth Human Rights Law," at: http://www.worldlii.org/int/cases/ICHRL/recentcases.html.

18. Cameroon Enhancing Structural Adjustment Facility Medium Term Economic and Financial Policy Framework Paper, (1999/200-2001/02) at http://www.imf.org/ external/NP, for more details. See also, "The IMF: Selling the Environment Short In Africa (2) at http://www.foe.org/camps/intl/imf/selling/africa2.html; see in addition, Cameroon (01/05), article suggesting that Cameroon and two other African states—were devalued by 50 percent in January 1994, The government failed to meet the conditions of the first four IMF

programs" article is slightly misleading and less informed since in most cases, salaries of civil servants were cut by up to 100 percent and in some cases, as in those of the military and other paramilitary units, police and gendarmes were instead raised! For details see: http://www.state.gov/r/pa/ei/bgn/26431.htm. See also Mbuh, J. (2005): Ingredients of International Conflict Viewed from: Inside Contemporary Cameroon Politics at: www.authorhouse.com for more details.

19. See Charles Cobb, Jr. S, article "Broader Approach Needed to Achieve Bush HIV/AIDS Plan Goals," at: http://www.allafrica.com/stories/200405180707.html. Accessed 18 March 2004.

20. See WHO publication titled "Global AIDS Epidemic shows no sign of abating; highest infections and deaths ever" at: http://www.who.int/hiv/en/ See also Mokgadi Moletsane and Mark W. DeLancey's article "HIV/AIDS: A Problem for Africa - A Special Problem for African Women" first published in *Asian Women Journal*, Vol. 15, (Seoul: Research Institute of Asian Women, 2003).

21. Reardon, "Women and Peace: Feminist Visions of Global Security", (Albany: State University of New York Press, 1993).

22. Russell and DeLancey, "African Women in Cabinet Positions."

Chapter 14

To Be or Not to Be a Mother

Anne Breneman

A discussion of any women's movement, whether local, national or global, would be incomplete without examining the primary social role women tradition-ally have played as mothers. Biotechnology notwithstanding, motherhood is not likely to disappear, though gender roles are adjusting to the egalitarian require-ments of a new millennium. While it is interesting to note various efforts to repli-cate women's functions as child bearers with various test-tube experiments, the biological instincts of women as mothers and the resulting maternal personality characteristics cannot be so easily replaced. One of the issues, which will be con-sidered here, is how the dramatic increase of women in the workforce outside of the home has affected the motherhood role of women and ultimately the devel-opment and welfare of their children and families.

Traditional Constructs of Motherhood

Concern about the changing nature of motherhood as a defining principle of women's identity is not a surprising one, since ancient societies tended to be ma-trifocal, valuing women on the basis of their fertility, childbearing, and child nur-turing capacities. In some societies, the matrifocal principle even took the form of mother-worship, of which the veneration of the Virgin Mother Mary in early Christian practice is an example. From ancient periods of history, India's reli-gious mythology involved female deities, as did African, European, and Asian cultures. Venus-like figurines, either carved or modeled from clay and dating back 30,000 years, have been found by archaeologists and interpreted in various ways, often from a male perspective.[1] Whatever the precise cultural meanings of such figurines, our ancestors were clearly concerned with survival, fertility and reproduction.

It seems likely that a division of labor based on biological differences devel-oped, though adapted to the culture, climate, beliefs, technology and circum-stances of each society and geographical circumstance. Both Durkheim and Engles studied and analyzed the beliefs and practices of a gender-derived division of labor in the family and, by extension, the society.[2] Religious revelations have contributed to the social constructions of motherhood, and correspondingly fa-therhood, in many societies.[3] Women have been taught generally, through relig-ion and custom, that motherhood is a sacred duty and to a great extent the *sine qua non* of womanhood, often their central occupation. On the other hand, men have been oriented toward a role of protector of women and children through the same religious teachings, though each culture has adapted these differently. On the other hand, many Native American tribes of North America have prioritized the mother role to such an extent that inheritance and identity are traditionally constructed on the basis of matrilineal clan organization.[4]

Chinese belief and tradition created a more patrilineal-based system, though women maintained their own identities by keeping the names derived from their mother's lineage. However, within their families of origin girls are not bearers of the family lineage; in their families of procreation girls are outsiders as well. Their value and social worth rested almost entirely on their childbearing capacities, particularly as bearers of sons to carry on the male lineage. Males inherited their father's clan and family names, and families lived with the paternal relatives, not the maternal.[5] On the other hand Europeans tended to have two parallel systems of gender construction, one which was patriarchal in name and lineage and another which may be a remnant of a matrifocal, goddess-worshipping society which existed prior to the invasion of the Indo-Europeans, a male-dominant, war-mongering group.[6]

African societies differ in their traditional social structures, from east to west, and north to south. The northern cultures seem to have developed, through both Islamic influence and European colonization, a more patriarchal, patrilineal culture, with some African adaptations to which Mbuh refers in chapter 8. Ancient Egyptian society may have valued males more than females in some eras, but archaeological findings suggest that there were also some egalitarian tendencies which permitted exceptional females to be held in esteem within their social contexts, though not necessarily through lineage or matriarchy.[7] In ancient Ethiopia, Queen Sheba created a royal lineage through her relationship with King Solomon of ancient Jerusalem. Through this legendary relationship, mentioned throughout the Torah, or Old Testament, requirements for Ethiopian royalty were established. If not descended from the union of Queen Sheba with King Solomon, a contestant could not claim the throne and title of "Lion of Judah." Further, Judaism became the official religion of the traditional Ethiopian Kingdom, until large numbers were converted to Christianity during the first century. However, wholesale conversion to Christianity didn't seem to influence the royal lineage requirement,[8] until the end of Haile Selassie's reign.[9] In this case, then, motherhood and lineage have been powerful influences in Ethiopian government until recent times.

Mesopotamian legends refer to a goddess rather than a god as the supreme deity, "Queen of Heaven." Eisler, who also mentions Sumerian and Babylonian legends and prayers extolling Nammu, the "Mother who gave birth to heaven and earth," argues that the prevailing social structure, prior to conquest by male-dominated, hierarchic and warlike barbarians about 3000 years ago, was one which valued peace, creativity and the life-sustaining powers of the goddess aspect of divinity.

In her extensive analysis of this process of replacing the "chalice" of civilization with the "blade" of aggression, force and war, Eisler implies that motherhood was once viewed as a power as well as an organizing principle of society. However, as a dominator culture spread its repressive influence, through war and conquest, societies such as the Minoan, which once valued more feminine qualities associated with the arts, love of beauty, goodness, compassion and spirituality, succumbed to the brute force of the invaders. Under such masculine domination, motherhood became something that bestowed status, controlled by the male-headed family and used to reinforce patriarchy.

In this light it may be useful to examine how motherhood fared in those societies that maintained either a matrilineal or matrifocal social structure after the dramatic change from hunting and gathering to pastoral and horticultural societies. Examples can be found among the Malay, the Thai and Filipino in Southeast Asia, Native Americans in North America and the Waadabe of northern Africa. In these cultures motherhood *is* family organization and infants and small children treasured, regardless of gender. Women with their offspring work in fields and marketplaces and contribute to the community's welfare and prosperity. If the father is absent through death, work-related travel, or divorce, the family continues to focus around the mother and her children, supported by the matrilineal clan.

Motherhood is also valued in patriarchal societies such as the Middle East. However, the ultimate value of a woman and her motherhood have been inextricably linked with the masculine gender of her offspring, as discussed in chapter 2, and women operate, to a great extent, within a cocoon of masculine dominance within the majority of Islamic societies. While the intricately woven threads may be silken, the cocoon of male control prevents girls growing up in Islamic cultures from aspiring to and developing capacities beyond the needs of the cocoon. Thus motherhood, especially in relationship to sons, may be fulfilling, in as much as bearers of sons are rewarded, but not bearers of daughters or barren women.

What Is the Value of Motherhood in Contemporary Society?

Women play a role in building and maintaining society, which has often been overlooked or dismissed in the European modeled modernization process. English Anthropologist Ashley Montague argued in his classic treatise on the role of women,[10] that the unique characteristic of women, emanating from motherhood, constitutes a primary civilizing force within any society. His viewpoint echoes that expressed by Anna Julia Cooper who in 1892, spoke of the role of educated mothers in pulling an enslaved people out of degradation:

> Not by pointing to sun-bathed mountaintops do we prove that Phoebus warms the valleys. We must point to homes, average homes, homes of the rank and file of horny handed toiling men and women of the South lighted and cheered by the good, the beautiful, and the true,—then and not till then will the whole plateau be filled with light.

Cooper's point in her essay, "The Colored Women's Office," was not that a woman of color, or any other woman for that matter, should confine her energies to the domestic sphere, but that her most direct influence on the upliftment of society is in the "office" of the enlightened daily management of her own home and family, a task which has far-reaching implications for her children and for society when one views the family as the basic social unit of any society. A daughter of a freed slave, Cooper herself was a graduate of Oberlin College in the US and an educator who completed her PhD at the age of 65 at the Sorbonne in France.[11]

Motherhood has become a somewhat unpopular topic among many feminists, who have focused their concerns around the equality of women through education, career opportunity, and control of one's body and reproduction.[12] Indeed, many women have opted out of the marriage institution altogether, preferring a career track instead of family life as a mother and wife. Others, increasingly fewer in number in the U.S., have chosen the more traditional role of working at home with their children, and in a growing number of cases, homeschooling them in order to counteract the increase of violence, materialism and immorality in public schools, to raise them in a more moral or religious environment, or to use a more individualized approach to developing human potential.[13]

On the other hand, divorce rates have risen everywhere as women have gained economic independence and legal support for human rights both nationally and internationally. Women of the new millennium are less likely to tolerate long lasting repression, violence and control by husbands once they become empowered to find jobs, housing and security independently of their husbands. Some researchers have revealed alarming statistics indicating that the new marital freedom has contributed to societies in which as much as 1/3 of its children and their mothers live in poverty. The United States is an example of the feminization of poverty, in which more liberal standards have led to both an increased number of divorces and out of wedlock births. Though not all societies would assume that children of divorce belong with their mothers, this has been a common assumption in American society and has resulted in a greater number of absentee fathers than might otherwise have occurred. According to recent research, fathers of divorce generally follow a pattern of decreasing contact with their children, which often produces growing alienation, anger and resentment on the part of the children.[14] This leads to an issue that will be addressed below.

Who Will Raise the Children?

As essential and significant as the goals of equality and empowerment are, must they be pursued at the cost of women's role as first teachers and trainers of the future generations? It is difficult to imagine a more significant role, though admittedly not a high paying or status-bestowing one. The U.S. census reports indicate an increase of stay-at-home fathers and single fathers, yet the numbers are negligent compared with those of single mothers. In 1970 1.8 percent of parents were single fathers, which grew to 2.5 percent by 2000. Compare this with 10.1 percent single mothers in 1970 and the jump to 22.9 percent by 2000. The loss of two-parent families was more dramatic during three turbulent decades, from 83.4 percent in 1970 to 60.4 percent in 2000. The same census indicated that what Andrew Hacker refers to as "happenstantial" births was at an all-time high, 1,347,043 in 2000.[15]

Hacker examined the success women have in sustaining families without fathers. One of the most notable disadvantages is the lack of financial resources one out of five single mothers in the US must cope with, compared with single fathers, who often experience an increase of income. The average once-married single mother household income drops 27 percent following divorce, while divorced fathers on the average experience a 10 percent rise in income.

A category which is of even greater concern, however, is that of unwed mothers; in 2001. 33.4 percent of American infants, one out of three, was born to unmarried girls and women, compared with one out of twenty in 1960. The average income in these single mother households is only half of the single, divorced mother households.[16] Such trends are creating an unprecedented number of children being raised in relative poverty. Compare these figures with those in two-parent homes who are enjoying the benefits of greater prosperity than has been available to any children anywhere in recent history. On the average, two-parent incomes are more than double that of one parent, which, combined with the decline in offspring, creates a formula for economic prosperity.

Research reports on childbearing across the world community indicate that as the education of women becomes more equal to that of men, birth rates tend to drop, sometimes dramatically. Within the U.S., the contrast in age of mothers at birth of their first baby is dramatic when correlated with college graduates. Only 22.4 percent college women under 25 gave birth to their first children in 1970 compared with the average American woman, of whom 81.2 percent gave birth to their first child before reaching the age of 25. By 2000 only 5.6 percent of college women, compared with 51.8 percent of all women, gave birth to their first child by age 25. In 1960 American women on the average gave birth to 3-4 children during their lifetime, compared with 2 or less by 2000.[17] With the discovery of more scientific methods of birth control, women have begun to take more control of the number of children to which they are willing to give birth.[18]

Compared with women around the world, the American rate of fertility is almost a median rate, with women in Yemen, Congo, Iraq and Uganda bearing an average of 7 children in their lifetimes, women in Guatemala, Iraq, Pakistan and Madagascar averaging 4-5, and women in Canada, Japan, Greece, Hong Kong, Russia and Bulgaria bearing only 1-2 children.[19] While the changes in birth control technology provide more choices for women, a significant factor in the drop of birthrates, many women in the world community are unwilling to forego the role of motherhood altogether in order to achieve success in a career. A growing number of women are combining their childrearing tasks with work in factories, businesses, cottage industries and professional careers. More than in the past, women are seeking leadership roles at local and national levels of government. Activism has been strongly encouraged by the United Nations through development of women's NGOs at the grassroots level. Women are becoming empowered as they work together toward common goals, experiencing the exhilaration of mutual support and achievement.

However, many adjustments need to be made to allow women to make choices, which will take into consideration new opportunities in education and careers, as well as giving attention to forming more egalitarian marriages with shared household and childrearing responsibilities. In fact, many have opted for a fuller life that includes both motherhood and career. In addition, some women have also managed to include community service, religious and recreational activities, and various forms of cultural enrichment into the spectrum of their lives. Where does this leave children? Can children actually benefit from the changes in family social structure and the resulting calibration of roles, power and economics?

Motherhood: a Social Construction?

As defining as motherhood has been for women in the past, it is often overlooked or brushed aside as a less important concern than the achievement of full equality and empowerment, particularly in North America. Johnston and Swanson[20] assert that". . . it is useful to recognize that motherhood is not biologically determined or socially ascribed: Motherhood is a social and historical construction." Their analysis of the role of the media in constructing motherhood ideologies reinforced their perspective of motherhood as a socially determined phenomena. Culture, in their view, mandates the meaning of motherhood within a given society, along with the norms that guide appropriate behavior, attitude, relationship and identity.

Among American college students of the first decade of a new millennium, few females plan to stay home to raise children even for the length of maternity leave, considering this as a less fulfilling alternative to pursuing a higher status, higher paying career in a profession. Some feminists consider nurturing children through their early years as a luxury afforded only by those in the upper, privileged classes, and as a perpetuation of patriarchy and the economic dependence of women.[21] Similarly such an ideology suggests that an American cult of traditional domesticity historically excludes African, Asian and Latino mothers from the ideal club of "good motherhood." Class may also influence the popular conception of what constitutes good motherhood. On the newsstands one finds themes of domesticity, beauty, race and consumerism in classic American women's magazines. How to make oneself pleasing and attractive are common topics. In contrast, career track women's magazines promote independence, political involvement, career focus, sexually active relationships, and consumer-driven beauty images.

Motherhood in the West suffered several major blows during the first half of the 20th century—the wholesale movement from the home into the workforce of working age women, the rise of divorce and single parent households headed by women, the increase of formal childcare for infants and preschoolers by non-family members, and the feminist movement itself, which favored career women with non-maternal identities and lifestyles. The overall effect has been a movement away from a family-oriented society to an adult-focused one obsessed with consumerism. Further the discovery of birth control devices provided women with a greater sense of personal choice regarding motherhood, but also moved sexuality away from a sacred act of procreation and toward a more banal and recreational function, the one intended by the slogan often heard on the streets and in the conversation of Americans, "Sex sells."

In speaking of motherhood one cannot ignore the primary beneficiaries of its quality. Ironically, just as women and men began to learn more about child psychology and pedagogy to improve the process of parenting, working mothers began to place their children in childcare facilities with unpredictable measures of quality. Consequently many children have been increasingly exposed to erratic preschool experiences, some of which may result in earlier reading achievement and social development, while others introduce toddlers to consumer conformity through peer pressure. The urge to wear clothing just like "Joshua" or "Sobrina's" and to act similarly to other children in a daycare can be overwhelming for children of preschool ages. Meanwhile Mothers find themselves working "double shifts," preparing meals, driving children to and from daycare, school and after-school lessons, doing laundry and housework while helping children with homework and bedtime routines, and preparing for the next day's work during their few hours at home. Children, especially infants and toddlers, must detach themselves from their mothers at a developmental stage when mother separation anxiety is already intense, due to a young child's complete dependency. While improved social skills are often cited as benefits of early childcare, so also is the earlier onset of peer pressure, which is more traditionally associated with school age children.

It is important to note that throughout the world women who have pursued careers outside of the home have utilized many alternative arrangements for care of children. One of the common traditional forms of non-parental childcare works well in extended families where grandparents either live in the same home with their grandchildren or within the neighborhood. Prior to industrialization, this common three-generation household lent itself to women working outside of the home, whether as cleaning women, farmers, businesswomen, midwives, or even "barefoot doctors." For this arrangement to work, there must exist a value placed on women working outside of their own households, and older relatives who are willing and able to serve as nannies. As modernization continues then, this structure becomes a segue for women to pursue higher education and careers, such as in some Latin American and Asian societies. In other societies, such as Malaysia and Singapore, women who have chosen careers outside of the home are comfortable with hiring "amahs" to care for their children and other servants to clean and cook. Indeed, it is considered selfish of an upper class working woman to not hire such persons to help her with her domestic work, as this is a way to share the wealth she is creating through wage labor.[22]

In the Russian and Chinese societies of 1976 to 1978, Bronfrenbrenner found that the governments developed policies in which all women were required to go into careers and to work outside of the home. Therefore the daycare programs were government sponsored as well and served as a means to socialize the post-evolution generations into communist values, behaviors and loyalty to the State above the family. Such programs began with infancy, much as contemporary western daycare programs which offer childcare from birth to primary school in many cases. The major difference is that in the State-sponsored childcare programs, the government made the decisions regarding which childcare and what curriculum children would be taught. Childcare was paid for by the state and the programs were fairly predictable, as they emphasized the party line and de-emphasized western liberal values such as individualism, free enterprise, critical thinking and personal decision-making.

In American society, where individualism has created uneven living arrangements, depending upon region, culture, ethnicity and class,—once the day-care stage ends with the beginning of public schools, children of working parents may find themselves shuffled from a 6-8 am daycare, to an 8 am-3 pm academic program, to a 3-5:30 pm after-school service. Tired working parents then pick their children up and drive them home for a few more hours of homework, dinner and bedtime. What this effectively creates for children of working parents is an average weekday of 14-15 hours, out of which approximately 20 percent is spent with family and 80 percent with peers and non-family members. Upper class parents, in the minority, are able to hire nannies and maids to help with their children and house work chores, while the great majority of American women share the double-shift syndrome of domestic and non-domestic work, using a variety of resources and networks to assist them with their multiple responsibilities.

Many parents may find themselves leaving their children at home with siblings and television after school. Unfortunately mothers are finding that most of what is offered on television and other media, such as computer games, cds and videos are not only unfit for their children, but even harmful, particularly in western countries, where the love affair with technology combines with freedom of speech values. Providing parents with such devices as "v chips" and filters which block swear words and some violence doesn't seem to make much of a dent in the swell of inappropriate material produced by the media for general consumption. Further, the question arises whether adults are immune from the negative effects of such meta-messages simply because they are no longer in the formative age of development. Numerous studies have confirmed what common sense has always suggested, that children who view violent and inappropriate sexual behaviors in the media are more likely to engage in "copycat" behaviors in their peer relationships than children who are not exposed to the material in question. But the influence of the media doesn't end with violence and sex, as an American group of protesting mothers point out.[23]

Mothers as Revolutionaries

In 2003 a group calling themselves "The Motherhood Project" organized a movement of mothers across America, protesting the pervasive reach of advertising campaigns into children's lives, retraining them to become primary consumers. According to a spokeswoman for the group, recent trends in marketing of various products directly to children, after the deregulation of children's television in 1984, has resulted in increased violence, obesity, family stress, negative values and eating disorders involving children. Enola Aird, expresses concerns that the media is actively competing with mothers and fathers in how they raise their children and what morals, mannerisms, and values the children adopt as they grow into adults:

> They target our children with a steady stream of messages that emphasize self-indulgence, instant gratification, and materialism. These attitudes are antithetical

to what most mothers and fathers seek to teach their children and antithetical to the attitudes and values that make for healthy living and democratic life.[24]

What mothers are universally known for, regardless of social, historical or geographical constructions, is their concern for the welfare of children, particularly their own. To deny the biological origins of motherhood, to dismiss the motherhood role as merely a socially constructed one, or one that is instrumental in nature and therefore replaceable by nannies, daycares, schools, or even fathers, is to ignore the evidence found even in the animal species. While exceptions abound in every species, it has been an experientially based understanding that mothers of young offspring can be more fiercely protective than their more powerfully built counterparts. Capacities for motherhood usually emerge during pregnancy, when the hormones are restructured to prepare a female for nurturing, feeding, training and protecting a helpless infant while enduring long hours with little sleep. The same instincts and concerns take the form of guardian, coach, teacher and counselor as a child grows through various stages of maturation to full adulthood. An elderly woman who had been orphaned during her early years described the value of a mother,

> I wasn't treated very nicely, but didn't expect nice treatment anyway. Coming up without a mother, I gave up my rights. A mother protects you and sees that you get the best, but she needs an education. My stepmother had no education— she was illiterate and mean. . . .There are so few good mothers, and they are so important.[25]

During the 1970s and 1980s, Urie Bronfenbrenner conducted a longitudinal study on motherhood, single parenting and the welfare of children brought up in father-absent families. As a social scientist, Bronfenbrenner was concerned with the effects of "latchkey" children raised with two-three times the exposure to peer culture than was the norm prior to World War II. Prior to that mid-century watershed, he observed, children were more likely to spend the greater portion of their day with adult family members and in adult-supervised social environments rather than with peers only. He noted that the movement of women from the home into the workplace during the twentieth century had created more peer dominated social environments for children than provided by traditional family arrangements. This trend has been compounded by the increase of single mother father-absent families.

One of the outcomes of his concerns and research findings was a White Paper prepared for the US Congress, documenting his concerns and recommendations. He described the development of healthy children in terms of functions and needs addressed in a traditional family, whether nuclear or extended, and concluded that if a single parent could arrange to provide such needs and functions, a child may yet grow up to be a healthy, contributing member of society, regardless of father or mother absence. Both parents make unique contributions to a child's development and maturation, though women are more likely to acknowledge the inadequacies of parenting alone and to seek help from relatives, friends and professionals.

Other research documents that the fullest development of a child's potential occurs when both parents are actively engaged in parenting and their child becomes deeply attached to both. Greater involvement of fathers is thought to contribute to a balance between individualism and the practice of justice in a child's development. In the U.S., the pattern has been that after divorce, children are gradually abandoned by their fathers. This manifests itself first as reduction of child support, irregular visits, and eventually moving away from their children. Ten years later, two thirds of divorced dads have lost contact with their children. Loss of financial support creates a dramatic change in lifestyle for children of divorce, who often suffer from the belief that they are a financial burden or even the cause of their parent's problems in the first place.[26]

In his landmark study of Russian children, Bronfenbrenner observed that following World War II the shortage of fathers was so widespread that the government found it necessary to provide state-sponsored boarding schools for infants and preschoolers to prevent widespread juvenile delinquency related to fatherless children roaming about the countryside.[27] Another aspect of the government plan was to train women for the numerous positions left open. Thus gender equality and government sponsored daycare in Russia were advanced by the government as a solution to the workforce gap following the carnage of a poorly prepared military operation for which Russia paid dearly in the number of male casualties. What effects have such arrangements, involving long periods of mother absence, had on Russian children? Bronfrenbrenner's research might well be extended to a longitudinal study to provide more understanding of the role of motherhood in the development of a good human being who is able to contribute positively to a given society, as well as to the next generation as a parent.

Other examples of collective expressions of mother revolutionaries can be found in societies as diverse as Argentina and Bosnia. Marguerite Bouvard studied a movement of Argentina mothers who protested the abduction, torture and disappearance of their children during the reign of a ruthless dictator.[28] Similarly in Bosnia during the beginning of the war, newspapers around the world carried photos and stories of groups of women surrounding government offices to protest their son's conscription as soldiers in a war they feared could only end in further violence and bloodshed. The sad ending to this story is historical record. If only the concerns of the mothers had been heeded.

Transforming Motherhood

As women have moved into the workplace during the past century, a greater number of women have also entered institutions of higher education. Fertility rates have decreased in proportion to the education and empowerment of women, who have become able to take greater control over the number of children they will bear with the advancement of birth control technology and participation in family decision-making. The issues associated with mothering have become more public in each society as the need for quality childcare has correspondingly increased. Clearly the functions of women as mothers have been a subject of greater scrutiny than in the past, when this function was assumed a natural part of the order of life. Further, the presence of grandparents who lived nearby or in the home made it possible for many women in traditional societies to move more freely to and from the home to the workplace, as opportunities evolved. However, this asset is diminishing in many societies as grandmothers are pursuing new careers, remaining longer in work positions or choosing such retirement options as travel, taking up a hobby or new career, volunteering or taking courses in various subjects.

Another important aspect of the mothering issue are new research findings on what interventions by parents can create the most intelligent, talented, capable child at each age of her development. When children were considered primarily as social security for parent's old age or as a significant part of the family work force, their training to "be seen and not heard" seemed adequate. Children could easily be evaluated in those terms. However, the accumulation of developmental psychology research findings over the past century and a half has motivated mothers, and to some extent fathers, more than ever to invest time, energy and other resources into developing their children's potential more fully by providing them with all of the latest learning materials, toys and technology. Upper class parents are at an advantage in this case.

Mothers who are able to stay at home to enrich their children's early childhood, at least during their formative years, are often able to succeed to a greater extent than those working mothers who must share their parenting with daycare workers or other child care agencies and thus have less control over what their children are learning and how much television they are watching. However, it would be a mistake to conclude that mothering is an either/or proposition: that is, either stay at home with one's children or pursue a career in the workplace and give up the primary functions of motherhood. In the Advancement of Women, Janet and Peter Khan[29] point out that the teachings of the most recent of the world's religions call for women to be invited to participate in all fields of human endeavor, to the extent that the concept of "women's work" and "men's work" will become irrelevant. They contrast the Bahá'í teachings on equality with religious/cultural practices of the past in which women were expected to occupy themselves almost exclusively with domestic pursuits, while men occupied themselves with public affairs, governance and the professions.

As the revolutionary movement of women into the workplace and public sphere has occurred, there has been a tendency to blame the breakdown of the family and the increase of adolescent crime and victimization on women's neglect of their family and children. Yet their entrance into fields that have been dominated by men, along with their participation in all aspects of society as equal decision-makers, can be viewed as a means of building amongst humankind the capacity for living together peacefully. Is it possible that the increase of crime and corruption among all ages and professions everywhere is symptomatic of the inadequacy of systems of thought and practice, which the world has outgrown? Searching for new paradigms, rather than yearning for the past to return, seems to offer better solutions for the globalized world community that is emerging. Among the many cultures of the world can be found those that have highly successful systems of childcare, which do not require a mother to "stay in the home," but rather rely on an extended family approach. This method works especially well in those communities that place a high value on children as their investment in the future.[30]

Among the outdated systems is the sort of education process that focuses on rote learning, competition, and superiority and credentialing agencies without concern for the development of humanity, ethics, consciousness, or understanding. Examples of outdated systems can be found everywhere. When a system of education is effective most of the graduates will succeed in becoming decent citizens and functioning members of society, with a reasonable percentage of exceptions. That is, basic concepts of trust, integrity, service, reliability, honor, tolerance of diversity,[31] respect, work, decency and concern for the welfare of others will be reflected in all of the social, political, economic and religious institutions and human affairs. It is natural to believe that mothers alone are responsible for such a state of grace. But it was Maria Montessori who traveled around the world between World War I and II to introduce the understanding that Peace must begin in the minds of men and women who have been given an education which develops their full intellectual and spiritual potential. She advocated an educational system that begins in early childhood, with both genders respected as individuals possessing unique talents and abilities to be developed. Though she is less remembered for her numerous peace talks, her influence can be reckoned in the number of Montessori programs and schools which have been established throughout the world and the students who have distinguished themselves in the various sciences and arts. In this system of education, motherhood and involvement in professions outside of the home, including positions of leadership, are presented as complementary aspects of a society which values its children, women and men equally. Teachers and parents work together to advance their children's progress in both the home and school settings, negating the notion of adversarialism which has grown up in many American schools, driving away both teachers and parents.

Bahá'í law requires that when parents or communities are unable to educate all children, the education of girls is to be prioritized so that when they become mothers their children will not suffer from ignorance. Clearly such new concepts imply reorganization of society so that motherhood and childcare is valued, but not at the expense of the full development of women's capacities to participate in the broader society.

A New State of Mind

The reorganization of society to place a greater value on the development of children's full potential, to encourage good mothers and good fathers, to give attention to quality child care, and the participation of both women and men in the domestic and public spheres seems a reasonable characteristic of a society which has shed its patriarchal armor in exchange for a more prosperous, egalitarian and cooperative family structure. From such beginnings, new generations are apt to emerge with beliefs, values, behaviors and expectations which support the concept that "each child is born into the world as a trust of the whole" and with basic human rights and obligations. In viewing the great variety of family types which exist throughout the world, it would seem that those with the greatest capacity to nurture, protect, guide and educate children to their full potential, with the least gender favoritism, will survive the revolution which is underway. Even the gender revolution would be self-defeating if the development and security of future generations were to be jeopardized. Therefore the topic of motherhood goes beyond that of equality to the survival of the human species, and to the full realization of its potential for prosperity. In this light the issue of whether one chooses motherhood or career success should be exchanged for one of the development of social structures, which encourage and fully support both. Not every woman wishes to become a mother, not every woman wishes to pursue a career, and many women wish to dissolve the boundaries between work and home. Similarly, some men are uncomfortable with children while others long to enjoy their company as fathers, brothers and uncles. Men have usually been freer to make choices regarding their potential roles as fathers, even to the extent of neglecting those they have helped to conceive. In a society that nurtures egalitarianism, such as the Mai of Malaysia, both males and females are involved with their children's care, support and upbringing. Our overly civilized western world may benefit from a deeper study of such societies, which often turn out to be among those that also value nonviolence, mutuality and peace.

Chapter 14 Notes

1. See C Renzetti & D Curran, *Women Men & Society*, 5th ed. (n.p.: Allyn & Bacon, 2002).
2. Friedrich Engels 1884, "The Patriarchal Family," in *Social Theory: the Multicultural and Classic Readings*, ed. Charles Lemert, (Boulder, CO: Westview Press, 1999); Emile Durkheim 1902, "Anomie and the Modern Division of Labor," *Social Theory:* Ibid.
3. e.g. J Khan & P Khan, "Advancement of Women: a Bahá'í Perspective," (Wilmette, IL USA: Bahá'í Publishing Trust, 1998).
4. Jensen, "Native American Women, Seneca.
5. See Chinese family structure and status of women within hierarchy in Ono Kazuko, *Chinese Women in a Century of Revolution, 1850-1959* (Stanford, CA: Stanford University Press, 1989)
6. Eisler, *Chalice and Blade.*
7. Gay Robbins, "Women in Ancient Egypt," in *Women's Roles in Ancient Civilizations,* (Westport, CT: Greenwood, 1999), 154-187; Tolagbye Ogunleye, "Women in Ancient West Africa," Ibid: 188-216.
8. i.e. to be a descendent of the Queen of Sheba and King Solomon.
9. Haile Selassie ("Tafari Makonnen") ruled from 1930 to 1936, was exiled from 1936 to 1941, and returned to rule as emperor of Ethiopia until his controversial death in 1975. Considered the last descendent of the "Lion of Judah" bloodline, Selassie's demise represented the end of monarchy in Ethiopia and the beginning of constitutional government with a socialist agenda, Chris Prouty & E. Rosenfeld, *Historical Dictionary of Ethiopia,* (London: Scarecrow Press, 1982).
10. Ashley Montague, *The Natural Superiority of Women*, 5th ed. (Walnut Creek, CA: AltaMira Press, 1999).
11. Cooper was an early Black American feminist writer and educator who taught at the

Washington DC M-Street School from 1887-1906. See Anna Julia Cooper, "The Colored Women's Office," in *Social Theory: the Multicultural and Classic Readings*, Charles Lemert, ed, (Boulder CO: Westview Press, 1999).

12. See e.g. Deidre D Johnston & Debra H Swanson. "A Content Analysis of Motherhood Ideologies & Myths in Magazines," in *Sex Roles: A Journal of Research*, July 2003.

13. 850,000 or 1.7% of US students, ages 5-17 are home-schooled, from *HomeSchooling in the US: 1999, see*
http://nces.ed.gov/pubs2001/2001033.pdf#search='HomeSchooling%20 in%20the%20US%201999'.

14. Hacker, *Mismatch.*

15. "Living Arrangements of Children" Bureau of Census 2001 (LAC), "Family Composition," Bureau of Census 1973 (FC)

16. "Money Income in the US" Bureau of Census 2001 (MI)

17. "Fertility of American Women" Bureau of the Census 2001 (FAW)

18. The World's Women 2000: Trends & Statistics, United Nations: NY 2000

19. UN Population Statistics Division (2002 BFD)

20. See Johnston & Swanson, "Invisible Mothers."

21. See Engels, "The Patriarchal Family"; Nancy Chodrow, "Gender Personality and the Reproduction of Mothering" in *Social Theory; The Multicultural and Classic Readings*, (Boulder, CO: Westview Press, 1999).

22. Field notes, Anne Rowley, 1977, Thomas Watson Fellowship

23. See Bandura's "Social Learning Theory."

24. Enola G Aird, Director of The Motherhood Project, Institute for American Values, Congressional Briefing 1/31/03, http://www.watchoutforchildren.org.

25. Vashti Smith, Notes: Personal Interview with Anne Breneman, 1990, Florence SC.

26. See Andrew Hacker, "Doing without Dads" in *Mismatch: the Growing Gulf Between Women and Men*, (New York: Scribner, 2003).

27. See Bronfenbrenner, *Two Worlds of Childhood.*

28. Marguerite G Bouvard, *Revolutionizing Motherhood: a Bahá'í Perspective* (Wilmette, IL: Bahá'í Publishing Trust, 1998, 2001).

29. Khan & Khan, *Advancement of Women.*

30. e.g. American Indian tribes, aboriginal tribes in Malaysia, and West African tribes often demonstrate a greater affection for children and desire to include them in their community life than many urban cultures which reflect a high level of work-achievement anxiety combined with time constraints

31. "Teaching Tolerance for All: Education Strategies To Promote Global Peace." *International Yearbook on Teacher Education 1995*. Proceedings from the World Assembly of the International Council on Education for Teaching (42nd, Darussalam, Brunei, July 3-7, 1995).

Chapter 15

Empowered and Equal:
How Do We Get There?

Anne Breneman and Rebecca Mbuh

In the preceding chapters we examined local, national and regional revolutions in the past century and a half, which led to the gradual emergence of an international women's movement supported by the United Nations and still gaining momentum. Social movements are more common in industrialized countries, particularly those with democratic process, than in more traditional authoritarian societies, where political participation is lower and repression of individual rights is higher. It has been observed by scholars such as C Wright Mills that, in order to form, social movements must manifest certain prerequisite conditions.[1] First among these is dissatisfaction with the status quo. In most cases the dissatisfaction of women has arisen out of the arrangements of patriarchy, in which societies have been organized around a principle of gender inequality that combines with traditions of power, authority, and privilege, as in Iran and the U.S..

Dissatisfaction

Gender social relations differ widely across the world community. In those societies in which patriarchy is prevalent as an ideology, dissatisfaction among women has been higher than in countries in which women enjoy higher status and greater participation in their communities. The subtleties of a patriarchal value system may socialize women and girls to participate in their own repression. During the early period of conquest and in the colonization of the Americas, Africa, Asia, and the islands, Riane Eisler suggests that *"dominator cultures"* imposed a veneer of patriarchalism on aboriginal hunting and gathering societies. That is, societies that had become more sedentary, with fixed male hierarchical structures of power, attempted to replace values and practices based upon more cooperative gender relations.

Sandra Bem believes that such patriarchal societies create cultural lenses of gender polarization and androcentrism that become the major basis of social organization.[2] The lenses are composed of a set of hidden assumptions about how members of a society should look, act, think and feel. That which is male is valued and preferred above that which is female. These assumptions are embedded in cultural discourses, social institutions, interrelationships, and individual psyches. Children are then enculturated systematically from infancy within their families, both through male and female members, to understand the resulting values that segregate and define gender roles and preferences as default responses to every aspect of their lives, from childrearing to family relations to the clan, tribe, community and nation. Throughout one's life, *"meta-messages"* provided by individuals, groups, institutions, and the media continuously reinforce the values of androcentrism. That is, what are considered by a society to be male experience and characteristics are used as normative standards through which even females are measured.

Eventually the patriarchal order of society becomes understood as "bio-essentialism." Bioessentialism creates the belief that the resulting gender segregation and its differential valuation of the sexes is natural and proper. Thus girls are clothed in pink (e.g. in America) and encouraged to engage in domestic activities and to concern themselves with the attraction of males to their persons. On the other hand, boys are clothed in blue (e.g. in America) and molded into emotionless warrior-hunter-protectors and sexual predators usually through sports enculturation. Because males are valued above females, it is acceptable and even desirable for girls to act as "tomboys," while it is highly undesirable for boys to manifest feminine behaviors and qualities. Aggression and assertiveness, for example, are considered desirable traits for success while compassion, intuitiveness and cooperation are not. America is a multicultural society, but nonetheless, the media promotes messages that tend to reinforce dominant patriarchal values.

In Islamic and many Western and African societies, primogeniture contributes to an androcentric individual identity by providing each member of society with one's father's name. Thus a woman's surname is in most cases, though not all, that of her father or her husband. In Islamic as well as many African societies, a woman's status rises when she gives birth to a son, whose name then becomes her primary identity e.g. *"Mother of Solomon."* In such a configuration, to be the daughter of her father carries more prestige than to be the daughter of her mother, regardless of the social status of either parent. In traditional Euro-American society, a woman was known by her father's name, then by her husband's when she married. As a married woman, her public identity completely submerged her personal identity i.e. "Mrs. Walter Jones." African American tradition permitted a somewhat more flexible adherence to androcentric traditions. Thus, an unmarried woman might carry either her mother's or her father's surname, particularly in the case of single parent families. Part of the concern with carrying one's father's name in an androcentric society is related to traditional norms concerning children born to unwed mothers. Such children were labeled as *"bastards"* and denied many rights associated with inheritance and social status. Since only males could own property in traditional American society, and not to own property was considered a manifest sign of unworthiness to participate in government, those without property were poor indeed.

Given such arrangements, what has happened to upset the status quo? In chapter 1 we discussed some of the conditions in selected areas of the world that gave rise to discontent among women. Among these were the development of liberal philosophies that led to revolutions against tyrants, including many monarchies of the seventeenth, eighteenth and nineteenth centuries. As these revolutionary ideas spread and social-political orders of the day were dismantled, women began to question both their repression and their inability to participate in the fruits of the revolutions. Greater freedom of speech, movement, and participation in decision-making, as well as individual rights to choose, gave hope to the hapless masses, half of whom were women. Only a small percentage of women were from privileged segments of society. Those who began to enjoy the benefits of literacy and even elementary or higher education began to speak out for the masses of women without voices. Outstanding among such women was scholar and poetess, Tahirih of Qazvin, Iran, whose bold example as the first female disciple of The Báb and advocate of women's education and emergence from purdah[3] won the admiration of the masses, but also the violent response of the Shah and Muslim clergy, resulting in her imprisonment and strangulation in 1852.[4]

Further examples include Elizabeth C Stanton, Angelina Grimke, Sojourner Truth, Seneca women of the Iroquois Confederation, Anna Julia Cooper,[5] the Trung Sisters of Vietnam, and Olympe de Gouges, who was sent to the guillotine in France for her circulation of *The Declaration of the Rights of Women and the Female Citizen.* The efforts of these courageous women and others referred to in earlier chapters, to organize other women and to speak out for their rights as citizens of what they saw as the emergence of a new social organization, created both seeds of discontent and visions of women as equal to men in capacity and possibility.

Such discontent on the part of women from societies with varying economic status contrasts with the assumption that gender equality is more prevalent to the extent a nation has moved from an agrarian to an industrial economy, and from an industrial to a postindustrial economy.[6] The Gender Empowerment Measure[7] was developed and used by the UNDP to correlate strength of religious belief, affluence, type of society, activism of women, work and family patterns to predict which nations are more likely to provide an encouraging environment for women's empowerment and gender equality.[8] This theme will be reexamined in our conclusions. During the early stages of a social movement, its momentum depends on its capacity to attract, engage, and mobilize adherents.

Mobilization and Engagement

If we are to view the movement of society from patriarchy to full equality as a social movement, then the second stage of its life course should focus on its capacity to mobilize others, recruit new participants, and engage the public's attention. This process was halting and irregular, according to the circumstances of each woman's life and the traditional restraints of her surrounding community, culture and society.

The Seneca Indian women who created their own *Declaration of the Rights of Women* at Cattaragus Reservation in Buffalo, New York earlier in 1848, just prior to the first organized women's rights convention in Seneca Falls, New York, were responding more, perhaps, to the oppressive European-American patriarchy, than to a sole concern with Seneca male dominance.[9] After all it was the former, which required Seneca women to relinquish their traditional agricultural work to the men in order to focus on European defined domestic tasks of sewing, cooking, and housekeeping. This forced resocialization of Seneca women resulted in the impoverishment of what had been a prosperous people.[10] The women protested to American political leaders the lack of respect accorded to those who provided for their people and from whom came their children. While their voices seemed to go unheard at that time, nonetheless history has recorded their appeal, which seemed to echo across the state of New York to take the form of protest by more privileged women against slavery and their lack of rights to vote its abolition.

Organization and dissemination of a women's movement crossed the globe according to each group of women's conditions. Some came from within a nation's social organization, such as that of Tahirih,[11] who unveiled herself, announced that a new age in which women would play a significant role was at hand and offered her life for the emancipation of women and the spread of the Bábi teachings in Persia (Iran). Other provocations came from without, as in colonization, with its transfer of patriarchy from the old world to the new and its dominant/subordinate relations between the conquerors and those conquered. Another kind of provocation for a women's movement is mentioned by Wu Xiaoqun in chapter 6. In the Communist revolution, part of the platform was to eliminate inequalities of gender, to reform the family structure, and to push women into the workforce along with men. A similar reorganization of gender relations was forced in Russia as the Communist revolution gained momentum, aided by the need to draw upon women to booster a workforce depleted by the loss of men during the wars. Hence in communist countries the women's movement was a gender equality movement owned and defined by the communist party, rather than by women awakening to their oppression. Nonetheless these events have provoked startling changes in gender relations in both societies and raise the question of how significant government policy can be in shifting power from one gender to another.

Institutionalization

The course of a social movement is typically characterized by a third stage of institutionalization. In this stage the principles of the movement become so widely accepted following a period of organized protest that those institutions representing the status quo begin to incorporate them into the social structure and provide the means for their enforcement. The authors would suggest that this stage has not been completely achieved in very many countries. The Gender Equality Scale relates modernization, affluence, education, religiosity, and type of society to gender equality among nations.[12] Can it be concluded that the more secular, the better educated, the more industrialized, the more affluent, the better educated, and the greater freedom a nation achieves, the more gender equality will be incorporated into a nation's institutions, social structure, relationships, values and life styles?

Has such a configuration been achieved in communist countries? To what extent have these factors contributed to the empowerment of women? While women's suffrage and the abolition of slavery were the focus of the women's movement which organized at Seneca Falls NY, in the U.S., in 1848, and were achieved in 1920 and 1863 respectively,[13] it has become increasingly apparent that the movement from a patriarchal to an egalitarian society has by no means been achieved. However, many western nations, including the U.S., have scored high on a modernization index. Among the key indices for modernization are economic prosperity, democracy, and participation of women in government. Yet the latter is yet to be achieved in most countries other than Scandinavia and the Caribbean, where women have achieved at least 30 percent of seats in parliamentary bodies.

"First Wave" and "Second Wave Feminism" have become terms used to acknowledge the limitations of the early period of women's awakening to work collectively toward tangible and politically achievable goals, such as women's suffrage, and to distinguish it from the more far-reaching and structural aims associated with the reawakening of women and, to some extent, men, to the realities of internalized oppressions of women and other victims of patriarchal societies.[14] The Second Wave is also associated in the U.S. with the conceptualization of the contemporary use of "feminism," which specifically attacks patriarchy and androcentrism in their many and varied forms. Feminism became a household word in America through the popularity of American authors such as Betty Friedan, who suggested that women's oppression extends into their bedroom relations and even their own socialized selves, as implied in her widely quoted phrase, "The personal is political."

However, it would also be possible to view the advancing global women's movement as evidence that institutionalization has been fully achieved or, at least, is well on its way toward becoming a standard for all nations of adherence to human rights and readiness for democracy. In this case the United Nations formation (1945), its subsequent adoption of the Declaration of Human Rights (1948), its first International Women's Conference in Mexico (1975), the series of global women's conferences which followed (1985, 1995, 2000), and the ratification of CEDAW by the majority of the member nations provide ample evidence of what has become the institutionalization of "indicators" of women's empowerment. That is, national governments have become accountable to the United Nations for compliance in areas of equality of educational opportunity, wages for equal work, seats in parliaments, access to health care, reduction of violence to women and girls, and establishment of national machinery and budgets for implementation of a national program to empower women.[15]

In the UN's "Millennium Forum Declaration of 2000," the UN, representing *"worldwide civil society,"* speaks of a *"vision of global inclusion and global prosperity."* It refers to the teachings of the world's religions prophesying a *"golden age of harmony and prosperity, peace and justice for all humanity"* and links this vision with great modern social movements and notable leaders, including Susan B Anthony and Mother Teresa:

> Moreover the impulse to war, peace and justice can be discerned in the abolition of slavery and the enfranchisement of women, to the struggle to throw off the yoke of colonialism, the great campaigns for racial harmony and economic jus-

tice, and the relentless efforts to establish world peace.[16]

It is the view of the authors that the global women's movement actually constitutes a Third Wave, since it transcends even the controversies of multiple and specific forms of feminisms, sweeping all into an inclusive movement toward "equality, development and education" of women everywhere. The "Third Wave" encourages each nation, culture or segment of women to work together toward common goals while defining through national machineries specific applications at the grass roots, including terminologies that apply.

Decline of the Women's Movement?

The last stage of a movement is that of decline. When the goals of CEDAW[17] have been completely achieved it might be said that the women's movement will have "declined." because it will have succeeded in achieving its aims. Indeed when egalitarian societies become structural, widespread and ordinary, and "dominator societies" become historic relics more than social realities, each society should begin to see a diminishing of issues associated with classism, racism, colonialism, sexism and patriarchalism. According to a document published by a NGO at the UN in 1995, as humankind begins to view its history as that of one human race and each infant born into the world as "a trust of the whole," as women and men view one another as "two wings of one bird" in need of mutual support to fly, as social problems are approached through consultation from the grass roots up rather than the more familiar top-down methods, as a vision of the possibility of celebrating unity in diversity emerges along with a concept of the entire earth as sharing the same environment—the "prosperity of humankind" will become a reality rather than a privilege enjoyed by a few.[18]

For such a fortuitous condition to be realized, each individual advocate of gender equality would have become committed to taking a few action steps towards the full equality of women and men within the scope of his or her own life, as well as within the framework of a nation's machinery for the implementation of CEDAW. The women's movement cannot achieve full success until men and boys have become equal partners in this endeavor.

A Global Revolution

When we speak of a movement from patriarchalism to egalitarianism or equality, we are in fact speaking of a revolution rather than merely a social movement. A revolution is described by social scientists as a radical perspective, one often associated with Marxist philosophy and theory. However, revolutions have occurred without Marxist influence as well. For example, when Christianity appeared in a Judaic and Roman society, when Protestantism swept through Europe and reorganized its religious, social and political worldview, or when Islam swept across Asia, Europe, and northern Africa and reorganized societies around the concept of nationhood and brotherhood. Going back further in time. "dominator" societies overtook cooperative societies and established permanent hierarchies of power based upon might, privilege and gender.

A revolution involves the uprooting of a certain pattern of economic, political and social institutions and beliefs and its replacement by a new set, which are in sharp contrast with what was in place before the revolution. Since the relationship between male and female is a fundamental aspect of any social organization, it seems reasonable to assume that the changes, which have been described and proposed in this book, collectively constitute a revolution in human affairs.

Although the women's movement may not at first thought seem to be a violent revolution, yet, if one reads section IV in this book on "Hazards of Growing up Female," there is evidence that this criteria has been met as well. Gender relations have largely been based upon male privilege and female subordinacy. As long as this pattern has been accepted and practiced, family relations have been described as fairly peaceful and harmonious. However, when the time-honored pattern is disrupted by new expectations and beliefs concerning equality and human rights,—friction, sometimes violence, becomes endemic and almost predictable. In viewing societies in Afghanistan or in some areas of the rural Southern U.S., or even large urban settings, the rules of male dominance and female subordinancy are enforced to such an extent that the streets are not safe for women and children to walk without fear of assault. This is certain to change as the new social, spiritual, political and economic forces which have been underway for more than a century and a half continue to break up traditional patterns of life and introduce new concepts such as universal communications and oceans of knowledge available to any one who is intelligent and computer-savvy.

That many women are already in the workforce, are in the government, are equally educated as men, are making decisions regarding their maternal choices, are writing and reading and speaking—indicates that the proverbial Pandora's Box cannot be closed with all of its content intact. It is in fact irreversible. All of the facts and figures which have been provided in each chapter and discussion are in fact trends, which continue to move toward more equality, more empowerment, more cooperation between women and men, and more incentives from governments to work toward a definition of progress that is based upon the progress of women.

To a large extent the next stage of the revolution must focus on developing mutual respect and cooperation between the genders, as men have more to lose of what has been their mistaken identity and privilege. Similarly the privileged peoples of the world, in terms of color, nation, wealth, status, and political clout, are in a position to develop a respectful relationship of cooperation with those members of society who perceive the privilege to have been gained at their expense. The decolonization of the world, the prosperity of humankind and the evolution of gender cooperation go hand in hand, particularly if we accept the notion that the origins of concepts of all political, economic and social inequalities may very well have begun with the concoction of inequality between the genders within the basic unit of society—the family. It is telling that the UN regards the Beijing Declaration of 1995 on Women as one of its nine most significant documents in advancing a vision of harmony and prosperity, peace and justice for all humanity. In identifying the way forward to the achievement of this vision, the UN calls for specific actions by the international community to address current gender inequities:

—firm and immediate action to protect women and children during war from physical depravation, use of child soldiers and rape as a form of terror*;
—recognition that the majority of the poor are women and children, and that society as a whole should take responsibility for institutionalized inequality and create equal opportunities for all people;
—inclusion of women's health in research and practice;
—recognition that gender-based violence, including female genital mutilation, armed conflict, domestic violence and other traumatic experiences contribute to chronic female physical and mental disorders and constitute a violation of their human rights;
—recognition that women's rights are human rights;
—women and men must be treated as equals. No tolerance of violations of women's rights should be entertained;
—trafficking of women and children should be ended via decisive action;
—harmful traditional practices such as female genital mutilation, child marriages and forced marriages should be combated;
—empowerment of women is essential for sustainable development;
—women must be fully empowered in all areas of decision-making.

The UN further urged world leaders to examine their paper on "The Challenges of Globalization: Achieving Equity, Justice and Diversity," expressing nine major concerns concerning the processes of globalization. Among these was one particularly relevant to what has been described extensively earlier, in chapter 10:

> We are concerned that the processes of economic globalization are taking a particularly heavy toll on women and children. Too often, women provide the bulk of cheap labor in the free trade zones, and there is little to ensure that safe working conditions and basic environmental standards are protected. Of special concern is the number of women who are the victims of sex trafficking and slavery, and the millions of children who are made to perform work that is hazardous or interferes with their health or physical, mental, spiritual, moral or social development.[19]

There is a tendency to become lost in the scale of these concepts at the macro level of society, particularly when referring to the global community. Yet these concepts seem little short of worthless if they cannot be boiled down to what each committed individual is capable of and committed to doing to achieve these objectives within the scope of ordinary lives and daily routines. How does one become empowered as a woman or assist others in becoming empowered? How can one promote gender equality in the daily lives each of us must live?

In Search of Empowerment

During the Beijing +5 conference in 2000 in Manhattan, a workshop was held entitled, "The Political Empowerment of Women." There were as many as 50 women from countries as diverse as Cameroon, Korea, Philippines, Japan, Russia, Uganda, Ghana and the U.S.. The authors participated in the workshop and recorded the discussion responses of our group to four questions posed by the workshop leader:

1) What does political empowerment mean to me?
2) How have you been involved at the local level to serve your community?
your family, and other women through decision-making and action?
3) How have you sought and created partnerships with other organizations
to show respect for the work of others?
4) What actions will you take when you leave the conference and return to
your community to empower women?

Some of the responses to Question 1 were:

decision making; learning not to become vacuumed into male agendas when in leadership roles; grassroots development of leadership capacities; confidence development from early childhood in girls; removal of impediments to empowerment from oneself; providing opportunity to work outside of the home; teaching respect for human life; providing equal education for both genders; learning to participate, network, and become involved; voting for issues which are important for women; enhancing women's ability to influence and negotiate power; training to raise consciousness of the spiritual and intellectual powers possessed by women and how to use these effectively.

Responses to Question 2 included, according to nation of origin:

Uganda: *Women organized themselves to support women candidates for positions in parliament, where the government has adopted an affirmative action policy to assure 33% women seats. The local counsels have become a way for women to develop the necessary skill for effective decision-making and consultation.*

Cameroon: *Local women organizations seek potential female candidates and rally support for them in elections, resulting in an increasing number of capable women in high offices.*

U.S.: *College students created and recorded a series of cds consisting of public service announcements using brief biographies of minority women who have risen above obstacles to achieve in various areas of human affairs. The project was created by a woman professor for a History course and used as a final exam.*

Ghana: *A group of lawyers formed a branch of the International Federation of Women Lawyers to train girls to defend their rights. They target women in churches and throughout the countryside to learn their rights and how to protect them. They also act as consultants for young girls, for lobbying to pass laws to protect women, such as banning female genital mutilation.*

Korea: *A Woman's Center for Policy Development has been founded to train girls and women in leadership skills, as well as policy awareness, and how to effectively change and create policies that will benefit women.*

Three responses were particularly relevant to Question 3 concerning women's skills in the areas of collaboration and networking:

Ghana: *The Federation of Women Lawyers collaborated with the Woman's Caucus in Parliament and a host of other groups to pass the law banning female genital mutilation in Ghana. These networks continue to grow as a means to approach other issues affecting women's rights. They have found that they have more power as networks of women's groups rather than as a single organization. For example they changed the way police stations handle girls and women who have been abused in domestic violence situations. Now there is a special room and a female officer available to provide respect, kindness and protection for the female victim in many Ghanaian towns Yet another example given is how this women's network acted to pressure the police department to begin an investigation of a series of female murders, which were considered of little significance to the police.*

Japan: *Several women's organizations have banded together to raise awareness re the horrors of sexual exploitation of women and girls. They are working on the passage of a law to prevent the molestation of women and girls. They are working on the passage of a law to prevent the molestation of girls currently, using the coalition as a basis for political pressure.*

Korea: *The Center for Policy Development works with other organizations that target women in their work in training women leaders, providing more resources for training than afforded by a single agency.*

Finally the women spoke to what actions they would personally take when they left the conference and returned to their respective communities to empower women. Their list included the following actions:

* *Try to remove impediments to the empowerment of women.*
* *Take time for yourself, rather than becoming so weakened and paralyzed by guilt and the desire to help everyone that you are unable to help yourself or anyone else.*
* *Seek to implement an affirmative action plan for women in leadership.*
* *Begin a support group for women in my workplace, encouraging more mature women to assist younger women to develop leadership skills, assume responsibilities, make goals and evaluate their progress toward achieving them.*
* *Work to overcome the immediate opposition.*

Empowerment may seem elusive to some, but the women who participated in the workshop were evidently already engaged in acts of empowerment, which included themselves and others. Any one of these reports of individual action could fan a revolution from a small spark into a raging fire capable of ravaging outworn shibboleths that have supported gender inequality and the oppression of women and girls for ages. While one may not personally wish to become a Member of Parliament, a mayor, a college president, a CEO, or a national leader, it is certainly within one's power to support and encourage those who do aspire to become effective leaders.

One does not necessarily need to become a public figure to work through all of the moments in one's daily life when small decisions have an accumulative effect on ones empowerment or disempowerment: what one says to a male member of one's family who has left most of the housework for more important tasks;

how one handles an intimate gender relationship; what decision one makes when being sexually harassed by an employer, colleague or family member; how one approaches one's employer to discuss fair work load, pay scale or maternity leave; the manner in which one conveys expectation of mutual respect to male family members and friends; how one trains sons and daughters in mutual respect and egalitarian modes of relationship. These are only a few examples of innumerable occasions at the micro-level of human relations, when gender tensions arise and are either resolved by some traditionally patterned response, often conflictive, or through the conscious application of the belief that women and men, as two wings of the same bird of humanity, are equal. But does empowerment lead to gender equality?

How Do We Get There?

How do we reconcile the findings of Inglehart and Norris, who concluded their study on gender equality and global cultural change with the propositions that secularization accompanies modernization, which in turn weakens religious values among younger generations and hence opens the door for relaxing traditional attitudes and beliefs regarding sexuality, marriage, family sex roles and divorce? They correlated UNDP indicators, such as percentage of women in professions, management, and parliament with women's education and reproduction and found that in agrarian societies, Catholics score higher in gender empowerment than Protestants, Buddhists or Muslims. In general, as societies move into the modernizing process of industrialization and post industrialization, the trend increases, paving the way for gender equality. This suggests that the less religious a society becomes, the more gender equality and empowerment will occur. However, with this trend usually comes demoralization and materialism. How can this paradox be understood?

One perspective, using Weber's analysis of modernization and secularization, is that modernization has a tendency to shift traditional values towards the acquisition of material goods and conveniences, providing a new measure of prosperity and success. The new measure is one requiring material wealth to gain status and dignity within a society. This is primarily gained in industrial and post-industrial societies through wage labor, rather than through the more traditional means involving networks, concern for the community's welfare, and sometimes trading of assets and services. Marx spoke bitterly of the process through which every aspect of life, even the sacred, can become reduced to dollars and cents as capitalism becomes the dominant economic philosophy of an industrialized society. Thus human trafficking and pornography becomes normal in a society that has abandoned traditional religious beliefs, values and practices. Individualism, drug sales and cruelty may become acceptable when these values are suspended in favor of profit and gain. Perhaps it would even be possible to suggest within such a vacuum of values that women and children who are trafficked have the opportunity to advance themselves and even make enough money to rise out of poverty and oppression by "playing their cards right" and exercising their choices? In this view even prostitution becomes a legitimate occupation, excusing the customers for their exercise of male privilege and ignoring the hazards to girls and women who have been employed in such activity.

Is it not possible that humankind has advanced to the point at which none of the existing theories of economic and political development are quite suitable? Similarly, many of the religious traditions referred to in the survey of gender equality suggest that adherents are operating within a religious framework which doesn't encourage individual development of conscience and relies on leaders of religion to define what is the acceptable way to practice religion, such as how many times a person should attend meetings, services or other official religious gatherings each week or month.

It is not surprising then that as individuals acquire more knowledge and education their willingness to be controlled by others gradually weakens and disappears, especially as they become aware of corruption among religious leaders. Traditionally women have exhibited more interest in spirituality and religion than men, but as women struggle to be esteemed as equals to men, paternal relationships with clergy may become more difficult to maintain, particularly if they reinforce inequality. Thus women have sought to become religious leaders themselves within the older religions, or to work from within the religious group to expand awareness of their growing belief in their own value as an individual with human rights that include equality.[20]

Equality doesn't imply sameness. Genuine application of equality as an empowering principle requires recognition of another principle found throughout the physical world—that of unity within diversity. Women are equipped with the same powers of intelligence and problem-solving capacities as men; however physiological research indicates that the unique capacities of women as child bearers and the primary nurturers of children extends female intelligence beyond the common denominator and even specializes their intelligence during childbearing and rearing toward a certain maternal genius. Education and development of such genius brings to the various fields of human endeavor, formerly closed to women, fresh insights and creativity. Management becomes less hierarchical and more cooperative, for example. Consultation becomes more essential to decision-making. The quality of education and childcare becomes more central to policy-making. Work places and methods become more flexible and less rigid. Leadership becomes less repressive and more empowering. Problem solving becomes more creative and less focused on "blame, shame, and humiliation" techniques.[21]

Women who rise to power in overwhelmingly androgynous societies are faced with misunderstandings regarding their approaches to leadership and problem solving, but may also prove their capacities to a point of provoking male fear, as discussed in chapter 1. The task of achieving full equality cannot be accomplished without revolutionizing the consciousness of both women and men. It has been recognized by the authors of the Charter of the UN that war begins in the minds of men, but it must also be understood that it is within the minds of both women and men that new concepts of relationship and partnership must develop. To a great extent this can be passed from mothers to sons and daughters, who will become a new generation of mothers and fathers, daughters and sons, sisters and brothers, and friends and lovers. These members of a new generation will also rise to leadership locally, regionally, nationally and internationally. This then is how a gender revolution can grow and gain momentum.

Might it not be said then that women have an immediate calling to the role of midwives of a better world, one capable of gender equality, kindness and tenderness, prosperity, justice and peace, in this new millennium? For according to an African proverb: *"He who wears the shoe knows how it pinches the foot."*

Chapter 15 Notes

1. C. Wright Mills, *The Sociological Imagination*, (New York: Oxford University Press, 1959); see also Herbert G Blumer, "Collective Behavior" in *Principles of Sociology*, Alfred McClung Lee, ed, (New York: Barnes & Noble, 1969); Charles Tilly, *From Mobilization to Revolution*, (Reading, MA: Addison-Wesley, 1978).
2. Bem, "Enculturated Lens Theory."
3. "Purdah" refers to the complete exclusion of women from public life, including the use of full covering from head to toe when males are present in any social setting outside of the home.
4. Root, *Tahirih.*
5. Cooper's list of "chieftains in the service" also includes: Francis Watkins Harper, Sarah Woodson early, Martha Biggs, Charlotte Fortin Grimke, Hallie Quinn Brown, Fannie Jackson Coppin (1892).
6. "UNDP Human Development Report 2000," Oxford University Press. Pooled World Values Survey/European Values Survey, 1995-2000.
7. The Gender Empowerment Measure combines economic participation and decision making, political participation and decision making, and power over economic resources (UN Human Development Report 2000)
8. Ronald Inglehart & Pippa Norris, *Rising Tide: Gender Equality and Cultural Change around the World*, (New York: Cambridge University Press, 2003).
9. See Chapter 1.
10. Jensen, "Native American Women."
11. See Chapter 2
12. See UN Human Development Report 2000
13. Women were permitted to vote by 1920. "The Emancipation Proclamation," which freed slaves in America, was issued in 1863.
14. Eisler, *Chalice and Blade*; Jane Ollenburger & H Moore, *The Intersection of Patriarchy, Capitalization & Colonization*, (Upper-Saddle, NJ: Prentice Hall, 1998); B Friedan, *The Feminine Mystique* (New York: Norton, 1963); B Friedan, *The Second Stage*, (New York: Summit Books, 1981).
15. See, for example, UNIFEM.
16. "The Millennium Forum Declaration": an Agenda of "We the Peoples...Millennium Forum," the *UN for the 21st Century*: Draft: May 18, 2000, 2.
17. i.e. the Beijing Platform version of CEDAW.
18. see *The Prosperity of Humankind*, (New York: International Bahá'í Community, UN, 1994).
19. Millennium Forum Declaration, Draft, May 18, 2000. (www.millenniumforum.org)
20. Among the world religions, only the Bahá'í Faith, the youngest (1844), promotes the equality of the sexes as a fundamental principle. However, this equality does not include homosexuality or promiscuity. Sexuality is regarded by Bahá'u'lláh, the Prophet-founder, as a sacred gift from the Creator to be used to assure the continuity of life and to confer beauty upon human relationships. Bahá'í laws discourage promiscuity outside of marriage

between one man and one woman. Homosexuality is regarded as a medical problem, which should be treated medically, and with compassion, but not as a social norm to be practiced and accepted.
21. John Naisbitt & Patricia Aburdene, *Megatrends 2000: Ten New Directions for 1990's*, (New York: Avon, 1991).

Appendixes

Fourth World Conference on Women Platform for Action

Mission Statement

1.   The Platform for Action is an agenda for women's empowerment. It aims at accelerating the implementation of the Nairobi Forward-looking Strategies for the Advancement of Women and at removing all the obstacles to women's active participation in all spheres of public and private life through a full and equal share in economic, social, cultural and political decision-making. This means that the principle of shared power and responsibility should be established between women and men at home, in the workplace and in the wider national and international communities. Equality between women and men is a matter of human rights and a condition for social justice and is also a necessary and fundamental prerequisite for equality, development and peace. A transformed partnership based on equality between women and men is a condition for people-centered sustainable development. A sustained and long-term commitment is essential, so that women and men can work together for themselves, for their children and for society to meet the challenges of the twenty-first century.

2.   The Platform for Action reaffirms the fundamental principle set forth in the Vienna Declaration and Programme of Action, adopted by the World Conference on Human Rights, that the human rights of women and of the girl child are an inalienable, integral and indivisible part of universal human rights. As an agenda for action, the Platform seeks to promote and protect the full enjoyment of all human rights and the fundamental freedoms of all women throughout their life cycle.

3.   The Platform for Action emphasizes that women share common concerns that can be addressed only by working together and in partnership with men towards the common goal of gender* equality around the world. It respects and values the full diversity of women's situations and conditions and recognizes that some women face particular barriers to their empowerment.

4.   The Platform for Action requires immediate and concerted action by all to create a peaceful, just and humane world based on human rights and fundamental freedoms, including the principle of equality for all people of all ages and from all walks of life, and to this end, recognizes that broad- based and sustained economic growth in the context of sustainable development is necessary to sustain social development and social justice.

5.   The success of the Platform for Action will require a strong commitment on the part of Governments, international organizations and institutions at all levels. It will also require adequate mobilization of resources at the national and international levels as well as new and additional resources to the developing countries from all available funding mechanisms, including multilateral, bilateral and private sources for the advancement of women; financial resources to strengthen the capacity of national, sub-regional, regional and international institutions; a commitment to equal rights, equal responsibilities and equal opportunities and to the equal participation of women and men in all national, regional and international bodies and policy- making processes; and the establishment or strengthening of mechanisms at all levels for accountability to the world's women.

* For the commonly understood meaning of the term "gender," see annex IV to the present report.

GLOBAL FRAMEWORK

6.   The Fourth World Conference on Women is taking place as the world stands poised on the threshold of a new millennium.

7.   The Platform for Action upholds the Convention on the Elimination of All Forms of Discrimination against Women and builds upon the Nairobi Forward- looking Strategies for the Advancement of Women, as well as relevant resolutions adopted by the Economic and Social Council and the General Assembly. The formulation of the Platform for Action is aimed at establishing a basic group of priority actions that should be carried out during the next five years.

8.   The Platform for Action recognizes the importance of the agreements reached at the World Summit for Children, the United Nations Conference on Environment and De-velopment, the World Conference on Human Rights, the International Conference on Population and Development and the World Summit for Social Development, which set out specific approaches and commitments to fostering sustainable development and inter-national cooperation and to strengthening the role of the United Nations to that end. Simi-larly, the Global Conference on the Sustainable Development of Small Island Developing States, the International Conference on Nutrition, the International Conference on Primary Health Care and the World Conference on Education

9.   for All have addressed the various facets of development and human rights, within their specific perspectives, paying significant attention to the role of women and girls. In addition, the International Year for the World's Indigenous People, the International Year of the Family, the United Nations Year for Tolerance, the Geneva Declaration for Rural Women, and the Declaration on the Elimination of Violence against Women have also emphasized the issues of women's empowerment and equality.

10.   The objective of the Platform for Action, which is in full conformity with the pur-poses and principles of the Charter of the United Nations and international law, is the em-powerment of all women. The full realization of all human rights and fundamental free-doms of all women is essential for the empowerment of women. While the significance of national and regional particularities and various historical, cultural and religious back-grounds must be borne in mind, it is the duty of States, regardless of their political, eco-nomic and cultural systems, to promote and protect all human rights and fundamental freedoms. The implementation of this Platform, including through national laws and the formulation of strategies, policies, programs and development priorities, is the sovereign responsibility of each State, in conformity with all human rights and fundamental free-doms, and the significance of and full respect for various religious and ethical values, cul-tural backgrounds and philosophical convictions of individuals and their communities should contribute to the full enjoyment by women of their human rights in order to achieve equality, development and peace.

11.   Since the World Conference to Review and Appraise the Achievements of the United Nations Decade for Women: Equality, Development and Peace, held at Nairobi in 1985, and the adoption of the Nairobi Forward-looking Strategies for the Advancement of Women, the world has experienced profound political, economic, social and cultural changes, which have had both positive and negative effects on women. The World Confer-ence on Human Rights recognized that the human rights of women and the girl child are an inalienable, integral and indivisible part of universal human rights. The full and equal participation of women in political, civil, economic, social and cultural life at the national,

regional and international levels, and the eradication of all forms of discrimination on the grounds of sex are priority objectives of the international community. The World Conference on Human Rights reaffirmed the solemn commitment of all States to fulfill their obligations to promote universal respect for, and observance and protection of, all human rights and fundamental freedoms for all in accordance with the Charter of the United Nations, other instruments related to human rights and international law. The universal nature of these rights and freedoms is beyond question.

12. The end of the cold war has resulted in international changes and diminished competition between the super-Powers. The threat of a global armed conflict has diminished, while international relations have improved and prospects for peace among nations have increased. Although the threat of global conflict has been reduced, wars of aggression, armed conflicts, colonial or other forms of alien domination and foreign occupation, civil wars, and terrorism continue to plague many parts of the world. Grave violations of the human rights of women occur, particularly in times of armed conflict, and include murder, torture, systematic rape, forced pregnancy and forced abortion, in particular under policies of ethnic cleansing.

13. The maintenance of peace and security at the global, regional and local levels, together with the prevention of policies of aggression and ethnic cleansing and the resolution of armed conflict, is crucial for the protection of the human rights of women and girl children, as well as for the elimination of all forms of violence against them and of their use as a weapon of war.

14. Excessive military expenditures, including global military expenditures and arms trade or trafficking, and investments for arms production and acquisition have reduced the resources available for social development. As a result of the debt burden and other economic difficulties, many developing countries have undertaken structural adjustment policies. Moreover, there are structural adjustment programs that have been poorly designed and implemented, with resulting detrimental effects on social development. The number of people living in poverty has increased disproportionately in most developing countries, particularly the heavily indebted countries, during the past decade.

15. In this context, the social dimension of development should be emphasized. Accelerated economic growth, although necessary for social development, does not by itself improve the quality of life of the population. In some cases, conditions can arise which can aggravate social inequality and marginalization. Hence, it is indispensable to search for new alternatives that ensure that all members of society benefit from economic growth based on a holistic approach to all aspects of development: growth, equality between women and men, social justice, conservation and protection of the environment, sustainability, solidarity, participation, peace and respect for human rights.

16. A world-wide movement towards democratization has opened up the political process in many nations, but the popular participation of women in key decision-making as full and equal partners with men, particularly in politics, has not yet been achieved. South Africa's policy of institutionalized racism - apartheid - has been dismantled and a peaceful and democratic transfer of power has occurred. In Central and Eastern Europe the transition to parliamentary democracy has been rapid and has given rise to a variety of experiences, depending on the specific circumstances of each country. While the transition has been mostly peaceful, in some countries this process has been hindered by armed conflict that has resulted in grave violations of human rights.

17. Widespread economic recession, as well as political instability in some regions, has been responsible for setting back development goals in many countries. This has led to

the expansion of unspeakable poverty. Of the more than 1 billion people living in abject poverty, women are an overwhelming majority. The rapid process of change and adjustment in all sectors has also led to increased unemployment and underemployment, with particular impact on women. In many cases, structural adjustment programs have not been designed to minimize their negative effects on vulnerable and disadvantaged groups or on women, nor have they been designed to assure positive effects on those groups by preventing their marginalization in economic and social activities. The Final Act of the Uruguay Round of multilateral trade negotiations underscored the increasing interdependence of national economies, as well as the importance of trade liberalization and access to open, dynamic markets. There has also been heavy military spending in some regions. Despite increases in official development assistance (ODA) by some countries, ODA has recently declined overall.

18.   Absolute poverty and the feminization of poverty, unemployment, the increasing fragility of the environment, continued violence against women and the widespread exclusion of half of humanity from institutions of power and governance underscore the need to continue the search for development, peace and security and for ways of assuring people-centered sustainable development. The participation and leadership of the half of humanity that is female is essential to the success of that search. Therefore, only a new era of international cooperation among Governments and peoples based on a spirit of partnership, an equitable, international social and economic environment, and a radical transformation of the relationship between women and men to one of full and equal partnership will enable the world to meet the challenges of the twenty-first century.

19.   Recent international economic developments have had in many cases a disproportionate impact on women and children, the majority of whom live in developing countries. For those States that have carried a large burden of foreign debt, structural adjustment programs and measures, though beneficial in the long term, have led to a reduction in social expenditures, thereby adversely affecting women, particularly in Africa and the least developed countries. This is exacerbated when responsibilities for basic social services have shifted from Governments to women.

20.   Economic recession in many developed and developing countries, as well as ongoing restructuring in countries with economies in transition, have had a disproportionately negative impact on women's employment. Women often have no choice but to take employment that lacks long-term job security or involves dangerous working conditions, to work in unprotected home-based production or to be unemployed. Many women enter the labor market in under-remunerated and undervalued jobs, seeking to improve their household income; others decide to migrate for the same purpose. Without any reduction in their other responsibilities, this has increased the total burden of work for women.

21.   Macro and micro-economic policies and programs, including structural adjustment, have not always been designed to take account of their impact on women and girl children, especially those living in poverty. Poverty has increased in both absolute and relative terms, and the number of women living in poverty has increased in most regions. There are many urban women living in poverty; however, the plight of women living in rural and remote areas deserves special attention given the stagnation of development in such areas. In developing countries, even those in which national indicators have shown improvement, the majority of rural women continue to live in conditions of economic underdevelopment and social marginalization.

22.   Women are key contributors to the economy and to combating poverty through both remunerated and unremunerated work at home, in the community and in the work-

place. Growing numbers of women have achieved economic independence through gainful employment.

23.   One fourth of all households world wide are headed by women and many other households are dependent on female income even where men are present. Female-maintained households are very often among the poorest because of wage discrimination, occupational segregation patterns in the labor market and other gender-based barriers. Family disintegration, population movements between urban and rural areas within countries, international migration, war and internal displacements are factors contributing to the rise of female- headed households.

24.   Recognizing that the achievement and maintenance of peace and security are a precondition for economic and social progress, women are increasingly establishing themselves as central actors in a variety of capacities in the movement of humanity for peace. Their full participation in decision-making, conflict prevention and resolution and all other peace initiatives is essential to the realization of lasting peace.

25.   Religion, spirituality and belief play a central role in the lives of millions of women and men, in the way they live and in the aspirations they have for the future. The right to freedom of thought, conscience and religion is inalienable and must be universally enjoyed. This right includes the freedom to have or to adopt the religion or belief of their choice either individually or in community with others, in public or in private, and to manifest their religion or belief in worship, observance, practice and teaching. In order to realize equality, development and peace, there is a need to respect these rights and freedoms fully. Religion, thought, conscience and belief may, and can, contribute to fulfilling women's and men's moral, ethical and spiritual needs and to realizing their full potential in society. However, it is acknowledged that any form of extremism may have a negative impact on women and can lead to violence and discrimination.

26.   The Fourth World Conference on Women should accelerate the process that formally began in 1975, which was proclaimed International Women's Year by the United Nations General Assembly. The Year was a turning-point in that it put women's issues on the agenda. The United Nations Decade for Women (1976-1985) was a world-wide effort to examine the status and rights of women and to bring women into decision-making at all levels. In 1979, the General Assembly adopted the Convention on the Elimination of All Forms of Discrimination against Women, which entered into force in 1981 and set an international standard for what was meant by equality between women and men. In 1985, the World Conference to Review and Appraise the Achievements of the United Nations Decade for Women: Equality, Development and Peace adopted the Nairobi Forward-looking Strategies for the Advancement of Women, to be implemented by the year 2000. There has been important progress in achieving equality between women and men. Many Governments have enacted legislation to promote equality between women and men and have established national machineries to ensure the mainstreaming of gender perspectives in all spheres of society. International agencies have focused greater attention on women's status and roles.

27.   The growing strength of the non-governmental sector, particularly women's organizations and feminist groups, has become a driving force for change. Non-governmental organizations have played an important advocacy role in advancing legislation or mechanisms to ensure the promotion of women. They have also become catalysts for new approaches to development. Many Governments have increasingly recognized the important role that non-governmental organizations play and the importance of working with them for progress. Yet, in some countries, Governments continue to restrict the abil-

ity of non-governmental organizations to operate freely. Women, through non-governmental organizations, have participated in and strongly influenced community, national, regional and global forums and international debates.

28.   Since 1975, knowledge of the status of women and men, respectively, has increased and is contributing to further actions aimed at promoting equality between women and men. In several countries, there have been important changes in the relationships between women and men, especially where there have been major advances in education for women and significant increases in their participation in the paid labor force. The boundaries of the gender division of labor between productive and reproductive roles are gradually being crossed as women have started to enter formerly male-dominated areas of work and men have started to accept greater responsibility for domestic tasks, including child care. However, changes in women's roles have been greater and much more rapid than changes in men's roles. In many countries, the differences between women's and men's achievements and activities are still not recognized as the consequences of socially constructed gender roles rather than immutable biological differences.

29.   Moreover, 10 years after the Nairobi Conference, equality between women and men has still not been achieved. On average, women represent a mere 10 per cent of all elected legislators world wide and in most national and international administrative structures, both public and private, they remain underrepresented. The United Nations is no exception. Fifty years after its creation, the United Nations is continuing to deny itself the benefits of women's leadership by their under representation at decision-making levels within the Secretariat and the specialized agencies.

30.   Women play a critical role in the family. The family is the basic unit of society and as such should be strengthened. It is entitled to receive comprehensive protection and support. In different cultural, political and social systems, various forms of the family exist. The rights, capabilities and responsibilities of family members must be respected. Women make a great contribution to the welfare of the family and to the development of society, which is still not recognized or considered in its full importance. The social significance of maternity, motherhood and the role of parents in the family and in the upbringing of children should be acknowledged. The upbringing of children requires shared responsibility of parents, women and men and society as a whole. Maternity, motherhood, parenting and the role of women in procreation must not be a basis for discrimination nor restrict the full participation of women in society. Recognition should also be given to the important role often played by women in many countries in caring for other members of their family.

31.   While the rate of growth of world population is on the decline, world population is at an all-time high in absolute numbers, with current increments approaching 86 million persons annually. Two other major demographic trends have had profound repercussions on the dependency ratio within families. In many developing countries, 45 to 50 per cent of the population is less than 15 years old, while in industrialized nations both the number and proportion of elderly people are increasing. According to United Nations projections, 72 per cent of the population over 60 years of age will be living in developing countries by the year 2025, and more than half of that population will be women. Care of children, the sick and the elderly is a responsibility that falls disproportionately on women, owing to lack of equality and the unbalanced distribution of remunerated and unremunerated work between women and men.

32.   Many women face particular barriers because of various diverse factors in addition to their gender. Often these diverse factors isolate or marginalize such women. They are,

inter alia, denied their human rights, they lack access or are denied access to education and vocational training, employment, housing and economic self-sufficiency and they are excluded from decision-making processes. Such women are often denied the opportunity to contribute to their communities as part of the mainstream.

33.   The past decade has also witnessed a growing recognition of the distinct interests and concerns of indigenous women, whose identity, cultural traditions and forms of social organization enhance and strengthen the communities in which they live. Indigenous women often face barriers both as women and as members of indigenous communities.

34.   In the past 20 years, the world has seen an explosion in the field of communications. With advances in computer technology and satellite and cable television, global access to information continues to increase and expand, creating new opportunities for the participation of women in communications and the mass media and for the dissemination of information about women. However, global communication networks have been used to spread stereotyped and demeaning images of women for narrow commercial and consumerist purposes. Until women participate equally in both the technical and decision-making areas of communications and the mass media, including the arts, they will continue to be misrepresented and awareness of the reality of women's lives will continue to be lacking. The media have a great potential to promote the advancement of women and the equality of women and men by portraying women and men in a non-stereotypical, diverse and balanced manner, and by respecting the dignity and worth of the human person.

35.   The continuing environmental degradation that affects all human lives has often a more direct impact on women. Women's health and their livelihood are threatened by pollution and toxic wastes, large-scale deforestation, desertification, drought and depletion of the soil and of coastal and marine resources, with a rising incidence of environmentally related health problems and even death reported among women and girls. Those most affected are rural and indigenous women, whose livelihood and daily subsistence depends directly on sustainable ecosystems.

36.   Poverty and environmental degradation are closely interrelated. While poverty results in certain kinds of environmental stress, the major cause of the continued deterioration of the global environment is the unsustainable patterns of consumption and production, particularly in industrialized countries, which are a matter of grave concern and aggravate poverty and imbalances.

37.   Global trends have brought profound changes in family survival strategies and structures. Rural to urban migration has increased substantially in all regions. The global urban population is projected to reach 47 per cent of the total population by the year 2000. An estimated 125 million people are migrants, refugees and displaced persons, half of whom live in developing countries. These massive movements of people have profound consequences for family structures and well-being and have unequal consequences for women and men, including in many cases the sexual exploitation of women.

38.   According to World Health Organization (WHO) estimates, by the beginning of 1995 the number of cumulative cases of acquired immunodeficiency syndrome (AIDS) was 4.5 million. An estimated 19.5 million men, women and children have been infected with the human immunodeficiency virus (HIV) since it was first diagnosed and it is projected that another 20 million will be infected by the end of the decade. Among new cases, women are twice as likely to be infected as men. In the early stage of the AIDS pandemic, women were not infected in large numbers; however, about 8 million women are now infected. Young women and adolescents are particularly vulnerable. It is estimated that by the year 2000 more than 13 million women will be infected and 4 million women will

have died from AIDS-related conditions. In addition, about 250 million new cases of sexually transmitted diseases are estimated to occur every year. The rate of transmission of sexually transmitted diseases, including HIV/AIDS, is increasing at an alarming rate among women and girls, especially in developing countries.

39.   Since 1975, significant knowledge and information have been generated about the status of women and the conditions in which they live. Throughout their entire life cycle, women's daily existence and long-term aspirations are restricted by discriminatory attitudes, unjust social and economic structures, and a lack of resources in most countries that prevent their full and equal participation. In a number of countries, the practice of prenatal sex selection, higher rates of mortality among very young girls and lower rates of school enrolment for girls as compared with boys suggest that son preference is curtailing the access of girl children to food, education and health care and even life itself. Discrimination against women begins at the earliest stages of life and must therefore be addressed from then onwards.

40.   The girl child of today is the woman of tomorrow. The skills, ideas and energy of the girl child are vital for full attainment of the goals of equality, development and peace. For the girl child to develop her full potential she needs to be nurtured in an enabling environment, where her spiritual, intellectual and material needs for survival, protection and development are met and her equal rights safeguarded. If women are to be equal partners with men, in every aspect of life and development, now is the time to recognize the human dignity and worth of the girl child and to ensure the full enjoyment of her human rights and fundamental freedoms, including the rights assured by the Convention on the Rights of the Child, universal ratification of which is strongly urged. Yet there exists world-wide evidence that discrimination and violence against girls begin at the earliest stages of life and continue unabated throughout their lives. They often have less access to nutrition, physical and mental health care and education and enjoy fewer rights, opportunities and benefits of childhood and adolescence than do boys. They are often subjected to various forms of sexual and economic exploitation, pedophilia, forced prostitution and possibly the sale of their organs and tissues, violence and harmful practices such as female infanticide and prenatal sex selection, incest, female genital mutilation and early marriage, including child marriage.

41.   Half the world's population is under the age of 25 and most of the world's youth - more than 85 per cent - live in developing countries. Policy makers must recognize the implications of these demographic factors. Special measures must be taken to ensure that young women have the life skills necessary for active and effective participation in all levels of social, cultural, political and economic leadership. It will be critical for the international community to demonstrate a new commitment to the future - a commitment to inspiring a new generation of women and men to work together for a more just society. This new generation of leaders must accept and promote a world in which every child is free from injustice, oppression and inequality and free to develop her/his own potential. The principle of equality of women and men must therefore be integral to the socialization process.

CRITICAL AREAS OF CONCERN

41.   The advancement of women and the achievement of equality between women and men are a matter of human rights and a condition for social justice and should not be seen in isolation as a women's issue. They are the only way to build a sustainable, just and developed society. Empowerment of women and equality between women and men are prerequisites for achieving political, social, economic, cultural and environmental security among all peoples.

42.   Most of the goals set out in the Nairobi Forward-looking Strategies for the Advancement of Women have not been achieved. Barriers to women's empowerment remain, despite the efforts of Governments, as well as non-governmental organizations and women and men everywhere. Vast political, economic and ecological crises persist in many parts of the world. Among them are wars of aggression, armed conflicts, colonial or other forms of alien domination or foreign occupation, civil wars and terrorism. These situations, combined with systematic or de facto discrimination, violations of and failure to protect all human rights and fundamental freedoms of all women, and their civil, cultural, economic, political and social rights, including the right to development and ingrained prejudicial attitudes towards women and girls are but a few of the impediments encountered since the World Conference to Review and Appraise the Achievements of the United Nations Decade for Women: Equality, Development and Peace, in 1985.

43.   A review of progress since the Nairobi Conference highlights special concerns—areas of particular urgency that stand out as priorities for action. All actors should focus action and resources on the strategic objectives relating to the critical areas of concern which are, necessarily, interrelated, interdependent and of high priority. There is a need for these actors to develop and implement mechanisms of accountability for all the areas of concern.

44.   To this end, Governments, the international community and civil society, including non-governmental organizations and the private sector, are called upon to take strategic action in the following critical areas of concern:

o   The persistent and increasing burden of poverty on women

o   Inequalities and inadequacies in and unequal access to education and training

o   Inequalities and inadequacies in and unequal access to health care and related services

o   Violence against women

o   The effects of armed or other kinds of conflict on women, including those living under foreign occupation

o   Inequality in economic structures and policies, in all forms of productive activities and in access to resources

o   Inequality between men and women in the sharing of power and decision-making at all levels

o   Insufficient mechanisms at all levels to promote the advancement of women

o   Lack of respect for and inadequate promotion and protection of the human rights of women

o   Stereotyping of women and inequality in women's access to and participation in all communication systems, especially in the media

o   Gender inequalities in the management of natural resources and in the safeguarding of the environment

o   Persistent discrimination against and violation of the rights of the girl child

Strategic Objectives and Actions
45.   In each critical area of concern, the problem is diagnosed and strategic objectives are proposed with concrete actions to be taken by various actors in order to achieve those

objectives. The strategic objectives are derived from the critical areas of concern and specific actions to be taken to achieve them cut across the boundaries of equality, development and peace—the goals of the Nairobi Forward-looking Strategies for the Advancement of Women—and reflect their interdependence. The objectives and actions are interlinked, of high priority and mutually reinforcing. The Platform for Action is intended to improve the situation of all women, without exception, who often face similar barriers, while special attention should be given to groups that are the most disadvantaged.

46.   The Platform for Action recognizes that women face barriers to full equality and advancement because of such factors as their race, age, language, ethnicity, culture, religion or disability, because they are indigenous women or because of other status. Many women encounter specific obstacles related to their family status, particularly as single parents; and to their socio-economic status, including their living conditions in rural, isolated or impoverished areas. Additional barriers also exist for refugee women, other displaced women, including internally displaced women as well as for immigrant women and migrant women, including women migrant workers. Many women are also particularly affected by environmental disasters, serious and infectious diseases and various forms of violence against women.

African Women's Views on Gender Relations and the Redefinition of Roles

Demographic Background:

1. a. Name:

   b. Address:

   c. Email address:

2. Date of Birth:

3. Marital Status:

4. Number of Children:

5. National/cultural background:

6. Religion:

7. Profession or occupation:

8. Highest level of education achievement:

Doctoral	Associate	Primary School Certificate
Masters	HS Diploma	Less Than 5 Years of Primary School
B.A. or B.S	Less than HS	Other:

Specific Research Questions:

9. Goals:
   a.   Personal:

    b.   Professional:

    c.   How much progress have you made toward achieving your goals?

10. Who are your favorite role models?

    Why?

11. What is the greatest change in gender relationships you have experienced in the past century?

12. How has this change affected. . .
    a.   Your life?

    b.   Your family life?

    c.   Your community life?

    d.   The world?

13. What changes would you make in the new millennium to improve gender relations in the family, the workplace, the community, the world?

14. a.   What role should men play in these changes?

    b.   What role should women play in these changes?

15. Could you sum up your philosophy of life in one or two sentences?

Two Wings of a Bird:
The Equality of Women and Men
by the
National Spiritual Assembly of the Bahá'í's of the United States of America

The emancipation of women, the achievement of full equality between the sexes is essential to human progress and the transformation of society. Inequality retards not only the advancement of women but the progress of civilization itself. The persistent denial of equality to one-half of the world's population is an affront to human dignity. It promotes destructive attitudes and habits in men and women that pass from the family to the work place, to political life, and ultimately to international relations. On no grounds, moral, biological, or traditional can inequality be justified. The moral and psychological climate necessary to enable our nation to establish social justice and to contribute to global peace will be created only when women attain full partnership with men in all fields of endeavor.

The systematic oppression of women is a conspicuous and tragic fact of history. Restricted to narrow spheres of activity in the life of society, denied educational opportunities and basic human rights, subjected to violence, and frequently treated as less than human, women have been prevented from realizing their true potential. Age-old patterns of subordination, reflected in popular culture, literature and art, law, and even religious scriptures, continue to pervade every aspect of life. Despite the advancement of political and civil rights for women in America and the widespread acceptance of equality in principle, full equality has not been achieved.

The damaging effects of gender prejudice are a fault line beneath the foundation of our national life. The gains for women rest uneasily on unchanged, often unexamined, inherited assumptions. Much remains to be done. **The achievement of full equality requires a new understanding of who we are, what is our purpose in life, and how we relate to one another,** an understanding that will compel us to reshape our lives and thereby our society.

At no time since the founding of the women's rights movement in America has the need to focus on this issue been greater. We stand at the threshold of a new century and a new millennium. Their challenges are already upon us, influencing our families, our lifestyles, our nation, our world. In the process of human evolution, the ages of infancy and childhood are past. The turbulence of adolescence is slowly and painfully preparing us for the age of maturity, when prejudice and exploitation will be abolished and unity established. The elements necessary to unify peoples and nations are precisely those needed to bring about equality of the sexes and to improve the relationships between women and men. The effort to overcome the history of inequality requires the full participation of every man, woman, youth, and child. Over a century ago, for the first time in religious history, **Bahá'u'lláh, the Founder of the Bahá'í Faith, in announcing God's purpose for the age, proclaimed the principle of the equality of women and men, saying: "Women and men have been and will always be equal in the sight of God."**[1] The establishment of equal rights and privileges for women and men, Bahá'u'lláh says, is a precondition for the attainment of a wider unity that will ensure the well-being and security of all peoples. The Bahá'í Writings state emphatically that "When all mankind shall receive the same opportunity of education and the equality of men and women be realized, the foundations of war will be utterly destroyed."[2]

Thus the Bahá'í vision of equality between the sexes rests on the central spiritual principle of the oneness of humankind. The principle of oneness requires that we "regard humanity as a single individual, and one's own self as a member of that corporeal form,"[3] and that we foster an unshakable consciousness that "if pain or injury afflicts any member of that body, it must inevitably result in suffering for all the rest."[4]

Bahá'u'lláh teaches that the divine purpose of creation is the achievement of unity among all peoples:

> *Know ye not why We created you all from the same dust? That no one should exalt himself over the other. Ponder at all times in your hearts how ye were created. Since We have created you all from one same substance it is incumbent on you to be even as one soul, to walk with the same feet, eat with the same mouth and dwell in the same land, that from your inmost being, by your deeds and actions, the signs of oneness and the essence of detachment may be made manifest.*[5]

The full and equal participation of women in all spheres of life is essential to social and economic development, the abolition of war, and the ultimate establishment of a united world. In the Bahá'í Scriptures the equality of the sexes is a cornerstone of God's plan for human development and prosperity:

> *The world of humanity is possessed of two wings: the male and the female. So long as these two wings are not equivalent in strength, the bird will not fly. Until womankind reaches the same degree as man, until she enjoys the same arena of activity, extraordinary attainment for humanity will not be realized; humanity cannot wing its way to heights of real attainment. When the two wings . . . become equivalent in strength, enjoying the same prerogatives, the flight of man will be exceedingly lofty and extraordinary.*[6]

The Bahá'í Writings state that to proclaim equality is not to deny that differences in function between women and men exist but rather to affirm the complementary roles men and women fulfill in the home and society at large. Stating that the acquisition of knowledge serves as "a ladder for [human] as-cent,"[7] Bahá'u'lláh prescribes identical education for women and men but stipulates that when resources are limited first priority should be given to the education of women and girls. **The education of girls is particularly important because, although both parents have responsibilities for the rearing of children, it is through educated mothers that the benefits of knowledge can be most effectively diffused throughout society.**

Reverence for, and protection of, motherhood have often been used as justification for keeping women socially and economically disadvantaged. It is this discriminatory and injurious result that must change. **Great honor and nobility are rightly conferred on the station of motherhood and the importance of training children.** Addressing the high station of motherhood, the Bahá'í Writings state, "O ye loving mothers, know ye that in God's sight, the best of all ways to worship Him is to educate the children and train them in all the perfections of humankind. . . ."[8] The great challenge facing society is to make social and economic provisions for the full and equal participation of women in all aspects of life while simultaneously reinforcing the critical functions of motherhood.

Asserting that women and men share similar "station and rank" and "are equally the recipients of powers and endowments from God,"[9] the Bahá'í teachings offer a model of equality based on the concept of partnership. Only when women become full participants in all domains of life and enter the important arenas of decision-making will humanity be prepared to embark on the next stage of its collective development.

Bahá'í Scripture emphatically states that women will be the greatest factor in establishing universal peace and international arbitration. *"So it will come to pass that when women participate fully and equally in the affairs of the world, when they enter confidently and capably the great arena of laws and politics, war will cease; for woman will be the obstacle and hindrance to it."*[10]

The elimination of discrimination against women is a spiritual and moral imperative that must ultimately reshape existing legal, economic, and social arrangements. Promoting the entry of greater numbers of women into positions of prominence and authority is a necessary but not sufficient step in creating a just social order. Without fundamental changes in the attitudes and values of individuals and in the underlying ethos of social institutions, full equality between women and men cannot be achieved. **A community based on partnership, a community in which aggression and the use of force are supplanted by cooperation and consultation, requires the transformation of the human heart.**

The world in the past has been ruled by force, and man has dominated over woman by reason of his more forceful and aggressive qualities both of body and mind. But the balance is already shifting; force is losing its dominance, and mental alertness, intuition, and the spiritual qualities of love and service, in which woman is strong, are gaining ascendancy. Hence the new age will be an age less masculine and more permeated with the feminine ideals . . . an age in which the masculine and feminine elements of civilization will be more evenly balanced.[11]

Men have an inescapable duty to promote the equality of women. The presumption of superiority by men thwarts the ambition of women and inhibits the creation of an environment in which equality may reign. The destructive effects of inequality prevent men from maturing and developing the qualities necessary to meet the challenges of the new millennium. "As long as women are prevented from attaining their highest possibilities," the Bahá'í Writings state, "so long will men be unable to achieve the greatness which might be theirs."[12] **It is essential that men engage in a careful, deliberate examination of attitudes, feelings, and behavior deeply rooted in cultural habit, that block the equal participation of women and stifle the growth of men.** The willingness of men to take responsibility for equality will create an optimum environment for progress: "When men own the equality of women there will be no need for them to struggle for their rights!"[13]

The long-standing and deeply rooted condition of inequality must be eliminated. To overcome such a condition requires the exercise of nothing short of "genuine love, extreme patience, true humility, consummate tact, sound initiative, mature wisdom, and deliberate, persistent, and prayerful effort."[14] Ultimately, Bahá'u'lláh promises, a day will come when men will welcome women in all aspects of life. Now is the time to move decisively toward that promised future.

Notes

1. Bahá'u'lláh, from a Tablet translated from the Persian and Arabic, quoted in Women: Extracts from the Writings of Bahá'u'lláh, 'Abdu'l-Bahá, Shoghi Effendi and the Universal House of Justice, comp. Research Department of the Universal House of Justice (Thornhill, Ontario: National Spiritual Assembly of the Bahá'ís of Canada, 1986), no. 54.

2. 'Abdu'l-Bahá, The Promulgation of Universal Peace: Talks delivered by 'Abdu'l-Bahá during His Visit to the United States and Canada in 1912, comp. Howard MacNutt, 2d ed. (Wilmette, Ill.: Bahá'í Publishing Trust, 1982), p. 175.

3. 'Abdu'l-Bahá, The Secret of Divine Civilization, trans. Marzieh Gail and Ali-Kuli Khan, 1st ps ed. (Wilmette, Ill.: Bahá'í Publishing Trust, 1990), p. 39.

4. 'Abdu'l-Bahá, Secret of Divine Civilization, p. 39.

5. Bahá'u'lláh, The Hidden Words, trans. Shoghi Effendi (Wilmette, Ill.: Bahá'í Publishing Trust, 1939), p. 20.

6. 'Abdu'l-Bahá, Promulgation, p. 375.

7. Bahá'u'lláh, Tablets of Bahá'u'lláh revealed after the Kitáb-i-Aqdas, comp. Research Department of the Universal House of Justice, trans. Habib Taherzadeh et al., 1st ps ed. (Wilmette, Ill.: Bahá'í Publishing Trust, 1988), 51.

8. 'Abdu'l-Bahá, Selections from the Writings of 'Abdu'l-Bahá, comp. Research Department of the Universal House of Justice, trans. Committee at the Bahá'í World Centre and Marzieh Gail (Wilmette, Ill.: Bahá'í Publishing Trust, 1997), 114.1.

9. Bahá'u'lláh,, Tablet translated from the Persian and Arabic, quoted in

Women, no. 2; 'Abdu'l-Bahá, Promulgation, p. 300.
10. 'Abdu'l-Bahá, Promulgation, p. 135.
11. 'Abdu'l-Bahá, quoted in Wendell Phillips Dodge, "Abdul-Baha's Arrival in America," in Star of the West 3 (April 28, 1912), no. 3, p. 4.
12. 'Abdu'l-Bahá, Paris Talks: Addresses Given by 'Abdu'l-Bahá in Paris in 1911, 12th ed. (London: Bahá'í Publishing Trust, 1995), 40.33
13. 'Abdu'l-Bahá, Paris Talks, 50.14.
14. Shoghi Effendi, The Advent of Divine Justice, p. 40.

Progress of the World's Women:
Toward the Millennium Development Goals

Goal 3 Promote gender equality and empower women (2015 target = education ratio to 100)

	Ratio of girls to boys in primary and secondary education		Ratio of literate females to males		Share of women employed in the non-agricultural sector		Women in parliament
	%		% ages 15-24		% of total employment in sector		% of total seats
	1990/91	2002/03	1990	2002	1990	2002	2004
World	87	93	87	92	35	37	15
High income	100	101	..	..	43	46	21
Low & middle income	84	91	86	91	33	34	14
East Asia & Pacific	89	97	96	99	38	39	17
Europe & Central Asia	98	97	100	100	46	46	12
Latin Amer. & Carib.	..	102	100	101	39	43	19
Middle East & N. Africa	82	94	77	85	19	..	6
South Asia	71	83	73	80	13	18	9
Sub-Saharan Africa	79	..	69	89	30	..	13
Afghanistan	..	52	..	..	5	..	..
Albania	96	102	94	100	40	40	6
Algeria	83	99	79	91	8	14	6
American Samoa	..	..	..	..	..	..	..
Andorra	..	..	..	..	43	46	14
Angola	..	..	..	..	35	..	16
Antigua and Barbuda	..	..	..	..	..	..	5
Argentina	..	103	100	100	37	46	31
Armenia	..	101	100	100	..	..	5
Aruba	..	99	..	..	..	..	..
Australia	101	99	..	..	45	49	25

Austria	95	97	..	..	40	44	34
Azerbaijan	100	97	..	..	41	48	11
Bahamas	..	102	102	102	49	49	20
Bahrain	101	103	99	100	7	13	0
Bangladesh	77	107	65	71	18	25	2
Barbados	..	100	100	100	46	49	13
Belarus	..	102	100	100	56	56	10
Belgium	101	107	..	..	40	45	35
Belize	100	100	101	101	38	41	3
Benin	48	66	44	53	52	..	7
Bermuda	..	..	..	..	49	49	..
Bhutan	..	88	..	..	12	..	9
Bolivia	90	98	93	98	36	37	19
Bosnia and Herzegovina	..	..	..	100	43	..	17
Botswana	109	102	110	109	48	45	17
Brazil	..	103	103	103	40	47	9
Brunei	99	103	101	101	40	..	..
Bulgaria	99	98	100	100	54	51	26
Burkina Faso	61	72	39	..	13	14	12
Burundi	82	79	77	97	10	..	18
Cambodia	73	85	81	90	41	53	10
Cameroon	83	85	88	96	24	..	9
Canada	99	100	..	..	47	49	21
Cape Verde	..	100	87	94	50	..	11
Cayman Islands	..	..	..	..	49	..	..
Cent. African Republic	60	..	60	67	36	..	7
Chad	41	59	65	84	4	..	6
Channel Islands	..	..	..	..	..	..	..
Chile	101	100	100	100	36	37	13
China	87	97	95	99	38	39	20
Hong Kong, China	103	100	99	101	41	46	..
Macao, China	100	100	97	100	43	50	..
Colombia	114	104	101	101	42	49	12
Comoros	71	82	78	79	16	..	..
Congo, Dem. Rep.	..	..	72	87	32	..	8

Congo, Rep.	85	87	95	99	33	..	9
Costa Rica	100	101	101	101	37	40	35
Côte d'Ivoire	66	..	62	74	23	20	9
Croatia	102	101	100	100	44	46	18
Cuba	106	97	100	100	37	38	36
Cyprus	100	101	100	100	36	42	11
Czech Rep.	98	101	..	..	46	47	17
Denmark	101	103	..	..	47	49	38
Djibouti	70	71	78	91	..	..	11
Dominica	..	100	..	..	..	..	19
Dominican Republic	..	108	102	102	35	35	17
Ecuador	..	100	99	100	37	40	16
Egypt, Arab Rep.	81	93	72	..	21	20	2
El Salvador	101	96	97	98	32	31	11
Eq. Guinea	..	83	92	97	13	..	5
Eritrea	..	76	68	77	..	..	22
Estonia	104	99	100	100	52	52	19
Ethiopia	68	69	66	82	40	..	8
Faeroe Islands	..	..	..	..	..	..	..
Fiji	..	103	100	..	30	35	6
Finland	109	106	..	..	51	51	38
France	102	100	..	..	44	47	12
French Polynesia	..	..	..	..	..	..	..
Gabon	..	..	..	..	43	..	9
Gambia	64	90	68	77	24	..	13
Georgia	98	100	..	..	45	47	7
Germany	99	99	..	..	41	46	32
Ghana	77	91	86	96	57	..	9
Greece	99	101	100	100	35	41	9
Greenland	..	..	..	..	..	..	..
Grenada	..	..	..	..	38	..	27
Guam	..	..	..	..	44	..	..
Guatemala	..	93	82	86	37	39	8
Guinea	44	69	..	..	30	..	19
Guinea-Bissau	..	..	43	64	11	..	8

Guyana	101	100	100	100	45	..	20
Haiti	95	..	96	101	40	..	4
Honduras	..	..	103	105	48	50	6
Hungary	100	100	100	100	46	47	10
Iceland	98	103	..	..	53	53	30
India	70	80	74	81	13	18	9
Indonesia	93	98	97	99	29	30	8
Iran, Islamic Rep.	85	96	88	96	18	..	4
Iraq	78	80	44	50	13	..	8
Ireland	104	104	..	..	42	48	13
Isle of Man	..	..	..	..	..	..	..
Israel	105	99	99	100	43	49	15
Italy	100	97	100	100	34	41	12
Jamaica	102	101	109	107	51	47	12
Japan	101	100	..	..	38	41	7
Jordan	101	101	97	100	23	22	6
Kazakhstan	102	100	100	100	60	48	10
Kenya	92	94	93	99	21	38	7
Kiribati	..	..	..	..	..	..	5
Korea, Dem. Rep.	..	..	..	..	50	..	20
Korea, Rep.	99	100	100	100	38	40	6
Kuwait	97	104	99	102	30	20	0
Kyrgyz Rep.	..	100	..	..	46	45	10
Lao PDR	75	83	76	85	42	..	23
Latvia	100	100	100	100	52	53	21
Lebanon	..	102	93	96	29	..	2
Lesotho	124	105	126	i19	40	..	12
Liberia	..	..	51	64	28	..	8
Libya	..	103	84	94	19	..	..
Liechtenstein	..	..	..	..	..	..	12
Lithuania	..	99	100	100	58	50	11
Luxembourg	..	103	..	..	35	38	17
Macedonia, FYR	99	99	..	..	38	42	18
Madagascar	98	..	86	93	26	..	4
Malawi	81	92	68	77	11	12	9

Malaysia	102	104	99	100	38	35	11
Maldives	..	102	100	100	21	40	6
Mali	58	71	45	52	36	..	10
Malta	95	99	103	102	26	34	9
Marshall Islands	..	..	..	..	..	..	3
Mauritania	67	94	65	73	43	..	4
Mauritius	100	101	100	102	37	38	6
Mayotte	..	..	..	..	..	..	..
Mexico	98	102	98	100	35	37	23
Micronesia, Fed. Sts.	..	..	..	..	..	..	0
Moldova	105	102	100	100	53	54	13
Monaco	..	..	..	..	..	..	21
Mongolia	109	110	100	101	49	47	11
Morocco	70	88	62	79	26	26	11
Mozambique	73	79	48	64	15	..	30
Myanmar	96	99	96	100	35	..	..
Namibia	111	104	104	104	39	50	26
Nepal	57	83	41	59	12	..	6
Netherlands	97	98	..	..	38	45	37
Netherlands Antilles	..	104	100	100	42	48	..
New Caledonia	..	..	..	..	..	..	..
New Zealand	100	103	..	..	48	51	28
Nicaragua	112	104	101	106	49	..	21
Niger	56	69	37	44	9	..	1
Nigeria	78	..	82	95	36	..	7
Northern Mariana Is.	..	..	..	..	..	..	..
Norway	102	101	..	..	47	49	36
Oman	89	97	79	98	19	25	..
Pakistan	..	71	49	..	7	8	22
Palau	..	..	..	..	..	..	0
Panama	99	100	99	99	44	44	10
Papua New Guinea	79	88	84	90	24	..	1
Paraguay	98	98	99	100	41	41	10
Peru	..	97	95	97	30	35	18

Philippines	100	102	100	101	40	41	18
Poland	101	98	100	100	47	48	20
Portugal	103	102	100	100	44	47	19
Puerto Rico	..	..	102	101	47	40	..
Qatar	98	100	105	..	17	14	..
Romania	99	100	100	100	43	45	11
Russian Fed.	104	100	100	100	50	50	10
Rwanda	96	95	86	97	17	..	49
Samoa	113	104	100	100	..	..	6
San Marino	..	..	..	..	40	42	17
São Tomé & Principe	..	92	..	..	..	..	9
Saudi Arabia	84	93	86	96	16	14	0
Senegal	68	87	60	72	28	..	19
Serbia and Montenegro	103	101	..	..	46	..	8
Seychelles	..	100	..	..	..	..	29
Sierra Leone	67	70	..	..	32	..	15
Singapore	95	..	100	100	43	47	16
Slovak Rep.	..	101	..	100	48	52	19
Slovenia	..	100	100	100	49	48	12
Solomon Is.	84	..	..	..	33	..	0
Somalia	..	..	..	..	28	..	..
South Africa	103	100	100	100	..	..	30
Spain	104	103	100	100	33	40	28
Sri Lanka	102	103	98	100	39	45	4
St. Kitts & Nevis	..	123	..	..	..	..	13
St. Lucia	103	107	..	..	..	..	11
St. Vincent & Grenadines	107	102	..	..	..	..	23
Sudan	77	86	71	88	22	15	10
Suriname	105	105	..	..	39	33	18
Swaziland	96	94	101	102	37	29	11
Sweden	102	112	..	..	51	51	45
Switzerland	97	96	..	..	43	47	25
Syrian Arab Rep.	85	93	73	84	14	18	12
Tajikistan	..	88	100	100	40	50	13
Tanzania	96	..	87	95	33	..	21

Thailand	95	95	99	100	45	46	9
Togo	59	..	60	75	47	..	7
Tonga	98	105	..	..	..	..	0
Trinidad & Tobago	101	102	100	100	36	41	19
Tunisia	86	100	81	93	20	..	12
Turkey	81	85	91	95	15	21	4
Turkmenistan	..	..	..	..	..	..	26
Uganda	77	96	76	86	43	..	25
Ukraine	..	99	100	100	51	53	5
United Arab Emirates	106	100	108	108	16	13	0
United Kingdom	98	116	..	..	48	50	18
United States	100	100	..	..	47	49	14
Uruguay	..	105	101	101	42	46	12
Uzbekistan	94	98	100	100	46	42	7
Vanuatu	94	100	..	..	..	..	2
Venezuela, RB	105	104	101	101	35	42	10
Vietnam	..	93	99	..	53	..	27
Virgin Islands (U.S.)	..	..	..	..	..	..	..
West Bank & Gaza	..	..	..	..	..	..	..
Yemen, Rep.	..	61	34	60	9	6	0
Zambia	..	91	88	95	36	..	12
Zimbabwe	96	95	95	97	15	21	10

Source: World Bank Group 2004

The data given indicates improvements made towards women's empowerment within the context of the Millennium Development Goals, a set of eight goals created by the international community in 2000 to focus global efforts to end poverty, hunger and inequality. The analysis of the indicators for Goal 3: *Promote gender equality and empower women'* - examines progress for women, or the lack of it, in education, literacy, nonagricultural wage employment and parliamentary representation.

BIBLIOGRAPHY

Abala L and C L Morna. "Target Practice: Africa Lags Behind." In *Flamme;* The African Daily Newspaper of Women". "Women 2000: Gender Equality, Development and Peace for the 21st Century." New York City, June 6, 2000.

Abdu'l-Baha, *Promulgation of Universal Peace.* comp. Howard MacNutt, end ed. Wilmette, IL: Bahá'í Publishing Trust 1982, 375.

Achebe, Chinua. *Things Fall Apart.* New York: McDowell Obolensky, 1959.

Adams, Melinda. *Women's Associations in Cameroon: the immediate Post-colonial and Contemporary Eras Compared.* Paper presented at the Annual Meeting of the Midwest Political Science Association, Chicago in April 2003. For more information visit: http://www.mwpsa.org

Adler, R. *Engendering Judaism.* New York: Jewish Publication Society, 1997.

Africa Recovery. "210 Million Africans Go Hungry." *Africa Recovery.* Vol. 12, No. 3. December 1998.

———. "AIDS: The Development Emergency." *Africa Recovery.* Vol. 13, nos. 2/3, September 1999, .30.

Aird, Enola G. Director of The Motherhood Project, Institute for American Values. Congressional Briefing 1/31/03. http://www.watchoutforchildren.org

All China Women's Federation (ACWF) and National Bureau of Statistics (NBS). "The Survey: Women's Status in Transformation." Beijing 1990.

Angelou, Maya. *I Know Why the Caged Bird Sings.* 1968 Reissue. New York, Toronto; Random House, 1970.

Arendt, Hannah. *The Recovery of the Public World.* Edited by M.A.Hill. New York: St. Martin's, 1979, XIII.

Asian Wall Street Journal, April 30, 2003, 1.

Asian Women 2002, Vol. 15. and *Research Institute of Asian Women (RIAW) 2002, Program 2002-06.*

Associated Press, July 2, 2002

Atkinson, Brooks ed. *The Selected Writings of Ralph Waldo Emerson.* New York: The Modern Library, 1992.

Baffoun, Alya "Research in the Social Sciences on North African Women: Problems, Trends and Needs." In *Social Science Research and Women in the Arab World.* Paris: UNESCO, 1984, 41.

Ball, Edward. *Slaves in the Family.* New York, Toronto: Ballantine Books, 1998.

Bandura, Alfred. "Social Learning Theory." Visit: http://www.mhhe.com/socscience/com m/bandur-s.mhtml.

Bem, Sandra. "Enculturated Lens Theory of Gender Formation." In *The Lenses of Gender: Transforming the Debate on Sexual Inequality.* New Haven, CT: Yale University Press, 1993, 139.

Blumer, Herbert G. "Collective Behavior." In *Principles of Sociology.*

Bouvard, Marguerite G. *Revolutionizing Motherhood: a Bahá'í Perspective.* Wilmette, IL: Bahá'í Publishing Trust, 1998, 2001.

Brákenhielm, C. R. "Christianity and Swedish Culture: A Case Study." International Review of Mission 84 (1995): 91-105.

Bray, R. S. *Armies of Pestilence: The Impact of Disease on History..* New York: Barnes and Noble, 1996.

Bronfenbrenner, Urie. New York: Russell Sage Foundation, 1970.

Browne, E.G, trans. *A Traveler's Narrative.* Cambridge: University Press, 1891.

Brownmiller, Susan. *Against Our Will.* 1975, Reprint. New York, Toronto: Ballantine, 1993.

Bryson, J C "Women and Economic Development in Cameroon." Prepared under contract No RDO 78/8 with USAID, Yaounde, 1979.

Cantow, Roberta. Dir. "Clotheslines." Buffalo Rose Productions, 1981. Documentary Film.

Charrad, Mounira. "State & Gender in the Maghrib." In *Women and Power in the Middle East.* Edited by Joseph Suad and Susan Slyomovics. Philadelphia: University of Pennsylvania Press, 2001.

Chesney-Lind, Meda. "The Female Offender." Cited in *Deviance, Crime and Social Control, Sociology,* 5th ed. Prentice Hall: NJ: John Farley, 2003, 269.

Chew, Phyllis G L. In "The Singapore Council of Women & the Women's Movement." Association of Women for Action & Research. Singapore University Press, 1999, 29.

Cheyne, TK. *The Reconciliation of Races and Religions.* London: Adam & Charles Black, 1914.

Chodrow, Nancy. "Gender Personality and the Reproduction of Mothering" In *Social The-*

ory; The Multicultural and Classic Readings. Boulder, CO: Westview Press, 1999.

CIA. "World Bank." *CIA World Factbook.* Washington, DC: Potomac Books, 2002.

Clark, P G. "A Gender View of the History of Professionalism in South Africa." In *Africa Development* vol. XXIII, Nos. 3 & 4 1998.

Clignet, Remi. "Social Change and Patterns of Sexual Differentiation in Two African Countries." In *Signs,* 1977.

Cobb, Charles Jr. S. "Broader Approach Needed to Achieve Bush HIV/AIDS Plan Goals." At: http://www.allafrica.com/stories/200405180707.html.

Collins, Emily. "Reminiscences of the Suffrage Trail (1881)." In *Women and the National Experience: Primary Sources in American History.* Edited by Ellen Skinner. New York: Longman-Addison Wesley, 2003, 79-81.

Commonwealth. Secretariat. Gender Affairs. "HIV AIDS: An Inherent Gender Issue." 2000.

Cooper, Anna Julia "The Colored Women's Office," in *Social Theory: the Multicultural and Classic Readings,* Charles Lemert, ed. Boulder CO: Westview Press, 1999.

Croll, Elizabeth. *Changing Identities of Chinese Women: Rhetoric, Experience and Self Precept in 20th Century China.* Atlantic Highlands, NJ: Humanities Press Int'l, 1995.

——. *Chinese Women since Mao.* Armonk, NY: ME Sharpe, 1984.

Daddieh, K. C. "Production and Reproduction: Women and Agricultural Resurgence in Sub-Sahara Africa". In *Women and Development in Africa: Comparative Perspectives.* Edited by J L Parpart. University Press of America, Inc.: Lanham: USA., 1989.

Dankelman I and J Davidson, "Women and Environment in the Third World: Alliance for the Future." London: Earthscan Publications Ltd., 1989.

Danticat, Edwidge. *Krik? Krak!* New York: Soho Press, 1994.

Davidson, B. *Modern Africa.* London: Longman, 1983.

De Oliveira, R.D. *In Praise of Difference: The Emergence of Global Feminism.* New Brunswick, NJ: Rutgers University Press, 1998, 62.

DeLancey, Mark. "Women's Cooperatives in Cameroon." In *African Studies Review,* 1987, vol. 30, 1, 1-8.

DeLancey, Virginia. "Agricultural Expansion for Women in Cameroon." Paper presented at the annual meeting of the African Studies Association, Los Angeles, October, 1984.

—— "The Economies of Africa." in April A. Gordon and Donald L. Gordon, Eds, *Understanding Contemporary Africa.* 3rd Ed. Boulder, CO: Lynne Rienner, 2001.

Denton, RK. *The Semai: A Nonviolent People of Malaysia.* Fieldwork, ed. New York:

Holt, Rinehart & Winston, 1979

Department of Economic and Social Affairs, UN. "The World's Women: Trends and Statistics." New York: UN Publishing, 2000.

Dhruvanajan, Vanaja and Jill Vickers. *Gender, Race and Nation: A Global Perspective.* University of Toronto Press, 2002

Diduk, S. "Moral Guardians and Women's Protests in the Grassfields of Cameroon." Paper presented at the 13th Satterthwaite Colloquium on African Ritual and Religion, Satterthwaite, UK, 1997.

Dinesen, Isak. *Out of Africa.* 1937 Reprint. New York: Random House, 1992.

Duncan, Cynthia M. *Worlds Apart: Why Poverty Persists in Rural America.* New Haven: Yale University Press, 1999.

Durkheim, Emile. "Anomie and the Modern Division of Labor, 1902." In *Social Theory: the Multicultural and Classic Readings*, Charles Lemert, ed. Boulder CO: Westview Press, 1999.

———. *Suicide: a Study in Sociology.* Orig in Fr 1897. Glencoe, IL: Free Press, 1964.

Easton, P. "Indigenous Knowledge for Development." University of Florida, Dec. 1998, 4.

Ebry, Patricia B. *Confucianism and Family Rituals in Imperial China: a social history of Writing about Rites*, Princeton, NJ: Princeton University Press, 1991.

Economic Commission for Africa. "Women of Africa: Today and Tomorrow." Addis Ababa: ECA, 1975. 22.

Effendi, Shoghi, trans & ed. *The Dawnbreakers: Nabil's Narrative.* Wilmette, IL: Bahá'í Publishing, 1932, 1970, 295.

Eisler, Riane. *The Chalice and the Blade: Our History, Our Future.* San Francisco: Harper & Row, 1988.

Elliot, Emory. gen. ed. *American Literature: A Prentice* Peterson *Hall Anthology,* New Jersey: Prentice Hall, 1991.

Endeley, J "Conceptualizing Women's Empowerment in Societies in Cameroon: How Does Money Fit In?" In *Gender and Development,* vol. 9, No. 1, March 2001.

Engels, Friedrich. *The Origin of the Family.* Orig 1884. Charles Kerr 1902.

Entwisle, Barbara and Gail Henderson. *Redrawing Boundaries: Work, Household and Gender in China.* Berkeley: University of California Press, n.d.

Errington, E A. *Wives and Mothers, Schoolmistresses and Scullery Maids: Working Women in Upper Canada, 1790-1840.* Montreal & Kingston: McGill-Queen's University Press, 1995.

Fafunwa, A Babs and J U Aisiku, eds. *Education in Africa: a Comparative Study.* London: George Allen and Unwin, 1982.

Finneran, Richard J. ed. *Collected Poems of WB Yeats.* New York: Scribner, 1996.

Fitzgerald, Robert, trans. Homer's *Odyssey.* New York: Doubleday, 1963.

FonJong, L. "Fostering Women's Participation in Development through Non-governmental Efforts in Cameroon." In *The Geographical Journal,* vol 167, No. 3, September 2001, 223-224.

Forsas, H. and Elin Wagner, *Vad tanker du mansklighet?/ What Do You Think, Humankind?* Stockholm: Norstedt, 1999, 31.

Forster, E M. *Passage to India.* 1924 Reprint. Orlando, FL: Harcourt/Harvest Books, 1965.

Freedman, Estelle B. *No Turning Back: the History of Feminism and the Future of Women.* New York: Random House-Ballantine, 2002.

Freeman, J. Unfinished Business: Kofi Annan on Opening Day: "Still Much Work to be Done.". June 6, 2000, p.1 & 5

Friedan, Betty. *The Feminine Mystique.* New York: Norton, 1963.

Friedan, Betty. *The Second Stage* New York: Summit Books, 1981.

Friedman, S A "Girls 2000: NGOs Report on Progress Since Beijing, 1995." New York: The Working Groups on Girls." New York: 6-7.

Gail, Marzeih. Rev. ed. *Tahirih the Pure.* By Martha Root. US: Kalimat Press, 1981. Orig. *Tahirih the Pure: Iran's Greatest Woman.* Karachi: Bahá'í Publishing, 1938.

Ghiglieri, Michael. *The Dark Side of Man.* New York; Perseus, 1999.

Giacamon, Rita Islah Jad, & Penny Johnson, "For the Common Good? Gender & Social Citizenship in Palestine." In *Women and Power in the Middle East.* Edited by Suad Joseph and Susan Slyomovics. Philadelphia: University of Pennsylvania Press, 2001.

Giddings, Paula. *When and Where I Enter: the Impact of Black Women on Race and Sex in America.* New York: William Morrow, 1984.

Gilman, Charlotte. "The Yellow Wallpaper." Boston, MA: Small & Maynard, 1899.

Gilmartin, Christine, Gail Hershatter, Lisa Rofel, Tyrene White. *Engendering China: Women, Culture and the State.* Cambridge, MA: Harvard University Press, 1994.

Gilmore, David D. *Misogyny: the Male Malady.* Philadelphia: University of PA Press, 2001.

Goheen, Miriam. *Men Own the Fields, Women Own the Crops: Gender and Power in the Cameroon Grassfields*. Madison, WI: The University of Wisconsin Press, 1996.

Göransson, S, ed. *Birgitta och hennes tid/Birgitta and Her Time*. Uppsala: Almqvist & Wiksell, 1973.

Gordon, April A and Donald L Gordon, eds. *Understanding Contemporary Africa*. 3rd ed. Boulder, Colorado: Lynne Rienner Publishers, Inc., 2001.

Gordon, April A. "Women and Development." in April A. Gordon and Donald L. Gordon, Eds, *Understanding Contemporary Africa*, 3rd Ed. Boulder, CO: Lynne Rienner, 2001, 127-129.

Graham-Brown, Sarah. "Women's Activism in the Middle East and North Africa." In *Women and Power in the Middle East*. Edited by Suad Joseph and Susan Slyomovics. Philadelphia: University of Pennsylvania Press, 2001.

Green, December. *Gender Violence in Africa*. New York: St. Martin's Press, 1999.

Grey, M. "Have the Wellsprings Run Dry? Re-Sourcing Tradition in Feminist Theology." *Feminist Theology* 3 1993: 38-52.

Grimke, Angelina. *An Appeal to the Women of the Nominally Free States, Issued by an Antislavery Convention of American Women*. 2nd ed. Boston: Isaac Knapp, 1838. 13-2.

Guttmacher, Alan. *Issues in Brief: Family Planning Improves Child Survival and Health*. Washington, DC: Alan Guttmacher Institute, 1997.

Habitat for Humanity International. "Habitat World." Americus, Georgia: February/March 2003, 20.

.Harding, S. *The Science Question in Feminism*. Ithaca & London: Cornell University Press, 1986, 88.

Harsch, E. "Child Labour Rooted in Africa's Poverty." Vol 15, no. 3. UN Department of Public Information, October 2001.

Hacker, Andrew. "Doing without Dads" In *Mismatch: the Growing Gulf between Women and Men*. New York: Scribner, 2003

———. "The Fragility of Masculinity." In *Mismatch: the Growing Gulf Between Women and Men*. New York: Scribner, 2003.

Hatcher, John. "The Emergence of a Global Religion." N.p. n.d.

Hedlund, E. Kvinnornas Europa/ The Europe of Women (Stockholm: Dagens Nyheter, 1993), 94

Heyzer, Noeleen. "Women's Participation and Leadership: Vital to Democratic Governance." Presented at the UNIFEM Summit on the Americas, Monterrey, Mexico, 13, January, 2004 at: http://www.unifem.org/speeches.php? f_page_pid=77&f_ pritem_pid=155.

.—— "Facing the Challenges: Commitments for the Future." June 21, 2001. At www.uni fem.undp.org/newsroom/speeched/ecosoc/June01.html.

——. "The Challenge to Sustainable Development in Africa: The Gender Dimension of HIV/AIDS, Peace and Economic Security." Presented to ECOSOC, June 21, 2001. At: www.unifem.undp.org/newsroom/speeches/ecosocJune21.html

.Hong, Fan. *Footbinding, Feminism: the Liberation of Women's Bodies in Modern China.* Essex, UK: Frank Cass Publishers, 1997.

Human Rights Watch. "Suffering in Silence: The Links between Human Rights Abuses and HIV Transmission in Zambia." London: Human Rights Watch, 2002, 1-2.

Inglehart, Ronald and Pippa Norris. *Rising Tide: Gender Equality and Cultural Change around the World.* New York: Cambridge University Press, 2003.

James, Stanlie M and Abena P Abusia. *Theorizing Black Feminisms: the Visionary Pragmatism of Black Women.* New Jersey: Routledge, 1993.

Janus, Christopher. "Slavery Abolished? Only Officially." *Christian Science Monitor,* 5/17/1996.

Jarlstrom, M. "Emilia Fogelklou-teologen/Emilia Fogelklou-the Theologian." Kvinnovetenskaplig tidskrift 2 (1989): 80-81.

Jensen, Joan M. "Native American Women and Agriculture: a Seneca Case Study." In *Unequal Sisters: A Multicultural Reader in US Women's History.* Edited by Vicki L Ruiz and Ellen C DuBois. New York: Routledge, 1994.

Jicai, Sha and Liu Qiming. *Women's Status in Contemporary China.* International Scholar's Press, 1996.

Joekes, Susan P "Women in the World Economy: An INSTRAW Study." New York: Oxford University Press, 1987, 63.

Johnston, Deidre D and Debra H Swanson. "A Content Analysis of Motherhood Ideologies & Myths in Magazines." In *Sex Roles: A Journal of Research,* July 2003.

Joseph, Suad and Susan Slyomovics, eds. *Women and Power in the Middle East.* Philadelphia: University of Pennsylvania Press, 2001.

Kang, Tien Ju. *Male Anxiety and Female Chastity: a Comparative Study of Chinese Ethical Values in Ming-Ching Times.* Boston: US: Brill Academic Publications, 1988.

Kaysen, Susanna. *Girl Interrupted.* New York: Random House/Vintage Books USA, 1994.

Kazuko, Ono. *Chinese Women in a Century of Revolution, 1850-1950.* Stanford, CA: Stanford University Press, 1989.

Kentor, Jeffrey. "The Long-term Effects of Globalization on Income Inequality, Population Growth, & Economic Development." *Social Problems.* Vol 48: 4, 11/2001, 435-55.

Khan, J and P Khan. "Advancement of Women: a Bahá'í Perspective." Wilmette, IL USA: Bahá'í Publishing Trust, 1998.

King, U. "Spirituality for Life." In *Women Resisting Violence: Spirituality for Life.* Edited. By M.J. Mananzan et al., Mary Knoll. New York: Orbis, 1996, 155.

Knapp, Bettina L. "Women in Myth" State University of New York, 1997.

Koenig, D E. "Sex, Work, and Social Class in Cameroon." Ann Arbor and London: University Microfilms International, 1977.

Koenig, Michael A. et al, "Domestic Violence in Rural Uganda: Evidence from a Community-based Study." Bulletin of the World Health Organization. Vol. 81, no. 1. January 2003, 53.

Konde, E. "Cameroonian women in national politics since the Second World War, 1945-85: An historical study of women and politics in a male-dominated society." Ann Arbor: UMI Dissertation Services, 1991.

Kyrkan, Svenska: Matrikel/Directory of the Church of Sweden. Stockholm: Verbum, 2000, 371.

League of Nations. "Statistical and Disarmament Document Collection." Evanston, IL: Northwestern University Library, N.p. n.d.

Leeyao, Esther S. *Chinese Women: Past and Present.* Irving, TX: Ide House, Inc; 1983.

Lemert, Charles ed. *Social Theory: the Multicultural and Classic Readings.* Boulder, CO: Westview Press, 1999.

—— ed. Friedrich Engels, 1884, "The Patriarchal Family," in *Social Theory: the Multicultural and Classic Readings.* Boulder, CO: Westview Press, 1999.

Lerner, G. *Why History Matters.* New York & Oxford: Oxford University Press, 1997, 118.

LeVine, V.T "The Cameroon Federal Republic." Ithaca, NY: Cornell University Press, 1963.

——. "The Cameroons from Mandate to Independence." Berkeley: University of California Press, 1964.

Levy, Howard S. *Chinese Footbinding: the History of a Curious Erotic Custom,.* London: Kegan Paul International Limited: 1966, 2001.

Ligomeka, Brian. "Malawi Fights Wife Inheritance," *Malawi Standard.* April 23, 2003.

Lilyxiao, Lee, ed. *Biographical Dictionary of Chinese Women: the Qing Period 1644-1911.* Vol I. Armonk, NY: ME Sharpe Inc., 1998.

Lobe, Jim. "Child Soldiers Abandoned in Angola." *Oneworld US*, April 29, 2003. Found at www.Oneworld.net.

Luke, N. and K. Kurz. "Cross-Generational and Transactional Sexual Relations in Sub-Saharan Africa: Prevalence of Behavior and Implications for Negotiating Safer Sexual Practices." 2002. Eldis Dossiers. At www.eldis.org

Madeleva. "Lecture in Spirituality." New York & Mahwah, NJ: Paulist, 2000.

Mail and Guardian. March 8, 1999.

Mailer, Norman. "The White Man Unburdened.". *The New York Review of Books*. July 2003: 4-6.

Mama, A. "Transformation Thwarted: Gender-Based Violence in Africa's New Democracies." N.p. n.d. 2000. ". http://www.uct.ac.2a/org/agi/newslet/vol6/transf.htr

Marton, Kati. "Protect Women, Stop a Disease." *International Herald Tribune*. March 4, 2003. At www.iht.com/articles/88504.html

Marx, Karl and F. Engels. *The Communist Manifesto*. 1848 Reprint. Mass Market Paperback: Signet Classics, 1995.

Matt, L M. "A Report on Women's Cooperatives in the Northwest and Southwest Provinces." N.p. 1979.

Mayberry, David. ed. *Tribal Millennium*, Alexandra, VA: Public Broadcasting Services, 1997. TV film.

Mayeski, M.A. "Reclaiming an Ancient Story: Baudonivia's Life of St. Radegund." In *Women Saints in World Religions*. Edited by A. Sharma. Albany: State University of New York Press, 2000, 71-88.

Mbuagbow, T E and R. Brain and R Palmer. *A History of Cameroon*. London: Essex: Group Ltd., 1987.

Mbuh, J. (2005) CHAPTER 5, "Redressing a Mismanaged Economy," at: http://docs.indymedia.org/twi/pub/Main/JusticeMbuh/ICCPC5.doc;see also "Recent Interights Commonwealth Human Rights Law," at: http://www.worldlii.org/int/cases/ICHRL/recent-cases.html.

———. *Ingredients of International Conflict Viewed from: Inside Contemporary Cameroon Politics*. At: www.authorhouse.com. 2005.

Mbuh, Rebecca N. "Women in Leadership: The Case of Cameroon." In *The Leadership Journal*. Spring 1998.
———. "African Women's Challenges in the 21st Century: an Overview." Seoul, Korea, 2002.

McCarthy, M A. "Report on Women's Cooperative Groups Activities for 1981. Kom Area Women's Cooperative. Peace Corps Volunteer, 1982.

McClung Lee, Alfred ed. New York: Barnes & Noble, 1969.

McCorduck, Pamela and Nancy Ramsey. *The Futures of Women-Scenarios for the 21st Century.* Reading, MA: Addison-Wesley, 1996.

McDonald, Joe "For Sale: baby girl, unwanted, cheap: illegal trade thrives in China." *Richmond Times Dispatch: Associated Press.* 3/26/2003, A7.

Merton, T. *No Man Is an Island.* San Diego & New York: Harcourt Brace, 1955, 150.

Mills, C. Wright. *The Sociological Imagination.* New York: Oxford University Press, 1959.

Ministry of Social and Women's Affairs. "Evaluation of the Implementation of the Nairobi Forward-Looking Strategies for the Advancement of Women and the Abuja Declaration on Participatory Development." Republic of Cameroon, September, 1995.

Mitchell, Margaret. *Gone With the Wind.* 1936 Reprint. New York: Scribner 1964.

Moletsane, Mokgadi and Mark W. DeLancey. "HIV/AIDS: A Problem for Africa - A Special Problem for African Women." In *Asian Women Journal.* Vol. 15, Seoul: Research Institute of Asian Women, 2003).

Moltmann-Wendel, E. *I An My Body.* New York: Continuum, 1995, 13.

Momen, Moojan, ed. *The Bábi's and the Bahá'í Faith, 1844-1944.* Oxford: George Ronald, 1981.

Momsen, J H. *Women and Development in the Third World.* London: Routledge, 1991.

Montague, Ashley. *The Natural Superiority of Women,* 5th ed. Walnut Creek, CA: AltaMira Press, 1999.

Mope Simo, J A. "The Political Economy of Cameroon: Historical Perspectives." Paper prepared for the African Studies Center-Cameroon Conference, Leiden, The Netherlands, June 1-4, 1988.

Morganthau, Hans. *Politics Among Nations: the Struggle for Power and Peace.* 5th ed. Revised. New York: Knopf, 1978.

—— "League of Nations Statistical and Disarmament Document Collection." Northwestern University Library: Evanston, IL, 1978.

Murdock, George. Human Relations Area Files (HRAF). Yale University.

Naisbitt, John and Patricia Aburdene. *Megatrends 2000: Ten New Directions for 1990's.* New York: Avon, 1991.

Nelson, H. D. et al., *Area Handbook for the United Republic of Cameroon*. Washington: U. S. Government Printing Office, 1974.

.Nessman, Ravi. "AIDS Main Killer of S. African Women." *Associated Press*. At cnn.news.com.

Niger-Thomas, M. "Women and the Arts of Smuggling." In *African Studies Review*, Sept. 2001, vol. 44 i2, 43.

O'Connor, Anna Marie. "New Lives for Women From Iran." *Los Angeles Times*, December 10, 1998, p.1, col.1.

OFUNC. "The Face of Women in Cameroon." Yaounde, Cameroon: AGRACAM, n.d., 67.

Ogunleye, Tolagbye. "Women in Ancient West Africa."

Olander A. and B. Stromberg. *Tusen svenska kvinnoar: Svensk Kvinnohistoria Fran Vikingatid till nutid! A Thousand Years of Swedish Women's History from the Time of the Vikings until Today*. Stockholm: Raben & Prisma, 1996, 11.

Ollenburger, Jane and H Moore. *The Intersection of Patriarchy, Capitalization & Colonization* Upper-Saddle, NJ: Prentice Hall, 1998.

Ovonji-Odida. "Do Ugandan Women Have any Good Deal on the Land Reforms?" In *Eastern African Initiatives*, No 1. Kampala, Uganda 1999 4.

Parpart, J L and K A Stuadt, eds. *Women and the State in Africa*. Boulder and London: Lynne Rienner Publishers, 1989.

Peiperl, Laurence. et al, Eds. "Women, Children, and HIV: Resources for Prevention and Treatment." CD. San Francisco, CA: Global Strategies for HIV Prevention and HIVInSite, 2002.

Pellauer, M.D. "Feminist Theology: Challenges and Consolations for Lutherans," Dialog 24 (1985):19-25.

Penn, Michael and Rahel Nardos. *Overcoming Violence Against Women and Girls: the International Campaign to Eradicate a Worldwide Problem*. Lanham, MD: Rowman & Littlefield Publisher, Inc. 2003.

Pinter, Frances. *Social Science Research and Women in the Arab World*. London: UNESCO, 1984.

Prouty, Chris and E. Rosenfeld, *Historical Dictionary of Ethiopia*. London: Scarecrow Press, 1982.

Reaney, Patricia. "Women Make up 50 Percent of AIDS Sufferers." November 26, 2002. Reuters at http://story.news.yahoo.com.

Reardon. "Women and Peace: Feminist Visions of Global Security." Albany: State University of New York Press, 1993.

Renzetti, C and D Curran. *Women Men & Society*, 5th ed. n.p.: Allyn & Bacon, 2002.

Ringa, Mathias, "HIV/AIDS: Men Urged to Shun Risky Activities," *East African Standard* Nairobi: April 6, 2003. All at www.allAfrica.com.

Robbins, Gay. "Women in Ancient Egypt." In *Women's Roles in Ancient Civilizations.* Westport, CT: Greenwood, 1999, 154-187;

Rodham Clinton, Hillary "Keynote Address to the Vital Voices of the Americas Conference." Uruguay: US State Department Archives, 10/1998.

Roesdahl, E. *The Vikings.* London: Allen Lane & Penguin, 1987, 58-60.

Root, Martha L. *Tahirih the Pure*. Rev. ed. Los Angeles: Kalimat Press, 1981, 98.

Rosaldo, Michelle Z. and L. Lamphere. *Women, Culture and Society.* California: Stanford University Press, 1974.

Rowley, Anne. Field notes, 1977. Thomas Watson Fellowship.

Russell, Catherine A. and Mark W. DeLancey. "African Women in Cabinet Positions— Too Few, Too Weak: A Research Report." *Asian Women.* Vol.15 2002, 147.

Sall, I. ed. *Women in Academia: Gender and Academic Freedom in Africa.* Council for the Development of Social Science Research in Africa *(CODESRIA).* Dakar, Senegal, 2000.

Santoli, Al. "Fighting Child Prostitution." *Freedom Review*, 1994. Vol 25: No 5, 5-8.

Sawyer, B. and P. Sawyer, *Medieval Scandinavia: From Conversion to Reformation, circa 800-1500.* The Nordic Series 17. Minneapolis & London: University of Minnesota Press, 1993, 104.

Schneiders, S. M. *With Oil in Their Lamps: Faith, Feminism and the Future.* New York and Mahwah, NJ: Paulist, 2000, 9.

Sengupta, Somini, "Congo's Warring Factions Leave a Trail of Rape." In *New York Times,* June 9, 2003 at www.nytimes.com/2003/06/09/international/ africa/09cong.

Silverberg, James and Thomas Gregor, eds. "The Rise, Maintenance & Destruction of Peaceable Polity." In *The Anthropology of Peace and Nonviolence.* New York; Oxford University Press, 1992, 214-270.

Sivard, R. *Women: A World Survey.* Washington, DC: World Priorities, 1985.

Skard, T. and E. Haavio-Mannila. A Equality between the Sexes: Myth or Reality in Norden? Daedalus 113:1 (1984): 141-167.

Skinner, Ellen ed., "Anne Hutchinson's Trial (1638)." In *Women and the National Experience: Primary Sources in American History.* New York: Longman-Addison Wesley, 2003. 2-5.

Smith, Sheila and Desmond Cohen. "Gender, Development and the HIV Epidemic." October 2000. www.undp.org/hiv/publications/gender/gendere.htm.

Smith, Vashti. Notes: Personal Interview with Anne Breneman. Florence SC: 1990.

Snyder, M C and M Tadesse. *African Women and Development: A History.* London: Zed Books Ltd., 1995 21.

Social Watch '99. Montevido, Uruguay: Instituto de Tercer Mundo in Progress of World's Women.

Stanton, Elizabeth C, Susan B Anthony, and Matilda J Gage, eds. "Women of Philadelphia (1848)." From "The Public Ledger and Daily Transcript," In *History of Women's Suffrage.* Edited by Elizabeth C Stanton, Susan B Anthony and Matilda J Gage. Rochester: Charles Mann, 1881.

——— , eds. "Declaration of Sentiments." In *History of Women's Suffrage.* Edited by Elizabeth C Stanton, Susan B Anthony and Matilda J Gage. Rochester: Charles Mann, 1881.

Statistical Yearbook of Sweden. Örebro: Statistics, 2000, 470-71.

Sterling, C. "Special report for the Development of Women's Cooperatives in the Southwest Province." Submitted to the Director of Cooperation, 1979.

Stiglitz, J E. *Globalization and its Discontents.* New York: W. W. Norton & Company Inc., .2002.

Stoddard, Ed. "History Holds Clues to AIDS Impact on Africa." *The Miami Herald.* July 29, 2002. At www.miami.com.

Stuart, E. "Experience and Tradition: Just Good Friends." In *Sources and Resources of Feminist Theologies.* Edited by D.A. Hartlieb and C. Methuen. Kampen: Kok Pharos, 1997, 49.

Sullivan, N P. "Mid-Service Report: Women's Cooperatives" Southwest Province, Meme Division, 1981.

Tabari, Azar and Nahid Yeganeh, eds. *In the Shadow of Islam: the Women's Movement in Iran.* ZED Press: London, 1982.

Tetchiada, S "Cameroon Women's Unemployment: A Great Injustice." ANB-BIA Supplement, Issue/Edition Nr. 433, 2002.

Tetreault, Mary Ann ed. *Women and Revolution in Africa, Asia and the New World.* Columbia, SC: USC Press, 1994, 8.

The Prosperity of Humankind. New York: International Bahá'í Community, UN, 1994.

Theroux, Paul, "Being a Man." In Linda H Peterson's, gen.ed., *The Norton Reader: An Anthology of Nonfiction Prose.* New York: W.W. Norton & Company, 2000.

Tilly, Charles. *From Mobilization to Revolution.* Reading, MA: Addison-Wesley, 1978.

Tjaden, Patricia and Nancy Thoennes, "Prevalence, Incidence, and Consequences of Violence Against Women." Washington, DC: National Institute of Justice, 2000.

Tran, My-Van. "The Position of Women in Traditional Vietnam." In *The Role of Women in an Advancing Civilization.* Edited by Starih Ala'I and C. Dowes. Australia: Association of Bahá'í Studies, 1989.

Truth, Sojourner. "Ain't I a Woman." In *History of Women's Suffrage.* Edited by Elizabeth C Stanton, Susan B Anthony and Matilda J Gage. Rochester: Charles Mann, 1881, 403-404.

UNAIDS. "The Global HIV/AIDS Epidemic 2002-2003." AIDS Epidemic Update, December 2002." Geneva: CD.

———. "New UNAIDS Report Warns AIDS Epidemic Still in Early Phase and Not Leveling off in Worst Affected Countries." July 2, 2002. At www.unaids.org

———. "UN Releases New Data Highlighting the Devastating Impact of AIDS in Africa." June 25, 2002. Press release at www.unaids.org;

UNDP "Human Development Report 2000." Oxford University Press. Pooled World Values Survey/European Values Survey, 1995-2000.

UNDP, *Human Development Report.* Oxford University Press, 1994.

UNESCO. "Africa Development Indicators, 2002." Statistical Yearbook, 2000.

UNFPA. "Population Numbers and Trends: HIV/AIDS: Impact and Prevention." At www.unfpa.org.

UNICEF, "Education For All: No Excuses." New York: UNICEF: Division of Communications, 2000. 2-4.

UNICEF. *The State of the World's Children.* New York: United Nations Publications, 2000, 10.

UNIFEM. "Bahá'í Project Raises Community Consciousness." in *The Greatness Which Might Be Theirs: Reflections on the Agenda & Platform for Action for the UN Fourth World Conference on Women.* Bahá'í International Community Office of the Advancement of Women, Beijing: 1995, 51-60.

UNIFEM. "Gender Equality Makes Headway."http://english.people.com.cn/200007/20/en g20000720_45966.html

UNIFEM. "Progress of Women Scoreboard." *Progress of the World's Women 2000,* Biennial Report, 83, Table 3.5.

UNIFEM. *Progress of the World's Women* New York: UNIFEM HQ, 2000.

United Nations Development Program. "Making New Technologies Work for Human Development." In *Human Development Report, 2001.* New York: Oxford University Press, 2001.

United Nations Office and Dept. of Public Information. *Everyman's United Nations.* New York: UN Publications, annual.

Universal House of Justice. *The Promise of World Peace.* 1985.

US. National Intelligence Council (USNIC), "The Next Wave of HIV/AIDS: Nigeria, Ethiopia, Russia, India, and China." September 2002. 7-23. At http://www.cia.gov.

USAID "HIV/AIDS in South Africa: A Country Profile." July 2002. At www.synergyaids.com

USA Today, July 7, 2002

Walker, S. "Walled Women and Women Without Walls Among the Fulbe of Northern Cameroon" In *Sage, 7,* 1990, 13-17.

Weber, Max. *Economy and Society.* Orig in German 1922. New York: Bedminister Press, 1968.

Wehrwein, Peter. "AIDS Leaves Africa's Economic Future in Doubt." At www.cnn.com/SPECIALS/2000/aids/stories/economic.impact.

WHO publication titled "Global AIDS Epidemic Shows No Sign of Abating; Highest Infections and Deaths Ever." At: http://www.who.int/hiv/en/

Wilbur, Richard. *New and Collected Poems.* Harcourt, Brace, Jovanovitch, 1988, p 193.

Winga, Imani L. "Why AIDS Takes Heavy Toll on Women." *Business Times.*Dar Salaam, April 4, 2003.

Wistrand, B. *Swedish Women On the Move.* Stockholm: The Swedish Institute, 1981.

Witcombie, C L C E. "Women in Egypt: Egyptian Queens and Pharaohs." Sweet Briar College, 1998. http://www.arthistory.sbc.edu/imageswomen/egyptmatriarch.html

Wittstock, Laura "We are All Members of One Family." In *Messengers of the Wind: Native American Women Tell Their Stories.* Edited by. Jane Kantz. New York: One World Ballantine, 1995, 111-112.

Wolfensohn, James. *Washington News on Africa,* vol. 22,: no. 2, 1996, 7.

Women's Feature Service, ed. *The Power to Change: Women in the Third World Redefine their Environment.* London: Zed Books Ltd., 1993, 43-44.

World Bank Report No. 8894. November, 1990.

World Council of Churches 8th Assembly. Harare, Zimbabwe. 3-14 December 1998, Document No. DE 8, 1998.

World Health Organization. "Women and Aids: Fact Sheet 242." June 2000. At www. who.int/inf-fs/en/fact242.html

Youngblood, Shay. *The Big Mama Stories.* Ithaca, NY: Firebrand Books, 1989.

Youth for Women's Rights. *The Realities of Young Women's Lives.* New York, March 17, 2000, 4.

Yu-Ning, Li ed. *Chinese Women through Chinese Eyes.* Armonk, NY: ME Sharpe, Inc. 1992.

Zumdorfer, Harriet, ed. *Chinese Women in the Imperial Past: New Perspectives.* Boston: Brill Academic Publishers, 1996.

"Changing Fortunes of Government Policies and its Implications on MIDENO2" at: http://www.njas.helsinki.fi/pdf-files/vol13num1/fonjong.pdf see also Highlights of the Nigerian Livestock Resources Report," at: http://www.odi.org.uk/pdn/papers/35d.pdf;

"Family Composition." Bureau of Census, 1973 (FC).

FEMNET. Commission on the Status of Women www.femnet.or.ke/documents/ csw.asp

"Fertility of American Women" Bureau of the Census 2001 (FAW)

"FGM in Africa: Statistics," at www.fgmnetwork.org/intro/stats.html

"Fresh Air." National Public Radio. US, January 26, 2004.

"Gender Equality, Development and Peace for the 21st Century." New York, June 6, 2000.

"Journal of the Royal Asiatic Society," article 6, (1889), 492.

"Kids of Disgrace Find Solace in Village." *Daily Press.* Hampton Roads, VA, USA: March 6, 2004, A10.

"Living Arrangements of Children." Bureau of Census, 2001 (LAC).

"Money Income in the US" Bureau of Census 2001 (MI)

"Progress of the World's Women 2000: A New Biennial Report." http://www.unifem. undp.org/progressww/2000/.

"Sex Trafficking Widespread." BBC News, April 1, 2003. At http://newsvote.bbc.co.uk.

"Teaching Tolerance for All: Education Strategies To Promote Global Peace." *International Yearbook on Teacher Education 1995.* Proceedings from the World Assembly of the

International Council on Education for Teaching. 42nd, Darussalam, Brunei, July 3-7, 1995.

"The IMF: Selling the Environment Short In Africa (2) at http://www.foe.org/camps/intl/imf/selling/africa2.html Cameroon (01/05), article.

"The Millennium Forum Declaration." An Agenda of "We the Peoples. . . Millennium Forum." the *UN for the 21st Century*: Draft: May 18, 2000, 2. www.millenniumforum.org.

"The Promise of World Peace." International Bahá'í Community, 1985, III.

"The World's Women, 2000: Trends & Statistics." United Nations: NY 2000.
"World Conferences: Developing Priorities for the 21st Century." *UN Briefing Papers.* New York: UN Dept of Pub Info, 1997.
A.CONF.157.23.En?OpenDocument

AVERT, "The History of AIDS", in 5 sections at http://www.avert.org/historyi.htm

Beijing Declaration and Platform for Action and Compliance with International Legal Instruments on Women as of 8/8/02. UN Dept for Economic & Social Affairs. http://www.un.org/womenwatch/daw/.

Beijing Declaration and Platform for Action, Fourth world Conference on Women. September 15, 1995, A/CONF.177/20 (1995) and A/CONF.177/ 20/Add.I (1995) at http://www.un.org/womenwatch/daw/beijing/platform/declar.htm..

Bureau of the Census. "Fertility of American Women." US 2001.

Cameroon Enhancing Structural Adjustment Facility Medium Term Economic and Financial Policy Framework Paper, (1999/200-2001/02) at http://www.imf.org/ external/NP,

Canadian Voice of Women for Peace at http://www.peace.ca/vowunesco.htm

Central Intelligence Agency Report 2000

Department of Reproductive Health and Research (RHR, WHO. visit http://www.who.int/reproductive-health/mpr/attendants

HomeSchooling in the US: 1999, see http://nces.ed.gov/pubs2001/2001033.pdf#search=Home Schooling%20in%20the%20US% 201999'

http://portal.unesco.org/education/en/ev.phpURL_ID=38873&URL_DO=DO_TOPIC&U RL_SECTION=201.html for a detailed discussion of UNESCO's goals for the education of girls and women human rights declaration

Report on Women in Power and Decision-Making http://secretary.state.gov/www/picw/2000commitment/americas_commitment.pdf for 2000

For U.S. State Department Information on Cameroon. http://www.state.gov/r/pa/ei/bgn/26431.htm.

For additional information on specific UNICEF programs.http://www.unicef.org/whatwe do/index.html.

Report entitled: "Endangered Development Through Gender Equality in Rights, Resources, and Voices." http://www.worldbank.org/gender/prr/.

Human Development Report, 2002. Available on line at htttp://www.undp.org.

National Bureau of Statistics: Third National Census in 1982. Beijing 1983

Organization for Economic Cooperation and Development. see http://www.oecd.org/data-oecd/30/28/2754929.pdf

Report of the World Conference of the UN International Women's Year, Mexico City, 19 June-2 July 1975: Equality, Development and Peace, E/Conf.66/34

"Rwanda Resurrects from Genocide." Eastern African Initiatives No. 1. Kampala, Uganda, 1999, p. 4.

Senegal Ban on FGM. University of PA, African Studies Center. 01/04/1999: http://www.sas.upenn.edu/African_Studies/Urgent_Action/apic_1499.html.

Statement on Women's Contributions to a Culture of Peace at http://www.unesco.org/cpp/ uk/declarations/wcpbei.htm.

Table "E Young People 2" in UNAIDS, The Global HIV/AIDS Epidemic 2002-2003, CD

The Buea University Newsletter, vol 1, no 3, January 1994, 12.

The Cyclic Theory of Abu-Ali Sina. Avicenna 980-1037 CE.

The Department of Gender and Women's Health at: http://www.who.int/gender/en/.

Transparency International,World Index on Corruption Report, 2003 at http://www .trans parency.org.

UN 1995a, Table 4.8 and Mexico: UNIFEM/CONMUJER 1999:65; Bangladesh: Zohir 1998.

UN Population Statistics Division. 2002 BFD.

Vienna Declaration and Program of Action at http://www.unhchr.ch/huridocda/huri-doca.nsf/(Symbol)/

Women in National Parliaments at: http://www.ipu.org/wmn-e/classif.htm

Women Leaders and other positions held visit: http://www.guide2womenleaders.com/ Cameroon_heads.htm

World religions see: http://www.refdesk.com/factrel.html

INDEX

308

About the Authors

Rebecca Mbuh is a professor of business administration at Sookmyung Women's University, Seoul, Korea since 2001. Born and raised in Cameroon, she received her BA in Business Administration from Allen University in 1988 and her Ph.D. in higher education administration and human resources management from the University of South Carolina in 1993. Dr. Mbuh worked at Allen University, Columbia, South Carolina first as Director of Institutional Research and Effectiveness and adjunct professor of Business Administration, then as Dean of Academic Affairs, and from 1999-2001 as Provost. She received a research grant through the United Negro College Foundation and spent her sabbatical year conducting research on women managers in Cameroon and Indonesia. She is the author of several articles and book chapters on women's issues (particularly African women) and has presented numerous papers at conferences in America and internationally. Dr Mbuh has been a regular contributor to articles to the South Carolina Black Media newspapers in the United States. She has nine years experience in consulting with small businesses and universities in America. Her current research interests are women in administration and business, gender inequalities in education and workplace, and African businesswomen in Asian communities.

Anne R Breneman is currently serving as an associate professor of Sociology at Hampton University, Hampton, Virginia, USA. As a Thomas Watson Fellow, she researched the anthropology of childhood and education in Southeast Asian cultures. Her doctoral research was an ethnographic study of a desegregated school and community in Georgia, resulting in a manuscript in progress, What We Inherit: Race, Economics and Education in a Rural School & Community. From 1989-1999 Dr Breneman served as a member of the National Bahá'í Education Task Force of the US and has been serving from 2001 to the present as an Area Coordinator for the Crimson Ark Regional Bahá'í Training Institute and an advisory board member of PRIDE (Pacific Rim Institute for Development and Education), promoting cultural and academic exchange between China and the US. She was serving as Chair of the Social Science Department at Allen University in Columbia, South Carolina when the idea for Women in the New Millennium was born. She is a mother, wife and grandmother and has written children's books and journal articles.